Interpretations

OF

AMERICAN HISTORY

VOLUME II

Interpretations

OF

AMERICAN HISTORY:

Patterns and Perspectives

VOLUME II

SINCE 1865

EDITED BY

Gerald N. Grob and George A. Billias

THE FREE PRESS, NEW YORK

Collier-Macmillan Limited, London

A DIVISION OF THE MACMILLAN COMPANY

Printed in the United States of America

COLLIER-MACMILLAN CANADA, LTD., TORONTO, ONTARIO

Library of Congress Catalog Card Number: 67-12834

SECOND PRINTING JUNE 1967

FOR

Bradford S., Evan D., and Seth A. Grob

Preface

THIS TWO-VOLUME WORK is based upon the authors' philosophy of teaching American history to college freshmen and sophomores. Simply stated, this philosophy holds to three basic premises: that the approach to history should be analytical rather than factual; that beginning students should be provided with a brief background so that they may fully appreciate the significance of the selections assigned as outside readings; and that reading assignments should be a joy rather than a chore and this is made possible because some of the best scholarship in the field is found among historians who write with a lively literary style.

The first purpose of this work, then, is to bring together scholarly selections which approach American history from an analytical point of view. In most instances the readings represent interpretive articles or pieces written about different problems and periods of America's past. Students will be struck, however, by a single thread that runs throughout the entire work and ties together the various readings. The selections reproduced here all illustrate one theme — that our view of American history has been a constantly changing one.

Generally speaking, new perspectives concerning America's past have arisen for two reasons. In writing about their nation's history, American scholars have often tended to reflect either consciously or unconsciously the predilections of the age in which they live. Each succeeding generation seems to have rewritten

American history to suit the needs of its own age. Secondly, historians of the same generation have often presented a contradictory picture of the past. Sometimes scholars of a given era have arrived at conflicting interpretations even when their research was based upon the same body of material. But in cases where they have done so it was because these historians had approached the same material with a different set of starting assumptions. In this work the authors have sought to show how the historian's assumptions and frame of reference have often influenced his interpretation of the data. This is not to argue, however, that history cannot be objective. For in the end, the authors believe that all students of history must face the difficult task of evaluating the data and interpretations of scholars dealing with the same problem and decide which represents a better portrayal of reality.

The selections in each instance are accompanied by chapter-length introductory essays. These essays, based upon the readings used to illustrate each problem or period, are designed to provide the beginning student with a brief historiographical background on the topic under discussion. Seeing the selections in their proper historical context will enable students to read their assignments with greater insight and understanding.

The third premise — that the readings should represent good writing as well as solid scholarship — was uppermost in the minds of the authors as they searched the literature for suitable selections. Some of the best historical writing in America has been done by scholars who are accomplished stylists. A conscious effort was made to seek out articles and chapters in which the point of view was expressed in an interesting and attractive manner. Within the pages of these two volumes, students will find selections by Vernon L. Parrington, Frederick Jackson Turner, J. Franklin Jameson, Charles A. Beard, Daniel J. Boorstin, Kenneth M. Stampp, Richard Hofstadter, Arthur M. Schlesinger, Jr., John Higham, John K. Galbraith, Henry Steele Commager, and Carl N. Degler — authors noted for their trenchant writing styles. Students are always pleasantly surprised when they encounter lively writing in an assignment and one of the purposes of this work is to introduce the readers to the richness of the literature in American history.

In preparing this work, we have had the advice and assistance of others. Prof. Ernest R. May of Harvard University in his capacity as general editor made many sound suggestions which improved the manuscript immeasurably. To Gordon Marshall,

Clark University graduate student, go our thanks for checking quotes and footnotes. Our wives helped by their patience in putting up with the demands on home life that were required to complete this project. Other members of our respective families also provided us with the incentive to see this task through to the end; to them, this book is affectionately dedicated.

G.N.G.
G.A.B.

Contents

Interpretations
OF
AMERICAN HISTORY

1

Introduction

"EVERY TRUE HISTORY IS CONTEMPORARY HISTORY." So wrote Benedetto Croce, the great Italian philosopher and historian, a half century ago. By this proposition Croce meant that history — as distinguished from chronicle — was meaningful only to the degree that it struck a sympathetic chord in the minds of contemporaries who saw in the past the problems and issues of their own day.

Croce's statement has special relevance to the writing of American history, for every generation of American scholars has reexamined and reinterpreted the past in terms of its own time. Why has this been so? One of the most compelling reasons, no doubt, has been the perennial tendency of scholars to reinterpret the past in the light of their own prevailing ideas, prejudices, and problems. Every age has developed its own climate of opinion — or particular view of the world — which, in turn, conditioned the way it looked upon its own past and present. Thus each succeeding generation in America rewrote the history of this nation in such a way as to suit its own image. Although there were other reasons for the continual reinterpretation of American history, the changing climate of opinion more than any other single factor caused historians to recast periodically their view of the past.

Changing interpretations resulted also from the changing structure of the American historical profession. Generally speaking, the writing of history in America has gone through three broad but distinct stages. In the first stage — the period of Puritan historians — historical writing was dominated by ministers and magistrates who were seeking to write a religious justification for their respective New World colonies. The second stage — the period of patrician historians — saw the best history being written by gentlemen of the patrician class from the early eighteenth to the late nineteenth century. These gentlemen-historians, often men of leisure and independent means, had little or no connection with the church or any other formal institution. They were motivated primarily by a strong sense of social responsibility and a sincere conviction that every individual had a moral obligation to utilize his talents for the benefit of mankind. While they were amateur historical writers for the most part, many patrician historians managed to achieve a high level of literary distinction and accuracy. Their works as a rule, however, reflected the ideology and outlook of their class. The third stage — the period of professional historians — emerged during the 1870's with the establishment of graduate schools which provided formal training in historical scholarship. Indeed, the period since the 1870's has been the age of the professional historian. Most of the major works produced in the period were by university professors for whom the writing of history was a specialized career.[1]

During each of these three stages of historical writing, the climate of opinion in America was markedly different. In the seventeenth century, the most competent histories were written by New England Puritan leaders who conceived of history as the working out of God's will. Theirs was a Christian interpretation of history which viewed events as the unfolding of God's intention or design. Borrowing the concept of a Chosen People from the ancient Hebrews, these historians viewed the colonization of America in Biblical terms. They cast the Puritans in the same role as the Jews in the Old Testament — a regenerate people who were destined to fulfill God's purpose. New England became for them New Canaan — the place which God had set apart for man to experiment in the ways of Christian living. Massachusetts became more than a mere colony. It was to be, in the words of John Winthrop, "a city upon a hill" — a universal model Utopia

1. John Higham, "The Construction of American History," in *The Reconstruction of American History,* John Higham, ed. (New York, 1962), pp. 10–11.

to demonstrate to the rest of the world that a City of God on earth along the lines of ideals set forth in the New Testament could be established.

The major theme of most Puritan historians — whether they were ministers or magistrates — was to demonstrate God's special concern for His Chosen People in their efforts to build a New Canaan in America. New England's history served their purposes best because it was here that God's mercy could be seen more clearly than in any other part of the globe. To the Puritans the history of the region was one long record of the revelation of God's providential dealings with His People. Their disasters as well as their triumphs were seen only in relation to God and the setbacks that occurred were viewed as evidence of God's wrath and disfavor.

Of all the Puritan histories, William Bradford's *Of Plimouth Plantation* was perhaps the preeminent work of art. Written in the 1630's and 1640's while Bradford was governor of the colony, the history told the tale of the small band of Pilgrims who fled first to Holland then to the New World. No other document reflected so perfectly the deep feeling of religious dedication of the early New England settlers. None illustrated better the Puritan ideal of a simple and plain literary style or mastered so well the rhythms of Biblical prose.

With the decline of the church as the focal point of American intellectual life, Puritan historians were succeeded by the patrician historians of the eighteenth century. The Christian theory of history with its emphasis on supernatural causes increasingly gave way to a more secular interpretation of history based upon the concepts of human progress, reason, and material well-being. Influenced by European Enlightenment thinkers, many American historians came to believe that man, through his reason, could control his own destiny and ensure his material and intellectual progress in this world. The patrician historians rejected the old Christian belief of man's progress in religious terms — a progress in which man was guided by God's hand toward some distant heavenly city. Instead, they pictured man's progress in secular terms toward a heavenly city here on earth.

Patrician historians in the eighteenth century were profoundly influenced also by the ideas derived from the writings of Sir Isaac

Newton. This seventeenth-century English scientist, by applying a rational, mathematical method, had arrived at certain truths, or "natural laws," concerning the physical universe. Newton's mathematical systematization of scientific thought led many to conclude that the same mathematical-scientific method could be used to formulate similar natural laws in other fields of endeavor. In order to develop a theory of history in keeping with Newtonian thought, writers began to postulate certain natural laws in the field of history. Thus, patrician historians abandoned the Christian theory of history where God determined events for a secular view of the universe in which natural laws were the moving forces in history.

This shift from a Christian interpretation of history to a more secular approach was reflected in the change of leadership among American historians. Minister-historians were increasingly replaced by members of the patrician class — political leaders, planter-aristocrats, merchants, lawyers and doctors.[2] In the eighteenth century, for example, America's outstanding historians included Thomas Hutchinson, member of the Massachusetts merchant aristocracy and royal governor of that colony; William Smith of New York, a well-to-do lawyer and colonial official; Cadwallader Colden of New York, doctor, landowner, and lieutenant-governor; and Robert Beverley and William Byrd of Virginia, planter-aristocrats, large landowners, and office-holders. Most of these men possessed a classical education, a good private library, and the leisure time in which to write. With the growth of private wealth and proliferation of the professions, more and more members of the upper classes were in a position to take up the writing of history as an avocation.[3]

The reaction against the Christian interpretation of history was particularly evident in the writings of Thomas Jefferson. In his *Notes on the State of Virginia,* first published in 1785, Jefferson stressed reason and natural law instead of divine providence as the basis for historical causation. Jefferson believed also that men were motivated by self-interest and he employed this concept as one means of analyzing the course of historical events. As he wrote in his history of Virginia, "Mankind soon learn to make interested uses of every right and power which they possess, or may assume."

2. Harvey Wish, *The American Historian* (New York, 1960), p. 25.
3. John Higham, *et al., History* (Englewood Cliffs, 1965), p. 3.

Jefferson's history showed the impress of yet another major influence — nationalism — which affected historical writing after 1776. As author of the Declaration of Independence, Jefferson felt a deep, patriotic pride in the free institutions that emerged from the Revolution. He was convinced that America as a democratic nation was destined to lead the way to a new era in world history. A whole new generation of patrician historians sprang up after the Revolution writing in a similar nationalistic vein — David Ramsay, Mercy Otis Warren, Jeremy Belknap, and Jared Sparks — who likewise contrasted the free institutions in America with what they considered to be the corrupt and decadent institutions of Europe.

During the first three quarters of the nineteenth century, the writing of history continued to be dominated by patrician historians who had no special training for the task. The influence of the romantic movement in the arts with its heightened appreciation of the past, emphasis upon pictorial descriptions, and stress upon the role of great men, caused history to be viewed increasingly as a branch of literature. Many outstanding men of letters — Washington Irving, Francis Parkman, Richard Hildreth, William H. Prescott, and John Lothrop Motley — wrote narrative histories about America, other lands, and other times, in a romantic style calculated to appeal to a wide reading public.

The romantic school of patrician historians who wrote about America were not content, however, to provide a mere narrative account of events. Writing within a developmental framework, their works were not only intended to provide a record of a single people or region, but attempted also to reveal some of the underlying principles of rational historical development. For the most part, their writings reflected certain assumptions common to many historians on both sides of the Atlantic during the first half of the nineteenth century: the idea that history was essentially the story of liberty; that man's record revealed a progressive advance of civil liberties throughout world history; and that the peoples of Anglo-Saxon origin had a special destiny to bring democracy to the rest of the world.

George Bancroft, the outstanding romantic historian of the mid-nineteenth century, organized his work on the history of the United States around these three themes. Studying in Germany during the early 1820's, Bancroft reflected the romantic interpretation of history of his European teachers. He believed in the progressive unfolding of human history toward a millennium in which all individuals would ultimately achieve complete freedom and liberty. This march of all mankind toward a greater freedom was in accordance with a preordained plan conceived by God. One phase of God's master plan could be seen in the way that ancient Germanic folkways served as "germs" from which there developed a superior Anglo-Saxon peoples with a distinctive set of democratic institutions. The United States, according to Bancroft, represented the finest flowering of such democratic institutions. American democracy, then, was the fruition of God's plan and the American people had a unique mission in history to spread democracy throughout the rest of the world. Such was the central theme of Bancroft's famous twelve-volume work, *History of the United States from the Discovery of the American Continent,* written between 1834 and 1882.

Francis Parkman, another of the romantic historians, held many assumptions similar to those of Bancroft. Writing about the intercolonial wars in his work, *France and England in North America,* Parkman portrayed the American colonists as democratic Anglo-Saxons of Protestant persuasion whose superior qualities enabled them to conquer the authoritarian-minded French Catholics in Canada. But in many other ways, the two writers were quite different. Parkman was more representative of the gentlemen-historians of the nineteenth century who, being drawn from the upper classes, usually reflected an aristocratic bias in their writings, advocated a conservative Whig philosophy, and were distrustful of the masses in America. Bancroft, on the other hand, believed fervently in the common man and was an ardent Jacksonian Democrat.

By the 1870's, two profound changes began to influence the writing of American history. The first of these was the change in leadership from amateur to professional historians. Until the last quarter of the nineteenth century, American history had been written almost exclusively by men who had no special training as historians — except, of course, for a few individuals like Bancroft. From this point on, however, the writing of history was dominated by professionally trained historians educated in the universities of Europe and America. Professionalization in the field was made possible by developments in higher education as graduate schools appeared in increasing numbers in America to train college history teachers. In the last three decades of the century, professionalization proceeded at a rapid rate: the Johns Hopkins University, the first institution devoted exclusively to postgraduate study and research, began its activities in 1876; the American Historical Association was founded in 1884; and the *American Historical Review* made its appearance in 1895.

The advent of professional historians brought about a marked transformation in the field. No longer was historical writing to be vested mainly in the hands of amateurs — though in fairness it should be noted that some of these men had been superb stylists, intelligent and creative scholars, and researchers who often made sound and judicious use of original sources. Nor would historians be drawn almost exclusively from the patrician class in the Northeast, particularly from New England. Professional historians came from all walks of life, represented a much broader range of social interests than the patricians, and hailed from various geographical regions. Finally, instead of being free-lance scholars as many patricians had been, professionals derived their financial support as teachers and researchers from universities, colleges, and educational institutions.

The second major development in the history field was the marked change in the climate of opinion. Under the impact of Darwinism and new discoveries in the natural sciences, historians began to think of history as a science rather than a form of art. Why could not the historian deal with the facts of history in much the same way that the scientist did with elements in the laboratory? If there were certain laws of organic development in the scientific field, might there not be certain laws of historical development? What historian, wrote Henry Adams, with "an idea of scientific method can have helped dreaming of the immortality that would be achieved by the man who should successfully apply Darwin's method to the facts of human history." [4]

The first generation of professional historians — who held sway from about 1870 to 1910 — was best exemplified by two outstanding scholars, Henry Adams and Frederick Jackson Turner. Henry

4. Henry Adams, "The Tendency of History," *Annual Report of the American Historical Association for the Year 1894* (Washington, D.C., 1895), p. 19.

Adams, a descendant of the famous Adams family that contributed American presidents, statesmen, and diplomats, had turned to history and literature as his avocation after being frustrated in hopes for high political office. In 1870 he was invited to Harvard and became the first teacher to introduce a history seminar at that institution. Adams pioneered in training his students in the meticulous critical methods of German scholarship and searched for a time for a scientific philosophy of history based on the findings in the field of physics. His nine-volume history of the United States during the administrations of Jefferson and Madison was destined to become one of the great classics in American historical literature. Although he left Harvard after a few years, his career symbolized the transformation from patrician to professional historians and the changing intellectual climate of opinion from romanticism to a more scientific approach in the writing of American history.

While Henry Adams was attempting to assimilate history and physics, Frederick Jackson Turner — perhaps the most famous and influential representative of the scientific school of historians to come out of the first generation of professional historians — was applying evolutionary modes of thought to explain American history. Born and reared in a frontier community in Wisconsin, Turner attended the University of Wisconsin, received his Ph.D. from the Johns Hopkins University, and then went on to a teaching career first at Wisconsin and later at Harvard. Like Adams, Turner believed that it was possible to make a science out of history and attempted, therefore, to apply the ideas of Darwinian evolution to the writing of history. Turner emphasized the concept of evolutionary stages of development as successive frontier environments in America brought about changes in the character of the people and their institutions. As one frontier in America was succeeded by another, each more remote from Europe than its predecessor, a social evolutionary process was working to create the American democratic individualist. The unique characteristics of the American people — their rugged individualism, egalitarianism, self-reliance, practicality, and materialistic outlook on life — all resulted from the evolutionary process of adapting to successive frontier environments, according to Turner. His famous essay, "The Significance of the Frontier in American History," written in 1893, was an outstanding example of the approach employed by the scientific school of historians.

The second generation of professional historians — who dominated the field from about 1910 to 1945 — were subject to different currents of thought that swept through American intellectual life during this era. Most of them were influenced in varying degrees by the reform movements then developing in contemporary American life. Rejecting the views of the older and more conservative patrician historians, they saw history as an ideological weapon that might explain the present and perhaps help to control the future. In sympathy with the aims and objectives of the Progressive reformers of the early twentieth century, these scholars wrote history in such a manner as to prepare the way for progress, change, and democracy.

Unlike the patrician historians of the nineteenth century, the scholars of the Progressive school tended to come from the Midwest and the South. These Progressives complained that in the past American history had simply been an extension of the history of New England. American civilization, they argued, was more than a transplanted English and European civilization; it had unique characteristics and a mission all of its own that distinguished it from its parent ancestors. But while the Progressive school was as nationalistic as the patrician school, it was a nationalism of a very different type. The patricians had conceived of nationalism as a stabilizing force, preserving order and thus assuring the continued ascendancy of the aristocratic elements in American life. The Progressives, on the other hand, considered nationalism a dynamic force. To them the fulfillment of democracy meant a continued and protracted struggle against those individuals, classes, and groups who had barred the way to the achievement of a more democratic society in the past.

In changing the direction of American historical writing, Progressive scholars drew upon the reform tradition that had grown out of the efforts to adjust American society to the new demands of an urban-centered and industrialized age. This tradition had originated in the 1880's and reached maturity in the early part of the twentieth century with the Progressive movement. Drawing upon various sources, the adherents of the Progressive movement rejected the idea of a closed system of classical economic thought which assumed that certain natural laws governed human society. Society, these reformers maintained, was open-ended and dynamic; its development was not determined by immutable laws, but by social and economic forces that grew out of the interaction between the individual and his environment.

Reacting against the older emphasis upon logic, abstraction, and deduction, these reformers sought a meaningful explanation of human society that could account for its peculiar development. Instead of focusing upon immutable laws, they began viewing society and individuals as products of an evolutionary developmental process. This process could be understood only by reference to the past. The function of the historian, then, was to explain how the present had come to be and to try and set guidelines for future developments. As a result of this approach, there was a drawing together of history and the other social sciences which were seeking to explain the realities of society by emphasizing the interplay of economic, technological, social, psychological, and political forces.

History, according to its Progressive practitioners, was not an abstract discipline whose truths could only be contemplated. On the contrary, the historian had an important role to fulfill in the construction of a better world. By explaining the historical roots of contemporary problems, historians could provide that knowledge and understanding necessary to make changes which would bring further progress. Like the Enlightenment *philosophes,* the historian could reveal the mistakes and errors of the past and thus liberate men from the chains of tyranny and oppression of the past. When fused with the social sciences, history would provide a powerful tool for reform. "The present has hitherto been the willing victim of the past," wrote James Harvey Robinson, one of the greatest exponents of Progressive history; but "the time has now come when it should turn on the past and exploit it in the interests of advance." [5]

Clearly, the sympathy of Progressive historians and scholars lay with change and not with the preservation of the *status quo.* Committed to the idea of progress, they saw themselves as contributing to the better and more humane world of the future. Consequently, they rejected the apparent moral neutrality and supposed objectivity of the scientific school in favor of a liberal philosophy of reform. In so doing, they rewrote much of American history, greatly widening its scope and changing its emphasis. Instead of

5. James Harvey Robinson, "The New History," in *The New History: Essays Illustrating the Modern Historical Outlook* (New York, 1912), p. 24.

focusing on narrow institutional studies or traditional political, diplomatic, and military history, they sought to delineate those determinant forces that underlay human institutions. In their hands, American history became a protracted and unceasing struggle between democracy and aristocracy, between the have-nots and the haves, between the underprivileged and the over-privileged; in short, between those committed to democratic and egalitarian ideals and those committed to a static conservatism.

Believers in inevitable progress, the Progressive historians assumed that America was continuously moving, in the words of Charles A. Beard, on an upward gradient toward a more ideal order. Not only was American society growing in affluence, but in freedom, opportunity, and happiness as well. The primary determinant of progress was unending conflict between the forces of liberalism and those of conservatism. Thus all periods in American history could be divided into two clear and distinct phases; periods of active reform and periods of conservative consolidation. As Arthur M. Schlesinger, Sr., wrote in 1939: "A period of concern for the rights of the few has been followed by one of concern for the wrongs of the many." [6]

Just as Henry Adams spoke for the scientific school of history, so did Frederick Jackson Turner, Charles A. Beard, and Vernon L. Parrington speak for the Progressives, each in his own way. After his epochal essay on the frontier in 1893—an essay that emphasized unity rather than conflict — Turner's interests turned elsewhere, particularly to the idea of sectional conflict. From the late 1890's until his death in 1932, he elaborated and refined his sectional conflict hypothesis. Turner and his students not only attempted to understand how a section came into being, but the dynamics of conflict that pitted the East against West, North against South, labor against capital, and the many against the few. Under Turner's guiding hand, American historians wrote a series of brilliant monographs as well as broad interpretive studies that emphasized the class and sectional divisions in American society. Although a few favored the conservative side, the overwhelming majority of historians made clear their preference for democratic liberalism and progress.

6. Arthur M. Schlesinger, Sr., "Tides of American Politics," *Yale Review*, XXIX (December, 1939), 220.

While Turner was developing and elaborating his sectional approach, Charles A. Beard was applying an overt class conflict hypothesis to the study of American institutions. In one of the most famous and influential books ever written by an American historian —*An Economic Interpretation of the Constitution* (1913)—Beard attempted to demonstrate that the Constitution, far from representing a judicious combination of wisdom and idealism, was actually the product of a small group of propertied individuals who were intent upon establishing a strong central government capable of protecting their interests against the encroachments of the great masses. In a series of books, culminating with the magisterial *Rise of American Civilization* in 1927, Beard argued that American history demonstrated the validity of the class conflict hypothesis. Time and again, he showed the paramount role that economic factors played in determining human behavior. Fusing his ardent faith in progress with a somewhat qualified economic determinism, Beard made clear that his sympathies lay with the forces of democracy as opposed to those of reaction and privilege.

The culmination of the Progressive school came with the publication of Vernon L. Parrington's *Main Currents in American Thought* (3 vols., 1927–1930). Using literature as his vehicle, Parrington portrayed American history in clear but unmistakable terms. The two central protagonists of Parrington's work were Jefferson and Hamilton. Jefferson stood for a decentralized agrarian democracy that drew its support from the great mass of people. Hamilton, on the other hand, represented a privileged and propertied minority seeking to maintain a dominant position. American history, according to Parrington, had witnessed a continual struggle between the liberal Jeffersonian tradition and the conservative Hamiltonian one. Underlying Parrington's approach was one major assumption that had governed also the thought of Turner and Beard: namely, that ideology was determined by the materialistic forces in history. Like Turner and Beard, Parrington clearly preferred the forces of reform and democracy, but there were times when he was much less certain of their eventual triumph than his two intellectual companions.

Until the end of World War II, the Progressive school continued to dominate the field of American historical scholarship. During these decades historians continued to interpret American history in terms of class and sectional conflict. Out of such conflicts, these scholars averred, progress would emerge triumphant. Even during those eras in American history when the forces of reaction triumphed — as in the post-Civil War period — their victory was only temporary; ultimately the forces of progress and good regrouped and thereby gained the initiative once again. Such an approach, of course, led to broad and sweeping interpretive syntheses of American history, for the basic framework or structure was clear and simple and the faith of historians in the ultimate triumph of good over evil remained unquestioned.

Beginning in the 1930's, however, and continuing especially in the 1940's, 1950's, and 1960's, the faith of American historians in progress began to undergo a profound change. The rise of Nazism in the 1930's and 1940's, and the menace of communism in the 1950's and 1960's, led to a questioning of older assumptions and generalities. How, some asked, could one subscribe to the optimistic tenets of liberalism after the horrors of Auschwitz, Buchenwald, Hiroshima, Nagasaki, and the threat of modern totalitarianism? Indeed, had not American historians, through their own optimistic view of history and their faith in progress, failed to prepare the American people for the challenges and trials that they would face during the middle of the twentieth century? Parrington himself had recognized as early as 1929 that the Progressive faith was under attack by those who did not subscribe to its basic tenets. "Liberals whose hair is growing thin and the lines of whose figures are no longer what they were," he wrote, "are likely to find themselves today in the unhappy predicament of being treated as mourners at their own funerals. When they pluck up heart to assert that they are not yet authentic corpses, but living men with brains in their heads, they are pretty certain to be gently chided and led back to the comfortable armchair that befits senility. Their counsel is smiled at as the chatter of a belated post-Victorian generation that knew not Freud, and if they must go abroad they are bidden take the air in the garden where other old-fashioned plants — mostly of the family *Democratici* — are still preserved." [7]

Since World War II, a third generation of professional his-

7. Vernon L. Parrington, *Main Currents in American Thought* (3 vols: New York, 1927–1930), III, 401.

torians appeared on the scene who gradually but clearly broke with the Progressive school of American historiography. Indeed, some of these modern scholars – the so-called neo-conservative school of historians – sharply revised the Progressive point of view. The term "neo-conservatives" was applied to these men because they seemed to hark back to the more conservative approach to history characteristic of the period prior to the rise of the Progressive school. What the neo-conservative historians did was to restudy American history in terms of consensus and continuity rather than in terms of conflict and change.

The neo-conservative historians – unlike the Progressive school – found Americans to be more united than divided and the American past characterized more by consensus than by conflict. They consistently de-emphasized class and sectional divisions and argued that there never was any class struggle in America in the European sense of the term. The tendencies that united Americans throughout their past were more important than those dividing them and it was this consensus that gave America its cohesiveness and a unique character of its own. If the political contestants of a period appeared to be at odds – such as during the Jeffersonian and Jacksonian eras – such disagreements took place within a broader framework where the beliefs held in common by the opponents were more powerful than the specific issues dividing them.

The neo-conservative historians also served a different role as commentators on American society. Rather than being critical of American society, they were fond of emphasizing its achievements. Although they did not deny the existence of social injustice within the United States, they tended to minimize somewhat its pervasiveness and seriousness. Unlike the Progressive historians, the neo-conservative scholars were not alienated from their culture. On the contrary, they played a vital role in assuring Americans that the society in which they were living was basically a harmonious one and, perhaps, had always been so in the past.

The results of such a complacent view of the American past were not difficult to identify. American history became relatively tame and placid; it was no longer a history marked by extreme group conflicts or rigid class distinctions. The heroes of American history—Jefferson, Lincoln, Wilson, Roosevelt – became less heroic because there was no head-on clash between individuals on the basis of ideas or ideology since all Americans seemed to share the same middle-class Lockean values. Conversely, the villains — Hamilton, Rockefeller, Carnegie — became less evil and more imaginative and constructive figures. The achievements of the business community — the bête noire of Progressive scholarship — were now glorified. Without the material achievements of America's great entrepreneurs, some argued, the United States could not have withstood the challenges to democracy in the two World Wars. The underdogs in American history — the reformers and working class — became less idealistic and more egocentric as neo-conservative historians sought to demonstrate that the ideology of these groups was no less narrow and self-centered than that of other groups.

In explaining the appearance of neo-conservative historians, commentators emphasized circumstances both within and without the United States. America, they noted, had entered upon a new phase of its history since the end of World War II. As leader of the free world, the United States had taken on new responsibilities in countering the rise of communism in such nations as the Soviet Union and China. The need for unity in the face of such threats to our national security had placed a greater premium than ever before upon conformity and consensus among the American people. Neo-conservative historians, some argued, had responded to the needs of their own generation by stressing the consensus thesis when writing about the American past in order to present the image of a nation that was strong and united throughout most of its history. The economic prosperity on the domestic scene since World War II likewise had an effect upon neo-conservative historians, according to these same commentators. Affluence in the postwar period dimmed the lines of class distinction in America, and neo-conservative scholars read the predilections of their own age back into America's past by de-emphasizing class conflict.

Whatever the reasons for the rise of the neo-conservative historians, it is clear that their influence was apparent in the historiography of every period of American history — the revival of the fileopietist approach to the Puritans; the treatment of the American Revolution as a conservative movement of little account; the conclusion that the Constitution was a document reflecting a middle-class consensus; the favorable, if not uncritical, attitude toward the founding fathers; the diminution in the traditional ideological conflict between Hamiltonianism and Jeffersonianism; the consensus view of the Jacksonian era; the enhanced reputation of America's business leaders; the renewed appreciation of such political leaders as Theodore Roosevelt; the inclination to play down the more radical aspects of the Progressive and New Deal periods; and the tendency to view contemporary American society in terms of a basic consensus — all attested to the new respect for tradition characteristic of the neo-conservative historians. Implicit in their approach to history was a fear of extremism, a yearning to prove national unity among the American people, and a longing for the security and way of life in the United States prior to World War II. In many ways, indeed, the neo-conservative scholars demonstrated the proof of Croce's dictum, "Every true history is contemporary history."

In attempting to understand the course of American history, therefore, it is important to keep in mind the fact that the interpretations of particular historians often reflect their own starting assumptions and ideology. History, after all, is more than an aggregation of discrete facts; it involves interpretation, meaning, and significance as well. To fully comprehend the writings of any given historian, then, it is essential to grasp the framework within which the data are being presented. In the final analysis, it is the historian who imposes order on the facts, not the reverse. Thus the study of American history involves not only a knowledge of empirical data in isolation, but also the structure that is used to explain such data.

2

The Reconstruction Era

Constructive or Destructive?

TO STUDENTS OF AMERICAN HISTORY, the Civil War years stand in sharp contrast to those of the Reconstruction era. The war years represented a period of heroism and idealism; out of the travail of conflict there emerged a new American nationality that replaced the older sectional and state loyalties. Although the cost in lives and money was frightful, the divisions that had plagued Americans for over half a century were eliminated in the ordeal of fire. Henceforth, America would stand as a united country, destined to take its rightful place as one of the leading nations in the world.

The Reconstruction era, on the other hand, conjures up a quite different picture. Just as the war years were dominated by heroism, the postwar period was characterized as being dominated by evil, power-seeking scoundrels, intent upon pursuing their narrow self-interest regardless of the cost to either the South or the nation. The result was a tragedy for all Americans — Northerners, Southerners, whites and Negroes alike. Nothing short of a revolution, it seemed, could displace the forces of evil from power and restore the South and the nation to its rightful rulers.

Between 1890 and 1930 few historians would have disagreed with this contrast of the two periods. If anything, most scholars during these years characterized Reconstruction in even harsher terms. Led by Professor William A. Dunning of Columbia University — who literally founded the school of Reconstruction historiography that still bears his name — the historical profession set out to prove that the years following the Civil War were marked by tragedy and pathos because men of good will were momentarily thrust out of power by the forces of evil. This period, in the words of one historian, "were years of revolutionary turmoil. . . . The prevailing note was one of tragedy. . . . Never have American public men in responsible positions, directing the destiny of the Nation, been so brutal, hypocritical, and corrupt. . . . The Southern people literally were put to the torture." [1]

Underlying the interpretation of the Dunning school were two important assumptions. The first was that the South should have been restored to the Union quickly and without being exposed to Northern vengeance. Most Southerners, it was argued, had accepted their military defeat gracefully and were prepared to pledge their good faith and loyalty to the Union. Secondly, responsibility for the freedmen should have been entrusted to white Southerners. The Negro, these historians believed, could never be integrated into American society on an equal plane with whites because of his former slave status and inferior racial characteristics.

Working within the framework of these two assumptions, historians in the Dunning school tradition proceeded to study Reconstruction in terms of a struggle between elements of good and evil. On one side stood the forces of good — Northern and Southern Democrats, and Republicans of the Andrew Johnson variety. These men, recognizing the necessity for compassion and leniency, were willing to forget the agonies of war and to forgive the South. On the opposing side were the forces of evil — scalawags, carpet-

1. Claude G. Bowers, *The Tragic Era: The Revolution After Lincoln* (Cambridge, 1929), pp. v–vi.

baggers, and above all, a group of radical and vindictive Republicans intent upon punishing the South by depriving the native aristocracy of their power and status, thereby ensuring the dominance of the Republican party in that section. Caught in the middle of this struggle were the helpless, impotent, and ignorant Negroes, whose votes were sought for sinister purposes by Radical Republicans who had little or no real concern for the welfare of the freedman once he had left the ballot box.

The result of such a political alignment in the South, according to the Dunning school, was disastrous. The Radical carpetbag state governments that came into power proved to be totally incompetent — in part because they included illiterate Negroes who were unprepared for the responsibilities of self-government. Still worse, these governments were extraordinarily expensive because they were corrupt. Most of them, indeed, left nothing but a legacy of huge debts. "Saddled with an irresponsible officialdom," one Dunning school historian concluded, "the South was now plunged into debauchery, corruption, and private plundering unbelievable — suggesting that government had been transformed into an engine of destruction." [2]

The decent whites in the South, the Dunning argument continued, united out of sheer desperation to force the carpetbaggers, scalawags, and Negroes from power. In one state after another Radical rule was eventually overthrown and good government restored. By the time of the presidential campaign of 1876 only three states remained under Radical control. When the dispute over the contested election was resolved, Hayes withdrew the remaining federal troops from the South, and the three last Radical regimes fell from power. Thus the tragic era of Reconstruction came to an end.

For nearly three decades after the turn of the century the Dunning point of view was the predominant one among most American historians. Many monographs on the history of individual Southern states were published, but most of them simply filled in pertinent details and left the larger picture virtually unchanged. All of these studies, despite their individual differences, agreed that the Reconstruction period had been an abject and

2. E. Merton Coulter, *The South During Reconstruction 1865–1877* (Baton Rouge, 1947), p. 148.

dismal failure. Not only had Reconstruction destroyed the two-party system in the South; it had left behind an enduring legacy of bitterness and hatred between the races.

The first selection, by Albert B. Moore, is a good example of a historian writing about Reconstruction within the Dunning tradition. The events between 1865 and 1877, Moore argues, had the effect of converting the South into a colonial appendage of the North. To put it another way, the Reconstruction period was simply one phase of the process whereby the North attempted to remake the South in its own image; it was an attempt by a victor to punish the vanquished. Rejecting completely the assertion that the North was lenient, Moore emphasizes property confiscations, mental torture, and vindictive military rule. The political enfranchisement of Negroes, which laid the basis for carpetbag government, is to Moore perhaps the most incredible event of an incredible era. The result was the continued exacerbation of Southern economic, political, and social problems. The South, he concludes, was still paying for the dark legacy of Reconstruction in the twentieth century.

In the late 1920's, however, historians began to look at the events between 1865 and 1877 from a new and different perspective. These revisionists — a term that distinguishes them from followers of the Dunning school — were much less certain that Reconstruction was as bad as had been commonly supposed. Influenced by the Progressive school of American historiography — which emphasized underlying economic factors in historical development — the revisionists began to restudy the entire Reconstruction period. As a result, they posed a sharp challenge to the Dunning school by changing the interpretive framework of the Reconstruction era.

Generally speaking, the revisionists accepted most, if not all, of the findings of the Dunning school. The disagreement between the two groups, therefore, arose from their different starting assumptions and the consequent interpretation of data rather than over disputed empirical data as such. Unlike the Dunningites, the revisionists could not view events between 1865 and 1877 in terms of a morality play that depicted Reconstruction as a struggle between good and evil, white and black, and Democrats and Radical Republicans. Nor were the revisionists willing to accept the view that responsibility for the freedmen should have been entrusted to native white Southerners. Given these differences, it was understandable that the revisionist interpretation should differ sharply from that of the Dunning school.

The second selection, written by Francis B. Simkins, a distinguished Southern historian who published with Robert Woody in 1932 one of the first revisionist state studies, illustrates the reaction against the Dunning position. Pointing out that the overwhelming majority of Southerners lived quietly and peacefully during these years, he emphasizes many of the constructive achievements of this era. Simkins, as a matter of fact, denies that the Radical program was radical within the accepted meaning of the word; indeed, the Radicals failed because they did not provide Negroes with a secure economic base. Past historians, he concludes, had given a distorted picture of Reconstruction because they had assumed that the Negro was racially inferior. The result was a provincial approach to Reconstruction that was based on ignorance and priggishness. Only by abandoning their biases could historians contribute to a more accurate understanding of the past, thereby making possible rational discussion of one of the nation's most critical dilemmas.

While the revisionists often disagreed as much among themselves as they did with the Dunning school, there were common areas of agreement that gave their writings a certain unity. Most revisionists viewed the problems of American society during these years in a broader context and concluded that they were national rather than sectional in scope. Corruption, to cite but one example, was not confined to the South. It was a national phenomenon in the postwar era and involved all sections, classes, and political parties alike. To single out the South in this regard was patently unfair and ahistorical.

Revisionist historians attempted also to refute many of the familiar assertions of the Dunning school. In the first place, they denied that the Radical governments in the South were always dishonest, incompetent, and inefficient. On the contrary, they claimed, such governments accomplished much of enduring value. The new constitutions written during Reconstruction represented a vast improvement over the older ones and often survived the overthrow of the men who had written them. Radical governments brought about many long-needed social reforms, including state-supported school systems for both Negroes and whites, a revision of the judicial system, and improvements in local administration. Above all, these governments operated — at least in theory — on the premise that all men, white and black alike, were entitled to equal political and civil liberties.

Secondly, the revisionists drew a sharply different portrait of the Negro during Reconstruction. They denied that developments in the postwar South resulted from Negro participation in government and that the freedmen were illiterate, naive, and inexperienced. In no Southern state, they pointed out, did Negroes control both houses of the legislature. Moreover, there were no Negro governors and only one state supreme court justice. Only two Negroes were elected to the United States Senate and fifteen to the House of Representatives. Such statistics hardly supported the charge that the supposed excesses of Reconstruction were due to political activities of the Negroes.

Indeed, the revisionists maintained that Negroes, as a group, were quite capable of understanding where their own interests lay without disregarding the legitimate interests of others. The freedmen were able to participate at least as intelligently as other groups in the American political process. As Vernon L. Wharton concluded in his pioneering revisionist study of the Negro in Mississippi after the Civil War, there was "little difference . . . in the administration of . . . counties [having Negroes on boards of supervisors] and that of counties under Democratic control. . . . Altogether, as governments go, that supplied by the Negro and white Republicans in Mississippi between 1870 and 1876 was not a bad government. . . . With their white Republican colleagues, they gave to the state a government of greatly expanded functions at a cost that was low in comparison with that of almost any other state." [3]

If Negroes were not the dominant group in most Radical governments, where did these governments get their support? In attempting to answer this question, revisionists again endeavored to refute the Dunning school contention that these governments were

3. Vernon L. Wharton, *The Negro in Mississippi 1865–1890* (Chapel Hill, 1947), pp. 172, 179–180.

controlled by evil, power-hungry, profit-seeking carpetbaggers and renegade scalawags who used Negro votes to maintain themselves in power. The stereotype of the carpetbagger and scalawag, according to revisionists, was highly inaccurate and far too simplistic. Carpetbaggers, to take one group, migrated to the South for a variety of reasons – including the lure of wider and legitimate economic opportunities as well as a desire to serve the former slaves in some humanitarian capacity. The scalawags were an equally diverse group. Within their ranks one could find former Southern unionists and Whigs, lower-class whites who sought to use the Republican party as the vehicle for confiscating the property of the planter aristocrats, and businessmen attracted by the promise of industrialization. The Radical governments, then, had a wide base of indigenous support in most Southern states.

Finally, the revisionists rejected the charge that the Radical governments were extraordinarily expensive and corrupt, or that they had saddled the South with a large public debt. It was true that state expenditures went up sharply after the war. This situation was due, however, to understandable circumstances and not to inefficiency or theft. As in most postwar periods, the partial destruction of certain cities and areas required an infusion of public funds. Deferring regular appropriations during the war years also meant that a backlog of legitimate projects had accumulated. Most important of all, the South for the first time had to provide certain public facilities and social services for the Negro. Southern states and communities had to build schools and provide other facilities and services for Negroes which did not exist before the 1860's and for which public funds had never been expended prior to this time. It is little wonder, then, that there was a rise in spending in the Reconstruction era.

In examining the financial structure of Southern governments between 1865 and 1877, the revisionists also found that the rise in state debts, in some instances, was more apparent than real. Grants to railroad promoters, which in certain states accounted for a large proportion of the increase in the debt, were secured by a mortgage on the railroad property. Thus, the rise in the debt was backed by sound collateral. The amount of the debt chargeable to theft, the revisionists maintained, was negligible. Indeed, the restoration governments, which were dominated by supposedly honest Southerners, proved to be far more corrupt than those governments controlled by the Radicals.

Although revisionists agreed that the Dunning interpretation of Reconstruction was inadequate — if not misleading — they had considerable difficulty themselves in synthesizing their own findings. If there was one idea on which the revisionists were united, it was their conviction that economic forces, which were related to the growth of an urban and industrialized nation, somehow played a major role during this period. Beneath the political and racial antagonisms of this era, some revisionists argued, lay opposing economic rivalries. Anxious to gain an advantage over their competitors, many business interests used politics as the vehicle to further their economic ambitions — especially since the South, like the North and West, was ardently courting businessmen. The result was that economic rivalries were often translated into political struggles.

Revisionists also emphasized the crucial issue of race. During Reconstruction many former Whigs joined the Republican party because of its pro-business economic policies. These well-to-do conservatives, at first, were willing to promise Negroes civil and political rights in return for their support at the polls. Within the Democratic party, however, lower-class whites, fearful of possible encroachments by the Negro upon their social status and economic position, raised the banner of race. Conservatives found their affiliation with the Republican party increasingly uncomfortable and slowly began to drift back into the Democratic party. The fact that both parties were under the control of conservatives made it easier for former Republicans to shift their political allegiance. One result of the political realignment was that it left the Negroes politically isolated and without allies among the whites. When the move to eliminate Negroes from political life in the South got under way, they could find little support among Southern whites. This political move came at a time when Northerners were disillusioned by the failure of the Radicals to achieve many of their idealistic aims for the freedmen. Tired of conflict and turmoil, Northerners became reconciled to the idea of letting the South work out its own destiny — even if it meant sacrificing the Negro people. Northern businessmen likewise became convinced that only Southern conservatives could restore order and stability and thus create a favorable environment for investment.

The result was both a polarization of Southern politics along racial rather than economic lines and the emergence of the Democratic party as the white man's party. For whites of lower-class background, the primary goal was to maintain the South as a white man's country. Upper-class whites were also contented with the existing one-party political structure because they were permitted the dominant role in determining the future economic development of their section.

The end of Reconstruction, according to the revisionists, was closely related to the triumph of business values and industrial capitalism. When the contested presidential election of 1876 resulted in an apparent deadlock between Rutherford B. Hayes, the Republican candidate, and Samuel J. Tilden, his Democratic opponent, some prominent Republicans saw an opportunity to rebuild their party in the South along new lines. Instead of basing their party upon propertyless former slaves, they hoped to attract well-to-do former Whigs who had been forced into the Democratic party as a result of events during Reconstruction. To accomplish this goal, a group of powerful Republican leaders began to work secretly to bring about a political realignment. If Southern Democratic congressmen would not stand in the way of Hayes' election and also provide enough votes to permit the Republicans to organize the House of Representatives, these leaders were willing to promise the South federal subsidies and also to name a Southerner as Postmaster General.

The "Compromise of 1877," as this political deal was called, was not fully carried out, but its larger implications survived unscathed. As C. Vann Woodward, the revisionist historian who propounded the thesis of such a political bargain, concluded, the Compromise "did not restore the old order in the South, nor did it restore the South to parity with other sections. It did assure the dominant whites political autonomy and nonintervention in matters of race policy and promised them a share in the blessings of the new economic order. In return the South became, in effect, a satellite of the dominant region. So long as the Conservative Redeemers held control they scotched any tendency of the South to combine forces with the internal enemies of the new economy — laborites, Western agrarians, reformers. Under the regime of the Redeemers the South became a bulwark instead of a menace to the new order." [4]

Since the early 1950's, a new school of Reconstruction historiography called the neo-revisionists has emerged. These historians emphasized the moral rather than the economic basis of Reconstruction. The differences between the revisionists and neo-revisionists are often minimal since the latter frequently rely upon the findings of the former to reach their conclusions and it is difficult, if not impossible, to categorize certain historians as belonging to one group or another. Generally speaking, while the neo-revisionists accepted many findings of the revisionists, they rejected the idea of interpreting Reconstruction in strictly economic terms. The Republican party, the neo-revisionists maintained, was not united on a pro-business economic program; it included individuals and groups holding quite different social and economic views.

In interpreting Reconstruction, the neo-revisionists stressed the critical factor of race as a moral issue. One of the unresolved dilemmas after the Civil War, they claimed, was the exact role that the Negro was to play in American society. Within the Republican party, a number of factions each offered its own solution to this question. Andrew Johnson, who had been nominated as Lincoln's running mate in 1864 on a Union party ticket despite his Democratic party affiliations, spoke for one segment of the party. To Johnson the Negro was incapable of self-government. Consequently, he favored the state governments in the South that came back into the Union shortly after the end of the war under his own plan of reconstruction and went along with the Black Codes that denied the Negroes many of their civil rights.

Although Johnson was President as well as titular head of the Republican party, there was a great deal of opposition to his policies by a group known as the "Radicals." Who were the Radical Republicans and what did they stand for? To the Dunning school the Radicals were a group of vindictive politicians who were utterly amoral in their quest after power; they were merely interested in the Negro for his vote. To revisionists the Radicals represented, at least in part, the interests of the industrial Northeast — men who

4. C. Vann Woodward, *Reunion and Reaction: The Compromise of 1877 and the End of Reconstruction* (Boston, 1951), p. 246.

wanted to use Negro votes to prevent the formation of a coalition of Western and Southern agrarian interests against the industrial capitalism of the Northeast.[5]

To the neo-revisionists, on the other hand, the Radicals were a much more complex group. Many of the Radicals, they claimed, had joined the Republican party in the 1850's for moral and idealistic reasons — their antislavery zeal — rather than for economic motives. These men, seeking to eradicate all vestiges of slavery, were consistent in their demands before and after the war that Negroes be given the same rights as other Americans. Their beliefs, of course, brought them to a face-to-face confrontation with President Johnson in the postwar period. In the ensuing struggle, the President, because of his political ineptness, soon found himself isolated. Taking advantage of the situation, the Radicals first won the support of conservative Republicans and then set out to remake Southern society by transferring political power from the planter class to the freedmen. The program of the Radicals, therefore, was motivated in large measure by idealism and by a sincere humanitarian concern.

In the third selection Kenneth M. Stampp analyzes the complex nature of radicalism in the 1860's. Stampp begins by rejecting the traditional stereotype of the average Radical as a figure motivated by vindictive considerations. He argues that the issues of the 1860's were not artificial ones, as the Dunning school had claimed. The central question of the postwar period was the place of the free Negro in American society. President Johnson and his followers believed in the innate racial inferiority of the Negro; therefore they rejected any program based upon egalitarian assumptions. The Radicals, on the other hand, took seriously the ideals of equality, natural rights, and democracy. Indeed, most of these men had been closely associated with the antebellum abolitionist crusade. Stampp does not deny that the Radicals had other motives as well, for he admits that they saw the Negro as a valuable addition to the Republican party. But most politicians, he argues, identify the welfare of the nation with the welfare of their party. To argue that the Radicals had invidious and selfish motives,

5. This point of view was best expressed by Howard K. Beale, one of the fathers of the revisionist school, in *The Critical Year: A Study of Andrew Johnson and Reconstruction* (New York, 1930).

Stampp concludes, does them a severe injustice and results in a distorted picture of the Reconstruction era.

The Radicals, according to the neo-revisionists, ultimately failed in their objectives. Most Americans, harboring conscious and unconscious racial antipathies, were not willing to accept the Negro as their equal. By the 1870's the North was prepared to abandon the Negro to the white South for three reasons: a wish to return to prewar relations between the sections; a desire to promote industrial investment in that section; and a growing conviction that the Negro was no longer worth further strife. The tragedy of Reconstruction, the neo-revisionists maintained, was not that it occurred, but that it had ended short of achieving the major goal sought by the Radicals.

The struggle over Reconstruction, nevertheless, had not been in vain. In addition to the many achievements of the Radical governments, the Radicals had succeeded in securing the adoption of the Fourteenth and Fifteenth amendments. These amendments, in the words of a leading neo-revisionist, "which could have been adopted only under the conditions of radical reconstruction, make the blunders of that era, tragic though they were, dwindle into insignificance. For if it was worth four years of civil war to save the Union, it was worth a few years of radical reconstruction to give the American Negro the ultimate promise of equal civil and political rights." [6]

The differences between the three schools of Reconstruction historiography may be explained in many respects in terms of the particular milieu in which each had grown to maturity. The Dunning point of view, for example, originated in the late nineteenth century and flowered in the early part of the twentieth. During these years the vast majority of white Americans assumed that Negroes constituted an inferior race and one that was incapable of being fully assimilated into their society. Most Southerners had come to this conclusion well before the Civil War; many Northerners had come to the same conclusion after the debacle of Reconstruction seemingly vindicated this belief. Racism in America was buttressed further by the findings of the biological and social sciences in the late nineteenth century. Influenced by evolutionary

6. Kenneth M. Stampp, *The Era of Reconstruction 1865–1877* (New York, 1965), p. 215.

concepts of Darwinism, some scientists argued that Negroes had followed a unique evolutionary course which resulted in the creation of an inferior race. The racial prejudices of many Americans thus received supposedly scientific justification.

Given these beliefs, it is not difficult to understand why the Dunning school interpretation gained rapid acceptance. The attempt by the Radicals to give equal rights to a supposedly inferior race did not appear to be sensible; state governments that included Negro officials and held power in part through Negro votes were bound to be inefficient, incompetent, and corrupt. Moreover, the Southern claim that responsibility for the Negro people had to be entrusted to whites seemed entirely justifiable. The findings of the Dunning school that Reconstruction was a tragic blunder doomed to failure from its very beginning came as no surprise to early twentieth century Americans, most of whom were prepared to believe the worst about the Negro.

The revisionist school, on the other hand, originated in a somewhat different climate of opinion. By the 1920's American historiography had came under the influence of the Progressive or "New History" school. This school, growing out of dissatisfaction with the older scientific school of historians that emphasized the collection of impartial empirical data and eschewed "subjective" interpretations, borrowed heavily from the new social sciences. The New History sought to explain historical change by isolating underlying economic and social forces that transformed institutions and social structures. In place of tradition and stability it emphasized change and conflict. Progressive and democratic in their orientation, New School historians attempted to explain the present in terms of the dynamic and impersonal forces that had transformed American society.

The revisionists, then, rejected the moralistic tone of the Dunning school. They sought instead to identify the historical forces responsible for many of the developments following the Civil War. Economic and social factors, they maintained, were basic to this era. The real conflict was not between North and South, white and Negro; it was between industrial capitalism and agrarianism, with the former ultimately emerging victorious. Thus, the question of the Negro in American society was simply a façade for the more basic conflicts that lay hidden beneath the surface. Reconstruction, they concluded, was the first phase in the emergence of the United States as a leading industrial and capitalist nation.

Finally, the neo-revisionist school, although owing much to the revisionists, was influenced by the egalitarian emphasis of the 1940's and the period following the Second World War. Indicative of changing attitudes toward the Negro was the publication in 1944 of the monumental study by Gunnar Myrdal and his associates, *An American Dilemma: The Negro Problem and Modern Democracy*. Myrdal, a distinguished Swedish sociologist, was commissioned by the Carnegie Foundation in the late 1930's to undertake a comprehensive study of the Negro in the United States. Although emphasizing that a variety of complex factors were responsible for the depressed condition of American Negroes, Myrdal argued that the problem was basically a moral one. Americans, he wrote, held a political creed that stressed the equality of all men. This ideal, however, was constantly confronted with the inescapable reality that in the United States white citizens refused to accept Negroes as their equals. Thus many Americans were caught in a dilemma between theory and practice, causing them to suffer an internal moral conflict. Myrdal's work anticipated, in part, the thinking behind the civil rights movement of the 1950's.

In evaluating events between 1865 and 1877, neo-revisionist historians began to shift the focus of previous schools. The issue of equal rights for the Negro, neo-revisionists maintained, was not a false one even though it was complicated by economic and other factors. In a real sense, the fundamental problem of Reconstruction was whether or not white Americans were prepared to accept the freedmen as equal partners. Even though the Radicals ultimately failed in achieving their egalitarian goals, they left an enduring legacy in the form of the Fourteenth and Fifteenth amendments. These amendments gave the Negro citizenship, promised him equal protection under the laws, and gave him the right to vote. That America did not honor these promises in the decades after Reconstruction in no way detracted from the idealism of those responsible for these amendments. Indeed, the importance of these amendments took on a new meaning as they gave legal sanction to civil rights after World War II.

Although it is possible to demonstrate that particular interpretations grew out of and reflected their own milieu, historians must still face the larger and more important problem of determining the accuracy or inaccuracy of each interpretation. Was Reconstruction, as the Dunning school argues, a tragedy for all Americans? Were the revisionists correct in stressing the achievements as well as the partial failures of this period, and emphasizing the fundamental economic factors? Or were the neo-revisionists justified in insisting that the major issue during Reconstruction was indeed a moral one?

To answer these questions, historians must deal also with a number of subsidiary issues. Should the North have forgotten that it had taken four years of bloody and expensive conflict to keep America united and welcomed the South back into the Union in 1865 with open arms? Or was it proper for Northern Republicans to lay down certain conditions to ensure that slavery, legal or implied, would never again exist within the United States? What should have been the proper policy for both the federal and state governments to follow with regard to the Negro? Were Southerners justified in their belief that the Negro was incapable of caring for himself and that his future should be left in the hands of white men? Or were the Radicals correct in insisting that the Negro had to be given the same legal and political rights that all Americans enjoyed?

The answers to some of these questions will, in large measure, determine the broader interpretive framework of the Reconstruction era. Although that period is nearly a century away from our own, some of the basic conflicts common to both remain unresolved and as pressing as ever. Time and circumstances may have changed; new leaders may have emerged; yet the fundamental dilemma of what role the Negro people should occupy in American civilization remains a controversial and vital one.

Albert B. Moore

THE SOUTH has long been, and to some extent still is, in the throes of being reconstructed by forces operating from outside the region. Ramifications of this reconstruction process account in large degree for certain conditions in the South today and for its place in the nation. They explain how the South has acquired a colonial status, not only in the economic system but also in the psychology, sentiment, culture, and politics of the nation.

While this address is concerned primarily with the reconstruction of the South after the Civil War, it takes cognizance of the fact that the reconstruction of the South by the North has been going on more than one hundred years. Prior to the Civil War it took the form of a savage attack upon slavery and southern society, though it had other connotations. The Northeast with its western extensions, possessed of what one writer called "egocentric sectionalism" – that is, the conviction that it was not a section but the whole United States and that, therefore, its pattern of life must prevail throughout the country–, undertook after 1830 to reconstruct the South into conformity and into a subordinate position. With furious denunciations and menacing gestures and actions it drove the South into secession and war, destroyed its power, and reconstructed it with a vengeance and violence remarkable in the history of human conflict. This is not to give the South a clear bill of health; but whatever the rights and wrongs of the controversy, the Civil War, broadly speaking, was the tragic drama of a movement to reconstruct the South.

"One Hundred Years of Reconstruction of the South," *Journal of Southern History,* IX (May, 1943), 153–65.

ALBERT B. MOORE (1887–   ) taught from 1923 to 1958 at the University of Alabama, where he also served as Dean of the Graduate School and Chairman of the Department of History. He is the author of several books on the history of the South. The selection reprinted above was his presidential address before the Southern Historical Association in 1942.

We have formed the habit of examining the phenomena of the reconstruction of the South after the Civil War — that is, the period 1865–1877 — in a very objective, almost casual, way and with little regard to their essence and their significance in southern and national history. While avoiding the emotional approach one should not forget that it was, after all, a settlement imposed by the victors in war, and should be studied in all its effects, immediate and far reaching, on its victims. An investigation of the effects on the victors themselves would also be an interesting adventure. It is a chapter in the history of the punishment of the defeated in war. The observations of a competent historian from another country, coming upon the subject for the first time, taking nothing for granted and making a critical analysis of its severity compared with the punishment of losers in wars in general, would make interesting reading.

The war set the stage for a complete reconstruction of the South. Furious hatred, politics, economic considerations, and a curious conviction that God had joined a righteous North to use it as an instrument for the purging of the wicked South gave a keen edge to the old reconstruction urge. The victories of bullets and bayonets were followed by the equally victorious attack of tongues and pens. Ministers mounted their pulpits on Easter Sunday, the day following President Lincoln's tragic death, and assured their sad auditors that God's will had been done, that the President had been removed because his heart was too merciful to punish the South as God required. An eminent New York divine assured his audience that the vice-regent of Christ, the new president, Andrew Johnson, was mandated from on high "to hew the rebels in pieces before the Lord." "So let us say," with becoming piety and sweet submissiveness he enjoined, "God's will be done." Whether the ministers thought, after they discovered that Johnson was opposed to a reign of terror, that the Lord had made a mistake is not a matter of record. As Professor Paul H. Buck has said, "It was in the churches that one found the utmost intolerance, bitterness, and unforgiveness during the sad months that followed Appomattox." Henry Ward Beecher, one of the more moderate northern preachers, thought the South was "rotten." "No timber," said he, "grown in its cursed soil is fit for the ribs of our ship of state or for our household homes." The newspapers spread abroad the preachers' gospel of righteous vindictiveness and expounded further the idea that drastic punishment of the South was essential for the security of the Union.

Many unfriendly writers invaded the South, found what they wanted, and wrote books, articles, and editorials that strengthened the conviction that the South must be torn to pieces and made anew. Books, journals, and newspapers stimulated the impulse to be vigilant and stern, to repress and purge. A juggernaut of propaganda, stemming from the various sources of public instruction, prepared the way for the crucifixion of the South. The South of slavery and treason, of continuous outrages against the Negroes and Northerners, of haughty spirit and stubborn conviction, and of superiority complex, must be humbled and made respectable or be annihilated, so that it could never become again a strong factor in national politics.

The South did little or nothing to neutralize Radical northern propaganda. To be sure, a few journalists, like A. T. Bledsoe, complained about "the cunningly devised fables, and the vile calumnies, with which a partisan press and a Puritanical pulpit have flooded the North," but their vituperative responses to vituperative attacks did more harm than good. There was, in the very nature of things, little that the South could do to disabuse the Radical northern mind that was disposed to believe evil of it. There was simply no escape for Southerners from an awful scourge. Even more courage and fortitude than they had displayed on the battlefield would be required to endure what was in store for them.

As much as Reconstruction has been studied in this country it should not at this late hour be necessary to point out its severity, its permanent effects upon the South, and its influence upon various aspects of our national history. Yet few have examined critically the harshness of it and its persistent and manifold effects. While crucifying the South, the dominant Radical group of the North, thanks to the blindness of hatred, believed it was being lenient. Because no lives were taken — but there are some things more agonizing than death — for the "crimes of treason and rebellion," the North has prided itself on its magnanimity; and its historians have been strangely oblivious of property confiscations and mental tortures. It seemed to the late James Ford Rhodes "the mildest punishment ever inflicted after an unsuccessful Civil War." But this was no ordinary civil war, if, indeed, it should be classed as a civil war. The thesis of leniency has oddly persisted. When the Germans protested to high heaven against the severity of the Versailles Treaty they had sympathizers in this country who compared the generosity of the North in its treatment of the South with the harshness of the Versailles Treaty. But the late Professor Carl Russell Fish of the University of Wisconsin, in his article on "The German Indemnity and the South," discredited the theory of generosity on the part of the North. He showed that the South was punished more than Germany, though he touched upon only a few phases of the South's burdens.

Professor Buck in his delightful and highly informative book, *The Road to Reunion,* recognized Reconstruction as "disorder worse than war and oppression unequalled in American annals," but made a serious error when he stated that "virtually no property" was confiscated. He overlooked the confiscation of large quantities of cotton – estimated in the minority report of the Ku Klux Klan Committee at two million bales – then selling for a very high price and most of which belonged to private citizens. The abolition of slavery wiped out about two billion dollars of capital and reduced the value of real estate by at least that amount. This was confiscation of property, and the repudiation of Confederate currency, the Confederate bonded debt, and the war debts of the states, all amounting to no less than three billion dollars, was confiscation of property rights. As inevitable as much of this was, it represented a frightful confiscation of property.

The freeing of the slaves not only cost the South two billion dollars but it also forced upon that section an economic and social revolution. It subverted a mode of life almost as old as the South itself. The repudiation of its debts impoverished the South and destroyed its financial relationships. While the South lost its debts, it had to pay its full share of the northern debts which amounted to about four-fifths of the total northern war expenses. The money for this debt was spent in the North for its upbuilding. It paid also its share of the $20,000,000 returned by the Federal treasury to the northern states for direct taxes collected from them during the war, and of extravagant pensions to Union soldiers. Professor James L. Sellers estimates that the South paid in these ways an indemnity of at least a billion dollars to the North.

The South accepted the results of the war — the doom of slavery and the doctrine of secession — as inevitable and its leaders sought to restore their respective states as speedily as possible to their normal position in the Union. But despite its acceptance in good faith of the declared aims of the North, the South was forced through the gauntlet of two plans of Reconstruction. The people conformed in good faith to the requirements of President Johnson's plan, but Congress repudiated this plan and forced the South to begin *de novo* the process of Reconstruction. Pending its restoration, it was put under the heel of military authority, though there was no problem that exceeded the power of civil authority to handle. Objectively viewed, it is a singular fact that it took three years to restore the South to the Union. It is little short of amazing that for a dozen years after the war Federal troops were stationed in the South among an orderly people who had played a leading role in the building and guidance of the nation since colonial times, and who now sought nothing so much as peace and surcease from strife. For much of the period government was a hodgepodge of activities by the civil authorities, the army, and the Freedmen's Bureau, with the President of the United States working through any or all of these agencies. Most of the serious problems of government were precipitated by outside influences and conspiracies.

The political enfranchisement of four million Negroes, from whose necks the yoke of slavery had just been lifted, is the most startling fact about Reconstruction, and a fact of tremendous impact in southern history. There is nothing in the history of democracy comparable to it. To give the Negroes the ballot and office — ranging from constable to governor — and the right to sit in state legislatures and in Congress, while depriving their former masters of their political rights and the South of its trained leadership, is one of the most astounding facts in the history of reconstruction after war. It was a stroke of fanatical vengeance and design. The basic purpose of this sort of political reconstruction was to vouchsafe for the North — while chastising the South — the future control of the nation through the Republican party. The South was never again to be allowed to regain the economic and political position which it had occupied in the nation prior to 1860.

Negro voting laid the basis for the Carpetbag regime. For eight years Radical northern leaders, backed by the Washington authorities and the army and aided by some native whites, pillaged and plundered and finished wrecking the South. Northern teachers who invaded the South to reconstruct its educational and social system, and northern preachers who came down to restore the unity of the churches by a reconstruction formula that required Southerners to bend the knee and confess their sins helped the politicians, the Freedmen's Bureau, and the Loyal League to undermine the Negroes' confidence in their white neighbors. The reconstruction policy of the churches did its part in stirring up both racial and sectional enmities. The *Nation* remarked, in 1879, the "Churches are doing their full share in causing permanent division." Reconstruction affected the religious life of the country for fifty years and more after the Radicals were overthrown. The character of the Carpetbag-Scalawag-Negro governments was well stated by the New York *Herald* which said the South is "to be governed by blacks spurred on by worse than blacks. . . . This is the most abominable phase barbarism has assumed since the dawn of civilization. . . . It is not right to make slaves of white men even though they have been former masters of blacks. This is but a change in a system of bondage that is rendered the more odious and intolerable because it has been inaugurated in an enlightened instead of a dark and uncivilized age."

It would be safe to say that the people of the North never understood how the South suffered during the Radical regime. The Radicals who controlled most of the organs of public opinion were in no attitude of mind to listen to southern complaints, and most people were too busy with the pursuit of alluring business opportunities that unfolded before them to think much of what was going on down South. In some respects conditions in the South at the end of the Radical regime remind one of the plight of the Germans at the end of the Thirty Years War.

The South staggered out of the Reconstruction, which ended *officially* in 1877, embittered, impoverished, encumbered with debt, and discredited by Radical propaganda. It had won after many frightful years the right to govern itself again, but there were still white men who could not vote and for many years there was danger of the federal regulation of elections and a resurgence of Negro power in politics.

The tax load had been devastating. The lands of thousands

upon thousands had been sold for taxes. Huge state and local debts, much of which was fraudulent, had been piled up. So many bonds, legal and illegal, had been sold that public credit was destroyed. The people stood, like the servant of Holy Writ, ten thousand talents in debt with not one farthing to pay. They had to solve the paradoxical problem of scaling down public debts — a bewildering compound of legal and illegal and far too large to be borne — while restoring public credit. Northern hands had imposed the debts and northern hands held the repudiated bonds. Repudiation became another source of misunderstanding between the sections and another basis for charges of "Southern outrages."

Reconstruction profoundly and permanently affected the political life of the South. It gave the South the one party system. The white people rallied around the Democratic party standards to overthrow the Radical regime, and their continued co-operation was necessary to prevent the Negroes from acquiring again the balance of power in politics. The terrible record of the Republican party during the Radical regime was an insuperable obstacle to its future success in the South. Hostility toward this party promoted devotion to the Democratic party. The complete domination of the latter party not only invested southern politics with the disadvantages of the one party system, but proved to be costly to the South in national politics. The Democratic party has been out of power most of the time in national politics and the Republican party naturally has not felt under obligation to do much for the South when it has had control of the national government. Even when the Democratic party has been in power the South has not had its share of patronage and appropriations, or of consideration in the formulation of national policies. The inequitable distribution of federal relief funds between the states since 1930 is an illustration in point. Political expediency has been the controlling consideration and not gratitude for party loyalty, which calls to mind an old Virginian's definition of political gratitude. Political gratitude, he said, is a lively appreciation of favors yet to be received.

Radical Reconstruction corrupted southern politics, and the prejudice aroused against Negro participation in politics led ultimately to the disfranchisement of most of the Negroes. Political habits formed in counteracting Carpetbag machinations and the presence of Negro voters continued to influence politics. Fraudulent methods were employed to control the Negro votes and when factions appeared among the whites they employed against each other the chicanery and frauds which they had used against the Radicals.

Reconstruction contributed to the proscription of the South in national politics and to provincialism in southern politics. Southerners so feared a recrudescence of Reconstruction in some form or other that for a generation they generally shrank from active participation in national affairs. Their attitude, generally speaking, was that if the North would leave them alone it could direct national affairs. This begat provincialism and made the continued proscription of the South easier. Such a situation was not good for either the South or the North.

Race friction and prejudice were engendered by Reconstruction, which was an unfortunate thing for both races and especially for the Negroes. It caused greater discriminations against the Negroes in politics and education, and in other ways. The Negroes had been so pampered and led as to arouse false notions and hopes among them and to make them for many years lame factors in the rebuilding of the South. The Negro after Reconstruction, and in large degree because of it, continued and continues to be a source of division between the North and South. The North either could not or would not understand the necessity of race segregation, and the idea that the Negro must have a definite place in the scheme of life was obnoxious. Disfranchisement of the Negro, occasional race riots, and the sporadic mobbing of Negroes accused of heinous crimes gave rise to continued charges of "Southern outrages." Criticisms from the North, generally based upon a lack of understanding of the problem, seemed more a matter of censure than of true interest in the Negro. Thus, those who expected to see sectional strife over the status of the Negro disappear with the emancipation of the slaves were disillusioned.

The Negro has been the cause of more misunderstanding and conflict between the sections than all things else. The North freed the Negro from slavery but by repressing and exploiting the South it has contributed much to conditions that have deprived him of some of the opportunities that a free man should have. If southern whites have suffered the pangs and restraints of poverty, the lot of the Negro has inevitably been worse. The shackles upon the

Negro's economic and cultural advancement have been formidable and deadening in their effects. Their inescapable lack of educational opportunities has been epitomized by the saying that the South has had the impossible task of educating two races out of the poverty of one.

In some respects the South has not pursued an enlightened policy toward the Negro. In ways it has exploited him. In the struggle for existence the Negro too often has been overlooked. Prejudice, too, resulting to a large extent from Reconstruction experiences, has done its part. Southerners, determined that the political control of Negroes back in the old Reconstruction days shall not be repeated, and probably too apprehensive about the breaking down of social barriers between the two races, have been conservative and slow to see adjustments that need to be made and can be made for the good of both races. Northerners with little information, but sure of their superior understanding, have scolded and denounced after the fashion of the old abolitionists. They have protested and cast sweeping aspersions without making constructive suggestions or troubling themselves to procure information upon which such suggestions could be based. Occasional violence against Negroes by ignorant mobs and discriminations against the Negroes in the enforcement of laws have evoked brutal and indiscriminating attacks from the northern press that remind one of journalism in the old Reconstruction days. Needless to say, such criticisms have contributed nothing to the southern Negro's welfare or to national unity.

The growing political power of the Negro in the North is adding to the Negro problem in the South. Many northern politicians to gain the political support of the northern Negroes — and, eventually, those of the South — are now supporting radical Negro leaders in their demand for a sweeping change in the status of the Negro in the South. But efforts to subvert the social system of the South will lead to more friction between the North and South and to bitter racial antagonisms.

The impoverishment of the people by Reconstruction and the heavy debt load imposed by it were most serious impediments to progress. They hindered economic advancement and educational achievement. Vast hordes of children grew to maturity unable even to read and write. It is impossible to measure the cost to the South of illiteracy alone resulting from the War and Reconstruction. Conditions brought about by Reconstruction also caused a tremendous loss of manpower. They caused a large exodus of the white people of the South to divers parts, and made the Negroes unfit to apply their productive powers. The loss of whites is well illustrated by Professor Walter L. Fleming's statement that Alabama lost more manpower in Reconstruction than it lost in the war.

The poverty attending Reconstruction laid the basis for the crop lien system and promoted sharecropping, and these more than all things else have hindered rural progress. Hundreds of thousands of both the landless and the landed had nothing with which to start life over and the only source of credit was cotton. Merchants, with the assistance of eastern creditors, advanced supplies to farmers upon condition that they would produce cotton in sufficient quantity to cover the advances made to them. The merchant charged whatever prices he chose to and protected himself by taking a lien upon the cotton produced. Under the system the great mass of farmers became essentially serfs. To throw off the shackles required more resources than most of them possessed.

Even at present a majority of southern tenant farmers depend for credit on their landlords, or on the "furnish merchants" for their supplies. The landlord, moreover, who stakes all on cotton or tobacco, is a bad credit risk. For this reason he pays interest rates as high as twenty per cent, and naturally his tenants pay more. It has been estimated that those who depend on the merchant for supplies pay as much as thirty per cent interest even on food and feed supplies. Credit unions and the Farm Security and Farm Credit Administrations have helped many of the farmers, but farm credit facilities are still sadly lacking in the South. Louis XIV's remark that "Credit supports agriculture, as the rope supports the hanged" has been abundantly verified in the South.

Thus, Reconstruction made a large contribution to the development of a slum-folk class in the rural South. The sharecropper-crop-lien farm economy of the South has produced a human erosion system more costly than soil erosion. In fact the two have gone hand in hand. These things always come to mind when in this day of national championships the South is referred to as the nation's "Economic Problem No. 1."

Reconstruction and its aftermath prevented the flow of population and money into the South. The 37,000,000 increase in population between 1870 and 1900 was largely in the North. The South's increase, except in Florida and Texas, was principally native and, as has been observed, it lost part of this increment. Northerners who moved and the millions of Europeans who came in either flocked to the industrial centers of the North or settled down on expansive fertile lands between Ohio and Kansas, made available by the Homestead Act. Most of the nation's capital and credit resources were put into railroad building and industrial and business pursuits north of the Mason and Dixon line. By 1890 the railroad pattern was laid and most of the roads had been built to feed the North. In every phase of economic activity the South was a bad risk compared with the North. Not the least of the things that kept men and money out of the South were its debt load and the stigma of debt repudiation. Northern newspapers and journals lambasted the South for the sin of repudiation and warned investors and emigrants to shun the South. In addition to other risks, they would find, the *Nation* said, that in the South the "Sense of good faith is benumbed, if not dead," and if they had anything to do with the South they would make themselves a part "of a community of swindlers." Even Henry Clews, who had conspired with the Carpetbag racketeers to sell shoddy reconstruction bonds to gullible buyers in the North and Europe, railed out against the spectacle of "Southern robbery." The notion of southern depravity was long-lived.

Between 1865 and 1900 a new republic of tremendous wealth and productive power was forged and concurrently there was a great educational development and a general advance in culture throughout the North. The South was a mere appendage to the new nation advancing through these epochal transformations; Reconstruction had assigned it a colonial status in all its relations with the North. J. M. Cross of New York City, for example, wrote to John Letcher of Virginia on March 8, 1867, that "Northern civilization must go all the way over the South, which is only a question of time." Some of those who had wanted to make the northern way of life the national way lived to see their wish a *fait accompli*. The patterns of national life were forming and henceforth were to be formed in the North and national unity was to be achieved by the conformity of the South to these patterns. Northerners have made little or no distinction between the North and the nation. The idea has become deeply imbedded throughout the country. For example, Professor Buck unconsciously expresses this attitude when he says, "The small farm worked in countless ways to bring Southern life into closer harmony with the major trends in national life" – that is, northern life. The same idea is carried in one of the chapter titles – "Nationalization of the South" – in Professor William B. Hesseltine's recent *History of the South*. When the South has failed to conform it has been stigmatized as backward, provincial, and sectional.

By 1900 the Old South was largely a thing of memory. Yearning for some of the good things of life, impulsive young men rejected antebellum traditions as inadequate to the needs of the new South which must be built. They sneered at "mummies," "mossbacks," and "Bourbons" who cherished the Old South. Others, just as avid about the future of business and industry, hoped to bring over into the New South of their dreams the best of the old and thus merge "two distinct civilizations" into a compound that some good day would surpass anything the North could show. They would leaven the lump of crass materialism with the leaven of graceful living. But to the older generation it seemed that those who were breaking loose from old moorings were bending "the knee to expediency" with little or no regard for principle.

Francis B. Simkins

THE ISSUES of most periods of American history have been so satisfactorily settled that they are now significant only as possible explanations of aspects of contemporary events and institutions. This is not true of the main issue of the Reconstruction period: the great American race question. It is almost as timely today as when it arose in 1865; as one of its prominent students says, like Banquo's ghost it will not down. Consequently, interpretations of the ten or twelve years following the Civil War seem destined, for an indefinite period, to have an influence beyond mere explanations of past events. The successful historian of Reconstruction, by revealing early phases of the still burning race question, arouses more attention among the reading public than is usually accorded historical works.

This continued survival of the leading issue of the post-bellum era explains why the interpretations of those years are so varied and numerous. Conservative scholars have described the follies and rascalities of Negro politicians and their Carpetbagger friends so as to make the reader thankful that such knavery cannot be repeated in his time. Less scrupulous writers have so effectively correlated the events of Reconstruction with those of their own times that their books have been best sellers. The outstanding example of this is Claude Bowers' *Tragic Era,* in which an attack upon the Republican enemies of Alfred E. Smith in 1928 is veiled behind attacks upon the Republican leaders of 1868, 1872, and 1876. At least one novelist has so effectively connected certain lurid aspects of Reconstruction with the race prejudices prevailing in the South in his times that the situations he described have become a part of the

"New Viewpoints of Southern Reconstruction," *Journal of Southern History,* V (February, 1939), 49–61.

FRANCIS B. SIMKINS (1897–1966) was Professor of History at Longwood College in Virginia. He also authored a number of major works on the history of the South, including (with Robert H. Woody) *South Carolina During Reconstruction* (1932) and *A History of the South* (1953).

Southern folk beliefs. The Ku Klux Klan is used as either a glamorous or sinister symbol for the arousal of issues of race, religion, and patriotism in which all Americans, radicals and reactionaries, Negro lovers and Negro haters, are vitally and perennially concerned. Reconstruction does not escape the attention of contemporary religionists; and even the Marxians, who would settle great social and economic issues, use Reconstruction experiences in their arguments.

A biased interpretation of Reconstruction caused one of the most important political developments in the recent history of the South, the disfranchisement of the blacks. The fraud and violence by which this objective was first obtained was justified on a single ground: the memory of the alleged horrors of Reconstruction. Later, amid a flood of oratory concerned with this memory, the white rulers of the South, in constitutional conventions of the 1890's and 1900's, devised legal means to eliminate the Negro vote. "Reconstruction," asserted the prime justifier of this act, "was this villainy, anarchy, misrule and robbery, and I cannot, in any words that I possess, paint it." These words of Ben Tillman were endorsed by all shades of white opinion from Carter Glass, Henry W. Grady, and Charles B. Aycock to Tom Watson, Hoke Smith, and James K. Vardaman.

Historians, sensing that the discrediting of the period in which the Negro most freely participated in politics justifies his subsequent exclusion from those activities, have condemned the Reconstruction measures as sweepingly as have the Southern politicians. They have called the military rule by which these measures were inaugurated "as brutish a tyranny as ever marked the course of any government whose agents and organs claimed to be civilized"; they have termed the best of the Carpetbaggers "infamous scoundrels"; and they have described the enfranchised freedmen as belonging to a race "incapable of forming any judgment upon the actions of men." The article on South Carolina in the eleventh edition of the *Encyclopaedia Britannica* in all seriousness concludes: "All the misfortunes of war itself are insignificant when compared with the sufferings of the people during Reconstruction."

The masses of white Southerners accept these judgments as axiomatic. White Southerners will argue the issues of the Civil War and even the merits of the Democratic party, but there is scarcely one in a position of authority who will debate Negro suffrage and the related issues of Reconstruction. The wickedness of this regime and the righteousness of the manner in which it was destroyed are fundamentals of his civic code. Such a condemnation or commendation justifies the settlement of questions of the immediate past and are invoked to settle issues of even the remote future.

This extremely partisan judgment of still timely historical events imposes upon the historian of Reconstruction a serious civic duty. He must foster more moderate, saner, perhaps newer views of his period. This the present writer attempts to do in the light of his investigations of the processes of Reconstruction in the state where they were applied most radically.

The capital blunder of the chronicler of Reconstruction is to treat that period like Carlyle's portrayal of the French Revolution, as a melodrama involving wild-eyed conspirators whose acts are best described in red flashes upon a canvas. Such a treatment creates the impression that Southern society was frenzied by misery. This is at best the picturesque pageantry of the artist; at worst, the cheap sensationalism of the journalist or the scenario writer. At all odds it is woefully one-sided and unhistorical. Of course the South during Reconstruction, like France during the Revolution, had its prophets of despair, its fanatical idealists, its unprincipled knaves. Luckily the behavior of these damned souls is not the whole story of Reconstruction, but merely a partial recording of the political aspects of the era. Some of the political acts were as sane and constructive as those of the French Revolution. They were concerned with educational, constitutional, and political reform, and were instrumental in putting the Southern states in line with the progressive spirit of the nineteenth century.

The aberrations of the Reconstruction politicians were not accurate barometers of the actual behavior of the Southern people. The Reconstruction governments were not natural developments from the conditions inherent in Southern life, but were, in a sense, artificial impositions from without. Frenzied politics did not necessarily reflect a frenzied social life. Despite strange doings in statehouses, the Southern people of both races lived as quietly and as normally during Reconstruction as in any politically disturbed period before or after. The defiance of the traditional caste division occasionally expressed in an official reception or in an act of the legislature was not reflected generally in common social relations. No attempt was made to destroy white supremacy in the social or economic sphere or to sanction interracial marriages. The political aggressiveness of the Negroes, characteristic of the period, did not extend to other phases of human relations. A staunch Republican voter was often a good servant in the house of a white Democrat. Negro officeholders who were aggressive politically were known to observe carefully the etiquette of the Southern caste system.

Moreover, in aspects of life not directly political there were achievements during the post-bellum era so quietly constructive that they have escaped the attention of most historians. This is true even of Du Bois, the colored author who ardently and extensively defends the Reconstruction record of his race.

Foremost among these achievements were agricultural reforms. While official agencies through Black Codes and the Freedmen's Bureau were making fragmentary and generally unsuccessful attempts to redefine a shattered rural economy, the freedmen bargained themselves into an agricultural situation unlike that of slavery and from their viewpoint advantageous. They worked beyond official purview. Although they were unable to gain legal title to the lands, they forced white competitors, for their labor in the expanding cotton fields, to establish them on separate farms in houses scattered over the land. This abandonment of the communal character of the Southern plantation bestowed upon the Negroes the American farmer's ideal of independent existence. This was a revolutionary reform more important in the actual life of the freedmen than the sensational but largely unsuccessful political changes attempted at the time. There followed the negotiation of share crop arrangements and other types of labor contracts between the freedmen and the landlords. These agreements soon became fixed by custom. They proved to be a satisfactory *modus vivendi* and demonstrated the possibility of the two races living together in harmony under a regimen of freedom.

Changes scarcely less significant took place in the religious sphere. Under slavery autonomous Negro churches had not been tolerated and blacks were forced to attend churches directed both administratively and doctrinally by the master race. During Reconstruction the freedmen successfully asserted religious freedom and established independent churches. This secession was accomplished with a minimum of ill feeling and without important doctrinal or ritualistic innovations by the seceding groups. But it was a momentous change in social relations. It has been permanent, having never been challenged by even the most reactionary social forces. Its importance to a people so intensely religious as are Southerners of both races is obvious. The existence of perfectly independent Negro churches has given the black race opportunity for self-expression studiously denied it since Reconstruction in political and other nonreligious fields.

Another radical but constructive change of a nonpolitical character was the development of a new commercial system. The breakup of the plantations into small units created much small trade and a consequent demand for small credit. This was met by the creation of the crossroads stores and the commercial villages and towns with stores and banks. These new institutions were owned by an emergent economic group, the storekeepers, who dominated the Southern community as effectively, if not as glamorously, as the planters had once done. The storekeepers were often also bankers, planters, church deacons, and sometimes state senators. Their power was based on large profits realized from the new system of credit advances on unharvested crops.

The assertion that the abnormalities of post-bellum politics did not adequately reflect the actualities of Southern life leads to the conviction that a balanced understanding of the period cannot be had without descriptions of social life. The social activities of both races remained relatively wholesome and happy; there was little of the misery, hatred, and repression often sweepingly ascribed to it by writers. There were camp meetings, dances, balls, tournaments, picnics, parades, agricultural fairs, lavish banquets, and indulgence in the vanities of personal adornment. There was, of course, much poverty, the shadow of the Lost Cause, and apprehension concerning possible events in the political world. But there were fresh memories of heroic events, and there were surviving warriors to give glamorous reality to these memories. Gaiety was disciplined by recent tragedy, but it was not dampened by the utilitarianism of a more progressive age.

The claim that the times were completely dominated by stark pessimism is refuted by the fact that during Reconstruction the optimistic concept called the New South was born. It is true that predictions concerning a new civilization springing from the ruins of slavery and the Confederacy were premature. It was ridiculous to call newspapers established amid the ruins of Columbia and the rice plantations *The Phoenix* and *The New South*. But the spirit of progress abroad in the land was not stifled by varied difficulties. It was fostered by some hopeful actualities — a new commercial life, the new banks, the high price of cotton, and the new agriculture made possible by the first extensive use of commercial fertilizer. An optimistic note was reflected in the newspapers. When in the 1880's this hopefulness germinated in the actualities of new industries and a philosophy of progress and reconciliation, it was from the seeds sown in the two previous decades.

In one sense, those who have essayed books on Reconstruction have closed their narratives before the actual reconstruction of the South began. The Northern reformers who arrived in the 1860's and 1870's carrying carpetbags were driven out by Southerners armed with shotguns before these outsiders could make their projects effective. But a later generation of Northern reformers, coming mostly in the twentieth century, have experienced a different reception. Riding in expensive automobiles, emanating an aura of wealth, this later generation have, through lavish expenditures, received the enthusiastic co-operation of Southerners. They have introduced Northern ideals of literature, architecture, and landscaping, and have instilled into the Southern mind a definite preference for Northern concepts of civilization.

Those of us who are not willing to accept this thesis that the true reconstruction did not come until years after the so-called Reconstruction, should nevertheless feel obligated to watch for evidence during the 1870's of the beginnings of the industrial, cultural, and psychical conquest by the North of the South which has shown itself so clearly in recent decades. Perhaps hidden beneath the seemingly premature and erratic actions of the Carpetbaggers were plans which have been executed by the rich Northerners of the twentieth century.

As has been suggested, one of the most striking features of Southern society is the color line. This division under slavery was not as sharp as it is today. The influences of reconstruction induced this sharpening. The aggressiveness of the blacks and their allies caused resentment among the whites and consequent estrangement between the races. This alienation in turn caused the blacks, especially in social and economic relations, to grow more independent. If this thesis is true, the careful student of the post-bellum period is obligated to isolate those interests and attitudes which account for the intensification of the caste division of Southern society. In doing this he will perhaps help explain the most important reality of interracial relations.

One of the accepted conventions of Reconstruction scholars is that the Carpetbaggers failed because their measures were excessively radical. We have often been told how the Four Million were suddenly hurled from slavery into freedom; how black barbarians were forced to attempt the roles of New England gentlemen; how seven hundred thousand of these illiterates were given the vote and the privilege of officeholding. But were these measures genuine radicalism, actual uprootings which inevitably led to fundamental changes in Southern society? The answer is that they were scarcely more than artificial or superimposed remedies from the outside which in no real sense struck at the roots of Southern life.

A truly radical program would have called for the confiscation of land for the freedmen. Land was the principal form of Southern wealth, the only effective weapon with which the ex-slaves could have battled for economic competence and social equality. But the efforts of the Freedmen's Bureau in the direction of land endowments for its wards were fitful and abortive. Conservative constitutional theory opposed any such meaningful enfranchisement. The dominant Radicalism of the day naïvely assumed that a people's salvation could be obtained through the ballot and the spelling book. The freedmen got these but were allowed to continue in physical want, and even lost the industrial skills and disciplines they had inherited from slavery. No wonder they carried bags in which to bear away their suffrage and expected education to place them at the tables of the rich and competent. They were realists and their so-called benefactors were the deluded ones. Wise Tory statesmen like Bismarck, Lord Salisbury, and Alexander II would have put something in their bags and endowed them with tangible social privilege.

In another vital respect the so-called Radicals of the 1860's lost an opportunity to attempt genuine radicalism. They did not try to destroy the greatest obstacle to the Negroes' salvation, the Southern caste system. Contemporary professions of such attempts lack sincerity. Anglo-Saxon race pride, New England standards of civilization, a respect for narrowly Protestant standards of morality were in the way. Attempts at fraternization between the races were stilted official affairs lacking in that unconscious informality on which true sociability must be based. No one was ever allowed to forget that race distinctions existed.

A distinguished Negro lecturer recently stated that the whole truth is not told by those books which assert that the blacks and their coadjutors were the sole aggressors of the Reconstruction period. Revolution was attempted on both sides. The blacks, of course, on their part, were sufficiently aggressive to demand the continuation of freedom and the vote and the liberties implied in these terms. But the whites also showed an aggressiveness which went beyond the maintenance of their traditional position in Southern society. They tightened the bonds of caste; they deprived the subordinate caste of many occupational opportunities enjoyed under slavery; they drove colored farmers from the land; they gradually deprived the blacks of a well-integrated position and imposed on them a status akin to pariahs whom many wished exiled. The disappearance of aristocratic prejudices against many forms of honest labor created the conviction that it was possible for Southern society to function without the despised African. Certainly an appraisal of the helplessness of the blacks at the close of the Reconstruction era makes one wonder why the whites are not more often adjudged the actual revolutionaries of the times. Victory was in white hands — the actuality as well as the sentiment and the tradition.

Several generations of historians have asserted that the Reconstruction governments were so grievously corrupt and extravagant that they checked all efforts at material rehabilitation. There was, of course, corruption and waste — expensive spittoons, thousand dollar bribes, fraudulent bonds, and so on. But the actual financial burdens of government which tolerated such acts have been exaggerated. Their expenditures seem small when compared with the budgets of twentieth-century states and extravagant only against the parsimony of the governments immediately preceding and following. The extravagant bond issues of the Reconstruction governments were not an immediate burden upon contemporaries and afflicted subsequent generations only to the extent to which they were not repudiated. The Radical governments, like the government of Louis XVI in France, failed not because their expenditures were burdensome but because they did not enjoy enough power and respect to force the taxpayers to yield funds sufficient to discharge the obligations of effective political establishments. There was a taxpayers' strike rather than a tax collectors' orgy. Some Reconstruction governments could not pay their gas bills.

A reinterpretation of the tax policies of the Radical regimes suggests a new explanation of the odious reputations possessed by these governments. Of course, a partial answer is that there was corruption and incompetence. Illiterate freedmen were easily seduced by unscrupulous Carpetbaggers and Scalawags. But were these malpractices the most serious offenses of the Reconstructionists? It seems that the worst crime of which they have been adjudged guilty was the violation of the American caste system. The crime of crimes was to encourage Negroes in voting, officeholding, and other functions of social equality. This supposedly criminal encouragement of the Negro is execrated ever more savagely as with the passing years race prejudices continue to mount. Mild-mannered historians declare that the assertiveness resulting therefrom was grotesque and abnormal, while the more vehement writers call it the worst of civic scandals. Attempts to make the Reconstruction governments reputable and honest have been treated with scorn, and the efforts of Negroes to approach the white man's standards of civilization are adjudged more reprehensible than the behavior of the more ignorant and corrupt. Social equality and negroism have not a chance to be respectable.

Such views logically grow out of the conviction that the Negro belongs to an innately inferior race and is therefore incapable by his very nature of exercising with sagacity the higher attributes of civilization. James Ford Rhodes gives the viewpoint of moderate historians by declaring the Negro to be "one of the most inferior races of mankind" and by endorsing Brinton's theory of the Negro's arrested development at adolescence. John W. Burgess voices the opinions of the more prejudiced when he says: "The claim that there is nothing in the color of the skin is a great sophism. A black skin means membership in a race of men which has never succeeded in subjecting passion to reason." Less critical writers take such statements as so obviously true that they need no specific affirmation.

The impartial historian, however, cannot so readily endorse this finding. His knowledge of the conclusions of modern anthropology casts grave doubts on the innate inferiority of the blacks. This knowledge, indeed, creates the necessity of explaining the conduct of the Negroes, during Reconstruction as well as during other times, on other than racial grounds. It also leads to the rejection of the gloomy generalization that the race, because of its inherent nature, is destined to play forever its present inferior role.

Loose assertions concerning Reconstruction as an attempt to return to the ideals of the jungle, as an effort to rebarbarize the Negro and to make South Carolina and Mississippi into African provinces, seem to have no basis in truth. Indeed, the exact opposite seems nearer the truth. Reconstruction can be interpreted as a definite step forward in the Anglicization or the Americanization of the blacks, certainly not their Africanization. The sagacious William A. Dunning tells the truth when he asserts that the newly-liberated freedmen were "fascinated with the pursuit of the white man's culture." This passion did not abate during the later years of Reconstruction; it is still a dominant feature of Negro life. The zeal with which the ex-slaves sought the benefits of literary education is unparalleled in history; this was the most obvious means of assimilating the white man's culture. Although Negro society during the first years of freedom tended to grow independent of white society, it continued to imitate the culture of the superior caste. Among the more cultivated Negroes, the more independent their society is of the whites', the stronger the resemblance. The radical changes in Negro religion which grew out of freedom were not in the direction of Africa, but rather in the direction of frontier or backwoods America, with some imitations of Fifth Avenue standards of clerical correctness. The misbehavior of Negro politicians had no African coloring. Their bad manners were those of American rustics and their vices were not unlike those of contemporary Tammany politicians. It is true that variations in the dialect of the Southern Negroes were most pronounced in the years after the war, or at least they were then best recognized; but even in the Gullah speech of the Sea Islands, African words did not predominate.

The efforts of certain Negroes of the post-bellum period to establish African connections were abortive. When cultured Negroes of the type of Martin R. Dulany tried to discover their African ancestors, they were guilty of a fatuous Americanism, different only in one respect from that of those Americans who trace their ancestors in England: the African quest could not be successful. The influences of slavery had resulted in such a thorough Americanization of the blacks that little African was left in their culture. This was the main reason why the efforts during Reconstruction to promote emigration to Liberia were a dismal failure. There was no more cultural affinity between the Southern Negro and his African blood kin than between the American Negro and the Chinese.

The aspersions on the freedmen for emulating the white man's culture have been as unfair as the criticisms of them for the alleged attempt to Africanize the South. Numerous writers have ridiculed sooty women for wearing veils and gloves, for carrying umbrellas, for calling themselves "Mrs." and "Miss," and for retiring from the fields to establish firesides and homes. Likewise, the spectacle of Negro politicians trying to talk like Daniel Webster or Charles Sumner has caused jest, and undue emphasis has been placed upon the impracticability of the attempt to load the curricula of Negro schools with items of classical culture adapted from New England. But are these criticisms just? It is granted that such aspirations after the white man's culture were often the result of uncritical enthusiasms and were beyond the immediate reach of an inexperienced people turned loose naked in the world. But measured according to the unescapable standards of American civilization, were these aspirations in the wrong direction? Were they not in the direction all Americans, including even those relegated to the lowest caste, seek to travel? The major problem of the American Negro is to attain the standards of American civilization. This is a decree of circumstances which the American Negro has accepted without reluctance. Therefore, the Reconstructionists who held Boston and Massachusetts up as ideals for the blacks were not giving the wrong advice. The fact that this advice moved the Negroes profoundly, if not always sagaciously, is a tribute to the sound instincts of these blacks and of their Reconstruction mentors.

Historians of the South should adopt a more critical, creative, and tolerant attitude toward so important a period in the annals of their section as Reconstruction. This will promote truth and scholarship in the austere sense of those terms. It will do more. It will banish that provincialism which is based on priggishness and ignorance of comparisons; it will fortify the sound provincialism born of better understanding of one's own province; and it will enrich those measured evaluations which are possible only after contact with other people's provinces. A better comprehension of the Reconstruction past will aid in the solution of the South's great race problem. Bias and passion should be explained in rational terms in order that contemporaries may better understand the forces motivating them. In this modest way the great civic obligation of the historian can be discharged.

Kenneth M. Stampp

FOR MORE than two years, from the convening of Congress in December 1865 to the President's impeachment trial in the spring of 1868, the radicals and the Johnsonians engaged in a fascinating dialogue. Some of the dialogue, to be sure, was shrill and irresponsible – a mere exchange of insults and false accusations. But much of it was an intensely serious discussion of several fundamental problems: the proper relationship of the legislative and executive branches, the legitimate areas of federal and state responsibility, and the terms that might justly be imposed upon the defeated South. . . .

On both sides, however, the central issue of the dialogue was the place of the free Negro in American society. This was the question that the radicals and Johnsonians always came to sooner or later. Between them they gave shape to the debate – its terms, its form, its assumptions – that has raged with varying degrees of intensity ever since.

When the Negro was the subject of the dialogue, President Johnson ranged himself on the side of the racists and, in effect, demanded that the South remain a "white man's country." In his third annual message he told Congress that the Negroes were entitled to be "well and humanely governed" and to be protected in their rights of person and property. But, he added, "it must be acknowledged that in the progress of nations negroes have shown less capacity for government than any other race of people. No independent government of any form has ever been successful in their hands. On the contrary, wherever they have been left to their

KENNETH M. STAMPP (1912–) is Morrison Professor of American History at the University of California at Berkeley. He has written a number of works on the Civil War era, including *And the War Came* (1950) and *The Peculiar Institution* (1956).

own devices they have shown a constant tendency to relapse into barbarism. . . . The great difference between the two races in physical, mental, and moral characteristics will prevent an amalgamation or fusion of them together in one homogeneous mass. . . . Of all the dangers which our nation has yet encountered, none are equal to those which must result from the success of the effort now making to Africanize the [southern] half of our country."

The rebuttal came from the radicals of the reconstruction era: "This is not a 'white man's government,' " said Thaddeus Stevens. "To say so is political blasphemy, for it violates the fundamental principles of our gospel of liberty. This is man's government; the government of all men alike." The goal of reconstruction, Stevens maintained, was to give Negroes perfect equality before the law and "to overcome the prejudice and ignorance and wickedness which resisted such reform." The South, said Charles Sumner, must be reconstructed in accordance with the principles of the Declaration of Independence, with government founded upon the consent of the governed. "If all whites must vote, then must all blacks." And, added Senator Henry Wilson, "we must see to it that the man made free by the Constitution . . . is a freeman indeed; that he can go where he pleases, work when and for whom he pleases; that he can sue and be sued; that he can lease and buy and sell and own propery, real and personal; that he can go into the schools and educate himself and his children; that the rights and guarantees of the . . . common law are his, and that he walks the earth, proud and erect in the conscious dignity of a free man." Horace Greeley, in the New York *Tribune*, denounced the state laws that prohibited marriages between Negroes and whites and advocated their repeal.

Demands for racial equality such as these went far beyond what the average white man, North or South, was then ready to support. . . . In their racial attitudes the radical Republicans were always a minority group, and it was only when they broadened their appeal — as the prewar abolitionists had done — that they managed for a time to win the general approval of the northern electorate.

Moreover, the conservative Johnsonians would never concede that the radicals were seriously concerned about the welfare of the Negro; nor would historians who wrote in the Dunning tradition.

The radicals, they said, used the rhetoric of equality, natural rights, and democracy as a camouflage to conceal the sordid purposes that lay beneath their pretended idealism. The conservatives apparently could not believe that any sane white man would actually favor the equality of the races and make this a genuine reason for opposition to Johnson's plan of reconstruction. Men who professed such a motive were either unbalanced fanatics or liars. The Johnsonians relegated a few of the radicals to the first of these categories but most of them to the second. In short, the typical radical had no sincere interest in the Negro at all — only a desire to exploit him. The vindictive radical would elevate the Negro to punish the southern white man; the ambitious radical would enfranchise the Negro to use him as a political tool; and the venal radical would mislead the Negro to protect the interests of northern businessmen.

These explanations of radical behavior introduce the extremely subtle and elusive problem of motivation. In the cases of Lincoln and Johnson this subject is often dealt with as if it were really no problem at all. The two Presidents were above guile; they were incapable of thinking of reconstruction in terms of strategies; they had no secret motives. Lincoln asked for a swift and painless reconstruction program because he was without malice and overflowed with compassion. Johnson vetoed measures to protect southern Negroes because he respected the rights of the states and feared the expansion of federal power. This is what they said, and this is what they meant — and, indeed, there is no reason to doubt that what they said was, in part at least, what they meant. But the radicals apparently *never* said what they meant; they were always guided by the unarticulated motive — or nearly always, save for those rare moments of candor when the mask was briefly lifted. Those moments of truth, the Johnsonians believed, occurred when the radicals betrayed some sordid purpose, not when they described some noble goal. The conservatives seldom doubted their capacity to understand why the radicals would protect the Negroes and overturn the Johnson governments in the South. But in actual fact they were about as reliable interpreters of radical motivation as the radicals were of conservative motivation.

This is not to say that the Johnsonians were altogether wrong in their appraisal of the radicals — when, for example, they accused the radicals of vindictiveness. "Hate, revenge, and persecution enter largely into their composition," wrote Gideon Welles. "These fanatics want a God to punish, not to love, those who do not agree with them." Indeed, these men, who had just emerged from four years of war, did have in them a streak of hatred and bitterness toward the South, a desire to punish her for her "treason." . . .

Gideon Welles described a second motive of the radicals: political advantage. He was convinced that "intense partisanship" rather than philanthropy was at the root of the movement for Negro suffrage. Four fifths of the radicals, he wrote, "are small party men . . . without any knowledge of the science of government or of our Constitution. With them all the great, overpowering purpose and aim are office and patronage. Most of their legislation relates to office and their highest conception of legislative duty has in view place and how to get it."

Since Welles had himself spent many years in public life, one need not take at face value his seemingly naïve dismay at discovering that radical politicians were, after all, motivated at least in part by considerations of practical politics. For surely they did search for means to keep their party in power and to consolidate its position. By 1865, the Republican party was no longer a spontaneous grass-roots movement as it had been to some extent at the time of its birth in the 1850's. It had now become institutionalized; it was dominated by professional politicians; and it had developed powerful political machines in the various northern states. Playing the political game according to a familiar set of rules, Republicans made the winning of elections and control of the patronage ends in themselves. And the radicals clearly believed that postponing the seating of southern Congressmen and repudiating the Johnson governments would serve these ends. Moderate as well as radical Republicans were afraid that southern and western agrarians might once more combine in the Democratic party, for this was the alliance that had dominated national politics most of the time in prewar years. Equally distressing was the fact that the South would now actually have greater power in the House of Representatives than it did before the war. When southern Negroes were slaves only three fifths of them were counted in the apportionment of Representatives; but with slavery abolished, they would all be counted, and southern representation would be increased by approximately fifteen. This, said the radicals bitterly, would be the South's reward for her treason!

The solution to this political dilemma, the radicals believed, was the enfranchisement of the Negroes and a vigorous campaign to win their votes for the Republican party. . . .

The third motive of the radicals, according to the Johnsonians, was to protect the interests of their northern business allies. "These Radical patriots are swindling the country while imposing on its credulity," wrote Welles. "The granting of acts of incorporation, bounties, special privileges, favors, and profligate legislation of every description is shocking." And, indeed, the Congress that repudiated the Johnson governments in the South did devote much of its time to economic legislation: to tariff laws in support of iron and wool manufacturers; to various proposals for direct or indirect subsidizing of commercial interests; to measures beneficial to railroad builders; and to policies that would protect investors in national banks and government securities. The Republican party had become, in part, the political agency of the northern middle classes and of northern business enterprise. The postwar era was the time of the Great Barbecue, when the federal government, under Republican control, generously turned the nation's natural resources over to individuals and corporations for private exploitation. But the agrarian interests in the South and West, ever suspicious of bankers, capitalists, and urban entrepreneurs generally, posed a serious threat to the economic groups the Republican party represented and to the legislation passed for their benefit. . . .

The Johnsonians and historians who wrote in the Dunning tradition thus demonstrated with abundant evidence that the radicals were something less than saints and that some of their motives were ignoble. But this leaves several aspects of the problem of radical motivation still unexplored. In the first place, even if one were to assume that radical motivation was entirely sordid, it does not necessarily follow that their program itself was reprehensible. Since their program included the granting of citizenship, civil rights, and the ballot to American Negroes, it may be that we are here confronted with a group which pursued objectives that were morally good for reasons that were morally bad. If that is the case, the historian will have to decide which has the greater historical significance: the praiseworthy program or the ignominious motive. He may, in fact, have to expand the classic moral dilemma of means and ends to means, *motives,* and ends.

But this is only part of the problem. For, as we have seen, the radicals in their public utterances, only rarely betrayed an unidealistic motive. . . .

But the most important question is whether the radicals, as the Johnsonians believed, were almost never motivated by genuine idealism. Were their rare confessions of dishonorable purposes the only occasions when they spoke the truth? Were their far more numerous professions of exalted motives just so much sham? Assuming that men in public life normally display at least a modicum of honesty and decency along with their presumed penchant for sly strategy, is there evidence to suggest that the radicals were below average in this respect? In answering these questions one ought not pretend to have read the minds of the radicals more successfully than the Johnsonians did, or to know the precise mixture of base and noble motives that underlay their reconstruction plans. But when a substantial body of men are accused of more than normal moral corruption, the burden of proof is on the accusers. As a matter of fact, such evidence does not exist; instead, there are a number of circumstances that suggest quite the opposite conclusion.

Back in the 1850's, when the Republican party was organized, a variety of groups were attracted to it. Among them were men who had been active in the reform movements, including abolitionism, that had flourished in the 1830's and 1840's. As heirs of the Enlightenment, these reformers believed in the doctrine of natural rights and in the equality of all men before the law and in the sight of God. Influenced by the romantic movement of the early nineteenth century, they had a transcendental faith in the essential goodness of man, in his ultimate perfectibility, and in his capacity to know truth intuitively. As nineteenth-century liberals, they believed in the autonomous individual — his right to control his own destiny — and therefore regarded slavery as the ultimate abomination. Moreover, they had an overpowering sense of personal guilt for the survival of evils such as slavery, and of duty to work for their eradication. They joined the Republican party in order to make it a political agency of moral reform, especially to convert it into an instrument of the antislavery crusade. Even in the 1850's the reformers were sometimes called radical Republicans; and though they were in a minority in the new party, they were the custodians of its conscience. Without them the party would have had no distinctive identity—it would have been, as one radical said, "*Hamlet* with Hamlet left out."

The radicals had great influence at the first Republican national nominating convention in 1856, when the party platform reaffirmed the principles of the Declaration of Independence, denounced slavery as a "relic of barbarism," and demanded that Congress exclude slavery from all new states and territories. During the next four years, the radicals opposed efforts to soften the platform of 1856 and to give greater emphasis to such mundane issues as the tariff, banking, and internal improvements. In 1860, they threatened to quit the party if it betrayed its antislavery principles; one radical described the new platform and the moderate Lincoln as representing a "superficial and only half-developed Republicanism." His strategy in that campaign was to "*assume* the whole movement to be antislavery, and *on that account* call on men to support it, and if any man fails, after election hold him up as an apostate from the faith."

During the secession crisis following Lincoln's election, the radicals, by threatening again to desert the Republicans, played a crucial role in defeating those who urged compromise with the South. "I helped to make the Republican party," vowed an Illinois radical, "and if it forsakes its distinctive ideas, I can help to tear it down, and help to erect a new party that shall never cower to any slave driver." James Russell Lowell advised Republicans to stand firm, reminding them that "material prosperity was never known to abide long in a country that had lost its political morality. . . . It is time that the North should learn that it has nothing left to compromise but the rest of its self-respect."

When Civil War followed, the radicals had no doubt about its fundamental cause. It was, they said, the result of a "blasphemous attempt to rear an empire on the cornerstone of human slavery"; hence there could be no domestic peace until slavery was abolished. To fight without this goal, argued Wendell Phillips, was to wage "a murderous and wasteful war . . . for no purpose at all." The moral fervor which radicals injected into the war, as well as the logic of events, eventually transformed what began as a struggle to preserve the Union into a crusade for freedom. Among their victories the radicals counted the Confiscation Acts, the Emancipation Proclamation, the decision in 1863 to accept Negro recruits in the Union Army, and, finally, the Thirteenth Amendment. In short, much of the nobility of the Civil War years, and most of the idealism of the Union cause, were supplied by the radical Republicans.

This being the case, it would be difficult to explain why their idealism suddenly should have died in 1865, when they turned against Johnson and demanded that Negro freedom be given federal support. The radicals of the reconstruction era were either the reformers of the prewar years or men who had been strongly influenced by their moral imperatives. In fact, radical reconstruction ought to be viewed in part as the last great crusade of the nineteenth-century romantic reformers. Since the radicals were in politics, we may assume that they had learned to accommodate themselves to some of the practical realities of public life and that their pristine innocence may have eroded in the passing years. Nevertheless, it is likely that the radicals were, if anything, somewhat *less* opportunistic in their purposes and a little *more* candid in their public utterances than the average American politician has been. Their pleas for justice for the Negro, their objection to the Johnson governments on the ground that the Black Codes were restoring a form of slavery, cannot be discounted as pure hypocrisy. To the practical motives that the radicals occasionally revealed must be added the moral idealism that they inherited from the abolitionists. . . .

Indeed, few of the radicals can be understood unless they are linked with the antislavery crusade, for that was the source of some of their goals and much of their rhetoric. Like the abolitionists they spoke of regenerating the South, of sacred duties, of the will of God, and of the evils of compromise. . . .

With this thread of idealism in mind, it is necessary to examine once more the radicals' alleged economic motive — their supposed identification with northern capitalist interests. Those who gave radical reconstruction an economic interpretation were often guilty of several oversimplifications. In the first place, they overlooked the fact that there was no clear division over questions of economic policy between Lincoln and the conservative Republicans on the one hand and the radical Republicans on the other. Lincoln favored the tariff, a national banking system, federal subsidies to the railroads, and federal appropriations for internal improvements; and he signed every measure for these purposes that Congress passed. Though President Johnson disapproved of these policies, the conservative Republicans who supported his reconstruction program usually did not. This is why Johnson made almost no attempt to stress economic issues in the congressional elections of 1866.

In addition, the economic interpretation is based on the assumption that the northern business community was united to promote a common economic program, whereas no such unity ever really existed. Iron and steel manufacturers favored high tariffs, but the railroad builders and shipping interests wanted the tariffs reduced. Wool manufacturers were protectionists – provided the duty on raw wool was not raised too high. Bondholders and most bankers (not all) demanded a quick return to the gold standard; but manufacturers, seeking capital for expansion, usually favored a moderate paper-money inflation. Divisions such as these troubled the radicals in Congress, too. For example, Thad Stevens favored high tariffs and inflation, as did his industrialist friends in Pennsylvania; while Charles Sumner favored tariff reduction and the gold standard. This does not mean that none of the radical Republicans were serving northern business interests, or that as a group they lacked economic motives. But it does discredit the idea of a vast conspiracy between the radical phalanx and a solid corps of capitalists to use reconstruction and Negro rights as a smokescreen to conceal a carefully planned program of economic aggrandizement.

Still another oversimplification of those who gave radical reconstruction an economic interpretation stems from their underlying conception of what is real and what is unreal in human affairs. When they discovered an economic motive, they seemed to feel that they were dealing with reality – with something that reflects the true nature of man. But when they were confronted with moral arguments, they seemed to feel that they were dealing with something that is slightly fraudulent, and they began searching for hidden meanings. This rather cavalier dismissal of man's moral and humanitarian impulses betrays not only a cynical but a superficial understanding of human behavior. As a matter of fact, for a few of the radicals — Sumner, for example — we might be nearer the truth if we stood the economic interpretation on its head. Sumner was probably revealing his *true* motive when he spoke in terms of moral principles. And when he argued that Negro suffrage was necessary to prevent a repudiation of the public debt, he may *then* have had a concealed motive — that is, he may have believed that this was the way to convert bondholders to his moral principles. In that case it would be the economic argument that was slightly fraudulent and had a hidden meaning.

Finally, insofar as the radicals were economically motivated, we cannot assume that their efforts to aid business enterprise were wholly devoid of a certain kind of idealism. For if economics is the Dismal Science, it is nevertheless often pursued with considerable moral passion. To be sure, one may question the wisdom of some of the fiscal measures that Congress passed during the reconstruction years; many of the radicals were blind to the abuses of the totally undisciplined and irresponsible businessmen of their day; and few of them could resist altogether the enticements of the Great Barbecue. But as far as motives are concerned, the important question is whether the radicals, through their economic program — to the extent that they had one — were consciously plotting to bring about socially undesirable results. By way of a partial answer, this much can be said at least: there is little in their public or private papers to indicate that this was the case, and much to suggest that such injuries to the public as occurred had been neither planned nor anticipated.

Most of the radicals who were committed to a high tariff, the national banking system, and subsidies to the railroads seemed to believe quite sincerely that these measures were designed to benefit and enrich not just special interest groups but the country as a whole. Public lands and mineral and timber resources could almost be given away to private entrepreneurs, because there was a general belief then that America's resources were inexhaustible and that this was the best way to put them to productive use. In this society of free farmers and growing industries, every man was presumed to have an equal chance for material success. With the abolition of slavery American labor had escaped a serious threat; and now, if the southern planters were crushed, the last vestige of an American aristocracy would be destroyed. . . .

These, then, were the practical and idealistic motives of the radical Republicans; for these reasons the Civil War had been fought and the South vanquished. But now, said the radicals, President Johnson, through his plan of reconstruction, threatened to deprive the North of the fruits of its costly victory. The fear of a revival of the southern rebellion, the desire to avoid having to fight the war over again, were crucial factors in determining northern postwar attitudes toward the South. "What we want, and what is our due, is indemnity for the past and security for the future," wrote a Vermont Republican. Schurz recalled that Northerners "asked themselves quite seriously whether there was not real danger that the legitimate results of the war, for the achievement of which they had sacrificed uncounted thousands of lives and the fruits of many, many years of labor, were not in grave jeopardy again. Their alarm was not artificially produced by political agitation. It was sincere and profound and began to grow angry." Indeed, this desire to preserve the fruits of victory, which has always helped to shape the immediate postwar policies of the victor toward the vanquished, was doubtless a major reason for northern support of radical reconstruction. In the words of a shrewd young contemporary French newspaperman, Georges Clemenceau: "When anyone has for four successive years joined in such a struggle as that which the United States has seen . . . [he desires] not to lose the dearly bought fruits of so many painful sacrifices. When the war ended, the North was concerned not to let itself be tricked out of what it had spent so much trouble and perseverance to win."

For the South to have gained almost immediate autonomy in its domestic affairs, as it would have under Johnson's program, would have required of its leaders extraordinary restraint, a quality for which they had not been distinguished in recent years. One of the radicals found consolation in this fact. In prewar years, he recalled, "whenever all looked gloomy for our cause, something of outrage or extravagant pretensions has been put forth on the part of the South which has brought our people to their senses." Now he expected — indeed hoped — that Southerners would "behave so outrageously as to awaken . . . the North once more." And the South obliged with its Black Codes, with major race riots in Memphis and New Orleans and smaller ones elsewhere, and by electing many distinguished Confederates to offices in the Johnson governments. . . .

The outcome of this raucous campaign was an overwhelming victory for the anti-Johnson Republicans. The proportions of the Republican victory were quite astonishing: they won control of every northern state legislature, won every northern gubernatorial contest, and gained more than two-thirds majorities in both houses of Congress.

Various explanations have been suggested for this result: that the Republicans deceived and misled the voters (though hardly more than the Johnsonians); that northern businessmen gave the Republicans a large campaign fund; and that the veterans, now organized in the Grand Army of the Republic, were mobilized behind the Republicans. All of this was true; but more important was the genuine fear that President Johnson, through his southern governments, was going to lose the peace — that unrepentant rebels were regaining control of the South and re-establishing slavery. When this appeared to be the likely outcome of Johnson's plan of reconstruction, northern voters turned to the Republicans and gave them a mandate to try a reconstruction plan of their own.

3

The American Businessman

Industrial Statesman or Robber Baron?

For many students of American history, the problems of war and peace appear to be the dominant ones in the years from 1850 to 1877. Yet during this same period the country was undergoing an industrial and urban transformation that inevitably resulted in profound changes in the structure of American society. Few individuals or institutions remained unaffected by the forces at work and the nation as a whole was destined to experience fundamental changes which enabled it to emerge as a leading world power by the close of the nineteenth century. "The old nations of the earth," Andrew Carnegie observed in 1886 with considerable pride, "creep on at a snail's pace; the Republic thunders past with the rush of the express. The United States, [in] the growth of a single century, has already reached the foremost rank among nations, and is destined soon to out-distance all others in the race. In population, in wealth, in annual savings, and in public credit; in freedom from debt, in agriculture, and in manufactures, America already leads the civilized world." [1] Industrial growth and the accumulation of wealth, Carnegie suggested, would lay the cornerstone of a better America, because ultimately material progress would lead to spiritual and intellectual progress.

Although this new burst of industrialism gave the United States one of the highest standards of living in the world, it was not always greeted with unrestrained enthusiasm. To some the new industrialism was destroying the very traits that had given America immunity from class strife, internal divisions, and rivalries that had long plagued Europe. Others feared the greed and ugliness that accompanied the industrial transformation. Walt Whitman, in *Democratic Vistas,* summed up the opposition. "The depravity of the business classes of our country is not less than has been supposed, but infinitely greater. The official services of America, national, state, and municipal, in all their branches and departments, except the judiciary, are saturated in corruption, bribery, falsehood, mal-administration; and the judiciary is tainted. The great cities reek with respectable as much as non-respectable robbery and scoundrelism. . . . In business, (this all-devouring modern word, business,) the one sole object is, by any means, pecuniary gain. . . . [M]oney-making is our magician's serpent, remaining to-day sole master of the field. . . . I say that our New World democracy, however great a success in uplifting the masses out of their sloughs, in materialistic development, products, and in a certain highly-deceptive superficial popular intellectuality, is, so far, an almost complete failure in its social aspects, and in really grand religious, moral, literary, and esthetic results." [2] In short, America was adversely affected by the material forces at work.

The differences between the views of Carnegie and Whitman were by no means atypical; Americans have always been ambivalent in their attitudes toward material affluence. While emphasizing the virtues of acquisitiveness, individualism, and competition, they have been unable to throw off the influence of their religious heritage and the sense that the nation as a whole has a mission. At

1. Andrew Carnegie, *Triumphant Democracy* (New York, 1886), p. 1.
2. Walt Whitman, "Democratic Vistas," in *Prose Works 1892,* Floyd Stovall, ed. (2 vols: New York, 1963–1964), II, 370.

times this dual heritage has created an internal conflict because attempts to harmonize American materialism and idealism have not always succeeded. Some Americans have dealt with this conflict by proclaiming that material well-being is a prerequisite of spiritual and intellectual achievement; others have criticized a system that emphasizes material values at the expense of other values; still others have insisted that America's abundance was proof of its superior moral character.

This ambivalent attitude toward our heritage has exercised a profound impact on the writing of American history. Historians, on the whole, have also displayed divided attitudes when studying the rise of industry and its implications for American society. Nowhere can this dichotomy of thought be better seen than in the changing image of such great entrepreneurs as Rockefeller and Carnegie. To many historians, these captains of industry represented more than the rise of industrialism; they symbolized some of the basic characteristics of modern American culture.

The first attempts to evaluate the achievements of these industrial giants occurred at the beginning of the twentieth century. Many of the early studies took their cue from the writings of Henry Demarest Lloyd. A journalist and a scholar, Lloyd until his death in 1903 played a significant part in reform movements that developed out of the social and economic unrest of that era. Critical of laissez faire and corporate monopoly, he insisted that the American people were confronted with a choice between reform or revolution. Public ownership of monopolies and an increased role for government were absolutely necessary, according to Lloyd, if the American people were to avoid the fratricidal class struggles that had wracked other nations in the Western world.

In 1894 Lloyd spelled out his case in *Wealth Against Commonwealth,* a book that anticipated the writings of later muckrakers and Progressive journalists and also set the stage for much of the controversy among historians over the captains of industry. The book ostensibly was a study of the Standard Oil Company and the techniques used by John D. Rockefeller to gain a virtual monopoly over the petroleum industry. Actually *Wealth Against Commonwealth* was an indictment of the entire capitalistic system as it then existed. Businessmen, wrote Lloyd, paid lip service to the ideal of competition, but their true purpose was to achieve monopoly. If the captains of industry continued to have their way, the results would probably be a violent and bloody class struggle. There was little time to act, declared Lloyd, for the nation was already faced with "misery, plagues, hatreds, national enervation." [3]

While Lloyd's principal purpose was to issue a call for national regeneration, he had drawn an unfavorable yet influential portrait of the typical industrial tycoon to make his point. His stereotype of the American businessman was in many respects similar to the one held by other American reformers, including the Populists as well as many Progressives. Much of the debate over reform in the years from 1900 to 1917, indeed, centered about the unbridled power and selfishness of the captains of industry — a group, many claimed, who were motivated only by a desire to amass great wealth regardless of the cost to the American people. The specific political issues of the Progressive era — monopolies, trusts, federal regulation — were all based upon the proposition that Americans could no longer afford to permit these autocratic barons to shape the nation's destiny.

Many of the studies dealing with the American businessman written prior to the First World War were done not only by historians, but by social scientists and, to a lesser extent, socialists seeking to prove that the system of capitalism was identified with social and individual selfishness and egoism. Among the social scientists were economists and sociologists like Thorstein Veblen and E. A. Ross, who implicitly denounced the predatory, profit-seeking, amoral businessman for refusing to recognize the pressing needs of society. In the latter category were Gustavus Myers and Algie Simons, who portrayed businessmen as malefactors of wealth and looked forward to their eventual extinction as the historical process reached its inevitable destiny in the emergence of a socialist utopia.

While the interpretation of the businessman as robber baron was being etched in the public's imagination, historians, under the influence of the "New History," were themselves beginning to inquire into the economic realities of capitalism in order to buttress their own predilection for democracy and reform. But not until the 1920's — a decade that was notable for the debunking activities

3. Henry Demarest Lloyd, *Wealth Against Commonwealth* (New York, 1894), p. 517.

of a small group of intellectuals – did historians turn their full attention to the study of the rise of American industry. With the publication in 1927 of Charles and Mary Beard's *Rise of American Civilization* and the first volume of Vernon L. Parrington's monumental *Main Currents in American Thought,* the scene was set for a radical reevaluation of the role of the businessman in American history.

Although the Beards refrained from any direct or outward condemnation of the industrial tycoon in their panoramic study of American civilization, their description suggested the analogy of a medieval baron – an individual who was despotic and autocratic within his own sphere. The story of American industry, they wrote, is "the story of aggressive men, akin in spirit to military captains of the past, working their way up from the ranks, exploiting natural resources without restraint, waging economic war on one another, entering into combinations, making immense fortunes, and then, like successful feudal chieftains or medieval merchants, branching out as patrons of learning, divinity, and charity. Here is a chronicle of highly irregular and sometimes lawless methods, ruthless competition, menacing intrigues, and pitiless destruction of rivals." [4]

Parrington, on the other hand, was much clearer and far less ambiguous in his description of postwar industrial developments. Writing within a Jeffersonian agrarian framework which stressed individualistic values, he sought to defend his particular vision of liberalism. In Parrington's eyes the predatory and materialistic tycoon of industry represented the greatest threat to those humane and democratic values that had made America great. Businessmen had created the America of the present, with "its standardized life, its machine culture, its mass-psychology – an America to which Jefferson and Jackson and Lincoln would be strangers." These giants of industry, Parrington wrote in colorful and emotion-laden terms, "were primitive souls, ruthless, predatory, capable; singleminded men; rogues and rascals often, but never feeble, never hindered by petty scruple, never given to puling or whining – the raw materials of a race of capitalistic buccaneers." [5]

4. Charles and Mary Beard, *The Rise of American Civilization* (2 vols: New York, 1927), II, 177.

5. Vernon L. Parrington, *Main Currents in American Thought* (3 vols: New York, 1927–1930), III, 12, 26.

The debunking atmosphere of the 1920's and depression years of the 1930's provided a favorable climate of opinion for the growing idea of the businessman as a robber baron. For decades the business community had taken great pains to convince the American people that the nation's greatness rested on the achievements of ambitious and energetic entrepreneurs. A. C. Bedford, a tycoon in the oil industry, made this point very clear in 1925. In his eyes, work was even of more importance than love, learning, religion, or patriotism. "I have come to the conclusion," he wrote, "that industry is the fundamental basis of civilization. The high office of civilization is to train men to productive effort." [6] Other business leaders during the 1920's echoed Bedford's observations; if anything, they were even more ecstatic in extolling the contributions of business to American civilization. With the exception of a dissenting minority of reformers, many Americans agreed with President Coolidge's dictum that "The business of America is business."

Having taken credit for the apparent prosperity of the 1920's, the business community, ironically enough, was forced to accept responsibility for the catastrophic depression of the 1930's. The capitalist free enterprise system, which supposedly accounted for the greatness of America, seemingly failed in 1929. Millions who sought work were unable to find jobs; bankruptcies increased at an astounding rate; and many Americans even faced a real threat of starvation. Indeed, the United States appeared to be on the threshold of disaster. For once the business community found that the time-honored cliché that wealth was the product of ambition, talent, and drive, no longer held true. Capitalism and free enterprise perhaps had come to the end of the road, many argued, and new approaches were required if the needs of a modern complex industrial society in America were to be satisfied.

Given these conditions, it was not surprising that much of the historical scholarship of the 1930's took an anti-business turn. Beard and Parrington had anticipated this development; their writings during the late 1920's echoed some of the critical literature of this era. Sinclair Lewis' unforgettable portrait of Babbitt, while not wholly intended to debunk businessmen, contributed to a stereotype already widely held. The massive attack on the image

6. Quoted in James W. Prothro, *The Dollar Decade: Business Ideas in the 1920's* (Baton Rouge, 1954), p. 67.

of the American businessman, however, came in the great depression. During the 1930's, the robber baron idea came to full bloom.

In presenting a highly unfavorable portrait of the industrial tycoon, most writers in this tradition were implicitly attacking an economic system that they thought had failed to live up to its promises and expectations. Oddly enough, many — though not all — of the critical studies during the 1930's were written by non-academic figures who were critical of capitalism rather than by academic historians. Thus Lewis Corey, a socialist, in his book *The House of Morgan* (1930), detailed the techniques whereby a major banking and investment concern exercised near dictatorial control over corporations having assets well in excess of twenty billion dollars. His lesson was not lost upon his readers. It was Corey's purpose to marshall as much evidence as possible to demonstrate the evil, selfish, and corrupting nature of industrial and finance capitalism. Other historical and literary writers, attracted by Marxian ideas, lent support to the growing body of critical studies of the American economic system.

The book that did the most to fix in American historical scholarship the enduring stereotype of the late nineteenth century industrialist, however, was Matthew Josephson's brilliantly written *The Robber Barons: The Great American Capitalists 1861–1901,* which appeared in 1934. Fittingly enough, Josephson dedicated his book to Charles and Mary Beard, who themselves had interpreted American history in terms of a struggle between haves and have-nots, debtors and creditors, agrarians and industrialists, workers and capitalists. Josephson set the tone of his work in his introduction. "This book," he began, "attempts the history of a small class of men who arose at the time of our Civil War and suddenly swept into power. . . . these men more or less knowingly played the leading roles in an age of industrial revolution. . . . Under their hands the renovation of our economic life proceeded relentlessly: large-scale production replaced the scattered, decentralized mode of production; industrial enterprises became more concentrated, more 'efficient' technically, and essentially 'cooperative,' where they had been purely individualistic and lamentably wasteful. But all this revolutionizing effort is branded with the motive of private gain on the part of the new captains of industry. To organize and exploit the resources of a nation upon a gigantic scale, to regiment its farmers and workers into harmonious corps of producers, and to do this only in the name of an uncontrolled appetite for private profit — here surely is the great inherent contradiction whence so much disaster, outrage and misery has flowed." Josephson conceded that the robber barons had many imposing achievements to their credit. On the other hand, the debits far outweighed the credits. Ultimately, he concluded, the "extremes of management and stupidity would make themselves felt. . . . The alternations of prosperity and poverty would be more violent and mercurial, speculation and breakdown each more excessive; while the inherent contradictions within the society pressed with increasing intolerable force against the bonds of the old order." [7] The implications of Josephson's ideas were obvious.

The popularity of the robber baron concept, nevertheless, was by no means limited to the depression years of the 1930's. Though modified and refined, it has continued to influence the writings of contemporary historians. In the first selection Chester M. Destler, a perceptive student of reform and protest movements after the Civil War and a recent biographer of Henry Demarest Lloyd, attempts to weigh the achievements of the late nineteenth century entrepreneurs. Taking a representative group, Destler portrays some of their outstanding characteristics. Although conceding that as a group these figures had certain achievements to their credit, he insists that the robber baron approach is still valid. These late nineteenth century industrialists were motivated by the hope of reaping monopoly profits and amassing power; other incentives played minor roles. The picture that Destler draws, therefore, remains an unfavorable one and within the robber baron tradition of American historiography.

At the same time that the robber baron concept was reaching maturity, another school of thought was emerging. Although it is difficult to give this school a particular name, the designation "business history" is not wholly inaccurate. The foundation of business history had already been laid by the 1930's. As a result of the work of Norman S. B. Gras and others at the Harvard Graduate School of Business Administration as well as the publication of a number of sympathetic biographies of individual business

7. Matthew Josephson, *The Robber Barons: The Great American Capitalists 1861–1901* (New York, 1934), pp. vii–viii, 453.

leaders, some historians and economists began to depart from the unfavorable stereotype of the American industrialist. Business history, however, was not merely a reevalution of the contributions of industrialists; it represented a radically new approach to the study of American economic history. Indeed, business historians by the 1950's — because of their differences with other academic historians — had created their own professional organization, developed a new vocabulary and research techniques, published their own journal, and in some cases had even founded new departments within the university separate from regular history departments.

Generally speaking, business historians insisted that the careers of industrial leaders were far more complex than earlier scholars had realized. Business leaders were not predatory money seekers. Indeed, in many cases they were talented individuals whose creative contributions to the economy — and to American society as a whole — were very great. Allan Nevins, who published a major revisionist biography of John D. Rockefeller in 1940, argued that much of the blame heaped on this man was unwarranted. It was true, Nevins conceded, that Rockefeller used methods that were of dubious moral character. On the other hand, the kind of monopoly control attained by Standard Oil was a natural response to the anarchical cutthroat competition of the period and reflected the trend in all industrial nations toward consolidation. To Nevins, Rockefeller was not a robber baron; he was a great innovator who imposed upon American industry "a more rational and efficient pattern." Rockefeller's objective was not merely the accumulation of wealth; he and others like him were motivated by "competitive achievement, self-expression, and the imposition of their wills on a given environment." [8]

Thirteen years later Nevins pushed this thesis even further when he published a second biography of Rockefeller. He was, Nevins forcefully argued, an "innovator, thinker, planner, bold entrepreneur." Taking a confused and disorganized industry, Rockefeller organized it with completeness, efficiency, and constructive talent; in his philanthropy he set a model for all to follow. Had it not been for men like him — men who helped to create within a brief span of time great and powerful industrial units in

8. Allan Nevins, *John D. Rockefeller: The Heroic Age of American Enterprise* (2 vols: New York, 1940), II, 707–714.

steel, oil, textiles, chemicals, electricity, and automotive vehicles — "the free world might have lost the First World War and most certainly would have lost the Second." [9]

The points that Nevins made about Rockefeller were not fundamentally different from those made by other students of business history. The great nineteenth century entrepreneurs, business historians emphasized, actually played a vital role in making the United States the greatest industrial power in the world and giving its people the highest standard of living. Far from being immoral, unethical, or evil individuals — although sometimes their methods involved questionable tactics — these industrial statesmen stepped into a disorganized, unstructured, anarchic economy, restored order and rationality, created giant organizations that were in a position to exploit fully the great natural resources of the nation, and took full advantage of the potentialities of the American economy.

Like students in the robber baron tradition of American historiography, business historians began with certain underlying assumptions that undoubtedly influenced the way in which they approached their subject. It is quite clear that they rejected the hostile critique of Progressive historians who believed that the social and economic costs of late nineteenth century industrialization could have been far lower and less painful and degrading to the great mass of Americans, and that the result need not have been a dangerous centralization of economic power that ostensibly threatened freedom and democracy. On the contrary, business historians tended to eulogize rather than to disparage the American economic system. Did not the growth and development of the large corporation, they maintained, give the American people the highest standard of living in the world and make possible the victory against totalitarianism? Was not America's industrial capacity responsible for the strength of a large part of the free world in the struggle with communism? To put it another way, these historians concluded that the large corporation, despite its monopolistic and

9. Allan Nevins, *Study in Power: John D. Rockefeller, Industrialist and Philanthropist* (2 vols: New York, 1953), I, viii–ix, II, 436. For a direct confrontation of views see the enlightening article "Should American History be Rewritten? A Debate Between Allan Nevins and Matthew Josephson," *Saturday Review,* XXXVII (February 6, 1954), 7–10, 44–49.

oligopolistic position, was far more of an asset than a liability. Unlike Progressive historians who feared the problem of democratic control and the menace of the concentration of economic power in the hands of a few, business historians minimized the threat of such dangers. In this sense business history was the product — perhaps unconsciously — of conservative historians interested in justifying the status quo rather than changing it.

The second selection by Alfred D. Chandler, Jr., is a good example of some recent trends in the writing of business history. Rather than concerning himself with the direct issue of the work of the great entrepreneurs themselves, Chandler attempts to delineate the forces that led businessmen to develop new products, new markets, and new sources of raw material. By 1900 these industrial leaders had created the modern corporation, which integrated the functions of purchasing, manufacturing, marketing, and finance. Each of the major processes was managed by a separate department, and all were coordinated and controlled by a central office. Such a complex organization was a response to the emergence of the urban market that followed the creation of a national railroad system. Minimizing the role of technological innovation, Chandler concludes that entrepreneurs like Rockefeller and others were successful because they correctly analyzed the economic situation and responded in a creative manner. Their contributions, he suggests, played an important role in the dramatic growth of the economy and the creation of an affluent society.

Although the interpretation of the business historians has been the dominant one since World War II — in part because the postwar years after 1945 have been marked by prosperity and conservatism — their views have not been accepted uncritically by other American scholars. Between the two extreme interpretations of the businessman as robber baron and the businessman as industrial statesman stands a third school of thought. It is sometimes difficult to identify historians affiliated with this school because they do not always agree on their interpretations or form a self-consciously united group of scholars within the profession. Nevertheless, they do share certain ideas in common. Specifically, these historians believe that late nineteenth century entrepreneurs were neither as bad as their critics claim nor as good as their defenders have argued. The balance sheet, they maintain, shows both debits and credits, and neither side can be neglected.

The third selection by Edward C. Kirkland is an excellent example of this middle ground approach. He points out that the typical businessman of the late nineteenth century was prone to separate his business and economic decisions from all other considerations, including morality, religion, and the welfare of society. But historians, argues Kirkland, are not justified in following along and therefore dividing and compartmentalizing the careers of these men because such a procedure leads to a distorted view of them as individuals as well as of their era. Business historians are in error when they confine themselves solely to a study of entrepreneurial decisions; the foes of business are equally in error when they focus only on the shortcomings of these figures. The character and activities of these businessmen must be studied as an interrelated whole, Kirkland maintains, in order to arrive at a complete and well rounded picture rather than a partial one.

In assessing the careers of businessmen, it is important to understand that differing interpretations often reflect diverging viewpoints regarding the very nature of economic development. Ironically enough, adherents of the robber baron concept implicitly extol the virtues of a competitive economy when they criticize the monopolistic objectives of most entrepreneurial leaders. Business historians, on the other hand, tend to argue that the movement toward consolidation arose out of a cutthroat and disorganized economy whose productive potential could never have been realized as long as industry remained highly competitive. Thus these admirers of American industry implicitly maintain that competition, far from being beneficial, was actually an impediment to progress.

Which of these viewpoints is correct? Was consolidation a necessary prerequisite for the emergence of a complex industrial economy? Is bigness synonymous with efficiency? On both these issues, the two opposing schools of thought give very different answers. The upholders of the robber baron approach insist that the monopolistic control that often accompanies large productive units frequently reflects the inability of these units to meet the challenges of smaller competitors who do not have such high overhead and fixed costs. Thus, consolidation actually reflects inefficiency rather than efficiency.[10] Some of these historians, moreover, argue that the movement toward consolidation was the result of bureaucratic business reorganizations rather than an effort to increase efficiency. Most business historians, on the other hand, reject this interpretation. They tend to correlate consolidation with order and efficiency; thus the great entrepreneurs are viewed as creative individuals interested not in profit per se, but in productive efficiency as well.

In the final analysis, any interpretation of the careers and accomplishments of American industrialists will depend on the starting assumptions and values of the individual making the particular judgment. Despite claims of objectivity, it is difficult, if not impossible, for historians to divest themselves of beliefs and standards that influence their analysis of this problem. In some ways an evaluation of the American businessman is even more controversial than that of any other symbolic figure in our nation's history. For underlying such an evaluation is the larger problem of the quality and meaning of the American experience. To some historians the significance of America is directly related to its productive capacity. America, they maintain, has demonstrated to the world that an affluent society is possible to achieve within a democratic capitalist framework. Thus the American economy — a creation of industrial pioneers and bold innovators — has far more to its credit than many have admitted. Other historians, however, argue in a much different vein. The social costs of industrialism, they maintain, could have been far lower had it not been for the greed and quest after power that marked this process. By placing a premium on

10. A recent variation of this point of view is reflected in the work of some historians who have attempted to demonstrate that the movement toward government regulation, rather than being opposed by industry, was actually inaugurated and promoted by large industrial concerns who saw in government regulatory agencies a legal means of limiting, if not eliminating, competition. Since these regulatory agencies were usually staffed by individuals sympathetic to the industry that it regulated, these agencies often acted in the interests of the industry instead of the public — which often was synonymous with the interests of the largest concerns in that particular segment of the economy. Thus the movement toward regulation, rather than being an anti-business movement, was actually a movement by business to eliminate competition. For an elaboration of this point of view see Gabriel Kolko's two recent books, *The Triumph of Conservatism: A Reinterpretation of American History, 1900–1916* (New York, 1963), and *Railroads and Regulation 1877–1916* (Princeton, 1965).

acquisitive and amoral values, by creating a system marked by great inequality of wealth, they conclude, these entrepreneurs contributed to the narrowness and the materialistic qualities of American life. Any judgment on this historical problem is, in the final analysis, a judgment on the nature and quality of American civilization itself.

Chester M. Destler

THIS PAPER is concerned with the semipiratical entrepreneurs who roamed the United States virtually unchecked before 1903, save for the opposition of a few publicists and some short-lived vigilante committees. Contemporaries, following Henry Demarest Lloyd and Carl Schurz, likened businessmen of this type to the nobles who infested the Medieval Rhine. The term "robber barons" has stuck to them through the years despite occasional attempts at rehabilitating one or another who stood out above the throng by virtue of his accumulations or philanthropy. Only recently, for example, Howard Mumford Jones distinguished between the "cruelty" and the "culture" of these magnates whose behavior in the commercial-political and the artistic-literary fields he prefers to liken to the "commercial tyrants" of the Renaissance. No one to date, so far as I know, has attempted to distinguish from their strictly buccaneering activities the permanent contributions made by these businessmen as a group to American business practices. Such is the purpose of this paper.

In order to interject as much objectivity as possible into the discussion, *The Dictionary of American Biography,* other biographical and secondary materials, and some primary sources have been drawn upon for data on the entrepreneurial activities and life histories of thirty-eight businessmen and five financiers, who were representative of the much larger element in the business community with which this analysis is concerned, during the period between the firing on Fort Sumter and the dissolution of the Northern Securities Company. The material thus gathered

"Entrepreneurial Leadership Among the 'Robber Barons': A Trial Balance," *The Tasks of Economic History* (Supplement), *Journal of Economic History,* VI [1946], 28–49. Reprinted by permission of the Economic History Association.

CHESTER M. DESTLER (1904–), before his retirement, was MacCurdy Professor of American History at Connecticut College. He is the author of several important historical works covering the late nineteenth century, including *Henry Demarest Lloyd and the Empire of Reform* and *American Radicalism 1865–1901.*

has been classified under some twenty-four categories. It will throw light, it is hoped, upon the origins, training, incentives, risks, advisers, and other aspects of the entrepreneurial activities of the group.

Before summarizing these findings, however, a word should be said in explanation of why the semipiratical type emerged so suddenly during Reconstruction to a position of great prominence if not of control over important segments of American economy. Then, after presenting the statistical material derived from the general analysis, the paper will conclude with a brief discussion of the activities of several groups of enterprisers whose individual members are included in the larger group.

[I]

Why did the semipiratical entrepreneur rise so swiftly to importance and economic power after Appomattox? Was it due entirely to novel circumstances that had appeared since the appeal to arms? Or can the protoype of the "robber baron" be discovered in the ante-bellum period in sufficient numbers to rule out the former possibility entirely? The historian's answer, like the politician's, must be neither, but some of both.

As the result of recent research it is possible to identify before the Civil War occasional businessmen and infrequent resort to amoral methods strikingly similar to the "robber barons" and their schemes. The promoter-speculator with his plea for government assistance, whom Mr. Dorfman's recent study of *The Economic Mind in American Civilization* shows to have been so prominent in American business history before 1860, may be regarded as their remote ancestor. More closely connected in the line of descent, however, were Robert Schuyler of the New York and New Haven Railroad and Edward Crane of the Vermont Central. Both men pointed the way to others who would profit by the looting of railroad corporations and default of fiduciary obligations. The Erie, as Thomas C. Cochran and William Miller have shown, was the football of Wall Street speculators before 1860. In use of the corporation for the conduct of industrial enterprises, as well as in their management by hired officers responsible to absentee owners in a distant metropolis, the Boston Associates gave lessons that all who ran might read.

More within the scope of post-bellum entrepreneurial methods, or at least those practiced by the "robber barons," were other activities. Occasional resort to the corruption of legislative bodies by promoters and lobbyists, whether in quest of subsidies for railroad construction projects, as in the case of the La Crosse and Milwaukee, or a tariff schedule favorable to the woolen industry, was certainly a harbinger of things to come. So were the bitter rate wars among rival steamship lines, whether on the Hudson River or the Isthmian route. Equally pregnant were the temporary pools between steamship operators on the Great Lakes and the grain-elevator pool at Buffalo that denied millers and consumers the benefit of progressive reductions in Erie Canal tolls. At Syracuse, New York, likewise, the Onondaga Company bound rival salt producers in an ironclad and extremely profitable pool which the Saginaw operators were quick to copy.

Neither manipulation of governments and corporations by promoters, with attendant corruption and betrayal of fellow stockholders, nor attempts to substitute monopoly for competition were dominant features of business before secession. Mercantile capitalism, although challenged by industrialism, was still regnant then. Business was highly competitive, organized in small units, most of which were individual enterprises or partnerships. Small business — genuinely free enterprise — foreign trade, and shipping dominated most men's thinking and calculations down to the panic of 1857, although a minority of shrewd entrepreneurs and stock-market operators saw that the future was with the railroads and with the home market, and industries catering to it.

Politically, the United States was governed until 1860 by a coalition of merchants, bankers, southern planters, and farmers, with a modicum of railroad promoters and their spokesmen. All these, and most politicians as well, were staunch churchgoers, adherents of old-fashioned Christianity and a code that laid less emphasis upon *caveat emptor* and unrestrained avarice than upon giving the customer and the public value for value received. The religious mold of American life, the ethics of mercantile-planter capitalism, the relatively small area of operations of individual firms, and the popular opposition to monopoly and special privilege were important factors that restrained the promoter-speculators and held the tariff to the low-water mark.

What an era of unbroken peace and orderly expansion after 1860 might have brought by way of the gradual modification or supercession of this regime will never be known. Its overthrow, in actual fact, was the result of a great domestic tragedy that synchronized chronologically with an intellectual revolution overseas.

All students know that the Civil War saved the Union at the expense of disrupting the merchant-planter-agrarian alliance, and leaving its separated elements helpless during a chaotic epoch of Reconstruction. The war ruined the great merchant marine, impaired the resources of the great importers, freed industry from mercantile leading strings, and opened the door wide to promoters in quest of government war contracts, or of land grants and money subsidies for railroads in the unsettled West, and to those who speculated on the nation's chances of ruin or survival. The speculators, the promoters, and the "shoddyites," encouraged by inflation and war contracts, tore great holes in the ante-bellum code of business, civic, and private ethics. As the idealists in the North joined the colors, the unprincipled, the bigoted, and the corrupt reached for the reins of political power, and the unscrupulous in a number of cases seized leadership in important fields of business. Before the war ended, the corrupt alliance that opened the door wide to the "robber barons" had been fashioned not only in Washington and New York City, but in the states that ranged from the Berkshires to San Francisco Bay. Castigated by Walt Whitman in his *Democratic Vistas* (1871), this regime of business politics and of entrepreneurs who sought special advantage through government favoritism or other forms of privilege lasted until it was terminated by Theodore Roosevelt's accidental rise to power.

Simultaneously, the Darwinian revolution placed American Protestantism on the defensive. Not only did the champions of evolution maneuver the clergy into the position of opposing freedom of teaching and of scholarship, but they also destroyed the religious sanction for morals by justifying ruthless methods in business and politics. "The survival of the fittest" became the rationale of those who shed moral scruples, in the business field at least, in their climb to wealth and economic power. As John D. Rockefeller declared to his Sunday school class, in rationalization of his own business career:

> The growth of a large business is merely a survival of the fittest. . . . The American Beauty rose can be produced in the splendor and fragrance which bring cheer to its beholder only by sacrificing the early buds which grow up around it. This is *not an evil* tendency in business. It is merely the working-out of a law of nature and a law of God.

Or, as Andrew Carnegie declared of his conversion to Darwinism:

> I remember that light came as in a flood and all was clear. Not only had I got rid of theology and the supernatural, but I had found the truth of evolution. "All is well since all grows better."

Finally, the conquest of the South, the isolation of the now helpless agrarian West, and the rapid opening up of the Great Plains and Rocky Mountains by means of the new trunk-line railroad, modern mining machinery, and novel milling and meat-packing processes rapidly expanded the geographic area of business operations to continental proportions. This tremendous increase in the geographic scope of business activity radiating out from the older business centers of the Northeast, much of it carried on now in raw frontier regions, made it impossible for champions of the older ethics to hold businessmen to ante-bellum standards. Instead, the frontier spirit moved east to coalesce with Social Darwinism and complete the rationale of a new school of business leadership. The widespread and prolonged moral collapse that accompanied these developments provided the milieu within which its members could operate to full advantage.

The growing ineffectiveness of the old mercantile code was not entirely due to impersonal forces. In New York, led by William Cullen Bryant, and in the Chicago Board of Trade, the merchants fought hard and long not only against free-booting on the exchanges but also against the spread of business amorality, special legislation, and political corruption. Lost sight of in the general preoccupation of historians with southern reconstruction or the struggles in Washington over the tariff and the currency, this losing battle throws light upon the historic process which ushered in the regime of the "robber barons." It suggests with great pertinency that unscrupulous men out for the main chance, representing newer, more aggressive interests than commerce, had much to do with shunting to one side such ethical considerations as stood in the way of their quest for wealth or economic power.

Leading separate spearheads in this attack upon the traditional order were the Erie ring, the Rockefeller coterie, the Huntington associates, and a fourth but less well-integrated group of midwestern railroad promoters and speculators. Of the first three, more anon. In the interim, let us turn to the more inclusive group of forty-three entrepreneurs, thirty-eight businessmen and five financiers, which has been selected for analysis.

Of these it can be stated that they exhibited the vigor, cleverness, and strength of will that have characterized the great entrepreneurs of each epoch of capitalist expansion, whether during the Renaissance, the commercial revolution, early industrialism, or the second industrial revolution in Europe. Whatever their amoralities and ruthlessness, they helped to lead American business into the stage of full capitalism, creating gigantic organizations capable of servicing the entire continent or several sections at least. They led in extending the corporation into new and important fields of enterprise, in employing hired executives for routine administration and specialized tasks, and in reserving to themselves exclusively entrepreneurial functions of planning, high strategy, and risk-taking. At the same time, particularly in the railroads, they developed a separation of capital ownership from management that was accompanied by such abuses that direct government intervention in business was agitated for the first time seriously as a remedy. Before the end of the period under consideration, more than one of the industrial magnates studied rose to the status of super-entrepreneur combining banking and industrial power, as did H. H. Rogers of the Standard Oil Company.

[II]

Of the forty-three men studied, classified by ordinary terminology, fifteen were railroad men. For two of this category, Daniel Drew and Jay Gould, stock-market speculation competed for first place with their formal affiliation with railroads. Two other enterprisers, Henry M. Flagler and Joseph E. Brown, were both railroad men and industrialists. Fourteen of the group were manufacturers. There were pre-eminently market speculators, James Fisk, Jr., Benjamin P. Hutchinson, and Russell Sage, although each was engaged in other business activities. Two, Marshall Field and John Wanamaker, were merchants, and two, John W. Gates and Judge William H. Moore, were promoters. Alexander J. Cassatt, a career man, is included in the railroad group, as is another careerist, Charles M. Schwab, among the industrialists. Five Standard Oil men, the California "Big Four," and three members of the Erie ring are studied individually. Five bankers are included, although by strict definition of entrepreneurship perhaps they should not be, because four of them invaded the industrial or railroad fields and promoted new forms of business organization.

An overwhelming majority of the group were new men. Twenty-nine, or 69 per cent, and an even higher proportion of the nonbanking members, belonged to the first generation of entrepreneurs. Thirteen of them were sons of farmers, one the son of a farmer-inventor, another the son of a wealthy German landed proprietor. Two were sons of lawyers, two of ministers, two from artisan families, two were sons of peddlers, another of a livery-stable keeper. Another was the son of a grocer and purchasing agent of the Concord Railroad. The origins of four remain obscure. Many were nurtured in poverty as well as in the stern school of American Protestantism. Few had more than limited formal education in the district school. Many were first employed at what would be regarded now as a tender age, out of sheer need to contribute to their own support. Only five of the forty-three, less than 12 per cent, were born outside the territorial limits of the United States.

The apprenticeship for larger administrative responsibilities served by twenty-one of the group was in the management of petty enterprises of their own. Fourteen first gained administrative experience in businesses operated by others. Two, Leland Stanford and Joseph E. Brown, may be said to have gleaned it from political office, although Stanford was a merchant in California before holding office as governor of the state. Three, Elbert H. Gary, William H. Moore, and James F. Joy, acquired similar training in connection with a practice in corporation law. Two, Cyrus McCormick and Henry Villard, first learned administration while developing their own giant enterprises.

The extreme youth at which many of the group first headed their own enterprises, or attained a partnership with others in them, is worth noting. Eleven did so before reaching their majority; two, Daniel Drew and Cornelius Vanderbilt, at the early age of sixteen. Eight attained this status at twenty-one, and twelve more before they reached thirty. Thus thirty-one out of forty-three had come to head their own businesses before they reached middle age. Jay Cooke, Henry Villard, Alexander J. Cassatt, James F. Joy, Joseph E. Brown, in order of age, were those who failed to head their own concerns before they reached their forties.

In attempting to classify the group according to mental type and range of activity, I have accepted Sombart's categories of expert and merchant, modified his financier into the financier-speculator to accord with American phenomena, and added the promoter as an indigenous product of first significance. As students familiar with the period would infer, very few of the entrepreneurs studied can be classed solely under these four headings. Two, Alexander J. Cassatt and Henry Clay Frick, were experts. Fourteen others combined this with one or more of the other functions. Two, Marshall Field and John Wanamaker, were merchants pre-eminently, although nineteen combined the characteristic feature of the businessman with other traits. Five were merchant-experts, for example. One was a merchant-expert-financier, and two were merchant-expert-promoters. Two, James J. Hill and Cornelius Vanderbilt, embodied all four traits with major emphasis upon the role of the expert. Four of our subjects were financier-speculators, preeminently, but seventeen others combined this with other functions. Finally, as might be expected, the role of promoter attracted the largest number, since some twenty-three united it with one or more other functions of entrepreneurial activity. Of this group, however, only Gates and Moore can be termed promoters exclusively, and Gates engaged in barbed-wire manufacturing for the sake of industrial and business-blackmailing profits before emerging in his final role.

In order to discover the major incentives that led our subjects to engage in and continue in their several fields of business, their motives, so far as they can be ascertained, have been classified under some twenty different headings. Each individual, of course, operated under the impulse furnished by one or more of them. Eleven of the twenty categories are different foci of the profit motive. Various fields of business as careers take up three more, family considerations two others, empire building and self-vindication another, and the last is business as the means to a larger cultural life.

Since we are dealing with an era when "the lack of quantitative limits to acquisition" and the pre-eminence of the acquisitive drive were as notable in American business as the ruthlessness with which this drive was expressed, the heaviest weighting of incentives is associated with the profit motive. Monopoly profits, fittingly, occupy first place with twenty-five entrepreneurs seeking them. Promoter's profits ranked third, with fifteen seekers, and manufacturing, transportation, and speculative profits tied for fourth place with twelve each. When to the great emphasis placed upon monopoly, promotion, and speculation is added the lure of easy profits from railroad construction for six men, profits from war contracts for two of the group, and the facile enrichment of at least three others by looting the corporations they controlled, the character of "robber baron" entrepreneurship becomes well defined. For this type of business leadership, it is plain, the profits from the routine production of goods and services for consumption held a decidedly tertiary place.

Ranking above it and pressing hard upon monopoly, promotional, and speculative profits for first place in the ascertainable motives of our forty-three entrepreneurs is imperialism. By this is meant more than ordinary emphasis upon the acquisition, extension, and retention of personal and corporate power. It was a major incentive for nineteen of the figures under examination, while empire building, close kin to it, held fifth place with ten practitioners. In the light of this evidence, and with due acknowledgement to Arthur H. Cole, the "robber barons" might better be entitled the "power entrepreneurs."

The other incentives mentioned were relatively unattractive. Self-vindication, as an inventor in the case of Cyrus McCormick, and in railroad administration for William H. Vanderbilt, motivated only two men. Business as a career attracted one each in banking, industry, and railroading. Family tradition and desire to found a family drew one each, and wealth as a means to a larger cultural life one, if we can take Andrew Carnegie's statements at their face value.

Death was the decisive determinant that ended the business career of at least seventeen and probably twenty-two of the group. Ill health led to the retirement of four, old age of three, and failure in business of three more. Desire for recreation was the cause of only two retirements. For the great bulk of the group, so far as the sources indicate, entrepreneurial activity was both work and play, although art collecting, a big house on Knob Hill or Fifth Avenue, and yachting served as secondary diversions for some. All told, these "robber barons" were outstanding exemplars of the activism that constitutes still a central dynamic of the American business community.

Less light has been cast by this analysis, so far as it was possible to push it, upon the ancillary institutions that supported the great entrepreneurs in our group. Ten were dependent upon local banks. Two out of the ten, Phillip D. Armour and Benjamin Hutchinson, founded their own to support, respectively, their manufacturing and speculating activities. John D. Rockefeller soon drew upon New York sources as well as upon the Cleveland banks for working capital. Railroads featured as important ancillary institutions. They were relied upon by six enterprisers, including George M. Pullman, Gould's telegraph enterprises, and three entrepreneurs in the late sixties who were heavily indebted to the Erie Railway for a swift, initial ascent up the ladder of "success" that soon produced the Standard Oil monopoly. Three of the enlarged Standard Oil group of later years figured as supporters of three other great enterprisers, Edward H. Harriman, James Stillman, and James B. Duke.

The United States government, as dispenser of money loans and subsidies in land, was a major reliance of six enterprisers. Political-party affiliations were important in the entrepreneurial careers of Leland Stanford and Joseph E. Brown. Stock and commodity exchanges, as institutions, were of major importance in the careers of five of the group. European banking connections were vital to Henry Villard as well as to John Pierpont Morgan, Jacob H. Schiff, and August Belmont. John Pierpont Morgan & Company, it may be added, was the chief reliance of only two of the men under consideration, and for one of these, James J. Hill, the

Bank of Montreal furnished the indispensable banking support of his early years.

Within the field of risks borne, there is considerable overlapping among categories since many of the group engaged in different activities or passed from one phase to another in the expansion of individual enterprises. The analysis indicates, however, considerable success in exploitation of business opportunities involving little or no risk. Monopoly risk was enjoyed by twenty-one of the group. Nine others profited from government subsidies or railroad-construction contracts, or both, that minimized risks for the enterprisers involved. Sixteen enterprisers experienced promoter's risks, and seventeen took speculative risks. Fourteen suffered normal competitive risks, five those of underwriting, two normal banking risks, and two the chances taken by the career man in a great enterprise. Two men faced the risks assumed by an inventor seeking to make business profits from the production and sale of his own invention.

So far as advisers are concerned, twenty-six of the forty-three relied primarily upon associates within their own organization or group. This number is swelled unduly, of course, by the inclusion of the Erie ring, the California "Big Four," and five of the Standard Oil men in the analysis. Six enterprisers relied upon a banker for advice, three on relatives, three on the Standard Oil group toward the close of the period, two on men in the same field but in independent enterprises. Other capitalists advised two men, and a corporation lawyer appears to have been the chief adviser of another.

In the type of organization employed, there was frequent shifting within the group from the partnership to the simple corporation, and to even more advanced forms of corporate organization. John D. Rockefeller, for example, experimented with several partnerships, then moved into a succession of corporations before launching the first trust, ultimately resorting to the holding company and to international cartels to satisfy the requirements of his expanding organization. Acknowledging the fact, then, that a given entrepreneur might be satisfied with a single type, or employ a variety of organizations, the analysis reveals that the corporation in various forms was used preponderantly. Five individual enterprises and twenty-four men resorting to partnerships compare poorly with employment of the simple corporation by thirty-six individuals, and resort to the trust by the Standard Oil five, whether in the parent organization or the succession of other industrial trusts that these men promoted. The holding company was employed by fifteen men, including the Standard Oil men, the Huntington group, James B. Duke, Elbert H. Gary, William H. Moore, John H. Inman, James J. Hill, Edward H. Harriman, and Henry Villard. The international cartel found American pioneers in the agreements made by the Standard Oil men with their Scottish and Russian competitors, and in Duke's agreement for a division of markets with the Imperial Tobacco Company some years later, after the turn of the century.

Leasing, as a means of achieving unified operation of separately incorporated railroad properties, was pioneered by Jay Gould, the Huntington group, and the Vanderbilts. To perpetuate banker control of reorganized railroads Morgan devised the voting trust as trustee acting without responsibility in the presumed interest of bond- and stockholders. At least fifteen of the forty-three men indulged in the operation of disguised, subsidiary companies in order to outmaneuver competitors or hide from a public devoted to free enterprise the realities of a monopoly position.

Sombart and Usher both stress the importance of the innovating function of the true entrepreneur, although the former insists that the inventing consists not so much of "technical innovations as of new forms of organization for production, transportation and marketing." Sombart would have added, if he had studied Jay Gould or some other of the more notorious "robber barons," that the inventing of traps for associates or competitors, of new ways of manipulating governments, and of new ways to bleed trusting stockholders or bilk consumers was part of the innovating function of great enterprise between 1860 and 1903.

To return to objectivity, if the last remark was a departure, our entrepreneurs may be analyzed in terms of their contribution to one or more of some thirteen types of innovation. Five, well over 10 per cent, seem to have been inactive in this important field of activity. Three, Cyrus McCormick, Henry H. Rogers before he joined Standard Oil, and George M. Pullman were genuine inventors. Only two, Andrew Carnegie and Gustavus Swift, seem to have made use of research technicians, a field in which twentieth-century American entrepreneurship has a far more notable record. Two,

Charles Crocker and James J. Hill, contributed to improving the methods of railroad construction. Six others improved production technology or processes in industry and railroading, with Benjamin P. Hutchinson, Gustavus Swift, and Phillip D. Armour vying with each other in the development of by-products of meat packing and the last two pioneering in dressed beef and use of refrigerator cars. Charles A. Pillsbury exploited the most improved milling processes. Vanderbilt the elder pioneered with the four-track trunk line. If somewhat chary of those contributed by outsiders, Carnegie made the most of improved methods of steel production worked out by his great lieutenant, Captain "Bill" Jones. Led by John D. Rockefeller and Henry H. Rogers, nine of the group contributed to the improvement of the over-all organization of their enterprises, while nine others, led by Gustavus Swift, Jay Cooke, John D. Rockefeller, James B. Duke, and Alexander J. Cassatt, were notable for improving marketing methods in their several fields. Jay Cooke and James Stillman, it may be added, were innovators in banking methods of first importance.

Some twelve men, led by the Standard Oil and Huntington groups, but including Jay Gould, Elbert H. Gary, John H. Inman, George M. Pullman, Cyrus McCormick, and Henry Villard, contributed to the development of monopoly techniques in American enterprise. Supporting this largest single group were eight who contributed to the art of corporate manipulation as a means to sudden wealth. Six made noted contributions to the refinement of speculative techniques. Five, Jay Gould, Collis P. Huntington, Leland Stanford, Jay Cooke, and Cornelius Vanderbilt, were notable for the developments that they introduced into the art of manipulating governments in the interest of their business ventures.

Only four of the forty-three, it should be noted, were distinguished for developing and practicing the principles of sound corporate finance. These were James J. Hill, Edward H. Harriman, John Pierpont Morgan, and John D. Rockefeller. Three others were notable for ensuring a supply of raw materials as a means of stabilizing and integrating their operations. These were Franklin B. Gowen, who secured ample anthracite coal reserves for future traffic on the Philadelphia and Reading, Henry Clay Frick whose purchases of Connellsville coal ensured him not only ample supplies of raw material for his ovens but a virtual coke monopoly, and Daniel Drew whose use of the corporate printing press made a unique and enduring contribution to the method of self-enrichment by watering down the equity holdings of fellow stockholders.

In adopting the latest technical improvements and putting them to effective use, at least fifteen of the thirty-eight nonbanking entrepreneurs were more or less alert to the advantage that this would give them in competition or in strengthening their general position.

Turning to other factors that contributed significantly to the business "success" of this group of "robber barons," it may be observed that railroad favors in rates or service were important for eleven of the group while railroad opposition was a partial and temporary obstacle to only one. Monopoly, partially or wholly, temporarily or more permanently achieved, was a significant or dominant feature of the entrepreneurial activity of at least thirty-six of the forty-three. This, it should be emphasized, is indicative of a basic deviation in entrepreneurial leadership away from the free-enterprise system that gave these men their opportunity.

Political corruption, as a means of securing favorable government action, was practiced by at least thirteen, a number that would be swelled if heavy campaign contributions were included in the definition of this practice. Marked hostility to the labor movement was exhibited by sixteen, including Andrew Carnegie, whose defenders would question his inclusion in the group, and the Standard Oil men. One, Joseph E. Brown, made a fortune employing convict labor. The "Big Four" employed Chinese coolies to keep down construction costs. Phillip D. Armour, Henry Clay Frick, and Gustavus Swift employed Pinkertons, and George M. Pullman was equally prominent in union smashing.

At least thirteen of these "robber barons" rigged the exchanges as a means of furthering their acquisitive urge or of promoting the welfare of the organizations that they controlled. Some sixteen milked their corporations by one means or another for their own personal profit. Fifteen, apparently, discriminated between favored and unfavored customers to the benefit of the former. One, Alexander J. Cassatt, was a leading opponent of this practice and three, Marshall Field, Cyrus McCormick, and John Wanamaker, won outstanding success in merchandising by following the contrary practice. Twenty-three charged exorbitant rates when a monopoly position or other factors made it possible. In this group the speculators, the promoters, and the Huntington and Standard Oil coteries were particularly prominent. James B. Duke, Alexander J. Cassatt, James J. Hill, Jay Cooke, and possibly Andrew Carnegie were those who achieved business success in part at least by following a contrary policy.

At least twenty-two, apart from the Rockefeller group and both Vanderbilts, who perhaps should be added to the number, speculated in opportunities created by the enterprises that they conducted. At least eleven speculated in the stock of their own companies. Of the eight who it is certain did not, six operated partnerships for the greatest proportion of their careers and could not have done so. Another died before the stock of his railroads became marketable, and the eighth preferred to speculate in grain.

Finally, although complete data could not be obtained on all the individuals under consideration, some thirteen profited from control and manipulation of the press. These were the Standard Oil group, the Huntington associates, Jay Cooke, Jay Gould, James J. Hill, and August Belmont through his personal and banking relations with Manton Marble before the Democratic endorsement of Horace Greeley in 1872. Further investigation would reveal, possibly, connections between the press and some of the promoters such as that which existed in Chicago between the *Inter Ocean* and Charles T. Yerkes, local representative of the Widener-Elkins-Whitney group of municipal traction magnates. Standard Oil was unique, not only in the propaganda that emanated from its members and in the press it subsidized in defense of monopoly and large-scale organization as such, but also in the subsidy it gave a supposedly learned journal, *The Social Economist,* and its editor, George Gunton, even after he became a professor at Columbia University.

If time and space permitted, inquiry might be made of the extent to which our group employed the business boycott in primary and secondary forms against competitors; of whether or not they sold adulterated or substandard products; and of their employment of the black list and "yellow dog" contract in labor relations.

It is possible, now, to differentiate to some degree among several different types of entrepreneurs in the group studied. Two of them at least, Alexander J. Cassatt and Charles M. Schwab, were prototypes of a new generation of business leaders who were to play an increasingly important role after the turn of the century.

Cassatt chose railroading as a career and during the days of Thomas A. Scott's administration rose from the ranks to the position of third and then first vice-president of the Pennsylvania Railroad. Eschewing the speculative and promotional aspects of railroading so prominent at that time, Alexander J. Cassatt evidently regarded the profits that accrued from efficient operation as the chief and legitimate ends of the business. Even more, during the heyday of Standard Oil's alliance with the eastern trunk-line association, Cassatt had the courage to denounce the rebate policy before the so-called Hepburn Committee in New York and to reveal payments of $10,000,000 in rebates to Standard Oil within a few months by the Pennsylvania Railroad alone.

Cassatt stood squarely on the common-law doctrine that carriers should treat all shippers alike, and upon the fiduciary obligations of corporate managers to the owners of the property that they directed. Retiring, temporarily, in 1882, he returned to become president of the Pennsylvania system in 1899, when he made a notable record as leader of the successful fight to abolish rebating and other forms of railroad favoritism, first through a community of interest based upon inter-trunk-line stockholdings and then in outstanding support of the Elkins Act. In rationalizing management, in improving equipment and operation, and in developing an enlightened labor policy. Cassatt heralded a new day in American business leadership.

The financiers, John Pierpont Morgan and Jacob H. Schiff, who stepped into railroading in the nineties to put an end to the abuses that were characteristic of the financial management of far too many corporations, stand far above such ordinary promoters as Judge William M. Moore and John W. Gates in their attempt to render a constructive solution for generation-old problems in the field of transportation. After the turn of the century, however, Morgan did not escape severe criticism for his stock-market manipulations accompanying the marketing of equities in new combinations that he promoted, and for the monopolistic and antilabor policies of some of these organizations that remained within the sphere of his influence.

For the bulk of the entrepreneurs studied and for many other contemporary business leaders, there is justification for Carl Schurz's epithet, the "robber barons," or Howard Mumford Jones' analogy with the Renaissance despot, because of the great weight which the statistics give to monopoly-promotional-speculative profits and to considerations of personal power, and the considerable number for whom there is evidence of resort to amoral methods to gain ends that they regarded as legitimate.

[III]

The outstanding representatives of this element, which was most strongly entrenched in the all-important railroad system, can be found in the Erie ring, the Standard Oil group, and Collis P. Huntington's associates in the Far West. If some measure of constructive contribution is conceded to Jay Gould for his opening parts of the Southwest by his railroads, and if due recognition is given the Napoleonic talents with which he operated, the remainder of his career and that of his two early associates on the Erie can be classified as outright freebooting without fear of effective denial. Profits through looting the corporations under his control, through cutting the melon raised by granting secret low rates to a few favored customers in a single business field, through rigging the markets and betting there on "a sure thing" were dominant traits of Gould's entrepreneurial activity, while he was not adverse to employing the threat of competition from his Pacific Mail line or from insolvent railroads to force better managed properties to accord him a blackmailer's reward in the renegotiation of the numerous pools that he entered in the seventies, eighties, and nineties.

The first generation of Standard Oil men, who alone fall within the scope of this inquiry, rate somewhat higher as entrepreneurs. It can hardly be denied, however, in light of recent discoveries, that they achieved their first great success by "muscling in" upon a highly competitive industry as allies of the Erie ring in one of the most extraordinary *coups de main* of modern industrial history. The daring, ruthlessness, and tactical skill with which this venture was carried out will long command admiration as a masterpiece of the piratical art. To the improvement of the basic technology of petroleum Standard Oil contributed little or nothing before the turn of the century. In S. F. Peckham's *Report on the Production, Technology, and Uses of Petroleum and Its Products,* which appeared in 1884, not a single reference is made to any Standard Oil contribution to improved technology or processes. Independent evidence indicates that up to that date the processes and technical devices employed by Standard Oil were those that had been worked out by others. Even the Frasch process for the purification of the Lima oils in the late eighties was the work of a research chemist of the then independent Imperial Oil Company, who was promptly lured into the employ of Standard Oil. The basic technology of the petroleum industry then, to be sure, was French in origin, but to it noted contributions had been made by the Downer Kerosene Company of Boston and Corry, Pennsylvania, by Samuel van Syckle, who fathered the pipe line and the process of continuous distillation, by the Empire Transportation Company's all-metal tank car, and by Byron D. Benson's long-distance pipe line. Monopoly, in the case of Standard Oil as in that of Western Union under Jay Gould, as Mr. Goldin indicates, had the effect of paralyzing interest in promoting technological improvements before 1900.

On the other hand, in the conduct of their business the Rockefeller group showed consummate skill in lowering production costs, in merchandising, and in maintaining the efficiency and altering the legal form of an organization that ramified like the green bay tree, and showed great tenacity of purpose in maintaining the monopoly that they had achieved by illicit methods. Here was proof of the talents of great entrepreneurship in the first era of mature capitalism which such contemporary critics as Simon Sterne, the Hepburn Committee, the Cullom Committee, and Henry D. Lloyd acknowledged while denying that the Standard Oil men possessed a monopoly of business talent in the petroleum industry and castigating the semipiratical methods that they employed until brought partially to book by the Progressive movement.

It may be observed, in parting, that the development of the organization and some of the merchandising innovations of Standard Oil were the result of force of circumstance. The petroleum-refining industry, when the Rockefellers seized control of it, though widely scattered was small in volume as well as in individual plant capacity. What none of group nor their Erie allies could have predicted was the rapid opening up of a succession of new and highly productive sources of crude oil. Compelled by their monopolistic policy to buy the product, to manufacture and distribute it, they were forced by their own ambitions, avarice, and monopoly position to pioneer in mass distribution of a basic commodity. That they succeeded in doing so, while maintaining a monopoly price for kerosene and perhaps for many by-products throughout an entire generation, was attested by contemporary critics and price analysts and admitted, inadvertently, by John D. Archbold before the Industrial Commission.

Long associated with Gould, like the Standard Oil men, and like him intimately allied with Standard Oil, the Huntington associates began operations as an independent group of railroad-construction promoters. They intended to sell their completed Central Pacific for a profit of $20,000,000 or more after rewarding themselves liberally for building it through construction contracts negotiated with themselves. Perhaps because of the panic of 1873, more probably because their railroad was highly speculative so far as operating revenues were concerned, the "Big Four" were obliged to operate the road they could not sell. Hiring men acquainted with the business to develop an adequate organization, the Huntington associates set out to monopolize transportation in California and the southwestern Rocky Mountain region by building the Southern Pacific, by employing a particularly ruthless system of exclusive service contracts with shippers while charging an extraordinarily high level of local rates, and by bribing Gould's Pacific Mail Steamship Company into a traffic pool on transcontinental traffic. As in the case of the Erie ring and the Rockefeller clique, the verdict of the careful historian of the Huntington group is that its effect upon the general level of business and civic ethics was seriously degrading.

The huge private fortunes of the "Big Four" were the measure of their success in reaping at little or no risk rich profits in construction and monopolistic operation, to which they added the returns from canny speculation in California real estate. As ruthless as Gould and the Standard Oil men, they contributed in the Far

West, by their long continued extortions and corrupt political activity, directly to the rise of a regional protest movement that in the next generation imposed stringent controls on railroad management there while joining in the larger movement to hold entrepreneurs everywhere to a proper consideration of the public interest.

Alfred D. Chandler, Jr.

THE HISTORIAN, by the very nature of his task, must be concerned with change. What made for change? Why did it come about when it did, and in the way it did? These are characteristically historians' questions. For the student of American business history, these basic questions can be put a little more precisely. What in the American past has given businessmen the opportunity or created the need for them to change what they were doing or the way they were doing it? In other words, what stimulated them to develop new products, new markets, new sources of raw materials, new ways of procuring, processing, or marketing the goods they handled? What encouraged them to find new methods of financing, new ways of managing or organizing their businesses? What turned them to altering their relations with their working force, their customers and competitors, and with the larger American public?

The question of what constitutes the dynamic factors in American business history, dynamic in the sense of stimulating change and innovation, can be more clearly defined if the country's land, natural resources, and cultural patterns are taken as given. Land and resources were the raw materials with which the businessmen had to work, and the cultural attitudes and values helped set the legal and ethical rules of the game they had to play. Within this cultural and geographic environment a number of historical developments appear to have stimulated change. These provide a framework around which historical data can be compiled and analyzed.

The following major dynamic forces are visible in the American

"The Beginnings of 'Big Business' in American Industry," *Business History Review,* XXXIII (Spring, 1959), 1–10, 14–20, 22–31. Reprinted by permission of the *Business History Review.*

ALFRED D. CHANDLER, JR. (1918–) is Professor of History at the Johns Hopkins University. He has published several books and many articles dealing with American business and economic history, including an important biography of Henry Varnum Poor.

business economy since 1815: the western expansion of population; the construction and initial operation of the national railroad network; the development of a national and increasingly urban market; the application of two new sources of power: the internal combustion engine and electricity, to industry and transportation; and the systematic application of the natural and physical sciences, particularly chemistry and physics, to industry through the institutionalizing of research and development activities.

The first, the westward expansion, appears to have provided the primary impetus, except possibly in New England, to business innovation in the years from 1815 to about 1850; the building of the railroads appears to have been the major factor from the 1850's to the late 1870's; the growth of the national and urban market from the 1880's until a little after 1900; the coming of electricity and the internal combustion engine from the early 1900's to the 1920's; and, finally, the growth of systematic and institutionalized research and development since the 1920's.

These five factors are essentially aspects of fundamental population changes and technological advances. There were, of course, other factors that encouraged business innovation and change. The coming of the new machines and mechanical devices may have been a more important stimulant to innovation in New England than the growth of her markets and sources of supply in the expanding South and West. Wars usually precipitated change. The business cycle, flow of capital, government policy and legislation all played a significant part in business innovation. But such political and financial developments appear to have intensified or delayed the more basic changes encouraged initially by fundamental population shifts and technological achievements.

The purpose of making such a list is, however, not to argue that one development was more dynamic than the other. Nor are these five factors to be considered as "causes" for change; nor are they "theses" to be argued as representing reality, nor "theories" to provide an over-all explanation of change or possibly of predicting change. They are, rather, a framework on which historical information can be tied and inter-related. They provide a consistent basis upon which meaningful questions can be asked of the data. . . .

The purpose of this article then is, by using the framework of basic, dynamic forces, to look a little more closely at the years that witnessed the beginnings of big business in American industry. What types of changes came during these years in the ways of marketing, purchasing, processing, and in the forms of business organization? Why did these changes come when they did in the way they did? Was the growth of the national market a major prerequisite for such innovation and change? If not, what then was? How did these innovations relate to the growth of the railroad network or the coming of electricity and the internal combustion engine?

In addition to secondary works on this period, the data used in seeking answers to these questions have been annual and other corporation reports, government documents, articles in periodicals, histories, and biographies concerning the 50 largest industrial companies in the country in 1909. Nearly all these companies . . . had their beginnings in the last years of the nineteenth century.

MAJOR CHANGES IN AMERICAN INDUSTRY AT THE END OF THE NINETEENTH CENTURY

Between the depression of the 1870's and the beginning of the twentieth century, American industry underwent a significant transformation. In the 1870's the major industries serviced an agrarian economy. Except for a few companies equipping the rapidly expanding railroad network, the leading industrial firms processed agricultural products and provided farmers with food and clothing. These firms tended to be small, and bought their raw materials and sold their finished goods locally. Where they manufactured for a market more than a few miles away from the factory, they bought and sold through commissioned agents who handled the business of several other similar firms.

By the beginning of the twentieth century, many more companies were making producers' goods, to be used in industry rather than on the farm or by the ultimate consumer. Most of the major industries had become dominated by a few large enterprises. These great industrial corporations no longer purchased and sold through agents, but had their own nation-wide buying and marketing organizations. Many, primarily those in the extractive industries, had come to control their own raw materials. In other words, the business economy had become industrial. Major industries were dominated by a few firms that had become great, vertically integrated, centralized enterprises.

In the terms of the economist and sociologist a significant sector of American industry had become bureaucratic, in the sense that business decisions were made within large hierarchical structures. Externally, oligopoly was prevalent, the decision-makers being as much concerned with the actions of the few other large firms in the industry as with over-all changes in markets, sources of supplies, and technological improvements.

These basic changes came only after the railroads had created a national market. The railroad network, in turn, had grown swiftly primarily because of the near desperate requirements for efficient transportation created by the movement of population westward after 1815. Except for the Atlantic seaboard between Boston and Washington, the construction of the American railroads was stimulated almost wholly by the demand for better transportation to move crops, to bring farmers supplies, and to open up new territories to commercial agriculture.

By greatly expanding the scope of the agrarian economy, the railroads quickened the growth of the older commercial centers, such as New York, Philadelphia, Cincinnati, Cleveland, and St. Louis, and helped create new cities like Chicago, Indianapolis, Atlanta, Kansas City, Dallas, and the Twin Cities. This rapid urban expansion intensified the demand for the products of the older consumer goods industries — particularly those which processed the crops of the farmer and planter into food, stimulants, and clothing.

At the same time, railroad construction developed the first large market in this country for producers' goods. Except for the making of relatively few textile machines, steamboat engines, and ordnance, the iron and nonferrous manufacturers had before 1850 concentrated on providing metals and simple tools for merchants and farmers. Even textile machinery was usually made by the cloth manufacturers themselves. However, by 1860, only a decade after beginning America's first major railroad construction boom, railroad companies had already replaced the blacksmiths as the primary market for iron products, and had become far and away the most important market for the heavy engineering industries. By then, too, the locomotive was competing with the Connecticut brass industry as a major consumer of copper. More than this, the railroads, with their huge capital outlay, their fixed operating costs, the large size of their labor and management force, and the technical complexity of their operations, pioneered in the new ways of oligopolistic competition and large-scale, professionalized, bureaucratized management.

The new nation-wide market created by the construction of the railroad network became an increasingly urban one. From 1850 on, if not before, urban areas were growing more rapidly than rural ones. In the four decades from 1840 to 1880 the proportion of urban population rose from 11 per cent to 28 per cent of the total population, or about 4 per cent a decade. In the two decades from 1880 to 1900 it grew from 28 per cent to 40 per cent or an increase of 6 per cent a decade. Was this new urban and national market, then, the primary stimulant for business innovation and change, and for the coming of big business to American industry?

CHANGES IN THE CONSUMERS' GOODS INDUSTRIES

The industries first to become dominated by great business enterprises were those making consumer goods, the majority of which were processed from products grown on the farm and sold in the urban markets. Consolidation and centralization in the consumers' goods industries were well under way by 1893. The unit that appeared was one which integrated within a single business organization the major economic processes: production or purchasing of raw materials, manufacturing, distribution, and finance.

Such vertically integrated organizations came in two quite different ways. Where the product tended to be somewhat new in kind and especially fitted for the urban market, its makers created their businesses by first building large marketing and then purchasing organizations. This technique appears to have been true of the manufacturers or distributors of fresh meat, cigarettes, high-grade flour, bananas, harvesters, sewing machines, and typewriters. Where the products were established staple items, horizontal combination tended to precede vertical integration. In the sugar, salt, leather, whiskey, glucose, starch, biscuit, kerosene, fertilizer, and rubber industries a large number of small manufacturers first combined into large business units and then created their marketing and buying organizations. For a number of reasons the makers of the newer types of products found the older outlets less satisfactory and felt more of a need for direct marketing than did the manufacturers of the long-established goods.

Integration via the Creation of Marketing Organization

The story of the changes and the possible reasons behind them can be more clearly understood by examining briefly the experience of a few innovating firms. First, consider the experience of companies that grew large through the creation of a nation-wide marketing and distributing organization. Here the story of Gustavus F. Swift and his brother Edwin is a significant one. Gustavus F. Swift, an Easterner, came relatively late to the Chicago meatpacking business. Possibly because he was from Massachusettes, he appreciated the potential market for fresh western meat in the eastern cities. For after the Civil War, Boston, New York, Philadelphia, and other cities were rapidly outrunning their local meat supply. At the same time, great herds of cattle were gathering on the western plains. Swift saw the possibilities of connecting the new market with the new source of supply by the use of the refrigerated railroad car. In 1878, shortly after his first experimental shipment of refrigerated meat, he formed a partnership with his younger brother, Edwin, to market fresh western meat in the eastern cities.

For the next decade, Swift struggled hard to carry out his plans, the essence of which was the creation, during the 1880's, of the nation-wide distributing and marketing organization built around a network of branch houses. Each "house" had its storage plant and its own marketing organization. The latter included outlets in major towns and cities, often managed by Swift's own salaried representatives. In marketing the product, Swift had to break down, through advertising and other means, the prejudices against eating meat killed more than a thousand miles away and many weeks earlier. At the same time he had to combat boycotts of local butchers and the concerted efforts of the National Butchers' Protective Association to prevent the sale of his meat in the urban markets.

To make effective use of the branch house network, the company soon began to market products other than beef. The "full line" soon came to include lamb, mutton, pork, and, some time later, poultry, eggs, and dairy products. The growing distributing organization soon demanded an increase in supply. So between 1888 and 1892, the Swifts set up meat-packing establishments in Kansas City, Omaha, and St. Louis, and, after the depression of the 1890's, three more in St. Joseph, St. Paul, and Ft. Worth. At the same time, the company systematized the buying of its cattle and other products at the stockyards. In the 1890's, too, Swift began a concerted effort to make more profitable use of by-products.

Before the end of the 1890's, then, Swift had effectively fashioned a great, vertically integrated organization. The major departments – marketing, processing, purchasing, and, accounting – were all tightly controlled from the central office in Chicago. A report of the Commissioner of Corporations published in 1905 makes clear the reason for such control:

> Differences in quality of animals and of their products are so great that the closest supervision of the Central Office is necessary to enforce the exercise of skill and sound judgement on the part of the agents who buy the stock, and the agents who sell the meat. With this object, the branches of the Selling and Accounting Department of those packing companies which have charge of the purchasing, killing, and dressing and selling of fresh meat, are organized in the most extensive and thorough manner. The Central Office is in constant telegraphic correspondence with the distributing houses, with a view to adjusting the supply of meat and the price as nearly as possible to the demand.

As this statement suggests, the other meat packers followed Swift's example. To compete effectively, Armour, Morris, Cudahy, and Schwarzschild & Sulzberger had to build up similar integrated organizations. Those that did not follow the Swift model were destined to remain small local companies. Thus by the middle of the 1890's, the meat-packing industry, with the rapid growth of these great vertically integrated firms had become oligopolistic (the "Big Five" had the major share of the market) and bureaucratic; each of the five had its many departments and several levels of management.

This story has parallels in other industries processing agricultural products. In tobacco, James B. Duke was the first to appreciate the growing market for the cigarette, a new product which was sold almost wholly in the cities. However, after he had applied machinery to the manufacture of cigarettes, production soon outran supply. Duke then concentrated on expanding the market through extensive advertising and the creation of a national and then world-wide-selling organization. In 1884, he left Durham, North Carolina, for New York City, where he set up factories, sales, and administrative offices. New York was closer to his major urban markets, and was the more logical place to manage an international advertising campaign than Durham. While he was building his marketing department, Duke was also creating the network of warehouses and buyers in the tobacco-growing areas of the country.

In 1890, he merged his company with five smaller competitors in the cigarette business to form the American Tobacco Company. By 1895 the activities of these firms had been consolidated into the manufacturing, marketing, purchasing, and finance departments of the single operating structure Duke had earlier fashioned. Duke next undertook development of a full line by handling all types of smoking and chewing tobacco. By the end of the century, his company completely dominated the tobacco business. Only two other firms, R. J. Reynolds & Company and P. Lorillard & Company had been able to build up comparable vertically integrated organizations. When they merged with American Tobacco they continued to retain their separate operating organizations. When the 1911 antitrust decree split these and other units off from the American company, the tobacco industry had become, like the meat-packing business, oligopolistic, and its dominant firms bureaucratic.

What Duke and Swift did for their industries, James S. Bell of the Washburn-Crosby Company did during these same years in the making and selling of high-grade flour to the urban bakeries and housewives, and Andrew J. Preston achieved in growing, transporting, and selling another new product for the urban market, the banana. Like Swift and Duke, both these men made their major innovations in marketing, and then went on to create large-scale, departmentalized, vertically integrated structures.

The innovators in new consumer durables followed much the same pattern. Both Cyrus McCormick, pioneer harvester manufacturer, and William Clark, the business brains of the Singer Sewing Machine Company, first sold through commissioned agents. Clark soon discovered that salaried men, working out of branch offices, could more effectively and at less cost display, demonstrate, and service sewing machines than could the agents. Just as important, the branch offices were able to provide the customer with essential credit. McCormick, while retaining the dealer to handle the final sales, came to appreciate the need for a strong selling and distributing organization, with warehouses, servicing facilities, and a large salaried force, to stand behind the dealer. So in the years following the Civil War, both McCormick and Singer Sewing Machine Company concentrated on building up national and then world-wide marketing departments. As they purchased their raw materials from a few industrial companies rather than from a mass of farmers, their purchasing departments were smaller, and required less attention than those in the firms processing farmers' products. But the net result was the creation of a very similar type of organization.

Integration via Horizontal Combination

In those industries making more standard goods, the creation of marketing organizations usually followed large-scale combinations of a number of small manufacturing firms. For these small firms, the coming of the railroad had in many cases enlarged their markets but simultaneously brought them for the first time into competition with many other companies. Most of these firms appear to have expanded production in order to take advantage of the new markets. As a result, their industries became plagued with overproduction and excess capacity; that is, continued production at full capacity threatened to drop prices below the cost of production. So in the 1880's and early 1890's, many small manufacturers in the leather, sugar, salt, distilling and other corn products, linseed and cotton oil, biscuit, petroleum, fertilizer and rubber boot and glove industries, joined in large horizontal combinations.

In most of these industries, combination was followed by consolidation and vertical integration, and the pattern was comparatively consistent. First, the new combinations concentrated their manufacturing activities in locations more advantageously situated to meet the new growing urban demands. Next they systematized and standardized their manufacturing processes. Then, except in the case of sugar and corn products (glucose and starch), the combinations began to build large distributing and smaller purchasing departments. In so doing, many dropped their initial efforts to buy out competitors or to drive them out of business by price-cutting. Instead they concentrated on the creation of a more efficient flow from the producers of their raw materials to the ultimate consumer, and of the development and maintenance of markets through brand names and advertising. Since the large majority of these combinations began as regional groupings, most industries came to have more than one great firm. Only oil, sugar, and corn products remained long dominated by a single company. By World War I, partly because of the dissolutions under the Sherman Act, these industries had also become oligopolistic, and their leading firms vertically integrated.

Specific illustrations help to make these generalizations more precise. The best-known is the story of the oil industry, but equally illustrative is the experience of the leading distilling, baking, and rubber companies. . . .

Thus United States Rubber, National Biscuit, and the Distillers Securities Company soon came to have organizational structures paralleling those of Swift and American Tobacco. By the first decade of the twentieth century, the leading firms in many consumers' goods industries had become departmentalized and centralized. This was the organizational concomitant to vertical integration. Each major function, manufacturing, sales, purchasing, and finance, became managed by a single and separate department head, usually a vice president, who, assisted by a director or a manager, had full authority and responsibility for the activities of his unit. These departmental chiefs, with the president, coordinated and evaluated the work of the different functional units, and made policy for the company as a whole. In coordinating, appraising, and policy-making, the president and the vice presidents in charge of departments came to rely more and more on the accounting and statistical information, usually provided by the finance department, on costs, output, purchases, and sales.

CHANGES IN THE PRODUCERS' GOODS INDUSTRIES

Bureaucracy and oligopoly came to the producers' goods industries somewhat later than to those making products for the mass market. Until the depression of the 1890's, most of the combinations and consolidations had been in the consumers' goods industries. After that, the major changes came in those industries selling to other businesses and industrialists. The reason for the time difference seems to be that the city took a little longer to become a major market for producers' goods. Throughout the 1880's, railroad construction and operation continued to take the larger share of the output of steel, copper, power machinery, explosives, and other heavy industries. Then in the 1890's, as railroad construction declined the rapidly growing American cities became the primary market. The insatiable demand for urban lighting, communication, heat, power, transportation, water, sewerage, and other services directly and indirectly took ever growing quantities of electric lighting apparatus, telephones, copper wire, newsprint, streetcars, coal, and iron, steel, copper, and lead piping, structures and fixtures; while the constantly expanding urban construction created new calls on the power machinery and explosives as well as the metals industries. Carnegie's decision in 1887 to shift the Homestead Works, the nation's largest and most modern steel plant, from rails to structures, symbolized the coming change in the market.

Also the new combinations and consolidations in the consumers' goods industries increased the demand for producers' products in the urban areas. Standard Oil, American Tobacco, Swift and other meat packers, McCormick's Harvesting Machinery and other farm implement firms, American Sugar, Singer Sewing Machine, and many other great consumer goods companies concentrated their production in or near major cities, particularly New York and Chicago.

The changes after 1897 differed from the earlier ones not only in types of industries in which they occurred but also in the way they were promoted and financed. Combinations and vertical integration in the consumer goods industries before 1897 had been almost all engineered and financed by the manufacturers themselves, so the stock control remained in the hands of the industrialists. After 1897, however, outside funds and often outside promoters, who were usually Wall Street financiers, played an increasingly significant role in industrial combination and consolidation. The change reflected a new attitude of investor and financier who controlled capital toward the value of industrial securities. Before the depression of the 1890's investment and speculation had been overwhelmingly in railroad stocks and bonds. The institutionalizing of the American security market in Wall Street had come, in fact, as a response to the needs for financing the first great railroad boom in the 1850's.

The railroads, however, had made a poor showing financially in the middle years of the 1890's when one-third of the nation's trackage went through receivership and financial reorganization. The dividend records of some of the new large industrial corporations, on the other hand, proved unexpectedly satisfactory. Moreover, railroad construction was slowing, and the major financial and administrative reorganizations of the 1890's had pretty well stabilized the industry. So there was less demand for investment bankers and brokers to market new issues of railroad securities.

Industrials were obviously the coming field, and by 1898 there was a rush in Wall Street to get in on this new business. The sudden availability of funds stimulated, and undoubtedly overstimulated, industrial combination. Many of the mergers in the years after 1897 came more from the desire of financiers for promotional profits, and because combination had become the thing to do, and less from the special needs and opportunities in the several industries. Moreover, as the financiers and promoters began to provide funds for mergers and expansion, they began to acquire, for the first time, the same type of control over industrial corporations that they had enjoyed in railroads since the 1850's.

The changes in the producers' goods industries were essentially like those in the consumer goods firms before the depression. Only after 1897 the changes came more rapidly, partly because of Wall Street pressures; and the differences that did develop between the two types of industries reflected the basic differences in the nature of their businesses. Like the companies making consumer goods, those manufacturing items for producers set up nation-wide and often world-wide marketing and distributing organizations, consolidated production into a relatively few large plants and fashioned purchasing departments. Because they had fewer customers, their sales departments tended to be smaller than those in firms selling to the mass market. On the other hand, they were more concerned with obtaining control over the sources of their supply than were most of the consumer goods companies.

Here a distinction can be made between the manufacturers who made semi-finished products from raw materials taken from the ground, and those who made finished goods from semi-finished products. The former, producing a uniform product for a few large industrial customers, developed only small sales departments and concentrated on obtaining control of raw materials, and often of the means of transporting such materials from mine to market. The latter, selling a larger variety of products and ones that often required servicing and financing, had much larger marketing and distributing organizations. These makers of finished goods, except for a brief period around 1900, rarely attempted to control their raw materials or their semi-finished steel and other metal supplies. They did, however, in the years after 1900, begin to buy or set up plants making parts and components that went into the construction of their finished products.

Except in steel, integration usually followed combination in the producers' goods industries. And for both makers of semi-finished and finished goods, integration became more of a defensive strategy than it was in the consumers' goods industries processing agricultural products. In the latter the manufacturers had an assured supply of raw materials from the output of the nation's millions of farms. In the former, on the other hand, they had to consider the threatening possibility of an outsider obtaining complete control of raw materials or supplies.

Integration and Combination in the Extractive Industries

By the early twentieth century nearly all the companies making semi-finished product goods controlled the mining of their own raw materials. The industries in which they operated can, therefore, be considered as extractive. This was also true of two consumers' goods industries: oil and fertilizer. The experience of these two provides a good introduction to the motives for integration and the role it played in the coming of "big business" in steel, copper, paper, explosives and other businesses producing semi-finished goods.

In both the oil and fertilizer industries, control over raw materials came well after combination and consolidation of groups of small manufacturing firms. The Standard Oil Trust, after its formation in 1882, consolidated its manufacturing activities and then created a domestic marketing organization. Only in the late 1880's, when the new Indiana field began to be developed and the older Pennsylvania ones began to decline, did the Trust consider going into the production of crude oil. Both Allan Nevins in his biography of John D. Rockefeller and the Hidys in their history of Standard Oil agree that the need to be assured of a steady supply of crude oil was the major reason for the move into production. Other reasons, the Hidys indicate, were a fear that the producers might combine and so control supplies, and the desire of the pipeline subsidiaries to keep their facilities operating at full capacity. Although neither Nevins nor the Hidys suggest that the desire to obtain a more efficient flow of oil from the well to the distributor was a motive for this integration, both describe the committees and staff units that were formed at the central office at 26 Broadway to assure more effective coordination between production, refining, and marketing. . . .

Defensive motives were certainly significant in the changes in the steel industry. Here the story can be most briefly described by focusing on the history of the industry's leader, the Carnegie Steel Company. That company's chairman, Henry C. Frick, had in the early 1890's consolidated and rationalized the several Carnegie manufacturing properties in and about Pittsburgh into an integrated whole. At the same time, he systematized and departmentalized its purchasing, engineering, and marketing activities. The fashioning of a sales department became more necessary since the shift from rails to structures had enlarged the number of the company's customers.

Then in 1896 the Carnegie company made a massive purchase of ore lands when it joined with Henry W. Oliver to buy out the Rockefeller holdings in the Mesabi Range. As Allan Nevins points out, the depression of the 1890's had worked a rapid transformation in the recently discovered Mesabi region. By 1896, the ore fields had become dominated by three great interests: the Oliver Mining Company, the Minnesota Mining Company, and Rockefeller's Consolidated Iron Mines. A fourth, James J. Hill's Great

Northern Railroad, was just entering the field. Frick's purchases, therefore, gave the Carnegie company an assured supply of cheap ore, as well as providing it with a fleet of ore ships. Next, Frick and Carnegie bought and rebuilt a railroad from Lake Erie to Pittsburgh to carry the new supplies to the mills.

Yet the steel company's managers did little to coordinate systematically the mining, shipping, and manufacturing units in their industrial empire. These activities did not become departments controlled from one central office but remained completely separate companies under independent managements, whose contact with one another was through negotiated contracts. This was the same sort of relation that existed between the Frick Coke Company and Carnegie Steel from the time Frick had joined Carnegie in 1889. If the Carnegie company's strategy had been to provide a more effective flow of materials as well as to assure itself of not being caught without a supply of ore and the means to transport it, then Frick and Carnegie would have created some sort of central coordinating office.

The steel industry responded quickly to the Carnegie purchases. In 1898, Chicago's Illinois Steel Company, with capital supplied by J. P. Morgan & Company, joined the Lorain Steel Company (with plants on Lake Erie and in Johnstown, Pennsylvania) to purchase the Minnesota Mining Company, a fleet of ore boats, and railroads in the Mesabi and Chicago areas. Again, little attempt was made to coordinate mining and shipping with manufacturing and marketing. In the same year, many iron and steel firms in Ohio and Pennsylvania merged to form the Republic and National Steel Companies. Shortly thereafter, a similar combination in the Sault Sainte Marie area became the Consolidated Lake Superior Company. These three new mergers began at once to set up their marketing organizations and to obtain control by lease and purchase of raw materials and transportation facilities. In 1900, several small firms making high-grade steel did much the same thing by the formation of the Crucible Steel Company of America. In these same years, the larger, established steel companies, like Lackawanna, Cambria, and Jones & Laughlin obtained control of more supplies of ore, coke, and limestone and simultaneously reorganized their manufacturing and marketing organizations. Like Carnegie and Federal, they at first made little effort to bring their mining and coke operations under the direct control of the central office. . . .

Changes and Integration in the Finished Producers' Goods Industries

Control of price and production was, on the other hand, much more of an obvious motive for combination and resulting consolidation in the industries manufacturing finished products or machinery from the semi-finished materials produced by the extractive firms. Concern over supply, however, was also a cause for change, for after 1898 the users of steel, copper, coal, and other semi-finished materials felt threatened by the growing number of combinations among their suppliers. In any case, between 1898 and 1900 there was a wave of mergers in these industries, largely Wall Street financed, which led to the formation of American Tin Plate, American Wire & Steel, American Steel Hoop, National Tube, American Bridge, American Sheet Metal, Shelby Steel Tube, American Can, National Enameling & Stamping Company and a number of other combinations among steel-fabricating firms. At the same time, there were many amalgamations in the power machinery and implement businesses, such as American Car & Foundry, American Locomotive, Allis-Chalmers, International Steam Pump, and International Harvester. The largest combination among the copper users, the American Brass Company, came a little later, in 1903, after the Guggenheims, Rogers, and Heinze had completed the major copper mergers.

Nearly all these combinations quickly consolidated their constituent companies into a single operating organization. Manufacturing facilities were unified and systematized, over-all accounting procedures instituted, and national and often world-wide distributing organizations formed. Many set up central traffic and purchasing departments; some even began to assure themselves control over supply by building up their own rolling mills and blast furnaces. As American Wire & Steel and National Tube began to make their own steel, they cancelled contracts with Carnegie and other semi-finished steel producers. This development, in turn, led Carnegie to develop plans for fabricating his own finished products.

The resulting threat of overcapacity and price-cutting led to the formation of the United States Steel Corporation. This giant merger, which included Carnegie, Federal and National Steel, and the first six of the fabricating companies listed above, continued on as a combination. Although the activities of the various subsidiaries were re-formed and redefined, there was no consolidation. United States Steel remained a holding company only, and the central office at 72 Broadway did comparatively little to coordinate the operations of its many subsidiary companies.

After 1901, the fabricators and the machinery manufacturers made little attempt to produce their own steel or copper. Nor did the makers of semi-finished products try, for some years to come, to do their own fabricating. Possibly the metal users realized that even with the formation of United States Steel they were fairly certain of alternative sources of supply. Also they may have found that once they had combined they had enough bargaining power to assure themselves of a supply of steel and other materials more cheaply than they could make it themselves.

While such firms no longer sought to control their basic materials, many, particularly the machinery makers like General Electric, Westinghouse, American Car & Foundry, International Harvester and, a little later, General Motors, began to purchase or set up subsidiaries or departments to make parts and components. Here again the motive was essentially defensive. Since much of their manufacturing had now become mainly assembling, they wanted to be sure to have a supply of parts available at all times. The lack of a vital part could temporarily shut down a plant. However, they expected to take only a portion of the output; a major share was sold to outsiders. One outstanding exception to this pattern was Henry Ford. He came to control his raw materials as well as his parts and components, and rarely sold such parts to outside companies. But Ford's insistence on having a completely integrated organization from mine to market, concentrated largely in one huge plant, proved to be one of the most costly mistakes in American business history.

Control of parts and accessory units led to a diversification of the types of products these manufacturing companies made and sold. Such diversification brought, over time, important changes in business organization. Even more significant for stimulating product diversification was the new "full line" strategy adopted by a number of these recently consolidated concerns. Such a policy, initiated largely to help assure the maximum use of the new departments, encouraged technological as well as organizational change.

Pioneers in developing "full lines" in the producers' goods industries were the two great electrical companies: General Electric and Westinghouse. Unlike almost any other of the leading American industrial companies in 1900, these two had begun as research and development rather than manufacturing organizations. Because of their origins, they had the skilled personnel and the necessary equipment to move, in the mid-1890's, from making lighting equipment alone to manufacturing many lines of electric traction and power machinery products. Allis-Chalmers, International Steam Pump, and American Locomotive began, shortly after their formation and subsequent consolidations, to develop new lines using electric and gasoline engines. International Harvester, building up a number of farm implement lines, also started to experiment with the use of the gasoline engine for machinery on the farm. In this same first decade of the twentieth century, rubber, explosive, and chemical companies began to turn to industrial chemistry in their search to develop broader lines of products.

Continuing diversification came, however, largely in industries where science, particularly chemistry and physics, could be most easily applied. And it was in these industries, and in those which were directly affected by the coming of two new sources of power, electricity and the internal combustion engine, that the major innovations in American industry came after 1900. The chemical, automotive, power machinery, rubber, and petroleum industries led the way to the development of new processes and products, new ways of internal organization and new techniques of external competition as the new century unfolded. The metals industries and those processing agricultural goods have, on the other hand, changed relatively little since the beginning of the century. In these industries, the same firms make much the same products, use much the same processes, and compete in much the same manner in the 1950's as they did in the 1900's. For them the greatest period of change came in the last decade of the nineteenth century.

CONCLUSION: THE BASIC INNOVATIONS

The middle of the first decade of the new century might be said to mark the end of an era. By 1903, the great merger movement was almost over, and by then the metals industries and those processing agricultural products had developed patterns of internal organization and external competition which were to remain. In those years, too, leading chemical, electrical, rubber, power machinery and implement companies had initiated their "full line" policy, and had instituted the earliest formal research and development departments created in this country. In this decade also, electricity was becoming for the first time a significant source of industrial power, and the automobile was just beginning to revolutionize American transportation. From 1903 on, the new generators of power and the new technologies appear to have become the dominant stimuli to innovation in American industry, and such innovations were primarily those which created new products and processes. Changes in organizational methods and marketing techniques were largely responses to technological advances.

This seems much less true of the changes during the 20 to 25 years before 1903. In that period, the basic innovations were more in the creation of new forms of organization and new ways of marketing. The great modern corporation, carrying on the major industrial processes, namely, purchasing, and often production of materials and parts, manufacturing, marketing, and finance — all within the same organizational structure — had its beginnings in that period. Such organizations hardly existed, outside of the railroads, before the 1880's. By 1900 they had become the basic business unit in American industry.

Each of these major processes became managed by a corporate department, and all were coordinated and supervised from a central office. Of the departments, marketing was the most significant. The creation of nation-wide distributing and selling organizations was the initial step in the growth of many large consumer goods companies. Mergers in both the consumer and producer goods industries were almost always followed by the formation of a centralized sales department.

The consolidation of plants under a single manufacturing department usually accompanied or followed the formation of a national marketing organization. The creation of such a manufacturing department normally meant the concentration of production in fewer and larger plants, and such consolidation probably lowered unit costs and increased output per worker. The creation of such a department in turn led to the setting up of central traffic, purchasing, and often engineering organizations. Large-scale buying, more rational routing of raw materials and finished products, more systematic plant lay-out, and plant location in relation to materials and markets probably lowered costs still further. Certainly the creators of these organizations believed that it did. In the extractive and machinery industries integration went one step further. Here the motives for controlling raw materials or parts and components were defensive as well as designed to cut costs through providing a more efficient flow of materials from mine to market.

These great national industrial organizations required a large market to provide the volume necessary to support the increased overhead costs. Also, to be profitable, they needed careful coordination between the different functional departments. This coordination required a steady flow of accurate data on costs, sales, and on all purchasing, manufacturing, and marketing activities. As a result, the comptroller's office became an increasingly important department. In fact, one of the first moves after a combination by merger or purchase was to institute more effective and detailed accounting procedures. Also, the leading entrepreneurs of the period, men like Rockefeller, Carnegie, Swift, Duke, Preston, Clark, and the DuPonts, had to become, as had the railroad executives of an earlier generation, experts in reading and interpreting business statistics.

Consolidation and departmentalization meant that the leading industrial corporations became operating rather than holding companies, in the sense that the officers and managers of the companies were directly concerned with operating activities. In fact, of the 50 companies with the largest assets in 1909, only United States Steel, Amalgamated Copper, and one or two other copper companies remained purely holding companies. In most others, the central office included the heads of the major functional departments, usually the president, vice presidents, and sometimes a chairman of the board and one or two representatives of financial interests. These men made major policy and administrative decisions and evaluated the performance of the departments and the corporation as a whole. In the extractive industries a few companies, like Standard Oil (N.J.) and some of the metals companies, were partly holding and partly operating companies. At Standard Oil nearly all important decisions were made in the central headquarters, at 26 Broadway, which housed not only the presidents of the subsidiaries but the powerful policy formulating and coordinating committees. But in some of the metals companies, the subsidiaries producing and transporting raw materials retained a large degree of autonomy.

The coming of the large vertically integrated, centralized, functionally departmentalized industrial organization altered the internal and external situations in which and about which business decisions were made. Information about markets, supplies, and operating performance as well as suggestions for action often had to come up through the several levels of the departmental hierarchies, while decisions and suggestions based on this data had to be transmitted down the same ladder for implementation. Executives on each level became increasingly specialists in one function — in sales, production, purchasing, or finance — and most remained in one department and so handled one function only for the major part of their business careers. Only he who climbed to the very top of the departmental ladder had a chance to see his own company as a single operating unit. Where a company's markets, sources of raw materials, and manufacturing processes remained relatively stable, as was true in the metals industries and in those processing agricultural goods, the nature of the business executive's work became increasingly routine and administrative.

When the internal situation had become bureaucratic, the external one tended to be oligopolistic. Vertical integration by one manufacturer forced others to follow. Thus, in a very short time, many American industries became dominated by a few large firms, with the smaller ones handling local and more specialized aspects of the business. Occasionally industries like oil, tobacco, and sugar, came to be controlled by one company, but in most cases legal action by the federal government in the years after 1900 turned monopolistic industries into oligopolistic ones.

Costs, rather than interfirm competition, began to determine prices. With better information on costs, supplies, and market conditions, the companies were able to determine price quite accurately on the basis of the desired return on investment. The managers of the different major companies had little to gain by cutting prices below an acceptable profit margin. On the other hand, if one firm set its prices excessively high, the other firms could increase their share of the market by selling at a lower price and still maintain a profit. They would, however, rarely cut to the point where this margin was eliminated. As a result, after 1900, price leadership, price umbrellas, and other evidences of oligopolistic competition became common in many American industries. To increase their share of the market and to improve their profit position, the large corporations therefore concerned themselves less with price and concentrated more on obtaining new customers by advertising, brand names, and product differentiations; on cutting costs through further improvement and integration of the manufacturing, marketing, and buying processes; and on developing more diversified lines of products.

The coming of the large vertically integrated corporation changed more than just the practices of American industrialists and their industries. The effect on the merchant, particularly the wholesaler, and on the financier, especially the investment banker, has been suggested here. The relation between the growth of these great industrial units and the rise of labor unions has often been pointed out. Certainly the regulation of the large corporation became one of the major political issues of these years, and the devices created to carry out such a regulation were significant innovations in American constitutional, legal, and political institutions. But an examination of such effects is beyond the scope of this paper.

Reasons for the Basic Innovations

One question remains to be reviewed. Why did the vertically integrated corporation come when it did, and in the way it did? The creation by nearly all the large firms of nation-wide selling and distributing organizations indicates the importance of the national market. It was necessary that the market be an increasingly urban one. The city took the largest share of the goods manufactured by the processors of agricultural products. The city, too, with its demands for construction materials, lighting, heating and many other facilities, provided the major market for the metals and other producers' goods industries after railroad construction slowed. Without the rapidly growing urban market there would have been little need and little opportunity for the coming of big business in American industry. And such a market could hardly have existed before the completion of a nation-wide railroad network.

What other reasons might there have been for the swift growth of the great industrial corporation? What about foreign markets? In some industries, particularly oil, the overseas trade may have been an important factor. However, in most businesses the domestic customers took the lion's share of the output, and in nearly all of them the move abroad appears to have come after the creation of the large corporation, and after such corporations had fashioned their domestic marketing organization.

What about the investor looking for profitable investments, and the promoter seeking new promotions? Financiers and promoters certainly had an impact on the changes after 1897, but again they seem primarily to have taken advantage of what had already proved successful. The industrialists themselves, rather than the financiers, initiated most of the major changes in business organization. Availability of capital and cooperation with the financier figured much less prominently in these industrial combinations and consolidations than had been the case with the earlier construction of the railroads and with the financing of the Civil War.

What about technological changes? Actually, except for electricity, the major innovations in the metals industries seem to have come before or after the years under study here. Most of the technological improvements in the agricultural processing industries appear to have been made to meet the demands of the new urban market. The great technological innovations that accompanied the development of electricity, the internal combustion engine, and industrial chemistry did have their beginning in these years, and were, indeed, to have a fundamental impact on the American business economy. Yet this impact was not to be really felt until after 1900.

What about entrepreneurial talent? Certainly the best-known entrepreneurs of this period were those who helped to create the large industrial corporation. If, as Joseph A. Schumpeter suggests, "The defining characteristic [of the entrepreneur and his function] is simply the doing of new things, and doing things that are already done, in a new way (innovation)," Rockefeller, Carnegie, Frick, Swift, Duke, McCormick, the DuPonts, the Guggenheims, Coffin of General Electric, Preston of United Fruit, and Clark of Singer Sewing Machine were all major innovators of their time. And their innovations were not in technology, but rather in organization and in marketing. "Doing a new thing," is, to Schumpeter a "creative response" to a new situation, and the situation to which these innovators responded appears to have been the rise of the national urban market.

There must be an emphasis here on the words "seem" and "appear." The framework used is a preliminary one and the data itself, based on readily available printed material rather than on business records are hardly as detailed or accurate as could be desired. More data, more precise and explicit questions, and other types and ranges of questions will modify the generalizations suggested here. For the moment, however, I would like to suggest, if only to encourage the raising of questions and the further compilation and analysis of data, that *the* major innovation in the American economy between the 1880's and the turn of the century was the creation of the great corporations in American industry. This innovation, as I have tried to show, was a response to the growth of a national and increasingly urban market that was created by the building of a national railroad network — the dynamic force in the economy in the quarter century before 1880. After 1900 the newly modified methods of interfirm and intrafirm administration remained relatively unchanged (as did the location of major markets and sources of raw materials) except in those industries directly affected by new sources of power and the systematic application of science to industry. In the twentieth century electricity, the internal combustion engine, and systematic, institutionalized research and development took the place of the national urban market as the dynamic factor in the American industrial economy.

Edward C. Kirkland

IN ORDER to dispel at once any mystery inherent in the title, this essay is primarily about the business generation of the "robber barons." I propose to explore not so much what the businessman of that era thought as the scheme of thought with which he chose to approach the problems of his day. Since this is the Mississippi Valley Historical Association, I shall at least be gracious enough to start my remarks in the West. Charles Elliott Perkins, president of the Chicago, Burlington and Quincy Railroad, provides my text. In 1885 he wrote in one of his frequent memoranda (for this was the manner in which he liked to express himself): "The question of political economy is not, What is noble? What is good? What is generous? What are the teachings of the Gospel? — But what, if anything, is it expedient for society, for government, to do about the production, distribution, and consumption of property, of wealth?" It is true, he continued, that "heroic example and noble obligation" are essential for a nation. "But these are individual, not governmental qualities. There is nothing noble, or generous, or heroic, or christian in a rich man's involuntary submission to taxation for the benefit of those who are less rich, if society shall deem it expedient to tax him for that object. . . . This is what some of the more recent writers call the old political economy, the economic law of Adam Smith, which they denounce as too cold and heartless for a Christian People."

The utterance was exceptional in its precision and force, but its ideas were commonplace among businessmen of that generation. Not only did they exalt the individual in the economic sphere, but they attempted to divide the individual into functions or compart-

"Divide and Ruin," *Mississippi Valley Historical Review,* XLIII (June, 1956), 3–17. Reprinted by permission of the Organization of American Historians.

EDWARD C. KIRKLAND (1894–) is Emeritus Professor of History at Bowdoin College. He is the author of several classic works in late nineteenth century American economic history, including *Men, Cities and Transportation* and *Industry Comes of Age.* This article was presented as the presidential address at the annual meeting of the Mississippi Valley Historical Association in 1956.

ments, which should as a matter of right and expediency have no relation to each other. In short, economic activity stood apart from the spheres of moral and personal considerations.

Businessmen demonstrated the application of this formula in labor policy. To the assertion of reformers and labor spokesmen that labor was entitled to a "living" wage, one which entitled the laborer to a "decent" or "respectable living," Perkins replied: "To say that a man is entitled to wages sufficient to maintain his family respectably is meaningless. What is the measure? Who is to decide what is enough to keep a man and his family respectable? Shall the labourer fix his own compensation and *somebody* be found to employ him? You may say society is morally bound to see that no honest man who is willing to work shall starve, and it may be admitted that it is better to give such men work than to give money without work. But that is public charity in either case, because if you do work which is not needed for the sake of giving employment, that is not *business*. It is easy to say that a man ought to be 'decently' paid, or 'well paid,' or 'reasonably' paid. But what is decent, or good, or reasonable pay? Is it what a man wants? Suppose two men apply for work. One says, 'I am careful, frugal, have an economical wife, can get along respectably on a dollar and a half a day, and am ready to go to work at that.' The other says, 'I am more frugal than number one. I can get along respectably on a dollar a day and am ready to go to work at that.' Both being equally capable of doing the job, which shall be taken?" The answer, according to the principles of political economy here defined, is obvious.

This response of the business community to the interrelation of wages and human considerations was automatically extended to cognate matters of labor welfare — pensions, relief societies, payments for injuries. The objections to these devices were numerous. They relieved the men of the care and responsibility for themselves, and care and responsibility were developmental. "The fact that some men are unfortunate does not change the rule. If a man put his hand over the fire, by accident or misfortune, he is burnt just as much as if he put it there intentionally." The one way to deal with these matters was to deal with them through the economic relation, the way of wages. Make the latter large enough so that men who chose to do so could take care of themselves, including emergencies. "No man can decide for another what he shall give away from motives of sympathy," wrote Perkins. "Stockholders employ agents to conduct their business affairs. If such gratuities (payment for injuries) are given, it must be for business policy or business expediency and not charity." Perkins denied that this attitude regarded men as commodities. "Of course men are not commodities . . . but their labor, when offered for sale, is just as much a commodity as the thing it produces, and all sympathy which leads people to think otherwise is doing more harm than good, like unwise charity." The capitalist not only divided himself, he divided the laborer as well.

Lest these be regarded as the self-interested rationalizations of employers, perhaps we should resort to academic economists to learn what they, in their detachment, thought on the matter. Arthur Lapham Perry of Williams College, author of one of the most widely used early texts in economic theory and a devout Christian as well, wrote of the wage contract: "When A hires B to work in his factory, this new relation is economical, not moral. . . . What is the economical relation? This. A desires the personal service of B in his factory purely for his pecuniary benefit, and assumes his own ability to make all the calculations requisite for determining how much he can (profitably to himself) offer B for his service; and B, who knows all about his own skill . . . wants to sell his service to A for the sake of the pecuniary return or wages. There is no obligation resting upon either. Man to man, each in his own right. There is no benevolence in the heart of either, so far as this matter goes. Benevolence is now an impertinence. It is a question of honest gain in broad daylight. Benevolence is blessed in its own sphere, but there is no call for it here and now. . . . The less either (A or B) thinks and talks and acts about the other in all the other relations of life, the better hope of good success to both in this relation. Church relations and social relations and political relations are all of consequence in themselves; but when any of these begin to get mixed up with labor-relations, there is soon a muss and a mess."

In the circumstances, it was natural that the businessman should have a dubious approach to the agencies, political and religious, which were trying to introduce into business affairs values and considerations which the businessmen thought had nothing to do with business. The laws of trade, sometimes vulgarized as "business principles," governed and should govern production, distribution, and consumption; statute laws, passed by legislatures and Congress, could have no bearing and no influence in this area. If they did, they acted only to distort and delay matters. The great tide of natural law would sooner or later break through and assert itself. Consequently businessmen, as a matter of principle, sought to stand outside the political process. Early in the 1880's, Henry Varnum Poor, the railroad expert and organizer of manuals, reached the heart of the matter: "Railroad Men form no political party. They are of all shades of parties. There is no possibility that they should be combined for any political object. They reject instead of craving political influence. They are as free from sinister political bias as our farmers, merchants, or manufacturers."

A few years later, when Lyman J. Gage, president of the First National Bank of Chicago and one of the most perceptive businessmen of that city, addressed the American Bankers' Association, he admitted that the general attitude of his hearers was that they should have no concern with politics or government and that the businessman thought of himself as "a business man, pure and simple." Certainly the historians who picture the businessman of this period in politics up to his last dollar would deny the justice of either adjective. But an illustration of the possible validity of the businessman's attitude was provided by Charles Francis Adams, Jr. As railroad commissioner of Massachusetts through the 1870's he was the advocate of general rather than special legislation for the railroads: general legislation would take railroad officials and the railroad lobby out of the legislature. In the 1880's, as president of the Union Pacific, his consuming objective was the passage by Congress "of such laws as will once and for all separate the government from the management of this or any other railroad corporation." And in the same strain, Edwin L. Godkin of the *Nation* argued for free trade to protect Congress against the lobby of manufacturers. "The way to arm them against temptation is to leave them as little as possible to sell of the things which capitalists are eager to buy."

Godkin was getting at the separation of business and politics through the back door. While individuals like Gage were urging participation by businessmen in the political process to do away with the "demagogue" and the "political trickster," the *Nation* was arguing that businessmen abjure membership in legislatures because, too "practical minded," they could not look at public issues comprehensively and they did not understand the interests of others. "Practical men will not make good laws; it demands theories." Whatever the favored approach to the matter of division, a New England banker, Henry Lee Higginson, expressed the business wish most pithily: "Let us ask Congress to do their work in their own way and let us [businessmen] do ours in our way."

The businessman on the whole was also sure that religion and business should be separated. Partly this was a result of a historic estrangement. Edward Atkinson, Boston cotton capitalist and a Unitarian – and perhaps not, therefore, a religious person – informed his readers: "For nearly fifty years I have been engaged in the practical work of this life, occupied in the functions of life which the priest in almost all churches and under all the various phases of religion has been apt to disparage and to hold in slight repute." Whether or not the antagonism between clergyman and businessman was historically inescapable, the growth of the social gospel after the Civil War and the liveliness of "ethical economists," the allies of its pastors, were sure to stimulate a reaction in the business community. The outlook of this new group was of course the exact opposite of that of the business community; it sought to introduce morals and values into economic operations, "to apply Christianity," as the phrase of one of its leaders, Washington Gladden, put it, to substitute for the word individual the concept social, as in "social justice," "social Christianity," "social gospel."

One answer of the business spokesmen was that such an objective was not the business of Christianity. The business of religion was the "old theological gospel," not the "gospel of social endeavor," the saving of souls and instruction in morals, not the "industrial millennium." On matters traditionally religious, clerics were scientific experts. "When Dr. Lyman Beecher took the charge of a group of 'anxious inquirers' out of the hands of Judge Gould at Litchfield, he did so as a professional man, just as a physician would have taken a case of typhoid out of the hands of an apothecary, and the church saw clearly the overwhelming necessity of the judge's deposition." But in matters of business and political economy, clergymen were not experts but amateurs. Andrew Carnegie announced: "Ecclesiastics . . . their attention being chiefly fixed upon the other world . . . seldom shine as advisers upon affairs pertaining to this." Generally he refused to include among his philanthropies gifts to churches. He made one exemption – church organs. The reason for this exceptional generosity – he gave 8,000 – he explained, "You can't always trust what the pulpit says but you can always depend upon what the organ says." Carnegie's anticlericalism and rationalism were well known. But on this point John D. Rockefeller, who generally suffered Baptist clergymen gladly, agreed: "I have sometimes been tempted to say that our clergymen could gain by knowing the essentials of business life better. . . . People who have had much to do with ministers and those who hold confidential positions in our churches have at times had surprising experiences in meeting what is sometimes practised in the way of ecclesiastical business, because these good men have had so little of business training in the work-a-day world."

So much for the true theory of the relationship between economics and religion. Departure from this theory of separation was bound to be damaging in practical affairs. A few surmises to the effect that the agitation of preachers and their lay readers, the "ethical economists," might in some way have been responsible for the Haymarket bomb outrage stiffened into certainty in the next decade. Both groups were blamed in a general way for the discontent of the 1890's and were held directly responsible for the Pullman outbursts. As Godkin wrote Charles Eliot Norton, "The labor craze fanned and promoted by 'ethical' professors and clergymen ended in the Chicago riots." Beyond the evil of particular circumstances, the social gospel weakened the qualities of character which the business world so highly esteemed. In a discussion of the morals of the future, Godkin grieved that public admiration was no longer given to "the just, austere, proud, and truthful man," but to the man of "brotherly kindness." Humanity had become more important than honesty. Whether because clerical criticism of business practices embraced a wider area or because its persistence was getting under the businessman's skin, the resentment of the latter seemed to increase as time went by. In the end Charles Elliott Perkins was reminding Henry Lee Higginson, "Without such mitigation by business of his [the workingman's] circumstances, no other kind of assistance is of the slightest use to a man — one who is hungry and cold can think of nothing else — no gospel touches him." Whatever the soundness of this observation in a historical sense, it would seem to cast some doubt on the business theory that religion and business could occupy separate spheres. Anyway, religion apparently should not bite the hand that fed it.

Just why so many members of the business community thought it feasible to isolate their various interests one from another is a problem. So pervasive an influence has been assigned in this era to phrenology that I am tempted to find here another reflection of its importance. "The mind," wrote Orson Fowler, one of the high priests of the phrenological movement, "is a plurality of innate and independent faculties — a congregate of distinct and separate powers." But probably any parallelism between the ideas of the business community and phrenology is whimsey. Somewhat more plausible is the idea that the businessman divided his interest into separate compartments because this was the correct way of logically arriving at sound conclusions. Perkins was fond of resorting to John Locke's dictum: "The greatest part of true knowledge lies in the distinct perception of things in themselves distinct." Rigorously applied, this aphorism should have restrained the habit of arguing by analogy so prevalent with Perkins and other businessmen. In their hands the statement really had another purpose. It was a method for reducing problems to their essentials, for stripping away irrelevancies. Since that business generation was confronted with the complex problems attendant upon rapid change, they had to use every device of exacting analysis to find the answers. "There is a great difference," wrote Perkins, "in attitudes and rules of conduct for an individual employer of small numbers of men and a corporation employing 10–20 thousand." The "distinct perception of things in themselves distinct" was one way of discovering the differences in these attitudes and rules.

Be that as it may, the decision to operate under the aegis of a "distinct perception of things in themselves distinct" was impossible. Chauncey M. Depew in an address before the New York State Chamber of Commerce found it was not easy for rich men to be philanthropists when they had acquired wealth under conditions which "dry up generous impulses and make the possessor hard, cold, and unsympathetic." Charles Elliott Perkins found in practice that the businessman was indivisible. Fighting his employees who had struck for higher wages in 1888, Perkins elected to stand on the high ground of principle. Faced with a delegation of workers, he wrote on a slip of paper which he passed to an associate, "As an officer, I can't sympathize with the men, but as an individual, I do sympathize with them."

Few incidents were more instructive of the impossibility of the program of a "distinct perception of things in themselves distinct" than the experience of Charles Francis Adams, Jr., when he was president of the Union Pacific. Here was a man of principle and honesty, a civil service reformer, and one who believed that it was advantageous for railroads and the state to have little to do with each other. Yet since the government had originally given the Union Pacific a land grant and financial assistance, and since representatives from the western states, especially Iowa, frequently voiced the anti-railroad feeling of their constituencies in Congress, Adams had to maintain a *de facto* office of the railroad in Washington, although "it will not do to have it suggested that we have a lobby on the spot." Nonetheless Adams and the Union Pacific's counsel, Moorfield Storey, were always going to the capital and in emergencies Adams sent General Grenville M. Dodge thither "to fix things up."

This concentrated mobilization did not work. As Adams wrote: "This gang of operators in Washington are certainly a most ingenious set of fellows. They every now and then put in a bit of work which I cannot but look upon with admiration. It is very much to me as if I were obliged to watch a set of burglars who were breaking into my vault, and unable to prevent their operations, yet from time to time deeply impressed with the skill with which the rascals went to work." Though he professed an inability to do anything about these raids, Adams was later offering to do favors in behalf of certain bills desired by the Iowa congressmen if they would vote for his, authorizing "employments to aid in procuring the passage" of legislation, and finally he was writing Dodge in Washington in a personal letter: "I wish you would see if you can do anything to expedite the matter. If you cannot do it in one way, do it in another. Anyhow let it be done. I know you are quite equal to the occasion. Simply advise me what has been done, I will remit to you." Whatever these confidences add up to, they at least reveal the pathetic, and in this case somewhat ludicrous, fate of a man bent on separating business and government. He was caught in the toils. In a later letter Adams attempted an explanation. He confided to Dodge, "Of course we do not wish to meddle in politics except in self-defence."

The policy with which the businessmen chose to approach their own problems and the problems of their day was not only impossible; it was ruinous on every score. In the field of labor relations there was bound to be an increasing degree of impersonalization as the scale of business and the size of labor forces was enlarged. The deliberate attempt to add a designed indifference and apartness to this inherent tendency simply made matters worse. Even if the relationship between employer and employee were economic and not one of benevolence, this did not mean that the employees liked it that way. Though they complained about wages and hours, a recurrent lament of the workers was that employers thought of men not as individuals but as part of the machines, that employees were known by number, not by name, and came into contact only with superintendents. The old friendly feelings were gone and society was crystallizing into classes. "Labor unions," said one of their partisans proudly, suggest remedies implying "something more than 'business principles'; they imply the subordination of what are regarded as 'business principles' to morality." In the final analysis the history of labor organization and of labor-management strife in the late decades of the nineteenth century revealed the folly of the business attitude.

The history of national legislation in the same period does not point to so sharp a failure. In spite of the common interpretation that the legislation after the Civil War was business orientated, actually business strategy in this area was directed to retaining advantages which it had won accidentally — say the tariff and the national banks during the Civil War — and to securing the veto or repeal of legislation it did not desire, such as the issue of legal tenders or the repeal of the Sherman Silver Purchase Act. A systematic reading of a business-minded journal, like the *Commercial and Financial Chronicle,* gives the impression of one long shriek on the political retreat. Commenting upon the congressional year 1874, the *Chronicle* sighed: "The season has not been a favorable one for financial wisdom, and any proposed law which does not carry with it the certainty of positive injury is regarded to a certain extent as a safety valve, by standing in the place of some other provision which would be still less propitious." For business *vis-a-vis* public legislation, these years were one long holding operation. The exhortations of Lyman Gage, toward the end of the period, advising the businessmen to organize as citizens and shopkeepers, not into "a political machine – that would be as unwise as it would be impossible, but if I could, I would make it an avenue through which should be poured in many streams over all the people the healthful influences of a better knowledge of the true laws of our politico-social-economic life," confessed the disadvantage of separating business from government.

Whether the ability of businessmen to take the church or leave it alone was equally ruinous for them, many would say was impossible to tell. It is not given to historians to see beyond the grave, nor has any arrangement yet devised bestowed infallibility in location theory upon Protestant clergymen, particularly the social gospel variety. Be that as it may, many men of the cloth were quite certain that here the theory of divide led, as it did elsewhere, to ruin. When J. P. Morgan died in 1913, an Episcopalian divine in Philadelphia preached a sermon, "Has J. P. Morgan gone to heaven? If not, why not?" and found that he had not, partly because he was neither Christian nor democrat; and somewhat more modestly the *United Mine Workers Journal* suggested an investigating committee to determine the dead financier's whereabouts. When John D. Rockefeller died in 1937, it was the labor press and spokesmen, rather than the pastors, who speculated whether the oil king had gone to heaven or hell and seemed to lean toward the latter destination. In view of the dearth of answers on the other side of this eternal question "Whither Bound?" here as elsewhere to divide was to ruin.

My exposition of the disadvantage of dividing his personality and his character, as the businessman sought to do, is in a sense a parable. In my estimation that experience carries a lesson for historians as historians. In the narrower field of writing about business and businessmen, it seems to me to be ruinous to accept the businessman's habit of division and to apply it to him. This is the defect, to my way of thinking, in much business history writing. While it is only redressing the balance to focus such narratives upon the entrepreneurial decision, written in terms of business documents, such procedure, without attention to the social and political context, ruins the picture. To segregate the criticism of a big business in separate, topical chapters near the end of a volume is a somewhat less obvious road to ruin. Such distortions are not necessarily committed only by the supporters of business enterprise as it was. The foes of business who focus upon only one aspect of what they criticize, who select opinions without attention to the whole life of the businessman and his achievements, can easily make a monster or caricature out of Stephen J. Field and William Graham Sumner, apologists for business freedom.

Nor need the caution "divide and ruin" be applied only to historians who write about business. It has relevance, I believe, to all practicing historians in the field of American history. I say practicing historians, for it is to this common man in the history field and to his difficulties that I wish to address my peroration. As long as I can remember, as an individual historian I have been exhorted and often scolded by presidents of historical associations, by the authors of numbered bulletins financed by foundations, and by sages emerging from the self-contemplation and intercommunion of committees and institutes, to do something: for example, either to embrace the contributions of other social sciences, to realize I cannot be objective because I have a frame of reference, or perhaps to acknowledge that I am studying or teaching something that does not exist, for there is no such thing as history or historical fact. Without wishing either to disparage or to deride these contributions — for I believe all intellectual activity to be commendable — I take consolation for my philistine attitude from the fact that few historians in their day-to-day work apparently pay much attention to these formulations, theses, and ultimatums; that is to say, I rarely hear these matters discussed informally among historians and even more rarely discover books written in accord with these wholesome prescriptions. Perhaps the reason is a failure of "communication," to borrow a word from the inventory of verbiage which this thought has accumulated.

While waiting upon the results of a study — an all-expense tour financed by one of our foundations that likes to grant its money to projects working along the frontiers of knowledge — I would like to hazard a guess as to why this body of preachment has had, comparatively, so little influence upon historians. One reason is because some of the assertions clearly are not true. For instance, the average historian, like other human beings, knows things happen to him and have happened to him. Equipped with this common experience, he quite rightly regards debates as to whether there is such a thing as history or a historical fact as simply for the stratosphere and the metaphysician. He proceeds on the sound assumption that he is studying and teaching something. The other reason for the negligible influence of thinking about history and of talk about historiography is that it has little bearing upon what the average practicing historian thinks is his job or duty. Throughout his apprenticeship and afterwards, he is engaged in trying, with the materials he has at hand, to become an honest observer and a trained diagnostician of what has taken place. This is an absorbing and exacting mission. I know that in the case of an American historian, the task does not generally involve the mastery of those recondite skills — epigraphy, and paleography, and the like — which our brethren in European history have to have at their finger tips, and perhaps can be accomplished without the knowledge of any other language than English. Furthermore the problems of long-time spans, with which President Lynn Thorndike dealt in his witty and erudite address before the American Historical Association last December, are not so frequently ours.

No matter how often we have been patronized because we deal with matters which are not unknown or mysterious or remote enough to be quite civilized or cultured, I believe we have a greater problem in becoming skilled and honest observers than our colleagues in European history. However partisan they may later become, they can at least approach ancient Tuscany or the medieval fair with relative detachment. If we are to secure a comparably serene view of our subject matter, we have to wrench ourselves out of our cultural environment and heritage and cut the political, economic, and social threads tying us to what we are talking about. Such a task, if it is to be bravely performed, requires dedication and discipline. On the whole the practitioners of American history, to their credit, have not taken the easy way of stretching out on the frame-of-reference theory and saying that as long as they acknowledge they are doing so, the affirmation explains and justifies their omissions and commissions. Seeking to be expert observers, they have sought to transcend rather than to accept their personal limitations.

In the attainment of such balance and freedom, it is essential to apply the same standards of judgment and appraisal to all groups and to all individuals: to realize, for instance, that success is no more a reason for denying a man or a cause a hearing than failure is a reason for granting it; to discard the sentimentalism that associates truth with one social class and error with another; to acknowledge that trade unions as well as corporations may use power arbitrarily. Since I have been talking about businessmen, perhaps I had better resort for the last time to a quotation from Charles Elliott Perkins. He was writing to a judge who had declared that we could not find truth unless we had the broadest sympathy with and care for the individual and the community. Perkins disagreed. He granted that "so far as sympathy is an attribute of the human mind, we must take it into account in trying to discover what individuals will as a rule do under given conditions. But I can't agree we cannot discover the truth 'if we go at it in cold blood.' The cooler we keep the better. The trouble is, as old John Locke points out in his Essay on the Understanding, that most people have too much sympathy either with their own preconceived ideas or with one side or the other of a controversy. To be a good judge you must not care *what* the truth is — only to find it, and the more you care what it is, the less likely you are to find it."

Surely a presidential address as old-fashioned as this should not conclude with a quotation from business. If it is to be true throughout to the context of the nineteenth century, where it belongs, it should include a bit of verse and a bit of Latin. I can kill two birds with one stone by acknowledging that about all I recall from my reading of Vergil's *Aeneid* is the line

Tros Tyriusque mihi nullo discrimine agetur

which my classic teacher, in order to communicate with a bunch of average high-school seniors, told us might be translated:

Democrats and Republicans I treat alike.

Fellow members of the Mississippi Valley Historical Association: Let us be on our guard lest, by dividing our standards, we ruin not only ourselves as practicing historians but also the heritage of American history which we are under obligation to honor, to explore, and to transmit.

4

The Progressive Movement

Liberal or Conservative?

THE RISE OF AMERICAN INDUSTRY in the decades following the Civil War was a development whose impact can hardly be exaggerated. It involved more than a shift from a commercial and agrarian economy to an urban and industrial one; indeed, it effected fundamental changes in the nature and quality of American society. The far-reaching technological and industrial innovations forced Americans to reexamine their traditional values and beliefs, many of which seemed obsolete, if not irrelevant, to the problems of a new age.

Traditionally, Americans were accustomed to think in terms of individualistic values. The rise of industry itself was often rationalized in the ideology of the self-made man who claimed he attained success by virtue of his own talents, drive, and ambition. By the end of the nineteenth century, however, it was becoming more difficult to conceive of industrial progress solely in terms of the achievements of a few creative individuals. The growth of a national transportation and communications system, which led to the rise of a national market, had stimulated the formation of large industrial units. This organizational revolution, to use Kenneth Boulding's convenient phrase,[1] was to have profound implications. Americans at the turn of the twentieth century found that their nation was being increasingly dominated by large corporations whose establishment arose partly out of a desire to curtail, if not abolish, competition — an aim that collided sharply with the dominant ideology of individualism.

The position of the individual within the nation's increasingly industrialized society became a major source of concern for many Americans. If America's greatness was related to individual achievement, what would happen as freedom and social mobility were more and more circumscribed by giant corporations with their impersonal and machinelike qualities? Did not the emphasis of corporations on efficient production and material objectives distort the human qualities that had been responsible for America's rise to greatness? Was not the growing disparity between rich corporations and poor workingmen creating a situation akin to that existing in many European countries where there was open class strife? These and similar questions led many Americans to advocate reforms that would restore dignity to the individual and give meaning to his life.

The forces of reform gradually gathered momentum in the last quarter of the nineteenth century. Although critics of American society could not agree upon a specific diagnosis, let alone remedial measures, they were united in a common conviction that some changes would have to be made if the United States was to survive with its historic values intact. The solutions presented were often diffuse. Many were all-embracing panaceas that called for the preservation of a competitive and individualistic society, but, at the same time, did not sacrifice the affluence associated with technological progress. Henry George, for example, gained international fame by presenting his single tax scheme in 1879 in his book *Progress and Poverty,* while Edward Bellamy, in his utopian novel *Looking Backward* (1886), argued that only the nationalization

1. Kenneth E. Boulding, *The Organizational Revolution: A Study in the Ethics of Economic Organization* (New York, 1953).

of all of the means of production and distribution would solve most of America's major problems. In a similar vein, many Protestant clergymen who were disturbed by the cleavages in American society offered their own answers in what came to be known as the Social Gospel. These religious critics argued that an immoral society was incompatible with the ideals of moral men. Society, therefore, would have to be remade in the form of a Christian socialist commonwealth, thereby offering individuals an opportunity to lead moral lives. Others, including the Populists, socialists, advocates of civil service reform, and academic critics also contributed to the swelling chorus of reform.

Between 1900 and 1917, these uncoordinated efforts at reform were institutionalized in what came to be known as the Progressive movement. Pluralistic rather than unitary, the Progressive movement was actually a series of movements operating at the local, state, and national levels of government and society. The movement consisted of a loose coalition of reformers who sought a variety of goals: political reforms such as the initiative, referendum, recall, and the destruction of urban political machines and corruption; economic reforms such as the regulation of public utilities and the curtailment of corporate power; and social reforms such as the Americanization of the immigrant, the amelioration of the lot of the urban poor, and regulation of child and woman labor, as well as many others. Among the symbolic leaders of the movement were two presidents, Theodore Roosevelt and Woodrow Wilson. These two men not only revived the moral authority and leadership-potential inherent in the presidency, but they supported the enactment of a series of laws embodying major social reforms.

Until the period after the Second World War, there was relatively little controversy among historians about the nature and character of the Progressive movement. Most American historians were writing within the tradition of the Progressive school. Consequently, they interpreted these reform movements and reformers within a liberal framework. In their eyes, the reformers in the movement had been challenging the dominant position of the business and privileged classes. The reformers' goals had been clear and simple: to restore government to the people; to abolish special privilege and ensure equal opportunity for all; and to enact a series of laws embodying principles of social justice. These reformers, Progressive historians emphasized, were not anticapitalist; they had not advocated the abolition of private property nor sought the establishment of a socialist society. On the contrary, they had taken seriously the American dream; their fundamental goal had been a democratic and humane society based on egalitarian ideals and social compassion. The real enemies of society were the businessmen, dishonest politicians, and "special interests," all of whom posed a serious threat to the realization of American democracy.

Such an approach put Progressivism squarely within the American liberal tradition and on the side of the "people" as opposed to the forces of wealth, self-interest, and special privilege. Vernon L. Parrington, one of the best known Progressive historians, saw Progressivism as a "democratic renaissance" – a movement of the masses against a "plutocracy" that had been corrupting the very fabric of American society since the Civil War. Thus, the movement concerned itself not only with political democracy, but with economic democracy as well. To Parrington Progressivism was a broad-based movement that included members of the middle class, journalists, and scholars – men, in other words, whose consciences had been aroused by the "cesspools that were poisoning the national household," and who had set for themselves the task of reawakening the American people.[2]

Implicit in this point of view was the conviction that the course of American history had been characterized by a continuous struggle between liberalism and conservatism, democracy and aristocracy, and equal opportunity and special privilege. Most historians writing in the Progressive tradition believed that reformers, regardless of their specific goals or the eras in which they appeared, were cast in the same mold because they invariably supported the "people" against their enemies. Such was the position of John D. Hicks, an outstanding American historian whose textbooks in American history were used by tens of thousands of high school and college students between the 1930's and 1960's. Hicks in 1931 published *The Populist Revolt,* the first major account of Populism based on wide research in the original resources. To Hicks the Populists carried the banner of reform in the 1890's and represented the first organized protest of the masses against the encroachments of a

2. Vernon L. Parrington, *Main Currents in American Thought* (3 vols: New York, 1927–1930), III, 406.

monopolistic plutocracy. Although the Populist movement ultimately failed, it was victorious in the long run, Hicks held, because much of its program was taken over by later reformers and enacted into law during the first two decades of the twentieth century. To a large extent his thesis rested on the assumption that American reform efforts drew much of their inspiration from the Jeffersonian agrarian tradition which had survived intact among the nation's farmers and rural population. The first selection is from Hicks' article "The Persistence of Populism," which takes substantially the same position as the concluding chapter in *The Populist Revolt,* and emphasizes the belief that there was a direct line of continuity from Populism to the Progressive movement.

Not all historians were as friendly and well-disposed toward Populism and Progressivism as was Hicks. Those historians writing within a socialist and Marxian tradition, for example, were highly critical of Progressivism because of its superficial nature and its refusal to adopt more radical solutions to meet the basic needs of American society. To John Chamberlain, a young Marxist who in 1932 published a devastating critique of American reform, the Progressive movement was an abysmal failure. Its adherents, claimed Chamberlain, were motivated by an escapist desire to return to a golden past where honesty and virtue had dominated over egoism and evil.[3]

Oddly enough, many of the detractors of the achievements of the reform movement from 1890 to 1917 were, like Chamberlain, within the Progressive school of history in that they accepted the idea that class conflict had been the major determinant of progress and social change in America. Many of them, particularly in the depression of the 1930's, condemned the Progressive reforms as being piecemeal and superficial in nature. The failure of the Progressive generation, these critics emphasized, had led to the reaction of the 1920's, which in turn had resulted in the disastrous depression of the 1930's. Disillusionment with the Progressive movement, however, did not necessarily imply disillusion with the efficacy of reform or with the aspirations and ideals of the liberal tradition in America. Even those intellectuals who flirted with Marxism during the depression did so out of their conviction that America could still be redeemed from the hands of its enemies.

3. John Chamberlain, *Farewell to Reform* (New York, 1932).

Beginning in the 1940's, and continuing in the 1950's and 1960's, the mood of American historians began to change. The increasing homogeneity of American society began to dissolve the sectional, class, and ethnic groupings that had been employed by the Progressive school of history. No longer did historians have to vindicate the claims of the West against the East, the South against the rest of the nation, or to establish conclusively the contributions of the Puritans, the immigrant, the working class, or the businessman. Such narrow loyalties appeared parochial in a milieu where national similarities seemed to be more significant than group differences.

The change in mood, however, was due to far more fundamental factors than a mere shift in the class and ethnic backgrounds of historians. Much more basic was the change in attitude and outlook that accompanied the revolutionary changes in the world since the 1940's. To scholars writing after 1940, the Progressive ideology appeared much too facile and simplified. Like many philosophers and theologians, they began to criticize Progressive historians for underestimating man's propensities for evil and for overestimating his capacity for good. In brief, these critics argued that the interpretation of the Progressive school of history rested on an unrealistic evaluation of human nature. The result, they concluded, was that Americans had been unprepared for the dilemmas and challenges that they faced in the great depression of the 1930's and the world-wide conflict of the 1940's because of their tendency to view history in terms of a simple morality play where good always triumphed over evil.

The challenge of democracy by communism since World War II has given rise to a new group of scholars — the neo-conservative historians — who have been critical of the Progressive school and who embarked upon their own reevaluation of the American past. Writing from a conservative point of view, these historians have stressed the basic goodness of American society and the consensus that has characterized the American people throughout most of their past. Thus these scholars have insisted that American history could not be written in terms of a struggle between democracy and aristocracy or the people against the special interests. On the contrary, they tended to stress the unity and homogeneity of the American past, the stability of basic institutions, and the existence of a monistic national character. While they did not deny that there have been conflicts and struggles between sections, classes, and special interest groups in the past, the neo-conservative historians insisted that such struggles were always fought within a liberal framework and that the protagonists were never really in disagreement over fundamentals. Moreover, these scholars were also much less certain about the value or desirability of social change. Having witnessed the effects of revolutionary movements in other parts of the world, the neo-conservatives questioned whether conflict and change would necessarily lead to a better society.

The result of this changed outlook was a sharp shift in the way that historians interpreted the Progressive movement. The Progressive school of history had looked upon the Progressive era as but one phase in the continuing struggle against special privilege and business. The newer neo-conservative school, in rejecting the older view, now began to ask new and different questions. If Progressivism was not in the Jeffersonian liberal tradition, in what tradition could it be placed? If Progressives were not necessarily moral individuals fighting on behalf of the masses, who were they and what did they stand for? If they did not democratize and reform America by their efforts, just what did they accomplish? Such were the questions raised by historians who rejected the older Progressive view.

The attack on the Progressive school interpretation of the Progressive movement was led by Richard Hofstadter, the distinguished Columbia University historian. Oddly enough, Hofstadter was writing within the Progressive tradition and as a liberal partisan. Yet he could not find very many constructive achievements to attribute to the American liberal tradition. Indeed, he found the liberal ideology to be narrow and deficient in many respects. In a number of brilliant books, Hofstadter attempted to expose, by historical analysis, the shortcomings, the inadequacies, and the failure of American liberalism.

In 1948 Hofstadter published *The American Political Tradition and the Men Who Made It*. In this book he attempted to delineate the basic characteristics of the American political tradition by studying the careers of nearly a dozen presidents and political leaders, including Andrew Jackson, John C. Calhoun, Abraham Lincoln, Theodore Roosevelt, Woodrow Wilson, and Franklin

Delano Roosevelt. Hofstadter's thesis was that the liberal tradition had failed because it was based upon the idea of a return to an ideology that emphasized acquisitive and individualistic values. Thus, the Populists and Progressives had similar deficiencies; neither had faced up to the fundamental problems of an industrialized and corporate America. Even Franklin Delano Roosevelt, who did not share the nostalgia common to the Progressive tradition, was a pragmatist whose attraction lay in the force of his personality rather than in any consistent ideology or philosophy.

Seven years later, Hofstadter spelled out his case in even greater detail in *The Age of Reform: From Bryan to F.D.R.* The Populists, he argued, were unsophisticated and simplistic reformers. Rather than approaching the farm problem within a broad national and international context, they placed the blame for their difficulties upon elements of American society which were alien to them — Easterners, Wall Street bankers, Jews, and foreigners. Associated with Populism, therefore, was a combination of attitudes made up of a curious blend of racism, nativism, and provincialism — attitudes that helped to explain the fears of agricultural and rural America that later manifested themselves in national paranoic scares. "The Populists," Hofstadter emphasized, "looked backward with longing to the lost agrarian Eden, to the republican America of the early years of the nineteenth century in which there were few millionaires and, as they saw it, no beggars, when the laborer had excellent prospects and the farmer had abundance, when statesmen still responded to the mood of the people and there was no such thing as the money power. What they meant — though they did not express themselves in such terms — was that they would like to restore the conditions prevailing before the development of industrialism and the commercialization of agriculture." [4]

Nor were the Progressives, according to Hofstadter, very much more sophisticated. Traditionally, Progressivism had been viewed by historians as a liberal reform movement aimed at readjusting American institutions to the imperatives of a new industrial age. To Hofstadter, on the other hand, Progressivism was something quite

4. Richard Hofstadter, *The Age of Reform: From Bryan to F.D.R.* (New York, 1955), p. 62.

different. Borrowing heavily from the work of behavioral scientists, he argued that Progressivism was related to other influences, notably status anxiety. Playing down the role of economic factors in individual and group motivation, Hofstadter maintained that to a large extent American political conflicts reflected the drive of different ethnic and religious groups for a secure status in society. By the latter third of the nineteenth century, a number of groups — clergymen, lawyers, professors, older Anglo-Saxon Protestant families — were finding themselves displaced from the seats of power and their traditional positions of leadership by a dangerous plutocracy and new political machines under the control of alien elements. The response of this displaced elite was a moral crusade to restore older Protestant and individualistic values — the Progressive movement. This crusade was based on the simple idea that only men of character — the "right sort of people" — should rule. Few Progressive leaders, including Theodore Roosevelt and Woodrow Wilson, were realistic in their appraisals of and solutions to America's problems. "In the attempts of the Populists and Progressives to hold on to some of the values of agrarian life, to save personal entrepreneurship and individual opportunity and the character type they engendered, and to maintain a homogeneous Yankee civilization," Hofstadter wrote, "I have found much that was retrograde and delusive, a little that was vicious, and a good deal that was comic." [5] Blinded by their moral absolutism and their righteous convictions, the Progressives were unable to foresee that much of their ideology was narrow and undemocratic and would prepare the groundwork for a later reaction that would threaten the very fabric of American liberty.

The implications of Hofstadter's interpretation were indeed striking. In brief, his line of thought led to the conclusion that American liberalism was not a liberal movement, but a movement by fairly well-to-do middle class groups alienated from their society because of technological and industrial changes. There is no doubt that Hofstadter himself was writing from the left of the political spectrum, but it is clear also that he felt strongly that the United States never had had a viable and constructive liberal tradition. Implicit in his views, therefore, was the assumption that American

5. *Ibid.*, p. 11.

history occurred within an illiberal or conservative mold, that a genuine struggle between classes — as portrayed by the Progressive historians — had never taken place.

The second selection by George E. Mowry represents the changing historical interpretation of Progressivism. Author of a number of important books on Theodore Roosevelt and the Progressive movement, Mowry was one of the first historians to see Progressivism as a movement by a particular class aimed at reasserting its declining position of leadership. Motivated by an intense faith in individualistic values, these groups opposed the rapid concentration of power in the hands of large corporate entities and the consequent emergence of an impersonal society. The Progressives, Mowry concluded, sought to recapture and reaffirm the older individualistic values, but they attempted to do so without undertaking any fundamental economic reforms or altering to any great extent the structure of American society.

While the specific formulations of the Mowry-Hofstadter thesis have not been universally accepted,[6] most recent historians seem to agree that the older interpretation of Progressivism as a struggle between the people and special interests is oversimplified, if not erroneous. Thus Louis Hartz in his fascinating book, *The Liberal Tradition in America: An Interpretation of American Political Thought Since the Revolution* (1955) argued that because America never had a feudal tradition, it did not experience the struggles between conservatives, reactionaries, liberals, and Marxians that characterized the history of most European countries. On the contrary, the United States had a three-century-long tradition of consensus, wherein all Americans subscribed to the Lockean tenets of individualism, private property, natural rights, and popular sovereignty. The differences between Americans, Hartz maintained, have been over means rather than ends. Thus, Americans never had a conservative tradition in the European and Burkean sense of

6. A number of historians have pointed to what they regard as a methodological flaw in the Mowry-Hofstadter analysis. To argue — as Mowry and Hofstadter have done — that the Progressives were a cohesive group requires that they show that the anti-Progressives represented a quite different social and economic group. One recent historian who did a study of the anti-Progressives in one state found that their social and economic and ideological characteristics were almost identical with those of the Progressives. See Richard B. Sherman, "The Status Revolution and Massachusetts Progressive Leadership," *Political Science Quarterly,* LXXVIII (March, 1963), 59–65.

the term, because American liberalism, by virtue of its continuity, was a conservative tradition. To view American history in terms of class struggle, said Hartz, was to misunderstand the basic agreements that united all Americans.

As a result of the rise of the neo-conservative school of historians, the Progressive movement has begun to be interpreted in a new and different light. Some of these scholars, for example, neatly reversed the Progressive school approach. Instead of seeing early twentieth-century Progressivism as a liberal movement, they argued that it was essentially conservative in nature — a characteristic that was a source of strength rather than of weakness. Thus the historical stature of Theodore Roosevelt rose as historians such as John M. Blum saw him as a conservative though responsible president who was flexible enough to deal with the major issues of the day in a constructive yet practical manner. Conversely, the reputation of Woodrow Wilson among some historians tended to decline because of his righteous moralism. Wilson's New Freedom, they wrote, was unrealistic because of its worship of a bygone age where all individuals had equal opportunity in the economic sphere. His foreign policies also turned out to be dismal failures because they rested on an exclusively moral foundation that omitted any appreciation of the national interest or the realities of international affairs.

Because they denied that Progressivism could be interpreted in terms of a liberal-conservative dichotomy or a class-conflict framework, neo-conservative historians were forced to formulate other hypotheses to explain this reform movement. Some neo-conservative historians, therefore, advanced the thesis that Progressivism represented largely an attempt to govern society in accordance with the newer ideals of scientific management and efficiency. The conservation movement, to take one concrete illustration, was not — as historians of the Progressive school had maintained — a struggle by the American people and their champions against special interests and large corporate enterprises bent on depriving the nation of its natural resources and despoiling the landscape. On the contrary, the conservation movement, according to Samuel P. Hays, was a movement of scientists and planners interested in "rational planning to promote efficient development and use of all natural resources." Frequently, large corporations — which were profoundly influenced by the ideals of scientific management – were ardent supporters of conservationist policies because of their interest in long-range resource planning. Conversely, small farmers, small cattlemen, homesteaders, and other groups that Progressive historians equated with the democratic masses, often opposed conservation because it conflicted with their hopes of becoming rich quickly. "The broader significance of the conservation movement," Hays concluded, "stemmed from the role it played in the transformation of a decentralized, nontechnical, loosely organized society, where waste and inefficiency ran rampant, into a highly organized, technical, and centrally planned and directed social organization which could meet a complex world with efficiency and purpose." [7] Implicit in this approach was the assumption that conservation had little or nothing to do with the liberal-conservative categories of the Progressive school of historiography.

In stressing the role of the "expert" and the ideals of scientific management as basic to an understanding of the Progressive era, neo-conservative historians also reinterpreted other aspects of early twentieth century American history. Many of the Progressive reforms, they stressed, were directed not at making the government more democratic and responsive to the wishes of the American people, but to making it and the economy more efficient. The movement for federal regulation of business was not, as the Progressive school of historians had argued, motivated by fear or hatred of large corporate enterprise. Its goal, according to neo-conservative historians, was the elimination of senseless and destructive competition in the economic system by making business and government partners in the effort to eliminate the ups and downs of the business cycle. Progressivism, therefore, reflected the desire of various professional groups to substitute planning for competition, to raise the "expert" to a position of paramount importance, and to end the inherent defects of democratic government by making government conform to the ideals of efficiency and rational planning.

The decline of the older view of the Progressive era was also evidenced in the changing historical interpretation of business and businessmen. For a good part of the twentieth century, the liberal assumptions of most historians led them to portray the business

7. Samuel P. Hays, *Conservation and the Gospel of Efficiency: The Progressive Conservation Movement, 1890–1920* (Cambridge, 1959), pp. 2, 265.

community not only as monolithic in character, but as being made up of men who were grasping, selfish, and narrow in their outlook. In recent scholarship, on the other hand, the businessman has been studied within a quite different framework. Business historians, as we have already seen, found in the careers of great entrepreneurs a creative and constructive leadership that brought into being America's phenomenal industrial capacity. Similarly, neo-conservative historians denied that the business community was necessarily reactionary or that all businessmen held a common ideology. Instead, they attempted to demonstrate that businessmen divided into various groups with conflicting ideas and that many of the Progressive reforms of the early twentieth century were actually introduced, supported, and endorsed by businessmen.

Conversely, the reputation of many American reformers suffered as a result of the writings of neo-conservative historians. Rather than writing about their contributions and achievements, historians have shown the shortcomings and failures of various reform leaders. They have exposed the personal and selfish factors that supposedly motivated the behavior of reformers and implicitly determined their unrealistic approach to contemporary problems. Above all, such historians scored the reformers for accepting an optimistic moralism based on their faith in progress. According to neo-conservative scholars, Progressive reformers tragically misunderstood man's propensity for evil and thereby failed to prepare Americans for the inevitable reaction that followed their failure to establish a democratic utopia at home and a peaceful international community of nations abroad in the first two decades of the twentieth century.

The reaction against the liberal interpretation of the Progressive movement, however, has not been shared by all historians. While admitting that older historians may have been wrong in their emphasis on a class conflict of the people versus the special interests, some scholars continue to see Progressivism as an attempt to deal effectively with many social and economic problems that grew out of industrialism and the resulting concentration of power in the hands of a few individuals and groups.

In the third selection, J. Joseph Huthmacher explicitly rejects the Mowry-Hofstadter idea that Progressivism was a middle class movement dominated by a system of values espoused by rural-

Yankee-Protestant groups. On the contrary, Huthmacher maintains that Progressivism was much more broadly based, and that lower class groups played an important role in the movement. Implicitly rejecting the neo-conservative thesis, Huthmacher argues that Progressivism was an attempt to cope with the complex dilemmas of an urban-industrial society. Although he clearly rejects the Jeffersonian agrarian interpretation of Progressivism, his point of view is essentially a modification and elaboration of the Progressive school that saw the reform movement of 1900–1920 as a continuing phase in the perennial struggle of liberalism versus conservatism.

Oddly enough, virtually all historians, whether they are in the older Progressive or the newer neo-conservative tradition, seem to be in agreement on at least one major point; namely, that Progressivism was an urban rather than a rural-centered movement. Once again, historians seem to have been reflecting their milieu. In the past many of the major historians had come out of an environment dominated by rural and agrarian values; their attitude toward cities was partly conditioned by the prevailing view that American democracy was the creation of a rural agrarian society. Within the past two or three decades, however, the majority of historians have tended to come from a society and regions of the country much more concerned with the problems of urban life. They do not share the anti-urban attitudes held by many of their predecessors. As a result, these historians have written about the contributions of cities and growing urban areas to American history. In this respect, they have shared the mounting concerns of most present-day Americans with the problems of an urban society.

As the historiography of the Progressive movement shows, it is difficult to evaluate the specific contributions of the movement without dealing with certain moral values that inevitably influence the historical judgments of scholars studying the subject. To the Progressive school of historical scholarship, Progressivism was one of the first efforts to adjust American values to an industrialized society wherein the concentration of economic power was thwarting the workings of American democratic institutions as well as corrupting the moral fibre of its citizens. Since they agreed with the goals of reformers who were attempting to ameliorate this situation, the writings of the Progressive school of historians on the movement tended to be a favorable one. More recent scholars, on the other hand, operated within quite a different value structure. Business and other neo-conservative historians, precisely because they emphasized the constructive achievements of American business, did not see much good in a movement which they believed was based on superficial knowledge, amateurism, and demagoguery. Because these historians were more complacent, even proud, of the accomplishments of American society, they saw less need for *radical* reforms in America's past history. Hence, they either emphasized the conservative nature of Progressivism or else pointed to its lack of realism or its optimistic illusions in order to show why the movement failed. Oddly enough, some historians who identified themselves with the liberal tradition, also argued that American liberalism fell far short of enacting truly meaningful reforms during the Progressive era. Thus it was possible for both neo-conservative and liberal scholars to be critical of the Progressive movement from their respective viewpoints.

The problem of evaluating the nature of the Progressive movement, therefore, is by no means easy or simple. Despite considerable research on this important era of American history, the divisions among historians are not necessarily disappearing. On the contrary, these divisions are in some respects growing sharper because of differences among historians pertaining to the nature and meaning of the American liberal tradition. In the final analysis, when historians are assessing Progressivism, they are assessing also the ability of Americans to adapt themselves to new problems in any given era.

Aside from the ideological and philosophical conflicts among historians, there are several major questions and problems that must be dealt with in evaluating the Progressive movement. Was there a relationship between the Progressive movement and earlier as well as later reform movements, including Populism and the New Deal? Who were the Progressives and what did they represent? Similarly, what groups opposed Progressivism and why did they do so? Were the reforms that were enacted between 1900 and 1917 constructive? What impact, if any, did they have upon American life? Why did the Progressive movement come to an end as an organized movement, or did it, indeed, come to an end at all?

These are only a few of the questions that historians have dealt with in an effort to understand the development of American society during the first two decades of the twentieth century. It is difficult, if not impossible, to avoid addressing one's self to these issues because of the bearing they have upon the larger question of understanding the nature of the American experience.

John D. Hicks

EARLY IN 1890, when the People's party was yet in the embryo stage, a farmer editor from the West set forth the doctrine that "The Cranks Always Win." As he saw it,

> The cranks are those who do not accept the existing order of things, and propose to change them. The existing order of things is always accepted by the majority, therefore the cranks are always in the minority. They are always progressive thinkers and always in advance of their time, and they always win. Called fanatics and fools at first, they are sometimes persecuted and abused. But their reforms are generally righteous, and time, reason and argument bring men to their side. Abused and ridiculed, then tolerated, then respectfully given a hearing, then supported. This has been the gauntlet that all great reforms and reformers have run, from Gallileo to John Brown.

The writer of this editorial may have overstated his case, but a backward glance at the history of Populism shows that many of the reforms that the Populists demanded, while despised and rejected for a season, won out triumphantly in the end. The party itself did not survive, nor did many of its leaders, although the number of contemporary politicians whose escutcheons should bear the bend sinister of Populism is larger than might be supposed; but Populistic doctrines showed an amazing vitality.

In formulating their principles the Populists reasoned that the ordinary, honest, willing American worker, be he farmer or be he laborer, might expect in this land of opportunity not only the chance to work, but also as the rightful reward of his labor a fair degree of prosperity. When, in the later eighties and in the "heart-

"The Persistence of Populism," *Minnesota History,* XII (March, 1931), 3–20. Reprinted by permission of the Minnesota Historical Society.

JOHN D. HICKS (1890–) is Professor Emeritus at the University of California at Berkeley. He is the author of many books on American history, the most recent of which is *Republican Ascendency 1919–1933* (1960).

breaking nineties," hundreds of thousands – perhaps millions – of men found themselves either without work to do, or having work, unable to pay their just debts and make a living, the Populists held that there must be "wrong and crime and fraud somewhere." What was more natural than to fix the blame for this situation upon the manufacturers, the railroads, the money-lenders, the middlemen – plutocrats all, whose "colossal fortunes, unprecedented in the history of mankind" grew ever greater while the multitudes came to know the meaning of want? Work was denied when work might well be given, and "the fruits of the toil of millions were boldly stolen."

And the remedy? In an earlier age the hard-pressed farmers and laborers might have fled to free farms in the seemingly limitless lands of the West, but now the era of free lands had passed. Where, then, might they look for help? Where, if not to the government, which alone had the power to bring the mighty oppressors of the people to bay? So to the government the Populists turned. From it they asked laws to insure a full redress of grievances. As Professor Frederick J. Turner puts it, "the defenses of the pioneer democrat began to shift from free land to legislation, from the ideal of individualism to the ideal of social control through regulation by law." Unfortunately, however, the agencies of government had been permitted to fall into the hands of the plutocrats. Hence, if the necessary corrective legislation were to be obtained, the people must first win control of their government. The Populist philosophy thus boiled down finally to two fundamental propositions: one, that the government must restrain the selfish tendencies of those who profited at the expense of the poor and needy; the other, that the people, not the plutocrats, must control the government.

In their efforts to remove all restrictions on the power of the people to rule the Populists accepted as their own a wide range of reforms. They believed, and on this they had frequently enough the evidence of their own eyes, that corruption existed at the ballot box and that a fair count was often denied. They fell in, therefore, with great enthusiasm when agitators, who were not necessarily Populists, sought to popularize the Australian ballot and such other measures as were calculated to insure a true expression of the will of the people. Believing as they did that the voice of the people was the voice of God, they sought to eliminate indirect elections, especially the election of United States senators by state legislatures and the president and the vice president by an electoral college. Fully aware of the habits of party bosses in manipulating nominating conventions, the Populists veered more and more toward direct primary elections, urging in some of their later platforms that nominations even for president and vice president should be made by direct vote. Woman suffrage was a delicate question, for it was closely identified with the politically hazardous matter of temperance legislation, but, after all, the idea of votes for women was so clearly in line with the Populist doctrine of popular rule that it could not logically be denied a place among genuinely Populistic reforms. Direct legislation through the initiative and referendum and through the easy amendment of state constitutions naturally appealed strongly to the Populists – the more so as they saw legislatures fail repeatedly to enact reform laws to which a majority of their members had been definitely pledged. "A majority of the people," declared the Sioux Falls convention, "can never be corruptly influenced." The recall of faithless officials, even judges, also attracted favorable attention from the makers of later Populist platforms.

To list these demands is to cite the chief political departures made in the United States during recent times. The Australian system of voting, improved registration laws, and other devices for insuring "a free ballot and a fair count" have long since swept the country. Woman suffrage has won an unqualified victory. The election of United States senators by direct vote of the people received the approval of far more than two-thirds of the national House of Representatives as early as 1898; it was further foreshadowed by the adoption in a number of states, beginning in 1904, of senatorial primaries the results of which were to be regarded as morally binding upon the legislatures concerned; and it became a fact in 1913 with the ratification of the seventeenth amendment to the Constitution. The direct election of president and vice president was hard to reconcile with state control of the election machinery and state definition of the right to vote, hence this reform never caught on; but the danger of one presidential candidate receiving a majority of the popular vote and another a majority of the electoral vote, as was the case in the Cleveland-Harrison contest of 1888, seems definitely to have passed. Late elections may not prove that the popular voice always speaks intelligently; but they do seem to show that it speaks decisively. In the widespread use of the primary election for the making of party nominations, the Populist principle of popular rule has scored perhaps its most telling victory. Benjamin R. Tillman urged this reform in South Carolina at a very early date, but on obtaining control of the Democratic political machine of his state, he hesitated to give up the power which the convention system placed in his hands. At length, however, in 1896 he allowed the reform to go through. Wisconsin, spurred on by the La Follette forces, adopted the direct primary plan of nominations in 1903, and thereafter the other states of the Union, with remarkably few exceptions, fell into line. Presidential preference primaries, through which it was hoped that the direct voice of the people could be heard in the making of nominations for president and vice president, were also adopted by a number of states, beginning with Oregon in 1910. Direct legislation by the people became almost an obsession with the Populists, especially the middle-of-the-road faction, in whose platforms it tended to overshadow nearly every other issue; and it is perhaps significant that the initiative and referendum were adopted by South Dakota, a state in which the Populist party had shown great strength, as close on the heels of the Populist movement as 1898. Other states soon followed the South Dakota lead, and particularly in Oregon the experiment of popular legislation was given a thorough trial. New constitutions and numerous amendments to old constitutions tended also to introduce much popularly made law, the idea that legislation in a constitution is improper and unwise receiving perhaps its most shattering blow when an Oklahoma convention wrote for that state a constitution of fifty thousand words. The recall of elected officials has been applied chiefly in municipal affairs, but some states also permit its use for state officers and a few allow even judges, traditionally held to be immune from popular reactions, to be subjected to recall. Thus many of the favorite ideas of the Populists, ideas which had once been "abused and ridiculed," were presently "respectfully given a hearing, then supported."

Quite apart from these changes in the American form of government, the Populist propaganda in favor of independent voting did much to undermine the intense party loyalties that had followed in the wake of the Civil War. The time had been when for the Republican voter "To doubt Grant was as bad as to doubt Christ," when the man who scratched his party ticket was regarded as little if any better than the traitor to his country. The Farmers' Alliance in its day had sought earnestly to wean the partisan voter over to independence. It had urged its members to "favor and assist to office such candidates only as are thoroughly identified with our principles and who will insist on such legislation as shall make them effective." And in this regard the Alliance, as some of its leaders boasted, had been a "great educator of the people." The Populist party had to go even further, for its growth depended almost wholly upon its ability to bring voters to a complete renunciation of old party loyalties. Since at one time or another well over a million men cast their ballots for Populist tickets, the loosening of party ties that thus set in was of formidable proportions. Indeed, the man who became a Populist learned his lesson almost too well. When confronted, as many Populist voters thought themselves to be in 1896, with a choice between loyalty to party and loyalty to principle, the third-party adherent generally tended to stand on principle. Thereafter, as Populism faded out, the men who once had sworn undying devotion to the Omaha platform were compelled again to transfer their allegiance. Many Republicans became Democrats via the Populist route; many Democrats became Republicans. Probably, however, most of the Populists returned to the parties from which they had withdrawn, but party ties, once broken, were not so strong as they had been before. The rapid passing of voters from one party to another and the wholesale scratching of ballots, so characteristic of voting today, are distinctly reminiscent of Populism; as are also the frequent nonpartisan ballots by which judges, city commissioners, and other officers are now chosen wholly without regard to their party affiliations.

In the South the Populist demands for popular government produced a peculiar situation. To a very great extent the southern Populists were recruited from the rural classes, which had hitherto been politically inarticulate. Through the Populist party the "wool hat boys" from the country sought to obtain the weight in southern politics that their numbers warranted but that the "Bourbon" dynasties had ever denied them. In the struggle that ensued both sides made every possible use of the Negro vote, and the bugaboo of Negro domination was once again raised. Indeed, the experience of North Carolina under a combination government of Populists and Republicans furnished concrete evidence of what might happen should the political power of the Negro be restored. Under the circumstances, therefore, there seemed to be nothing for the white Populists to do but to return to their former allegiance until the menace of the Negro voter could be removed. With the Democratic party again supreme, the problem of Negro voting was attacked with right good will. Indeed, as early as 1890 the state of Mississippi, stimulated no doubt by the agitation over the Force Bill, adopted a constitution which fixed as a prerequisite for voting two years' residence in the state and one year's residence in the district or town. This provision, together with a poll tax that had to be paid far in advance of the dates set for elections, diminished appreciably the number of Negro voters, among whom indigence was common and the migratory propensity well developed. To complete the work of disfranchisement an amendment was added to the Mississippi constitution in 1892 which called for a modified literacy test that could be administered in such a way as to permit illiterate whites to vote, while discriminating against illiterate, or even literate blacks. The Tillmanites in South Carolina found legal means to exclude the Negro voter in 1895; Louisiana introduced her famous "grandfather clause" in 1898; North Carolina adopted residence, poll tax, and educational qualifications in 1900; Alabama followed in 1901; and in their own good time the other southern states in which Negro voters had constituted a serious problem did the same thing. Some reverses were experienced in the courts, but the net result of this epidemic of anti-Negro suffrage legislation was to eliminate for the time being all danger that Negro voters might play an important part in southern politics.

With this problem out of the way, or at least in process of solution, it became possible for the rural whites of the South to resume the struggle for a voice in public affairs that they had begun in the days of the Alliance and had continued under the banner of Populism. They did not form again a third party, but they did contest freely at the Democratic primaries against the respectable and conservative descendants of the "Bourbons." The Tillman machine in South Carolina continued to function smoothly for years as the agency through which the poorer classes sought to dominate the government of that state. It regularly sent Tillman to the United States Senate, where after his death his spirit lived on in the person of Cole Blease. In Georgia the struggle for supremacy between the two factions of the Democratic party was a chronic condition with now one side and now the other in control. Ex-Populists, converted by the lapse of time into regular organization Democrats, won high office and instituted many of the reforms for which they had formerly been defamed. Even Tom Watson rose from his political deathbed to show amazing strength in a race for Congress in 1918 and to win an astounding victory two years later when he sought a seat in the United States Senate. For better or for worse, the political careers of such southern politicians as James K. Vardaman of Mississippi, the Honorable Jeff Davis of Arkansas, and Huey P. Long of Louisiana demonstrate conclusively the fact that the lower classes in the South can and sometimes do place men of their own kind and choosing in high office. In these later days rural whites, who fought during Populist times with only such support as they could obtain from Republican sources, have sometimes been able to count as allies the mill operatives and their sympathizers in the factory districts; and southern primary elections are now apt to be as exciting as the regular elections are tame. Populism may have had something to do with the withdrawal of political power from the southern Negro, but it also paved the way for the political emancipation of the lower-class southern whites.

The control of the government by the people was for the thoughtful Populist merely a means to an end. The next step was to use the power of the government to check the iniquities of the plutocrats. The Populists at Omaha, when they were baffled by the insistence of the temperance forces, pointed out that before this or any other such reform could be accomplished they must "ask all men to first help us to determine whether we are to have a republic to administer." The inference is clear. Once permit the people really to rule, once insure that the men in office would not or could not betray the popular will, and such regulative measures as would right the wrongs from which the people suffered would quickly follow. The Populists believed implicitly in the ability of the people to frame and enforce the measures necessary to redeem themselves from the various sorts of oppression that were being visited upon them. They catalogued the evils in their platforms and suggested the specific remedies by which these evils were to be overcome.

Much unfair criticism has been leveled at the Populists because of the attitude they took toward the allied subjects of banking and currency. One would think from the contemporary anti-Populist diatribes and from many subsequent criticisms of the Populist financial program that in such matters the third-party economists were little better than raving maniacs. As a matter of fact, the old-school Populists could think about as straight as their opponents. Their newspapers were well edited and the arguments therein presented usually held together. Populist literature, moreover, was widely and carefully read by the ordinary third-party voters, particularly by the western farmers, whose periods of enforced leisure gave them ample opportunity for reading and reflection. Old party debaters did not tackle lightly their Populist antagonists, and as frequently as not the bewhiskered rustic, turned orator, could present in support of his arguments an array of carefully sorted information that left his better-groomed opponent in a daze. The injection of the somewhat irrelevant silver issue considerably confused Populist thinking, but, even so, many of the "old-timers" kept their heads and put silver in its proper place.

The Populists observed with entire accuracy that the currency of the United States was both inadequate and inelastic. They criticized correctly the part played by the national banking system in currency matters as irresponsible and susceptible of manipulation in the interest of the creditor class. They demanded a stabilized dollar and they believed that it could be obtained if a national currency "safe, sound, and flexible" should be issued direct to the people by the government itself in such quantities as the reasonable demands of business should dictate. Silver and gold might be issued as well as paper, but the value of the dollar should come from the fiat of government and not from the "intrinsic worth" of the metal. It is interesting to note that since the time when Populists were condemned as lunatics for holding such views legislation has been adopted which, while by no means going the full length of a straight-out paper currency, does seek to accomplish precisely the ends that the Populists had in mind. Populist and free silver agitation forced economists to study the money question as they had never studied it before and ultimately led them to propose remedies that could run the gauntlet of public opinion and of Congress. The Aldrich-Vreeland Act of 1908 authorized an emergency currency of several hundred million dollars to be lent to banks on approved securities in times of financial disturbance. A National Monetary Commission, created at the same time, reported after four years' intensive study in favor of a return to the Hamiltonian system of a central bank of the United States; but Congress in 1914, under Wilson's leadership, adopted instead the Federal Reserve system. The Federal Reserve Act did not, indeed, destroy the national banks and avoid the intervention of bankers in all monetary matters; but it did make possible an adequate and elastic national currency varying in accordance with the needs of the country, and it placed supreme control of the nation's banking and credit resources into the hands of a Federal Reserve Board, appointed, not by the bankers, but by the president of the United States with the consent of the Senate. The Populist diagnosis had been accepted and the Populist prescription had not been wholly ignored.

Probably no item in the Populist creed received more thorough castigation at the hands of contemporaries than the demand for subtreasuries, or government warehouses for the private storage of grain; but the subtreasury idea was not all bad, and perhaps the Populists would have done well had they pursued it farther than they did. The need that the subtreasury was designed to meet was very real. Lack of credit forced the farmer to sell his produce at the time of harvest when the price was lowest. A cash loan on his crop that would enable him to hold it until prices should rise was all that he asked. Prices might thus be stabilized; profits honestly earned by the farmers would no longer fall to the speculators. That the men who brought forward the subtreasury as a plan for obtaining short-term rural credits also loaded it with an unworkable plan for obtaining a flexible currency was unfortunate; but the fundamental principle of the bill has by no means been discredited. Indeed, the Warehouse Act of 1916 went far toward accomplishing the very thing the Populists demanded. Under it the United States department of agriculture was permitted to license warehousemen and authorize them to receive, weigh, and grade farm products, for which they might issue warehouse receipts as collateral. Thus the owner might borrow the money he needed; not, however, from the government of the United States.

In addition to the credits that the subtreasury would provide, Populist platforms usually urged also that the national government lend money on farm lands directly at a low rate of interest. This demand, which received at the time an infinite amount of condemnation and derision, has since been treated with much deference. If the government does not now print paper money to lend the farmer with his land as security, it nevertheless does stand back of an elaborate system of banks through which he may obtain the credit he needs. Under the terms of the Federal Reserve Act national banks may lend money on farm mortgages – a privilege not enjoyed in Populist times – and agricultural paper running as long as six months may be rediscounted by the Federal Reserve Banks. From the Farm Loan Banks, created by an act of 1916, the farmers may borrow for long periods sums not exceeding fifty per cent of the value of their land and twenty per cent of the value of their permanent improvements. Finally, through still another series of banks – the Federal Intermediate Credit Banks, established by an act of 1923 – loans are made available to carry the farmer from one season to the next, or a little longer, should occasion demand; the intermediate banks were authorized to rediscount agricultural and livestock paper for periods of six months to three years. Thus the government has created a comprehensive system of rural credits through which the farmer may obtain short-term loans, loans of intermediate duration, or long-term loans, whichever his needs require, with the minimum of difficulty and at minimum interest rates. It would be idle to indulge in a *post hoc* argument to try to prove that all these developments were due to Populism; but the intensive study of agricultural problems that led ultimately to these measures did begin with the efforts of sound economists to answer the arguments of the Populists. And it is evident that in the end the economists conceded nearly every point for which the Populists had contended.

More recent attempts to solve the agricultural problem, while assuming the responsibility of the government in the matter as readily as even a Populist could have asked, have progressed beyond the old Populist panacea of easy credit. Agricultural economists now have their attention fixed upon the surplus as the root of the difficulty. In industry production can be curtailed to meet the demands of any given time and a glutted market with the attendant decline of prices can in a measure be forestalled. But in agriculture, where each farmer is a law unto himself and where crop yields must inevitably vary greatly from year to year, control of production is well-nigh impossible and a surplus may easily become chronic. Suggestions for relief therefore looked increasingly toward the disposal of this surplus to the greatest advantage. The various McNary-Haugen bills that came before Congress in recent years proposed to create a federal board through which the margin above domestic needs in years of plenty should be purchased and held or disposed of abroad at whatever price it would bring. Through an "equalization fee" the losses sustained by "dumping" the surplus in this fashion were to be charged back upon the producers benefited. This proposition, while agreeable to a majority of both houses of Congress, met opposition from two successive presidents, Coolidge and Hoover, and was finally set aside for another scheme, less "socialistic." In 1929 Congress passed and the president signed a law for the creation of an appointive Federal Farm Board whose duty it is, among other things, to encourage the organization of coöperative societies through which the farmers themselves may deal with the problem of the surplus. In case of necessity, however, the board may take the lead in the formation of stabilization corporations which under its strict supervision may buy up such seasonal or temporary surpluses as threatened to break the market and hold them for higher prices. A huge revolving fund, appropriated by Congress, is made available for the purpose, loans from this fund being obtainable by the stabilization corporations at low interest rates. There is much about this thoroughly respectable and conservative law that recalls the agrarian demands of the nineties. Indeed, the measure goes farther in the direction of government recognition and aid to the principle of agricultural coöperation than even the most erratic Allianceman could have dared to hope. Perhaps it will prove to be the "better plan" that the farmers called for in vain when the subtreasury was the best idea they could present.

To the middle-western Populist the railway problem was as important as any other — perhaps most important of all. Early Alliance platforms favored drastic governmental control of the various means of communication as the best possible remedy for the ills from which the people suffered, and the first Populist platform to be written called for government ownership and operation only in case "the most rigid, honest, and just national control and supervision" should fail to remove the "abuses now existing." Thereafter the Populists usually demanded government ownership; although it is clear enough from their state and local platforms and from the votes and actions of Populist officeholders that, pending the day when ownership should become a fact, regulation by state and nation must be made ever more effective. Possibly government ownership is no nearer today than in Populist times, but the first objective of the Populists, "the most rigid, honest and just national control," is as nearly an accomplished fact as carefully drawn legislation and highly efficient administration can make it. Populist misgivings about governmental control arose from the knowledge that the Interstate Commerce Act of 1887, as well as most regulatory state legislation, was wholly ineffectual during the nineties; but beginning with the Elkins Act of 1903, which struck at the practice of granting rebates, a long series of really workable laws found its way upon the statute books. The Hepburn Act of 1906, the Mann-Elkins Act of 1910, and the Transportation Act of 1920, not to mention lesser laws, placed the Interstate Commerce Commission upon a high pinnacle of power. State laws, keeping abreast of the national program, supplemented national control with state control; and through one or the other agency most of the specific grievances of which the Populists had complained were removed. The arbitrary fixing of rates by the carriers, a commonplace in Populist times, is virtually unknown today. If discriminations still exist as between persons and places the Interstate Commerce Commission is likely to be as much to blame as the railroads. Free passes, so numerous in Populist times as to occasion the remark that the only people who did not have passes were those who could not afford to pay their own fare, have virtually ceased to exist, except for railway employees. Railway control of state governments, even in the old "Granger" states, where in earlier days party bosses took their orders direct from railway officials, has long since become a thing of the past. The railroads still may have an influence in politics, but the railroads do not rule. Governmental control of telephones, telegraphs, and pipe lines, together with such later developments as radio and the transmission of electric power, is accepted today as a matter of course, the issues being merely to what extent control should go and through what agencies it should be accomplished.

For the trust problem, as distinguished from the railroad problem, the Populists had no very definite solution. They agreed, however, that the power of government, state and national, should be used in such a way as to prevent "individuals or corporations fastening themselves, like vampires, on the people and sucking their substance." Antitrust laws received the earnest approval of Alliancemen and Populists and were often initiated by them. The failure of such laws to secure results was laid mainly at the door of the courts, and when Theodore Roosevelt in 1904 succeeded in securing an order from the United States Supreme Court dissolving the Northern Securities Company, it was hailed as a great victory for Populist principles. Many other incidental victories were won. Postal savings banks "for the safe deposit of the earnings of the people" encroached upon the special privileges of the bankers. An amendment to the national constitution in 1913, authorizing income taxes, recalled a decision of the Supreme Court that the Populists in their day had cited as the best evidence of the control of the government by the trusts; and income and inheritance taxes have ever since been levied. The reform of state and local taxation so as to exact a greater proportion of the taxes from the trusts and those who profit from them has also been freely undertaken. Labor demands, such as the right of labor to organize, the eight-hour day, limitation on the use of injunctions in labor disputes, and restrictions on immigration, were strongly championed by the Populists as fit measures for curbing the power of the trusts and were presently treated with great consideration. The Clayton Antitrust Act and the Federal Trade Commission Act, passed during the Wilson régime, were the products of long experience with the trust problem. The manner in which these laws have been enforced, however, would seem to indicate that the destruction of the trusts, a common demand in Populist times, is no longer regarded as feasible and that by government control the interests of the people can best be conserved.

On the land question the Populist demands distinctly foreshadowed conservation. "The land," according to the Omaha declaration, "including all the natural resources of wealth, is the heritage of all the people and should not be monopolized for speculative purposes." Land and resources already given away were of course difficult to get back and the passing of the era of free lands could not be stopped by law; but President Roosevelt soon began to secure results in the way of the reclamation and irrigation of arid western lands, the enlargement and protection of the national forests, the improvement of internal waterways, and the withdrawal from entry of lands bearing mineral wealth such as coal, oil, and phosphates. At regular intervals since 1908 the governors of the states have met in conference to discuss the conservation problem, and this one-time dangerous Populist doctrine has now won all but universal acceptance.

It would thus appear that much of the Populist program has found favor in the eyes of later generations. Populist plans for altering the machinery of government with but few exceptions have been carried into effect. Referring to these belated victories of the Populists, William Allen White – the same who had asked, "What's the matter with Kansas?" – wrote recently, "They abolished the established order completely and ushered in a new order." Thanks to this triumph of Populist principles, one may almost say that in so far as political devices can insure it, the people now rule. Political dishonesty has not altogether disappeared and the people may yet be betrayed by the men they elect to office, but on the whole the acts of government have come to reflect fairly clearly the will of the people. Efforts to assert this newly won power in such a way as to crush the economic supremacy of the predatory few have also been numerous and not wholly unsuccessful. The gigantic corporations of today, dwarfing into insignificance the trusts of yesterday, are in spite of their size far more circumspect in their conduct than their predecessors. If in the last analysis "big business" controls, it is because it has public opinion on its side, and not merely the party bosses.

To radicals of today, however, the Populist panaceas, based as they were on an essentially individualistic philosophy and designed merely to insure for every man his right to "get ahead" in the world, seem totally inadequate. These latter-day extremists point to the perennial reappearance of such problems as farm relief, unemployment, unfair taxation, and law evasion as evidence that the

Populist type of reform is futile, that something more drastic is required. Nor is their contention without point. It is reasonable to suppose that progressivism itself must progress; that the programs which would solve the problems of the one generation might fall far short of solving the problems of a succeeding generation. One may not agree with the contention of some present-day radicals that only a revolution will suffice, and that the very attempt to make existing institutions more tolerable is treason to any real progress, since by so doing the day of revolution may be postponed. But one must recognize that when the old Populist panaceas can receive the enthusiastic support of Hooverian Republicans and Alsmithian Democrats, their once startling reforms have passed from the left to the right and are no longer to be regarded as radical measures at all. One is reminded of the dilemma that Alice of Wonderland fame encountered when she went through the looking-glass. On and on she ran with the Red Queen, but "however fast they went they never seemed to pass anything."

> "Well, in our country," said Alice, still panting a little, "you'd generally get to somewhere else – if you ran very fast for a long time, as we've been doing."
>
> "A slow sort of country!" said the Queen. "Now, *here,* you see, it takes all the running *you* can do to keep in the same place. If you want to get somewhere else, you must run at least twice as fast as that!"

George E. Mowry

CONSIDERING THE fact that the origins of early twentieth-century progressivism lay in the agrarian Middle West, California in 1905 did not seem to be the logical place for the projection of the doctrines first associated with the names of William J. Bryan, Robert M. La Follette, George W. Norris, and Albert B. Cummins. For in almost every important particular, the state offered more contrasts to the land of William Allen White than it did similarities. As opposed to the relatively homogeneous population of the corn and wheat belt states, there existed in California a veritable welter of first and second generation immigrants. Contrasted with the middle western one-farm, one-family type of staple agriculture, the California countryside was characterized by the tremendous holdings of corporations and cattle and lumber men on the one hand, and by the smaller but intensively cultivated fruit and vegetable plats on the other. Irrigation on the latter was but one factor in producing extremely high cost land as well as a high rate of absentee ownership and an itinerant labor force. By 1905 factories in the fields had already made their appearance south of the Tehachapi and in the San Joaquin and lesser valleys of the state.

By 1910, 60 per cent of California's population was urban, and to make the comparison with the progressive Middle West a little sharper, almost one half of the state's population in the same year lived in the three metropolitan counties of San Francisco, Los Angeles, and Alameda. Moreover, throughout these urban districts organized labor was on the move as it was in few other places in the nation After the general strike of 1901, San Francisco was

"The California Progressive and His Rationale: A Study in Middle Class Politics," *Mississippi Valley Historical Review,* XXXVI (September, 1949), 239–50. Reprinted without footnotes by permission of the Organization of American Historians.

GEORGE E. MOWRY (1909–   ) is Professor of History and Dean of the Social Science Division of the University of California at Los Angeles. He is the author of several works on the Progressive era, including *The California Progressives* (1950) and *The Era of Theodore Roosevelt* (1958).

often called "the most closed shop city in the country." And while Harrison Gray Otis and the Los Angeles Merchants and Manufacturers Association had managed to preserve an open shop town, organized labor never gave up its fight to break through this anti-union domination. In fact, one of the two basic state-wide conflicts in California from 1905 to 1916 was the continuous and often bloody struggle between organized capital and organized labor.

The second great state-wide clash of interests in California during these years was the one between the Southern Pacific Railroad and the state's farmers, shippers, merchants, and the ratepaying public. Until Hiram Johnson's victory in 1910, the one constant and almost omnipotent factor in California politics was the railroad. So deep were the tentacles of the "Octopus" sunk into the commonwealth that its agents even selected the receiving surgeons of city hospitals to insure favorable medical evidence whenever acidents occurred on the company's property. During the years before 1910, numerous economic and political groups had fought the railroad. But through its own powerful political machine, through extensive nonpartisan corruption, and through careful nurture of the state's widespread gambling, liquor, and vice interests, the Southern Pacific weathered every popular storm. Until 1910 its rule was disputed only in a few local communities and in San Francisco.

In the Paris of the West, as San Francisco proudly styled itself, the Union Labor party ruled from 1901 to 1911. But far from contributing to honest, efficient, and responsible government, the Union Labor machine, under the able but cancerously corrupt Abraham Reuf, turned out to be a partner in pelf with the railroad. Often for a cash consideration Reuf's "pack of hounds" supplied the votes for the continuing control of the Southern Pacific. The only other force in the state, with the exception of the rising progressives, capable of voicing much protest was the Socialist party. At the crest of their power in 1911, the California Socialists elected a mayor of Berkeley and came within an eyelash of winning control of the city of Los Angeles. But for one reason or another the Socialists were never able to summon up the strength to win a major victory, and it remained for the progressives alone to challenge the Southern Pacific machine.

Just what was a California progressive before he took office in 1910 and before power and the exigencies of politics altered his beliefs? What were his springs of action, his personal aspirations, and his concepts of what constituted the good society? The rest of this paper is devoted to an attempt to answer these questions in the hope that it may shed some light on the origins of progressivism, not only in California but in the rest of the nation as well, and perhaps even direct a few faint rays on the class structuring of American politics before 1917.

Fortunately, the men who first organized the California progressive movement were both literate and historically minded. The nine solid collections of personal manuscripts they so considerately left behind them, the diaries, documents, and innumerable published articles afford the historian perhaps an unrivaled opportunity in recent American history to inquire into the origins of a grass roots movement. Moreover, this group was small. Fewer than a hundred men attended the two state-wide progressive conferences in 1907 and 1909 before victory swelled the number of the organization's would-be leaders. Of this number, the author has been able to discover biographical data on forty-seven men, which produces in total a striking picture of similarity in background, economic base, and social attitudes. Compositely, the California progressive was a young man often less than forty years old. A majority of them was born in the Middle West, principally in Indiana, Illinois, Wisconsin, and Iowa. A good minority was native to the state. Almost all carried north European names and many of them, with two notable exceptions, were of old American stock.

The long religious hand of New England rested heavily upon California progressivism as it has on so many American movements. Of the twenty-two progressives indicating a religious affiliation in their biographies, seven were Congregationalists, two were Unitarians, and four were Christian Scientists. Three of every four had a college education, and three of the group had studied in European universities. Occupationally, the California progressive held a significant niche in the American economic structure. In the sample obtained, there were seventeen attorneys, fourteen journalists, eleven independent businessmen and real estate operators, three doctors, and three bankers. At least one half of the journalists owned their own papers or worked for a family enterprise, and the lawyers, with two exceptions, were not practicing politicians. In the entire group apparently only two had any connection with a large industrial or financial corporation save for the ownership of shares. Obviously this was a group of traditional small independent free enterprisers and professional men.

While not wealthy, the average California progressive was, in the jargon of his day, "well fixed." He was more often than not a Mason, and almost invariably a member of his town's chamber of commerce. Finally, by all available evidence he usually had been, at least until 1900, a conservative Republican, satisfied with William McKinley and his Republican predecessors.

Naturally, some fundamental questions arise about these fortunate sons of the upper middle class. Inheriting a secure place in society, earning a reasonably good living and certainly not radical by temperament, what prompted their political revolt and what did they want? The answer to the first of these questions, of course, is clear. The California progressive reacted politically when he felt himself and his group being hemmed in and his place in society threatened by the monopolistic corporation on one side and organized labor and socialism on the other. Proof for this general conclusion is not hard to find. The earliest manifestation of what later became progressivism in California is apparent in two local movements starting in 1906, one aimed against the Southern Pacific political machine in Los Angeles and the other against the control of the Union Labor party in San Francisco. From that time until victory in 1910, the progressive literature was full of criticism for both politically organized capital and politically organized labor.

The adverb "politically" in the last paragraph is important, for the progressive revolt was not alone a matter of economics. It might be pointed out that progressivism arose in an extremely prosperous period in California, and that the men who really organized the movement were not employers of any significance. In addition, far from beggaring these lawyers, journalists, and real estate operators, a good case can be made out that the Southern Pacific Railroad actually befriended many of them economically. Moreover, the California progressives never attacked the corporate form of business organization or the labor union as such. And although they believed that the closed shop was "anti-social, dangerous and intrinsically wrong," many of them repeatedly went to the union's defense when industry organized to break the unions and create open shops.

"Modern politics," Henry Adams wrote in his *Education*, "is a struggle not of men but of forces. The men become every year more and more creatures of force massed about central power houses." With the struggle for power between capital and labor penetrating to almost every level of California life in the period, and with the individual more and more ignored, the California progressive was increasingly sensitive to that drift and increasingly determined to stop it if possible. This was obvious in the progressive obsession with the nightmare of class consciousness and class rule. "Class government is always bad government," the progressive Los Angeles *Express* vehemently declared as it exclaimed that "unions had no more right to usurp the management of public affairs than had the public service corporations." Chester Rowell, probably the most intelligent of the California progressives, went on to gloss that statement. "Class prejudice among the business men," he wrote, "excuses bribery and sanctifies lawlessness and disorder among labor. When the spectre of class rule is raised, then all questions of truth, right, and policy disappear, and the contest is no longer over what shall be the government but wholly who shall be it." This class spirit on both sides, the editor of the Fresno *Republican* lamented, "is destroying American liberty." When it became predominant he predicted American institutions would have to be changed. "For upon that evil day reform ends and nothing but revolution is possible."

Clearly what troubled these independent progressives about both organized capital and labor was not alone a matter of economics but included questions of high politics, as well as group prestige, group morality, and group power. Involved also was the rising threat to an old American way of life which they represented and which they enthusiastically considered good.

The progressives were members of an old group in America. Whether businessmen, successful farmers, professional people, or politicians, they had engaged in extremely individualistic pursuits and had since the decline of the colonial aristocracy supplied most of the nation's intellectual, moral, and political leadership. Still confident that they possessed most of society's virtues, the California progressives were acutely aware in 1905 that many of society's rewards and badges of merit were going elsewhere. Although finely educated, they were all but excluded from politics unless they accepted either corporate or labor domination, a thing they were exceedingly loath to do. Their church, their personal morality, and their concept of law, they felt, were demeaned by the crude power struggle between capital and labor. Before the days of the Rotarians and kindred organizations they were excluded from, or did not care to participate in, either the Union League Club or the union labor hall.

On the defensive for the first time since the disappearance of the old aristocracy, this class of supreme individualists rationally enough developed a group consciousness themselves. Although generally overlooked by the historian, this consciousness had already evolved among some farming elements in the Populist period. Nothing else can be concluded from the words of the official organ of the Michigan State Farmers' Alliance. "It has been truly said," remarked that paper, "that the People's Party is the logical and only nucleus for every element of the American population that stands for social stability and constitutional rights. It is the bulwark against anarchy of the upper and lower scum of society." Now in the twentieth century, flanked by organized labor on the one side and organized capital on the other, the urban California progressives took up that song. Their letters, journals, and speeches are full of the phrases, "Our crowd," "the better element," and "the good people of the state." Even their political enemies recognized their separateness as indicated by the names they conferred upon them. The phrases "Goo-goo" and "Our Set" dripped with ridicule. But they also indicated an awareness of the progressives' claim to ethical and political superiority. Finally, no clearer expression of the progressives' self-confidence in their own moral elevation and their contempt for the classes above and below them can be found than that in an editorial of their state-wide organ, the *California Weekly*. "Nearly all the problems which vex society," this illuminating item ran, "have their sources above or below the middle class man. From above come the problems of predatory wealth. . . . From below come the problems of poverty and of pig-headed and of brutish criminality." Despite the fact that it was made up of extremely individualistic elements, this was unmistakably an expression of a social group on the march.

The California progressive, then, was militantly opposed to class control and class consciousness when it emanated from either below or above him. This was his point of opposition. What was his positive creed? In the first place this "rank individualist," as he gladly styled himself, was in most cases an extremely religious man. His mind was freighted with problems of morality, his talk shot full of biblical allusions. He often thought of the political movement he had started as a part of the "Religion Forward Movement." As early as 1903 Arthur J. Pillsbury, who was later to become a leading progressive, praised Theodore Roosevelt for coming nearer "to exemplifying the New England conscience in government than any other president in recent times."

But if the religion of the California progressive was old American in its form, much of its content was a product of his recent past. Gone was the stern God of the Puritan, the abiding sense of tragedy, and the inherent evilness of man. As William Allen White later wrote, the cult of the hour was "to believe in the essential nobility of man and the wisdom of God." With an Emersonian optimism, the California progressive believed that evil perished and good would triumph. Under the influence of Darwinism, the rising social sciences, and a seemingly benign world, the progressive had traded some of his old mystical religion for a new social faith. He was aware that evil still existed, but it was a man-made thing and upon earth. And what man created he could also destroy. For the then present sinful condition of man was the result of his conditioning. As Fremont Older's San Francisco *Bulletin* editorialized, "the basic idea behind this age of liberalism is the simple one that all men, prisoners and free, rich and poor are basically alike in spirit. The difference usually lies in what happens to them." And from that, one could conclude that when all men were given justice most of them would return justice to society. The progressive, then, not only wanted to abolish a supernatural hell; he was intent upon secularizing heaven.

There were, of course, individual variations from these generalizations. Chester Rowell, for one, while agreeing that men should not be treated as free moral agents, protested against considering them as "mere creatures of environment." "If we try to cure the trouble by curing the environment," Rowell argued, "we shall never go far enough, for however much we protect men from temptation there will be some left and men will fall to that. . . . Dealing with society the task is to amend the system. But dealing with the individual man the task is to reiterate forever, 'thou shall not steal' and tolerate no exceptions." But Rowell was more of a child of his age than even he himself realized. Despite his strictures on the sinfulness of man, one found him writing later that William H. Taft's peace treaties made international war impossible because "the moral influence on nations (for peace) would be tantamount to compulsion."

"The way to have a golden age," one progressive novelist wrote, "is to elect it by an Australian ballot." This was an extreme affirmation of democracy, but it followed logically from the progressive belief in the fundamental goodness of the individual. For according to progressive thought, behind every political question was a moral question whose answer "could safely be sought in the moral law." Since all men were moral agents, then public opinion was the final distillate of moral law. "It was a jury that can not be fixed," according to Lincoln Steffens, and indeed to some progressives, "God moving among men." Thus Charles D. Willard objected to Theodore Roosevelt's characterization of democracy as just a means to an end. To Willard democracy was a positive moral force in operation, a good in itself. "It is," he wrote, "a soul satisfying thing."

Back in the 1890's Senator John J. Ingalls of Kansas had remarked that "the purification of politics is an iridescent dream." Dream or not, that was one of the major goals of the California progressive a decade later. There was but one law for him — that of the churchgoing middle class — and he was convinced that it should be applied equally to the home, to government, and occasionally even to business. It was in this spirit that Hiram Johnson admonished his followers to forget how to make men richer and concentrate on how to make them better. This attitude helps to explain much of the progressive interest in sumptuary legislation. Individualism was a sacred thing as long as it was moral individualism; otherwise it needed to be corrected. Thus the progressive proposals for the abolition of prize fighting, "a form of social debauchery," gambling, slang, "since it is a coverup for profanity," prostitution, and the liquor traffic. And thus their demands for the censorship of literature, the drama, and social dancing.

In protest against these "holier than thou people" among his fellow progressives, Charles J. McClatchey, owner of the Sacramento *Bee,* wrote that he was his "brother's keeper only in so far as I should set him a good example." And though most progressives vehemently denied the full import of this statement when applied to morality, the majority of them was not in complete disagreement with McClatchey's views when they were applied to economics. Good Christian as he was, and on the whole benevolent, the California progressive did not quarrel with the doctrine of wardship provided it was not pushed too far. Thus he stood ready in 1910 to protect obviously handicapped individuals. And he was ready and even eager to eradicate what he called "special privilege," which to his mind was the fundamental factor in limiting opportunity for the man on the bottom to make his way economically upward. A few individuals on the left of the movement, like Congressman William Kent, felt that soon "property rights were going to tumble about the heads of the men who had built themselves pyramids of money in a desert of want and suffering." And Older raised the disturbing question of why men should be paid fortunes who had been lucky enough to be born with brains or in fortunate environments. One might as well go back to the feudal system, Older answered himself, because there was no more personal merit "in having talent than in having a noble lineage." But for the most part, the progressive majority was content with the basic concepts of the economic system under which 1910 American capitalism awarded its profits and pains.

What the progressive did object to in the year of his triumph was not 1910 capitalism as such but rather the ideological, moral, and political manifestations arising from that system. He was confident, at least in 1910, that there was not an inevitable causal relation between them. And he felt confident that he could cure these ills of society through the political method and through preaching and legislating morality.

The California progressive, then, wanted to preserve the fundamental pattern of twentieth-century industrial society at the same time he sought to blot out the rising clash of economic groups, and for that matter, the groups themselves as conscious economic and political entities. But he sought to do all this, at least before he had actually taken power, without profound economic reform. "The people," Rowell wrote sometime after the sweeping progressive victory in 1910, "elected Governor Johnson to get moral and political reform." The word "economic" was significantly absent from the statement.

From today's dark vantage point, the progressive aim of a capitalist commonwealth,

> Where none were for a class and all were for the state,
> Where the rich man helped the poor and the poor man loved the great,

may seem incredibly naïve. His stress on individualism in a maturing industrial economy was perhaps basically archaic. His refusal or inability to see the connection between the economic institutions and the rising class consciousness indicated a severe case of social myopia. His hopes to avert class strife by political and moral reform alone was scarcely realistic. And paradoxical in extreme was his antipathy to the class consciousness of organized capital and labor without his being aware of his own intense group loyalties.

When the California progressives confidently took control of the state in 1910, the road ahead was uncertain indeed. What, for example, would happen to the fundamental beliefs of this group if they found their ends could not be achieved without substantial economic reform, or, if in spite of their efforts, labor through one program or another threatened their economic and political estate, or if many of them became economically and psychologically absorbed by the advancing corporate system, or again in a less prosperous age than 1910, if the clash between economic groups for a livelihood created an intense social friction? Would their moral calculus, their spirit of benevolence, their faith in men, and their reverence for democracy still persist? The answers to these questions, of course, lay beyond 1910 and belong to another story, another chapter.

But the composite California progressive in 1910 was perhaps the best his economic and social group produced. He was educated, intelligent, able. A man of unquestioned sincerity and public integrity, he was also benevolently aware of the underprivileged groups around him. Devoted to the extension of political democracy and civil rights, he stood as a worthy representative of that long historical lineage of Americans who had dreamed and worked for a better commonwealth. If such a small group is ever able to amend or to alter a little the drift of society, the California progressive's chances seemed better than an even bet.

J. Joseph Huthmacher

Pop

MOST HISTORIANS of twentieth-century America would agree that the effective beginnings of the present-day "people's capitalism" — the present-day liberalism — can be traced back to the Progressive Era. And most of them would agree that the essential ingredient which made possible the practical achievement of reforms at that time was the support given by city dwellers who, at the turn of the century, swung behind reform movements in large numbers for the first time since America's rush into industrialism following the Civil War. True, the Populists and other agrarian radicals had done spadework on behalf of various proposals in the late nineteenth century, such as trust regulation, the income tax, and direct election of senators. But their efforts had gone unrewarded, or had been frustrated by enactment of half-way measures. Not until the reform spirit had seized large numbers of urbanites could there be hope of achieving meaningful political, economic, and social adjustments to the demands of the new industrial civilization.

Between 1900 and 1920 American statute books became studded with the results of urban-oriented reform drives. The direct primary, the initiative, the Seventeenth Amendment; the Clayton Act, a revived Interstate Commerce Commission, and the Federal Trade Commission; workmen's compensation, child labor laws, and Prohibition — these and many other achievements testified to the intensity of Progressivism. It is admitted, of course, that not everything done in the name of reform was desirable. Some measures, notably Prohibition, are counted today as being wrongheaded, while some political panaceas like the direct primary elicited an undue degree of optimism on the part of their exponents.

"Urban Liberalism and the Age of Reform," *Mississippi Valley Historical Review,* XLIX (September, 1962), 231–41. Reprinted without footnotes by permission of the Organization of American Historians.

J. JOSEPH HUTHMACHER (1929–) is Associate Professor of History at Georgetown University. He is the author of *Massachusetts People and Politics 1919–1933* (1959).

Nevertheless, the Progressive Era did witness America's first modern reform upsurge, and much of substantial worth was accomplished. Moreover, it established patterns and precedents for the further evolution of American liberalism, an evolution whose later milestones would bear the markings "New Deal" and "New Frontier."

In accounting for the genesis and success of urban liberalism in the Progressive Era, however, the historians who have dominated its study thus far have concentrated on one population element, the urban middle class, and its Yankee-Protestant system of values. "The great majority of the reformers came from the 'solid middle class,'" Professor George E. Mowry tells us. "If names mean anything, an overwhelming proportion of this reform group came from old American stock with British origins consistently indicated." Professor Richard Hofstadter adds that "the key words of Progressivism were terms like *patriotism, citizen, democracy, law, character, conscience* . . . terms redolent of the sturdy Protestant Anglo-Saxon moral and intellectual roots of the Progressive uprising." The component parts of this amorphous middle class, and the reasons for their new interest in reform at the turn of the century, have been described by various scholars. We have been told about the "white collar" group which saw, in the increasing bureaucratization of big business, the blotting out of its traditional belief in the American "rags to riches" legend. Some writers have dwelt upon the middle-class intellectuals — writers, publicists, ministers, college women, professors — who, in response to changing patterns of social thought represented by the rise of "realism" in literature, religion, and the social sciences, determined to uplift the living conditions of their less fortunate brothers. Others have examined the "Old Aristocracy" threatened by a "status revolution," and fighting to maintain the degree of deference that had been theirs before the rise of the newly rich moguls of business and finance.

Imbued with this mixture of selfish and altruistic motives, reinforced by the pocketbook-pinching price inflation that got under way in 1897, the urban middle-class reformers set out to right the wrongs of their society. They introduced a variety of new democratic techniques into our political mechanics, in an attempt to break the grip of the corrupt bosses who manipulated irresponsible immigrant voters and unscrupulous businessmen in ways that subverted good government. They augmented the government's role as watchdog over the economy, either to maintain the traditional "small business" regime of competitive free enterprise, or at least to make sure that oligopolists passed on to consumers the benefits of large-scale operation. Through the activities of their philanthropic organizations, coupled with support of paternalistic labor and social welfare legislation, the middle-class reformers also sought to uplift the standards of the alien, slum-dwelling, urban working class to something more closely approximating the Yankee-Protestant ideal. So runs the "middle-class" interpretation of Progressivism, an interpretation which has set the fashion, by and large, for scholarly work on the subject.

There is no doubt, of course, that discontented elements among the urban middle class contributed much to Progressivism, or that the historians who have explored their contributions and their motives deserve the plaudits of the profession. Nevertheless, it may be pertinent to ask whether these historians have not overstressed the role of middle-class reformers, to the neglect or exclusion of other elements — such as organized labor — who have had something to do with the course of modern American liberalism. More particularly, a number of circumstances call into question the assertion that "In politics . . . the immigrant was usually at odds with the reform aspirations of the American Progressive." If such were the case, how does one explain the drive and success of Progressive Era reform movements in places like New York and Massachusetts — states that were heavily populated with non-Protestant, non-Anglo-Saxon immigrants and sons of immigrants? How could reformers succeed at the polls or in the legislatures in such states if, "Together with the native conservative and the politically indifferent, the immigrants formed a potent mass that limited the range and the achievements of Progressivism"? Moreover, how does one explain the support which individuals like Al Smith, Robert F. Wagner, James A. Foley, James Michael Curley, and David I. Walsh gave to a large variety of so-called Progressive measures in their respective office-holding capacities? Surely these men do not conform to the middle-class, Yankee-Protestant "Progressive Profile" as etched by Professor Mowry.

If the Progressive Era is to be considered a manifestation of the

Yankee-Protestant ethos almost exclusively, how does one explain the fact that in the legislatures of New York and Massachusetts many reform bills received more uniform and consistent support from representatives of the urban lower class than they received from the urban middle-class or rural representatives? Some of the most effective middle-class reformers, such as social worker Frances Perkins, realized this fact at the time and charted their legislative strategy accordingly. It may be pointed out also that, even when submitted to popular referendums, typically Progressive measures sometimes received more overwhelming support in the melting-pot wards than they received in the middle-class or rural constituencies. This was the case, for example, in Massachusetts when, in 1918, the voters passed upon a proposed initiative and referendum amendment to the state constitution. Such circumstances become especially compelling when we remember that reform measures, no matter how well formulated and publicized by intellectuals, cannot become effective in a democracy without skillful political generalship and — even more important — votes.

Marshaled together, then, the foregoing evidence suggests that the triumphs of modern liberalism in the Progressive Era, and in subsequent reform eras, were owed to something more than a strictly middle-class dynamism. It indicates that the urban lower class provided an active, numerically strong, and politically necessary force for reform — and that this class was perhaps as important in determining the course of American liberalism as the urban middle class, about which so much has been written.

Today's liberals look to the "northern" Democrats and the "eastern" Republicans — those whose elections are due largely to the votes of the urban working class — for support of their proposals. If, as is contended, this phenomenon of urban lower-class liberalism can be traced back beyond the election of 1960, beyond the New Deal, and to the Progressive Era, then the probing of its chronological origins and the operational details of its emergence present wide fields for fruitful research. In the process of such studies, many other questions will present themselves to the investigator. What were the sources of lower-class interest in reform? How did its sources affect its nature, specific content, and practical effects? How, if at all, did urban lower-class liberalism differ in these respects from urban middle-class liberalism? At the risk of premature generalization, tentative suggestions, indicated by research thus far conducted, may be set forth regarding these matters.

The great source of urban working-class liberalism was experience. Unlike the middle-class reformers, who generally relied on muckrakers, Social Gospelers, and social scientists to delineate the ills of society, the urban working class knew at first hand the conditions of life on "the other side of the tracks." Its members and spokesmen grew to manhood "in the midst of alternately shivering and sweltering humanity in ancient rat-infested rookeries in the swarming, anonymous, polyglot East Side, an international center before the U.N. was dreamed of," where "souls and bodies were saved by the parish priest, the family doctor, and the local political saloonkeeper and boss who knew everyone and was the link between the exploited immigrant and the incomprehensible, distant law." Such people were less imbued than the middle class with the "old American creed" which expounded individualism, competition, and laissez-faire free enterprise as the means of advance from "rags to riches." Their felt needs, largely of the bread and butter type, were of the here and now, and not of the middle-class variety which fastened upon further advancement to a higher station from one already fairly comfortable. Moreover, their constant immersion in the depths of human misery and frailty, and the semi-pessimistic nature of their religious psychology, limited their hopes for environmental improvement within the bounds of reasonable expectation. Their outlook tended to be more practical and "possibilistic" than that of some middle-class Progressives who allowed their reform aspirations to soar to Utopian heights, envisaging a "Kingdom of God on Earth" or a perfect society to be achieved by means of sociological test tubes. Finally, the previous political experience of the immigrant workers, centering about their security-oriented relations with a paternalistic ward boss, conditioned them to transfer the same functional conception to the city, state, and national governments as they became progressively aware of their ability, through their voting power, to make those governing bodies serve their needs. Consequently, their view of government was much less permeated with fears of paternalism and centralization than that of traditionally individualistic middle-class reformers, many of whom abated their attachment to the laissez-faire principle with only the greatest trepidation.

The influence of these conditioning factors seems clearly discernible in the specific types of reform programs to which the urban lower class and its spokesmen lent greatest support. It is commonplace to say, for example, that the immigrants were not interested in political machinery reforms simply as reforms. Unlike the remaining middle-class "genteel reformers," they did not look upon political tinkering as the be-all and end-all of reform. Yet it is an injustice to imply that the immigrants' attitude on this matter was due to an inherent inability to comprehend the Yankee-Protestant concept of political behavior, and that they were therefore immune to all proposals for political reform. These lower-class voters seemed willing enough to support specific proposals which would enable them to secure the voice necessary to satisfy their economic and social needs, recognizing, quite properly, that the latter were the real sources of society's maladjustment. Since the rural areas of Massachusetts generally controlled the Bay State legislature, the urban working class supported the initiative and referendum amendment which might enable them to by-pass tight-fisted rural solons. Since the same situation prevailed in the New York legislature, the New York City delegation was glad to secure popular election of United States senators. In brief, it would seem that the line-up on such questions depended more upon local conditions of practical politics than upon the workings of a Yankee-Protestant ethos.

In the realm of economic reform, pertaining particularly to the problem of "big business," indications are that the urban lower class tended – unwittingly, of course – to favor the "New Nationalism" approach of Herbert Croly and Theodore Roosevelt over the "New Freedom" of Wilson and the trust-busters. Its members had seldom experienced the white collar group's "office boy to bank president" phenomenon themselves. They had never been part of the "Old Aristocracy," and hence had not suffered a downward revision in status at the hands of big business moguls. They shared few of the aspirations of the industrial "small businessman" and, indeed, recognized that the latter was all too frequently identified with sweatshop conditions. Consequently, the urban lower class was little stirred by Wilsonian cries to give the "pygmies" a chance. To workers the relative size of the employer's establishment was quite immaterial so long as he provided job security and adequate wages and working conditions, and passed some of the benefits of large-scale production on to consumers in the form of lower prices. Governmental stabilization of the economy and regulation of big business might well prove more successful in guaranteeing these conditions than would government antitrust drives. As a result, we find urban lower-class representatives introducing a large variety of business regulatory measures on the local and state levels during the Progressive Era. And it is symbolic, perhaps, to find Senator Robert F. Wagner introducing the National Industrial Recovery Act in 1933, while Senator David I. Walsh of Massachusetts had sponsored somewhat similar, forerunner, measures in Congress during the 1920's.

What has been said above indicates the basis for urban lower-class interest in the many types of social welfare and labor measures which became novelties, and then commonplace enactments, during the Progressive Era. If the middle class faced the fear of insecurity of status, then the working class faced an equally compelling fear of insecurity of livelihood and living conditions. The precarious condition of the lower class had now become known even to those on the better side of the tracks and, partly for humanitarian reasons and partly to defend their own civilization against a "revolution from below," middle-class reformers had become interested in social justice movements — which involved "doing things for others." But the recipients of this benevolence might surely be expected to show at least an equal interest in such movements — which involved doing something for themselves. That such was the case is clearly indicated by study of the legislative history of measures like workmen's compensation, widows' pensions, wages and hours legislation, factory safety legislation, and tenement laws in the legislatures of New York and Massachusetts during the Progressive years. The representatives of lower-class constituencies were the most active legislative sponsors and backers of such bills and, in collaboration with middle-class propagandists and lobbyists, they achieved a record of enactments which embraced much of the best and most enduring part of the Progressive Era's heritage.

The operations of the New York State Factory Investigating Commission are a case in point. Established by the legislature following the tragic Triangle Shirtwaist Company fire in 1911, the

Commission recommended and secured passage of over fifty labor laws during the next four years, providing a model factory code that was widely copied in other states. The Commission's most active legislative members were State Senator Robert F. Wagner and Assemblyman Alfred E. Smith, two products of the East Side, while its most effective investigator and lobbyist was Miss Frances Perkins, a middle-class, college trained social worker. (It should be noted also that the Commission received notable assistance from Samuel Gompers and other leaders of organized labor.) Again it is rather striking to observe that the Social Security Act of 1935, which began the transfer of industrial security matters from the state to the national level, was introduced by Senator Wagner, to be administered by a federal Department of Labor headed by Miss Perkins.

Effective social reform during the Progressive Era, and in later periods, seems thus to have depended upon constructive collaboration, on specific issues, between reformers from both the urban lower class and the urban middle class (with the further co-operation, at times, of organized labor). Of course, such co-operation could not be attained on all proposals that went under the name of social "reform." When, during the Progressive Era, certain old-stock, Protestant, middle-class reformers decided that the cure for social evils lay not only in environmental reforms, but necessitated also a forcible "uplifting" of the lower-class immigrants' cultural and behavior standards to "100 per cent American" levels, the parting of the ways came. Lower-class reform spokesmen had no use for compulsory "Americanization" through Prohibition, the closing of parochial schools, or the enforcement of puritanical "blue laws." Nor had they any use for immigration restriction laws which were based upon invidious, quasi-racist distinctions between allegedly "superior" and "inferior" nationality stocks. To them reform, in so far as the use of government compulsion was concerned, was a matter of environment. The fundamentals of a man's cultural luggage — his religion, his emotional attachment to his "old country" and its customs, his habits and personal behavior — were of concern to himself and his God, and to them alone. The lower-class reformers were products of the melting pot, and most of them took seriously the inscription on the base of the famous statue in New York harbor. True, there were many religious and ethnic differences among the component elements of the lower class, which often resulted in prejudice and violence. But each of these elements resented the Old Stock's contention that all of them were equally inferior to the "real Americans" of Yankee-Protestant heritage, and they resisted the attempts, which grew as the Progressive Era wore on, to enforce conformity to a single cultural norm.

In so far as conformity-seeking "cultural" reforms were enacted in the Progressive years, then, the responsibility must be assigned to urban middle-class reformers, joined in this instance by their rural "bible belt" brethren. The lower class can share no part of the "credit" for reforms like Prohibition. But in resisting such movements, were they not waging an early fight on behalf of what we today call "cultural pluralism" — acceptance of which has become a cardinal tenet in the standard definition of "liberalism" in the modern world? Indeed, it may not be too much to say that in all three fields of reform — the political and economic, as well as the social — indications are that the urban lower-class approach was more uniformly "advanced" than that of the middle class, in the sense of being more in line with what has become the predominant liberal faith in modern America. After all, does not the lower-class reform impulse, as outlined above, resemble the "hard-headed," realistic, and pluralistic liberalism for which spokesmen like Reinhold Niebuhr and Arthur Schlesinger, Jr., plead today, so that the "Children of Light" might not fall easy prey to the "Children of Darkness"?

It is not contended, of course, that all members of the urban working class became interested in reform during the Progressive Era, any more than it can be contended that all members of the urban middle class did so. The same "sidewalks of New York" that produced Al Smith and Robert Wagner continued to produce their share of "unreconstructed" machine politicians, whose vision never rose above their own pockets. Nor is it argued that the nature and zeal of lower-class attachment to liberalism remained constant throughout the twentieth century, or that the degree of co-operation attained with other reform minded elements remained unchanging. In the 1920's, for example, mutual suspicion and distrust, based largely on ethnic or "cultural" differences, seem to have displaced the former mood of limited collaboration between lower- and middle-class spokesmen, and in these changed circumstances Progressive-type measures found little chance of enactment. It is also possible that the high level of general prosperity prevailing since 1941 has vitiated urban working-class devotion to economic reform, and that the increasing degree of acceptance enjoyed by ethnic elements formerly discriminated against is causing their members to forget the lessons of cultural pluralism. All of these matters deserve further study.

The last-mentioned problems, dealing with the contemporary scene, may lie more properly within the realm of the political scientist and sociologist. But surely the evolution of America's twentieth-century liberal society, from the Progressive Era through the New Deal, is a province for historical inquiry. It is suggested that the historians who enter it might do better if they modify the "middle-class" emphasis which has come to dominate the field and devote more attention to exploring hitherto neglected elements of the American social structure. Such exploration necessitates tedious research, focusing at first on the local and state levels, in unalluring source materials such as local and foreign-language newspapers, out-of-the-way manuscript collections, and the correlations between the make-up and voting records of small-scale election districts. In the course of this research, however, our conception of the Progressive Era, and of recent American history as a whole, may undergo change. In fact, it may even begin to appear that "old fashioned" political historians, if they inform their work with up-to-date statistical and social science skills, still have as much to contribute to our knowledge of ourselves as do the intellectual and social historians, who are, perhaps, sometimes prone to over-generalize on the basis of historical psychoanalysis.

5

America's Entry into World War I

Needless or Necessary?

FOR MOST AMERICANS World War I posed a dilemma that conflicted sharply with what they felt was their national heritage. Traditionally Americans regarded themselves as a peace-loving nation destined to serve as a model for mankind. War itself was considered as an aberration from the normal course of events. After each of its previous foreign wars — the War of 1812, the Mexican War, and the Spanish-American War — bitter self-recrimination had followed as Americans sought to fix the blame on some person or party for involving this peace-loving nation in combat. How had the nation been drawn into conflict with foreign countries, when war itself seemed contrary to the cherished American ideal of peace? To this question many answers were given. Some pointed to blundering statesmen; some alleged evil conspiracies by groups that stood to benefit from war; and some argued that a strong sense of moralism blinded America's leaders to the realities of international affairs. But whatever answer was given, it was usually accompanied by a great debate concerning the proper role of the United States in world affairs — a debate that transcended the immediate specific issue of war causation or responsibility.

When armed hostilities broke out in the summer of 1914, most Americans, although concerned over events abroad, showed little or no inclination to become involved. President Wilson echoed the desires of most of his fellow citizens when he called upon them to remain neutral in thought as well as deed. Yet the hope of remaining neutral was soon to encounter formidable obstacles that placed a severe strain upon American diplomacy.

One of the basic problems confronting Wilson and his advisers was the fact that new weapons and total war had created a situation where past precedents and rules defining the duties, responsibilities, and rights of a neutral in time of war simply did not apply. In attempting to redefine the long-established rules of neutrality, Wilson soon found himself facing a dilemma. Both the Allies and the Central Powers sought to force America to adopt a policy of ostensible neutrality that would in fact be beneficial to their own national interests.

Britain, who controlled the seas by virtue of her predominant naval strength, wanted to exercise maximum restraint on neutral trade with the Central Powers. A naval blockade was established at the start of the war to intercept neutral vessels trading with Germany and the scope of the blockade was gradually expanded until it virtually covered all neutral commerce with the continent. To allow Britain to employ her naval might to this degree, America would be forced to relinquish some of its rights as a neutral, which was clearly to the disadvantage of Germany.

Germany, on the other hand, attempted to counter the impact of the British blockade by various means which also raised problems insofar as America's neutrality was concerned. Submarines, then a novel means of naval warfare, soon became the center of the controversy. Being relatively defenseless on the surface, submarines dared not investigate neutral and belligerent shipping too closely, nor could they always make adequate provision for the safety of the crews and passengers. Under these conditions there was bound to be indiscriminate destruction of both ships and lives. Early in 1915 the German Admiralty announced a blockade of the waters around the British Isles, declaring that all enemy vessels in the area would be sunk without warning by German submarines. Given the manner in which submarine warfare was being conducted, there was no doubt that American lives would be threatened.

The policies of both belligerents placed Wilson in a difficult position. If he accepted the British regulations, it would favor the Allied cause; if he obeyed the German blockade it would nullify Britain's naval advantage and favor Germany's strength on the continent. A total embargo against all belligerents would clearly redound to the advantage of the Central Powers because Britain rather than Germany was the beneficiary of the trans-Atlantic trade. Thus, genuine neutrality was impossible and even an American embargo raised implications of an unneutral policy.

President Wilson ultimately decided that German submarine warfare presented America with a far greater danger than did the restrictions imposed by the British. When Germany decided at the end of 1916 that its national interests demanded a resumption of unrestricted submarine warfare against belligerent and neutral shipping, Wilson concluded that he had no real alternatives. Following the sinking of several American vessels, he went before Congress to ask for a declaration of war. Despite isolated opposition, Congress concurred with the President's request, and on April 7, 1917, the United States entered the war on the Allied side.

Although the overwhelming majority of citizens agreed with Wilson that the United States had no choice but to defend itself, there was some scattered opposition throughout the country. In Congress six senators and fifty representatives voted against the declaration of war. Outside Congress some intellectuals and socialists also opposed America's participation. Nevertheless, the conformity brought on by the war resulted in silencing much of the opposition. It was only well after the war was over that serious discussion got under way regarding the reasons for America's involvement.

The discussion of America's entry into war that began in the early 1920's did not reflect the traditional assumptions that had given rise to the Progressive school of historiography. One of the reasons for this was the fact that domestic issues played a relatively minor role in the decision for war. But like historians of the Progressive school, the diplomatic historians who wrote about America's entry into the First World War had their own set of assumptions. These assumptions usually revolved around such questions as the proper role of the United States in world affairs and the desirability of American involvements in foreign conflicts. More than anything else, the divisions among those historians who dealt with American diplomacy from 1914 to 1917 reflected differing views as to what America's policy should have been.

Generally speaking, most of the contemporary or near-contemporary accounts — none of which were based upon wide research in the sources simply because relevant manuscript materials were as yet unavailable — took a favorable view of America's diplomatic moves between 1914 and 1917. The two most widely read works in this regard in the 1920's were semi-autobiographical accounts that dealt with the careers of Walter Hines Page, the American ambassador to England, and Colonel Edward House, Wilson's close friend and advisor. Both men had advocated intervention; both had shown concern lest America's policy obstruct the Allies; and both were of the opinion that German militarism would have represented a real threat to American democracy if the Central Powers had emerged victorious. When the United States entered the war, they argued, it did so for reasons of morality and self-interest, both of which coincided in 1917.

The controversy over the Versailles peace treaty and the growing disillusionment with Wilsonian idealism, however, set the stage for a reexamination of the problem of America's entry into the war. During the 1920's a new school of historians known as the revisionists emerged to offer different explanations for America's involvement. John K. Turner, a veteran socialist writer who published a book entitled *Shall It Be Again?* in 1922, was among the first of the revisionists. Rejecting the interpretation that the United States had intervened to protect commerce and lives and to uphold national honor and international law, Turner argued that Wilson, a pseudo-liberal, had gone to war because of the greed of Wall Street bankers. His book, however, had little influence at the time of its publication, one possible reason being its polemical tone.

A few years later a more significant statement of the revisionist point of view was presented by Professor Harry Elmer Barnes, who had become interested in the general problem of war guilt. In 1926 Barnes published his *Genesis of the World War* in which he repudiated the idea that Germany had been responsible for the outbreak of war in 1914. He contended that America's participation in the war had been a mistake brought about by Wilson's acquiescence in Britain's illegal maritime restrictions and his misguided desire to save the Allies from defeat. By throwing American power into the conflict on the side of the Allies, Wilson set the stage for the disastrous and one-sided Versailles peace settlement that followed.

Barnes continued for over forty years to reiterate his belief that the United States should have stayed out of World War I. Implicit in his point of view was the assumption that America had had no stake in the European conflict and that a much fairer peace between the warring powers could have been negotiated had American power not thrown the balance in favor of England and the Allies. In the first selection in this chapter, Barnes spells out his case in detail. Wilson started off as a neutral, he argues, but his Anglo-Saxon perspective and the fact that most of his advisers were pro-Allied and distorted the case against Germany caused the President ultimately to take an unneutral stand. One of the reasons for Wilson's change of mind was the growing munitions trade with the Allies upon which America's prosperity rested, in part, at the time. This trade—which according to Barnes was unneutral and illegal — forced Germany to resort to unrestricted submarine warfare and led to America's involvement in the war. Because of our unneutral policy, Barnes concluded, the United States entered the conflict without any clear legal or moral basis for doing so.

During the 1920's and 1930's the revisionists continued to build up their thesis that America had entered the war because of Wilson's unneutral diplomacy. C. Hartley Grattan, one of Barnes' former students at Clark University, published a long and detailed revisionist work in 1929. Working on the assumption that neither the world nor the United States had gained anything from the war, Grattan in his book *Why We Fought* examined in detail the circumstances that had led to American involvement. He pointed to Wilson's shift in policy from true neutrality to a pro-Allied position — a shift brought about by Anglophilism, the influence of capitalists, financiers, and munition makers who had an economic stake in an Allied victory, and the skill of British propagandists. In view of America's pro-English policy by late 1916, Grattan concluded, Germany had no choice but to counter with the submarine.

The revisionists found a very receptive climate of opinion for their views in the 1930's because of the deterioration in the world situation. By this time it was evident that the international structure erected at Versailles and at various conferences in the 1920's was failing to keep the peace. In Italy Mussolini and the fascists exercised dictatorial control; in Germany Hitler was well on the road to rebuilding Germany's war potential; and in the Far East Japan was already beginning its policy of expansion on the mainland of Asia.

To many Americans these developments were particularly distressing. After all, the United States had gone to war in 1917 not only to protect its own interests, but also, as Wilson had so eloquently put it, "to make the world safe for democracy." More than ever before, the rise of dictatorships abroad seemed to be making a mockery of the high idealism with which America had entered the First World War.

The disillusionment of the American people in the 1930's was reflected in their growing distrust and suspicion of foreign nations. As a result, the United States entered a period of semi-isolationism. In its foreign policy moves, America seemed to be intent upon cutting itself off from membership in the community of nations as much as possible. At the same time, steps were taken to prevent a repetition of the mistakes many felt had been made in the period prior to America's entry into the First World War. In the mid-1930's a series of neutrality acts were passed in an obvious effort to prevent history from repeating itself. For example, the Johnson Act of 1934 forbade American citizens from lending any money to a nation which was in default of its war debts to America. The intent of this act, in part, was to prevent the establishment of an American financial interest in the survival of any foreign country. The three neutrality acts written between 1935 and 1937 had other provisions to prohibit aid to belligerent nations in time of war.

The isolationist mood of the 1930's was further strengthened as a result of the Senate investigation of the American munitions industry. A Senate committee headed by Senator Gerald P. Nye of North Dakota was given the task in 1934 of investigating the influence of munitions makers on American foreign policy. Although the evidence gathered by the committee came closer to refuting rather than supporting the thesis that the munitions industry had played a Machiavellian role in influencing foreign policy, the findings of the committee were used indirectly by some revisionist historians to buttress their case against Wilsonian diplomacy.

Coupled with the rise of isolationism was that of pacifism. The pacifist movement in this era was a potent force in shaping the minds of many Americans and creating an intense desire throughout the nation for peace. Many American citizens became convinced that war was to be avoided at all costs because of its immoral nature, its threat to civilization, and its failure as a means of achieving any worthwhile objectives.

The desire to avoid involvement in any future European war had the effect of reawakening interest in the reasons why America had entered World War I. How had America become involved in the war and who was responsible? In asking a question of this nature, many historians started with the assumption that America's entry into the war had been a gross error that could have been avoided. By revealing the process whereby the United States had undertaken a mistaken commitment, the revisionists hoped to provide contemporary statesmen and diplomats of the 1930's with the knowledge and wisdom to avoid similar pitfalls in the future.

Some of the revisionists deplored America's participation on different grounds. These historians felt that war and liberal reform were incompatible. War, they argued, always sounded the death knell of domestic reform and often inaugurated periods of conservatism or reaction. The First World War, for example, had weakened if not destroyed the commitment to liberal values that had been characteristic of the Progressive era.

Such was the thesis presented by Charles A. Beard during the 1930's. Although Beard did not write specifically on Wilsonian diplomacy, he was one of the most articulate of the anti-war critics. In his book *The Open Door at Home,* which was published in 1934, as well as in testimony before Congressional committees, he argued that America's strength and character had derived from its relative isolation from European power politics and chicanery. Committed to a program of liberal reform, Beard staunchly opposed America's involvement in any future European war. His position seemed to support by implication the revisionist critique of American foreign policy between 1914 and 1917, though for different reasons.

By the mid-1930's the writings of the revisionist school of historians had reached a peak. Edwin Borchard and W. P. Lage in an important book, *Neutrality for the United States,* written in 1937, attributed American involvement in 1917 to the failure of the Wilson Administration to observe recognized rules of neutrality. "There is no doubt," they wrote, "that the administration desired to see the Allies win and declined to take any action even in defense of American neutral rights which would seriously interfere with that objective. Perhaps the objective is understandable . . . but to suggest that the objective was consistent with the maintenance of American neutrality is a travesty of the truth. We were unneutral and we paid the price." [1]

The most mature and complete revisionist account came when Charles C. Tansill published his massive work *America Goes to War* in 1938. In writing this book, Tansill explored a huge mass of manuscript and printed material. Tansill believed that there were multiple causes for America's entry into the war: he stressed the great growth of the munitions trade with the Allies; the unneutral biases of Lansing, House, and Page; and the inability of Wilson to cope with the pressures put on him. But above all, Tansill's argument rested mainly on one premise — that the United States had no valid reason for helping the Allies and opposing Germany and that a German victory would have been a lesser evil than American participation. Reflecting the disillusionment of the 1930's and the intense desire of the nation to avoid any future conflict, Tansill's work seemed to offer conclusive evidence for support of the revisionist thesis.

There were a number of historians in the 1930's, however, who took issue with the revisionist point of view. The outstanding opponent of the revisionists was Professor Charles Seymour of Yale University who edited *The Intimate Papers of Colonel House* (4 vols.,

1. Edwin Borchard and William P. Lage, *Neutrality for the United States* (New Haven, 1937), pp. 33–34.

1926–1928), published *American Diplomacy During the World War* in 1934, and *American Neutrality, 1914–1917* in 1935. Unlike the revisionists, Seymour never discussed the issue of whether or not the United States *should* have gone to war; he approached the question of America's entry into the war as a historical problem rather than a moral issue. Nor were Seymour's writings in a didactic vein; he was not concerned with the problem of how America might stay out of a future conflict. Seymour succeeded, therefore, in ridding his work of the present-mindedness that had characterized the writings of many other historians on this issue.

As a result of his approach, Seymour came to certain conclusions regarding Wilson's diplomacy that differed sharply from those of the revisionists. Seymour admitted that Wilson and his advisers were pro-English in their sympathies, but he felt that the President made a determined effort to follow the principles of international law. Indeed, Seymour pointed out, there were periods when America's relations with the Allies were far more vexatious and troublesome than those with Germany. At certain times in the course of the war, Wilson had seriously considered the possibility of imposing economic sanctions against the Allies.

Seymour's major thesis, however, was that the United States had gone to war primarily because of Germany's decision to wage unrestricted submarine warfare. If Germany was permitted to have her own way, the economic well-being of neutral nations and the lives of their citizens would have been seriously threatened. Since Wilson was unwilling to surrender to German demands, Seymour concluded, he had no alternative — given Germany's intransigence on the submarine issue — but to ask Congress for a declaration of war.

The second selection in this chapter, that of Walter Millis, reveals the wide range of opinion that existed among historians in the 1930's regarding America's involvement in the First World War. A graduate of Yale and an editorial writer for the New York *Herald Tribune,* Millis became interested in the period of American diplomacy from 1914 to 1917. He published in 1935 *Road to War: America, 1914–1917,* a book that caused a stir because the author refused to pinpoint precisely the reasons why America had entered the war. In the article reprinted here, however, Millis was more explicit. After examining the events from 1914 to 1917, Millis concluded that a conspiratorial thesis about Wilson and his advisers simply could not be proved and that the problem of causation was far more complex than anyone had imagined. In discussing the work of other historians on this problem, Millis observed that their interpretations often depended in large degree upon their starting assumptions regarding the nature of the state and upon their philosophy of international relations.

The outbreak of World War II tended to quiet for a time the debate over the reasons for America's participation in World War I. But one work — Walter Lippmann's *U.S. Foreign Policy: Shield of the Republic,* published in 1943 — touched upon the problem and cast the issue in a different light. Lippmann argued that America had gone to war in 1917 because a German victory ultimately would have threatened the nation's security. When Germany embarked on its campaign of unrestricted submarine warfare, Lippmann claimed, the United States responded by declaring war because it was unwilling to risk an Allied defeat which would have jeopardized America's safety. Lippmann admitted that Wilson had never educated the American people to the dangers involved in an Allied defeat nor clearly defined America's national interests. But the events of the Second World War were demonstrating that America could not afford to stand idly by while the rest of the Atlantic community was overrun by aggressors. With the United States fighting a two-front war against Germany and Japan at the time his book was published, it is not too difficult to understand why Lippmann wrote as he did.

Lippmann's work foreshadowed the position many historians were to take in the period after 1945 as well as to suggest some of the assumptions they would make. As a result of the epochal events in world affairs between 1933 and 1945, historians and political scientists began placing more emphasis upon power politics and the national interest as significant factors in the shaping of international relations. This tendency was reinforced by the increasingly important role that the United States was playing as leader of the free world after World War II. Many argued that America's foreign policy had to be based upon realistic rather than moral considerations and a keen appreciation of the national interest. Viewing America's diplomatic moves in the period prior to 1917 in these terms, some scholars were very critical of Wilson's foreign policy. Now Wilson began to be criticized not because America had entered the war in 1917, but because he had never clearly defined the reasons why the country had gone to war. His excessive moralism, some scholars claimed, prevented Wilson from defining America's national interest and placed him at a serious disadvantage when it came to writing a treaty of peace in the postwar period.

Such was the argument advanced by two writers, George Kennan and Hans Morgenthau, in 1951. According to both of these scholars, America's national interest required the preservation of a balance of power in Europe. If one accepted this premise, the United States indeed had had a vital interest in the outcome of World War I. America's national interest made it mandatory, as Kennan put it, that the war "be brought to an end as soon as possible on a basis involving a minimum maladjustment and as much stability as possible for the future." [2] Wilson's policy, on the other hand, had been founded on precisely the opposite assumption — that one of the aims of the war was to end once and for all the balance of power concept.

What was the result of the implementation of Wilson's policy? According to Kennan and Morgenthau, it resulted in diplomatic disaster for America. Wilson's policies fatally weakened the European balance of power and thereby prepared the way for the ultimate emergence of Fascism and Nazism. Germany, bitter and resentful over its treatment at Versailles, found that the breakup of its traditional institutions brought about a decade of profound social unrest; Austria-Hungary was dismembered and carved up into a series of unstable nation-states; Russia was no longer a potential ally of France to help contain German power; and England and France lay weakened by the vicissitudes of war and unable to do much to maintain world peace. Wilson's insistence upon the total destruction of German power, plus his reliance upon abstract moral principles, had isolated him from reality and caused him to embark on a mistaken policy. "If Woodrow Wilson erred," one political scientist has concluded, "it was not because he led the United States into war but because he failed to do everything in his power to prepare the people to see their entrance into a foreign war as an act consistent with imperative principles of national self-

2. George Kennan, *American Diplomacy 1900–1950* (Chicago, 1951), p. 66.

interest, as well as with national ideals and sentiments. . . . Armed intervention might well have been the wisest alternative from the long-run standpoint of American ideals and interests, but the great majority of the people did not choose war upon mature deliberation; they simply drifted into war, guided largely by impulses — some noble, some mean — with but a tenuous relation to broad and enduring national policy. Consequently, it is little wonder that the motives which led to war seemed inadequate in the perspective of peace, and that America's vaunted moral leadership revealed itself once more as the irresponsible outburst of a nation physically mature but emotionally and intellectually adolescent — a quick-tempered, good-hearted giant of a nation, moved by impulses it would later regret, undertaking commitments it would not fulfill, and never quite comprehending either the circumstances or the consequences of its erratic behavior."[3]

Realists like Morgenthau and Kennan, of course, judged Wilson in the light of their own philosophy of international relations. In one sense, their works were primarily intended to serve as a message to Americans after the Second World War. They were less interested in understanding Wilson and the dilemmas that he faced than they were in showing that America's foreign policy during the First World War had been based too much on moral grounds. Unlike the revisionists, the school of realists represented by Kennan and Morgenthau was not critical of Wilson because he had taken the United States into war; they criticized him instead because he had taken the nation into war *for the wrong reasons.*

While the realists were evaluating Wilson in terms of what he should have done, other recent historians, following the approach of Charles Seymour, were examining in great detail the situation that Wilson actually faced. Taking a historical rather than a didactic approach, they were not interested in criticizing the diplomacy of 1914–1917; their primary objective was to understand and define the issues that the Wilson Administration had faced, the pressures imposed upon America's leaders, and how these leaders responded to such pressures. These historians did not have to deal specifically with the issue of whether the United States

3. Robert E. Osgood, *Ideals and Self-Interest in America's Foreign Relations: The Great Transformation of the Twentieth Century* (Chicago, 1953), pp. 262–263.

should have stayed out of war in 1917 or whether it should attempt to avoid any future conflicts because the problem of American intervention did not exist in the same form as it had at the time of the First World War. The profound change in America's international role and position after 1945 made any discussion of such an issue a meaningless one. Research by these recent historians was facilitated also by two other developments. The private papers of many public officials who played an active and important part in the Wilson Administration became available with the passage of time and materials in foreign archives were placed at their disposal. As a result, these historians were able to view the problem of America's entry into the First World War in a somewhat different light than earlier writers.

The picture drawn by these historians of the 1950's and 1960's — and since they did not establish a distinct school these scholars cannot be given a specific designation — was far more complex than that of their predecessors. Rejecting a moralistic or conspiratorial approach, they viewed Wilson as a leader confronted with a variety of pressures — pressures that limited his choices of alternative policies. They sought to understand how Wilson responded to the foreign and domestic problems that arose in rapid succession after the outbreak of war in Europe in 1914. In so doing they sketched a portrait of a wartime leader that was both tragic and sympathetic, but by no means uncritical.

Unlike the revisionists of the 1930's or the realists of the 1950's — both of whom wrote under the assumption that Wilson had considerable freedom in determining the nation's foreign policies — these more recent historians have emphasized the complexity of events following 1914. The third selection in this chapter is from Arthur S. Link's *Wilson the Diplomatist,* which were delivered as the Albert Shaw lectures at the Johns Hopkins University in 1956. Link's writings on this problem represent one of the best examples of this recent trend in historiography. Having spent over twenty years working on a multi-volumed biography of Wilson, Link had mastered virtually every important source bearing on the period from 1914 to 1917.

The picture of Wilsonian diplomacy that Link drew was anything but simple. He pointed to the many factors with which the President had to contend: the desire of most Americans to remain neutral; the pressure for continued trade, particularly with the Allies; the existence of pacifist, interventionist, and preparedness groups; the growing restrictiveness of the British maritime system; and the challenges posed by German submarine policy. Added to these problems was the fact that Wilson ardently desired to act as a mediator between the warring European powers in order to bring about a just peace. To Link, Wilson was not as simple a figure as he had been presented by the revisionists or realists. On the contrary, Wilson was a complex individual who combined both idealistic and realistic traits. Given the circumstances that he faced and the numerous pressures that were piled upon him, Link implied that Wilson had far less freedom than had been supposed in determining the course of events. Many of the major decisions were beyond his control and were made by the English and German leaders. The result was that by the spring of 1917, according to Link, Wilson reached the tragic conclusion that the United States had no alternative but to intervene once the Germans had decided to sink all vessels bound for Allied ports.

Several other historians have also argued that the range of choices open to Wilson was limited from the very beginning and that as time went on the available alternatives grew fewer and fewer. Considering that neither the Allies nor the Central Powers were willing to accept a peace without victory in 1917 and that the Germans believed that unrestricted submarine warfare could defeat the Allies before American aid became effective, Wilson had to accept either the sinking of American ships and the loss of American lives or else defend his nation's rights. Reviewing the history of this period, Ernest R. May, a Harvard historian, wrote in the late 1950's: "one has a sense that it could not have ended otherwise. . . . There was no way out. Triumph for the immoderates was only a matter of time. . . . Despite its tragic ending, the struggle [for peace] was heroic." [4]

In surveying the extensive literature covering America's entry into World War I, one is struck by the fact that the attitude taken by different generations toward war itself has played a significant role in determining the approach scholars have adopted in evaluating Wilson's diplomacy. The revisionists in the 1930's were con-

4. Ernest R. May, *The World War and American Isolation 1914–1917* (Cambridge, 1959), p. 437.

vinced that the United States had little to gain by foreign entanglements; thus, they tended to project their beliefs back to the period from 1914 to 1917. War was the great enemy of progress, and in their eyes Wilson was either a dupe at best or part of an evil conspiracy. The realists of the 1950's, on the other hand, felt that war and the use of force was an integral part of the prevailing international system. Their criticism of Wilson, therefore, was not that he took the nation into war, but that he did not make clear why the national interests of the United States required this action. Even recent historians like Arthur S. Link and Ernest R. May have looked upon war as part of the tragic human condition; they emphasized the limitations of political leaders in dealing with international problems.

As long as Americans continue to debate the proper role of their nation in world affairs, the events from 1914 to 1917 will continue to hold great interest for historians. In studying this problem, historians will continue to raise many of the same questions that their predecessors asked for nearly a half century. Should the United States have gone to war in 1917? Was America's national interest vitally threatened by Germany? Did American involvement arise out of its unneutral policy, its misguided sentimentalism and utopianism, and its desire to maintain the integrity of the Atlantic Community, or was its true interest to preserve the balance of power in Europe? These remain, in one form or another, the questions that will continue to be the object of future debate.

Harry Elmer Barnes

THE UNITED STATES could not have been more perfectly set up for neutrality than it was in July and August, 1914. President Woodrow Wilson was a lifelong and deeply conscientious pacifist. His convictions in this matter were not emotional or impressionistic, but had been based upon deep study and prolonged reflection. Moreover, he was married to a woman noted for pacific sentiments and firm convictions on such matters. She strongly backed up her husband in his pacific beliefs and policies. As Secretary of State, we had in William Jennings Bryan the world's outstanding pacifist. His pacifism was notably courageous; he was willing to stick by his guns even in the face of malicious criticism.

Moreover, Wilson was almost uniquely well informed as to the essentials of the European situation before war broke out in the summer of 1914. He had sent his personal representative, Colonel Edward M. House, to Europe to study the international situation and to report to him upon it. Whatever his later mistakes, Colonel House sized up matters in Europe with almost perfect sagacity and understanding in May, 1914. He concluded his observations with the statement that "whenever England consents, France and Russia will close in on Germany."

If one were to summarize, as briefly as this, the outcome of the years of scholarly study since 1918, with respect to responsibility for the World War, a more perfect estimate and verdict than Colonel House's phrase could not be rendered in the same number of words. Further, the Colonel pointed out that, whatever the Kaiser's emotional shortcomings, he wished for European peace.

"The World War of 1914–1918," in Willard Waller, ed., *War in the Twentieth Century* (New York: The Dryden Press, 1940), pp. 71–82, 96–98. Reprinted by permission of Harry Elmer Barnes.

HARRY ELMER BARNES (1889–) taught at Clark University, Smith College, and the New School for Social Research. He is the author of more than a dozen books in history and sociology and is also considered to be the father of World War I and World War II historical revisionism.

On the other hand, he stated candidly that George V of England was "the most pugnacious monarch loose in these parts."

When war broke out, President Wilson's statements were a model of neutral procedure. He issued a formally correct neutrality proclamation and went on to exhort his countrymen to be neutral in thought as well as in action. There is no doubt that he was completely neutral at heart in August, 1914. Less than three years later, however, in April, 1917, he went before Congress and told its members that "God helping her," this country could do no other than make war on Germany. Moreover, he returned from the Capitol to the White House and made statements to his secretary, Joseph P. Tumulty, indicating that, at the time of his war message, he had so far changed his attitude that he could not believe he ever had been neutral. He cited with approval an article by the correspondent of the *Manchester Guardian* stating that Mr. Wilson had always been sympathetic with the Allies and had wished to throw this country into war on their side just as soon as circumstances would permit.

We shall first briefly consider some of the reasons why Wilson altered his point of view, since no other set of circumstances could alone have forced us into the war, if Wilson had not been favorable to our entry by the spring of 1917.

First and foremost, we must take into account the fact that Wilson's intellectual perspective was predominantly Anglo-Saxon. He had little knowledge of, or sympathy with, continental European culture and institutions. His great intellectual heroes were such English writers as John Milton, John Locke, Adam Smith and Walter Bagehot. He did his graduate work in the Johns Hopkins University Seminar under Herbert Baxter Adams, where the "Anglo-Saxon Myth" reigned supreme. Wilson was a persistent student and admirer of the English constitution and frankly regarded the British system of government as superior to our own.

Then Wilson had in his cabinet and among his ambassadors men who were intensely pro-English or pro-Ally in their sympathies. Such were Secretaries Lindley M. Garrison and David F. Houston. Walter Hines Page, our ambassador in London, was even more intensely pro-English than Wilson. Indeed, he frequently went to such excesses as to annoy the President. When Bryan was succeeded by Robert Lansing, the most crucial post in the cabinet went to another vehemently pro-English sympathizer. The biases of Page and Lansing made it difficult to pursue forthright diplomacy with Great Britain.

Another major difficulty lay in the fact that President Wilson and Secretary Lansing did not formulate and execute a fair and consistent line of diplomatic procedure. They had one type of international law for England and the Allies, and quite another for Germany. They all but allowed Great Britain to run wild in the violation of international law and of our neutral rights, while they insisted on holding Germany "to strict accountability."

England started out in 1914 by making a scrap of paper out of the Declaration of London governing contraband in wartime. Next, we proceeded to allow her to make use of armed belligerent merchantmen as if they were peaceful commercial vessels. England violated our neutral rights far more extensively between 1914 and 1917 than she did before the War of 1812, even to the point of flying the American flag.

Wilson came to believe, however, that Great Britain was fighting for civilization and that so trivial a thing as international law must not be allowed to stand in her way. Wilson's Attorney-General, Thomas W. Gregory, tells of the rebuke which the President administered to certain cabinet members when they protested over the flagrant British violation of our neutral rights: "After patiently listening, Mr. Wilson said, in that quiet way of his, that the ordinary rules of conduct had no application to the situation; that the Allies were standing with their backs to the wall, fighting wild beasts; that he would permit nothing to be done by our country to hinder or embarrass them in the prosecution of the war unless admitted rights were grossly violated, and that this policy must be understood as settled." Bryan protested against our unfair and unneutral diplomacy and ultimately resigned because he could not square his conscience with it.

Secretary Lansing admits in his *Memoirs* that he made no real pretense of holding England to the tenets of international law. He tells us that after the sinking of the *Lusitania* he thought we should be fighting on the side of the Allies and that he was determined to do nothing which would prove embarrassing to us when we later took up our position as a military comrade of the Allied powers. He persisted in this attitude, even though he was honest enough to write after the war that in 1917 we had as good, if not better, legal grounds for fighting Britain as for fighting Germany.

Ambassador Page even went so far as to collaborate with Sir Edward Grey in answering the protests of his own government, an unparalleled procedure which, when revealed, outraged even so pro-Ally a journal as the *New York Times*.

We thus encouraged and perpetuated the illegally extensive British blockade, which provoked the German submarine warfare. In time, we made war on the latter, though it was our unneutral diplomacy which contributed, in large part, to the continuance of both the British blockade and the German submarine activities.

Wilson was deeply affected by the criticisms to which he was subjected by prominent Americans sympathetic with the Allies and in favor of intervention on their side. He was stung by the famous speeches of Theodore Roosevelt on "The Shadows of Shadow Lawn," and by the latter's reference to Wilson's diplomatic statements as examples of "weasel words." He was particularly annoyed by the statement of Elihu Root that "first he shakes his fist and then he shakes his finger."

On the other hand, Wilson was human enough to take note of the praise which was showered upon him by the press when he made a bellicose statement or led a preparedness parade. This contrasted sharply with the bitter criticism he evoked when he made a statesmanlike remark, such as that a country might be "too proud to fight," or that the only desirable peace would be "a peace without victory."

Wilson was also profoundly moved by the British propaganda relative to German atrocities and territorial ambitions. This was particularly true after Lord Bryce lent his name to the prestige and veracity of the propaganda stories as to German savagery. Of all living Englishmen, Bryce was probably the man whom Wilson most admired and trusted. When Bryce sponsored the propaganda lies, Wilson came to believe that they must have a substantial basis in fact. This helped on his rationalization that England was fighting the battle of human civilization against wild beasts.

Personal matters also played their rôle in the transformation of Wilson's attitude. His first wife died and a strong pacific influence was removed. He then courted and married a dashing widow who was sympathetic with the Allied side and friendly with Washington military and naval circles. She was also bitterly resentful of the criticism to which Wilson was subjected on account of his refusal to be stampeded into intervention. She appears to have wished him to take a stronger stand for intervention. The domestic influence on the President was, thus, completely transformed in character as a result of his second marriage. The publication of Mrs. Wilson's *Memoirs* does not make it necessary to modify this statement.

When, as an outcome of these various influences, Wilson had been converted to intervention, he rationalized his change of attitude on the basis of a noble moral purpose. As he told Jane Addams in the spring of 1917, he felt that the United States must be represented at the peace conference which would end the World War if there was to be any hope of a just and constructive peace. But Wilson could be at the peace conference only if the United States had previously entered the World War.

It is still asserted by many writers, such as Professor Charles Seymour, that the resumption of submarine warfare by Germany was the sole reason for Wilson's determination to enter the war on the Allied side. But we know that he had been converted to intervention long before January, 1917. A year earlier, he had sent Colonel House to Europe with a plan to put us in the war on the side of the Allies if Germany would not accept peace terms obviously unfavorable to her. But even such peace terms for Germany were rejected by the British leaders who felt sure of American aid anyway and were determined to crush Germany. Yet this British rebuff did not lead Wilson to lose heart in his efforts to put this country into the war.

His next step was taken in this country. Early in April, 1916, Wilson called into consultation Speaker Champ Clark of the House of Representatives and Congressional leaders Claude Kitchin and H. D. Flood, and sounded them out to see if they would support him in a plan to bring the United States into the war on the side of the Allies. This was the famous "Sunrise Conference" described later by Gilson Gardner in *McNaught's Monthly* of June, 1925. These men sharply refused to sanction any such policy, and Wilson allowed the campaign of 1916 to be fought out on the slogan, "He kept us out of war." Wilson did not dare to risk splitting the Democratic Party over entry into the war before the campaign of 1916 had successfully ended. The existence of the "Sunrise Conference" has been fully verified by Professor A. M. Arnett in his scholarly book on Claude Kitchin.

Wilson was convinced after the failure of the "Sunrise Conference" that there was no hope of getting the country into war until after the election. The sentiment of the nation was for peace. If he was elected as an exponent of peace and then went into war the country as a whole would believe that he had done his best to "keep us out of war." He would have a united country behind him. Hence, he and Colonel House sent Governor Martin Glynn of New York and Senator Ollie James of Kentucky to the Democratic National Convention at St. Louis, in June, 1916, with instructions to make keynote speeches emphasizing Wilson's heroic efforts to keep us out of war.

Thus was fashioned the famous slogan "He kept us out of war," which re-elected Woodrow Wilson to the presidency almost a year after Colonel House, following Wilson's directions, had declared that: "The United States would like Great Britain to do whatever would help the United States to aid the Allies."

The campaign and election of 1916 were very really a referendum on war, and the people voted against war. This is illuminating as an illustration of the fallacy that a war referendum, such as the Ludlow Amendment, would, by itself alone, suffice to keep us out of war, but the election of 1916 does offer definite proof that Wilson was not pushed into war by popular demand.

The influence exerted by American finance upon our entry into the World War has been revealed in Ray Stannard Baker's *Life and Letters of Woodrow Wilson,* in the volumes of the Nye armament investigation, and in Professor C. C. Tansill's *America Goes to War.*

At the outset, the international bankers were not by any means all pro-Ally. Some, like the Morgan firm, were pro-British, and had been for years, while others, like Kuhn, Loeb and Company, manned chiefly by men of German derivation, were pro-German. But the financial interests of all the bankers soon came to be pro-Ally, for credit and loans to Germany were discouraged, while large loans were presently being made to the Allied powers.

On August 15, 1914, at the beginning of the war, Bryan declared against loans to any belligerent, on the ground that credit is the basis of all forms of contraband. President Wilson backed him up. For the time being, this position did not operate seriously against the Allies, for the balance of trade and investment was against the United States, and the Allied countries could pay for their purchases by cancelling the debts owed abroad by Americans. This situation took care of matters for a few months. But Allied war purchases became so great that, by the autumn of 1914, there was a credit crisis. The National City Bank addressed Robert Lansing, then Counsellor of the State Department, on this matter on October 23, 1914. Short-term credits to European governments were advocated. Lansing talked the matter over with President Wilson at once, and the latter agreed that the government would not interfere with such an arrangement. This information was transmitted orally to Willard Straight of J. P. Morgan & Company at the Metropolitan Club in Washington on the same night.

Shortly afterwards, H. P. Davison of the Morgan firm went to England and signed a contract to become the British purchasing agent in America. A similar contract was soon made with France.

The short-term loans sufficed for some months, but by the summer of 1915 Allied buying had become so extensive that the bankers saw that they must float loans here for the Allied countries if the latter were to continue to buy American munitions on a large scale. So they made strong representations to Colonel House and to the Secretary of the Treasury, W. G. McAdoo.

On August 21, 1915, McAdoo wrote a long letter to President Wilson, pointing out that great prosperity had come to the country as a result of the sale of munitions to the Allies, but that this prosperity could not continue unless we financed it through open loans to the Allies – i.e. selling Allied bonds in our own financial markets.

On September 6, 1915, Secretary Lansing argued similarly in a letter to President Wilson, stressing the crisis that faced American business if the earlier ruling of Bryan and the President on American loans to belligerents was not rescinded. Colonel House supported this position. McAdoo and Lansing won their point. On September 8, 1915, Wilson assented to loans and the Morgan firm was once more given oral information. Very soon, the first public loan, the $500,000,000 Anglo-French loan, was floated.

The formal loans to the Allies – over $2,500,000,000 in all – financed their purchases for a little over a year, but their buying was so heavy that even the great investment banking houses could not take care of their needs. By January, 1917, the Allies had overdrawn their credit by nearly $500,000,000. Only Uncle Sam could save the great banking houses and the Allies. And Uncle Sam could help only if the United States were at war with Germany. We could not, as a government, lend money to a belligerent, unless we were at war with its enemy.

Just at this time the Germans renewed their unrestricted submarine warfare. The United States could now be led into the war, and the bankers would be repaid. They were repaid to the last cent. When the war was over, Mr. Thomas W. Lamont, of J. P. Morgan and Company, stated the facts relative to the attitude of his firm toward the World War and the belligerent powers:

> At the request of certain of the foreign governments the firm of Messrs. J. P. Morgan and Company undertook to co-ordinate the requirements of the Allies, and then to bring about regularity and promptness in fulfilling these requirements. Those were the days when American citizens were being urged to remain neutral in action, in word, and even in thought. But our firm had never for one moment been neutral: we didn't know how to be. From the very start we did everything we could to contribute to the cause of the Allies. And this particular work had two effects: one in assisting the Allies in the production of goods and munitions in America necessary to the Allies' vigorous prosecution of the war; the other in helping to develop the great and profitable export trade that our country has had.

Most American industrialists naturally shared the attitude of the bankers. Since England controlled the seas, our sales were mainly to the Allied powers. We wished to see the Allies continue the war and win it. Upon their purchases depended most of our sales and prosperity, and upon their success and solvency depended the prospect of their being able to pay us in the end. The trade in munitions carried us from a depression in 1914 to boom years in 1915 and 1916.

By abandoning his neutral financial and industrial policy in favor of the Allies, President Wilson made it possible for the Entente Powers to enjoy an enormous advantage over the Central Powers in getting war supplies. The only way for the Central

Powers to overcome it was to resume unlimited submarine warfare and try to sweep from the seas the ships that were carrying these supplies to the Allies.

It was our unneutral financing of the Allies that led to the resumption of German submarine warfare, and it was the resumption of this warfare which furnished the "incident" that enabled the war party in this country to put us into the conflict. It is, thus, perfectly clear that economic and financial pressure was the crucial factor which led us into war in 1917.

But no one need hold that President Wilson was moved primarily by any tender sentiments for the bankers. Both McAdoo and Lansing argued that it was essential to American prosperity to finance the Allies.

It was this general consideration of continued prosperity in 1915–16, and the relation of this to the prospects of the Democratic Party in the election of 1916, rather than any direct banker pressure on the White House, that bore in on Wilson's consciousness in the late summer of 1915, when he let down the gates to financing the Allies.

Yet, it is downright silly to contend that the bankers had no influence on Wilson's policy. If he did not listen to the bankers himself, he did listen very attentively to those who did heed banker pressure, namely, McAdoo, Lansing and House.

The active campaign for American preparedness and intervention was engineered by leaders of the war cult in the United States, such men as Theodore Roosevelt, Leonard Wood, Henry Cabot Lodge, "Gus" Gardiner, and the like. They led in the preparedness movement, the Plattsburg camp episode, and other steps designed to stimulate the martial spirit in America. The newspapers warmly supported this movement because of the circulation appeal which preparedness material supplied.

While there were notable exceptions, the majority of our newspapers were pro-Ally and pro-interventionist. Many of them were honestly sympathetic with the Allies. Others were deeply influenced by Allied propaganda. Some were heavily subsidized by the Allies. Still others were bought outright by Allied interests. Moreover, the Allies supplied all American newspapers with a vast amount of war-news material always favorable to the Allied cause. The newspapers also had a natural affinity for the bankers and industrialists who were their chief advertising clients. Finally, the newspapers were not unaware of the enormous circulation gains and increased advertising revenue which would follow our entry into the World War.

In the matter of propaganda the Allies had a notable advantage. They controlled the seas, the cables, and other means of communication. The Germans had only one crude and temporary wireless contact with the United States. Further, Allied propaganda was far better organized and more lavishly supported. It was also much more adroit than the German. As a result, a majority of Americans were led to believe in the veracity of the great batch of atrocity lies relative to the German invasion of Belgium, submarine warfare, and the like. This was particularly true after Lord Bryce put the force of his name and prestige behind the authenticity of such tales. Lord Northcliffe, who was in charge of British propaganda, in moments of unusual candor, stated that the Americans proved more gullible in such matters than any other people except the Chinese and called us "a bunch of sheep."

The ministers of the gospel also joined heartily in the great crusade to put us into the World War. Lining up behind such a stalwart as Newell Dwight Hillis, they preached a veritable holy war. They represented the Allies as divinely-anointed promoters of international decency and justice and the Central Powers as the servants of evil and the agents of savagery.

The net result of all this was that we entered the World War in April, 1917. We did so, even though there was no clear legal or moral basis for our so doing. If there ever was an instance in which the facts were clearly in accord with a neutrality policy it was in the spring of 1917. We should have fought both Germany and Britain or else neither. But the country went into war, with most of the citizens of the United States feeling that our self-respect and national honor demanded it. No other course seemed open to us. . . .

It was generally believed in 1917 and thereafter that the intervention of the United States in the World War on the side of the Allies saved human civilization. It was lauded as one of the most noble and fortunate episodes in the history of man on the planet. Today, there is a great deal of skepticism about any such judgment. There is a tendency now to see in American intervention one of the major calamities in modern history — a calamity for the Allies and the United States as well as for the Central Powers.

Let us assume the worst possible result of American neutrality in 1917–18. If we had not gone into the war the worst imaginable result would have been a German victory. But no sane person can very well conceive that the world would be any worse off today if the Germans had won under the Hohenzollerns.

We used to picture the horrors of a Germany and a Europe dominated by the Crown Prince and his followers. But, compared to Hitler, Mussolini and Company, the Crown Prince and his crowd now appears to be cultivated gentlemen, urbane democrats, and sincere pacifists. A more warlike world than the present could hardly have been created as a result of German victory, and certainly the economic situation in Europe since 1918 would have been far better under a Europe dominated by monarchist Germany.

But there is hardly a remote possibility that Germany would have won the war, even if the United States had not come in on the side of the Allies. Germany was eager to negotiate a fair peace arrangement at the time when Lloyd George's "knock-out victory" interview with Roy Howard put an end to all prospect of successful negotiations. We now know that the Lloyd George outburst was directly caused by his assurance that the United States was surely coming in on the side of the Allies. Had Wilson remained strictly neutral, there is little doubt that sincere peace negotiations would have been actively carried on by the summer of 1916.

There is every reason to believe that the result of American neutrality throughout the European conflict would have been the "peace without victory," which Woodrow Wilson described in his most statesmanlike pronouncement during the period of the World War. We would have had a negotiated peace treaty made by relative equals. This would not have been a perfect document but it would certainly have been far superior to the Treaty of Versailles.

Had we remained resolutely neutral from the beginning, the negotiated peace would probably have saved the world from the last two terrible years of war. Whenever it came, it would have rendered unnecessary the brutal blockade of Germany for months after the World War, a blockade which starved to death hundreds of thousands of German women and children. This blockade was the one great authentic atrocity of the World War period. In all probability, the neutrality of the United States would also have made impossible the rise of Mussolini and Hitler – products of post-war disintegration – and the coming of a second world war.

Not only was our entry into the World War a calamity of the first magnitude for Europe and contemporary civilization, it was also a serious disaster for the United States.

During the first Wilson administration an impressive program of social reform had been introduced, widely known as "The New Freedom." Had this continued until March, 1921, enormous and permanent improvements might have been made in the political and economic system of the United States. But when Wilson allowed himself to be slowly but surely pushed into war, the New Freedom perished overnight. Reaction and intolerance settled down on the country. Some of those who had earlier warmly supported Wilson's domestic policies were thrown into prison, and many others were bitterly persecuted.

The myth of a German menace and the crusading sanctity of the Allies was exploded by Wilson himself shortly before his death. On December 7, 1923, he told his friend James Kerney: "I should like to see Germany clean up France, and I should like to see Jusserand and tell him so to his face."

Walter Millis

THE CURRENT debate upon the question of how the United States is to avoid entanglement in the next war should naturally begin with the problem of how, in fact, we got into the last one. In confronting the future, the first guide is the experience of the past. As such, the experience of 1914–1917 has the defects of most historical experience. It is confused and baffling in the extreme. The deceptive simplicity of the facts conceals a matted jungle of motives, of conflicting economic and psychological influences, of unstated assumptions as to the proper bases of national action or the nature of the social process. Even to traverse this jungle to any purpose it is necessary first to agree upon certain fixed-datum points, concerning which there is today no agreement; to establish the "cause" of the American declaration of war in April 1917, one must solve an equation in innumerable variables, although there is as yet no consensus as to the values that should properly be attached to any of them.

It is not difficult to describe what happened. When the European complex exploded in August 1914, the shock to the American economy was almost as violent as that to the American emotions. The situation was in both respects something with which American opinion and American statesmanship were utterly unprepared to deal. The government issued its formal proclamation of neutrality and consigned the problems of our practical relationship with the warring powers to the uncertain and contradictory principles of international law. The more influential and more vocal elements of public opinion took refuge in an attitude of hostility towards the

"How We Entered the Last One," *The New Republic,* LXXXIII (July 31, 1935), 323–27.

WALTER MILLIS (1899–) spent many years working as a journalist. At present he is a staff director at the Fund for the Republic. He also is the author of more than half a dozen books, including *The Martial Spirit* (1931), *Road to War* (1935), and *Arms and Men* (1956).

Central Powers — as reactionary, autocratic governments that had willed the war in the hope of achieving world hegemony — and of sympathy for the Entente as the defenders of ideals and political institutions similar to our own against a brutal and unwarranted aggression. If the government, however, was willing to leave the future to international law, this majority opinion was no less willing to leave it to the Allies. There were very few, in or out of the government, who either grasped the possibility that the United States might be involuntarily entangled or saw any reasons of national interest that might compel us to become a participant. The United States proposed to take up the role of interested spectator.

Immediately, however, as one writer has recently put it, "the truism that the world is economically interdependent became grimly apparent." It did not appear, it is important to note, in the form of a question as to whether the United States should retreat into a prudent isolation until the storm had passed. We found ourselves isolated with a devastating abruptness. European selling forced the New York Stock Exchange to close on July 31, 1914, and it dared not reopen until December. Practically the whole of our trans-Atlantic commerce came to a standstill; and if the two belligerents had been equally able to interfere with each other's trade, we might have found ourselves cut off for an indefinite time from all our more important foreign markets. Germany's geographical disadvantage and the overwhelming superiority of the British navy combined to prevent this; the seas were soon reopened, but not to commerce with the Central Powers. Cotton, one of our two great export crops, of which Germany was a heavy taker, could not be sold, and the South was brought to the verge of ruin. At the same time, the normal trade with the Entente countries was, of course, seriously dislocated; and the late summer and fall of 1914 saw our already somewhat depressed economy sinking towards prostration.

The first economic problem presented by the war, consequently, was not one of eschewing the excess profits of death; it was one of regaining some of the ordinary profits of peace. The unemployed, who were filling the streets in the latter part of 1914, had to be provided for no less than the stockholders. Two methods presented themselves. The State Department devoted itself to reopening, so far as possible, the normal channels of trade with the civil population of the Central Powers. The businessmen, and subsequently the bankers, turned with a greater realism to develop from the war needs of the Entente a substitute for the markets of which they had been deprived in Germany and Austria.

The State Department's attempt to obtain the adoption of the Declaration of London was essentially an attempt to confine the savage violence of the European War within the gentlemanly limits which the Great Powers had in the past been able to impose upon such private quarrels as that between Russia and Japan in 1904. While the armies fought, the normal business of the world would be conducted as usual. The attempt promptly failed, partly because our diplomatists had no conception of the pressures they would have had to apply if it was to succeed; but the department continued to work to the same end by insisting upon strict construction of the elaborate precedents concerning blockade and contraband, which are supposed to establish the rights of neutrals in time of war. It was continuously baffled, both by the elusive and frequently inapplicable nature of the precedents and by the practical fact that the British navy possessed the physical power to enforce its own interpretation of them.

Upon this solid basis of sea power, the Allies had, by the beginning of 1915, erected an intricate structure of controls over American foreign commerce. It amounted to a practically complete blockade of our direct trade to and from the Central Powers and a hardly less complete interdiction upon trade by way of the European neutrals. Many of these controls were indirect, maintained by threats and promises rather than by official action, and policed by the "voluntary" undertakings of American businessmen themselves. It is difficult to say that any of the main features of this system were flatly "illegal," although the British were hard put to it to defend a number of important details from the bitter protests launched against them by the State Department. Whether the controls were legal or illegal, however, it is possible that the United States could have compelled their relaxation had it applied economic pressure or the threat of war; it is certain that, given the preponderant naval power of the Entente, it could have kept the seas more or less open in no other way.

Such pressures, however, were never seriously applied. Here

was the first important consequence of the fact that the majority sentiment of the country had not actually been neutral from the outbreak of the war. The President, his more influential advisers, all the important people in the foreign service (except Secretary Bryan), shared the hostility toward Germany and the sympathy for the Entente that filled every leading newspaper and the after-dinner speeches of most public figures. These sentiments were now being powerfully reinforced by the Entente propaganda; they were likewise being reinforced in another way. American business had turned to solve the problems of war depression by seeking war markets in the Entente. By the end of 1914 it was beginning to find them. The United States started out to supply the Entente because the Entente markets alone were open and because the United States badly needed business. But as the war demand rapidly developed (after the end of the 1914 campaign had revealed to the belligerents the colossal material requirements of the new warfare), it began to be realized that the United States had stumbled upon a gold mine. The Allies' power to offer or withhold these stupendous contracts became one of their most useful instruments in organizing American enterprise to enforce the boycott of Germany while serving the needs of the Entente. The contracts themselves, needless to say, intensified the emotional fervor of all the leading elements of the community for the Entente cause; just as the original sympathy for the Entente had facilitated the development of the war-supply business.

For the State Department to exert any serious pressure upon the Allies in order to keep open some trade with Germany early became a political, a psychological and an economic impossibility; while the unexpected, seemingly miraculous, appearance of the huge war-supply business removed the original economic motive for such an attempt. Many different and intricately interrelated factors (not all of which need by any means operate in the same way in the event of another foreign war) had combined to produce this result, almost accidentally. Not because of any conscious policy — rather indeed because of the lack of any sufficiently conscious policy — the United States had become a chief source of supply for one side in a life-and-death struggle, at the same time acquiescing in the complete exclusion of the other side from her markets.

The other side inevitably sought for some means of reacting

against this situation; and in the spring of 1915 a means was discovered. Here again there is an accidental element in the sequence of events. Had the Germans earlier developed the submarine as a commerce destroyer, it is possible that our economic alliance with the Entente would not have become established as it did; if, on the other hand, they had waited to perfect the weapon before resorting to it, American policy might more clearly have recognized its importance and adjusted itself to the new factor. From the American point of view, the German declaration of the submarine war zone in February 1915 came at just the wrong time. It was too late then to revert to the original policy of forcing open the seas for commerce with the civil populations of the belligerents; it was too early to realize the immense strategic value of the new weapon. President Wilson summarily ordered the Germans not to use their submarines as they proposed to do against the American traffic with the Allies. Only later was he to perceive the difficulty of enforcing such an order.

This refusal to accept, or at the least to discuss, the German theory of a maritime war zone must be ascribed in part to the personal temperament of Mr. Wilson, a strong moralist who was at bottom emotionally enlisted on the side of the Allies; in part to the similar temper of the public; in part to the resultant political considerations that made it difficult for any official to seem to favor Germany; in part to Allied propaganda, which discounted the submarines as strategically ridiculous. Though the Germans had a legal case for this use of the submarine, it was, at any rate on the surface, a much weaker one than the Allies' case for their blockade measures; it challenged the conventional ideas of national right in a much more dramatic way, while the whole issue was of course profoundly obscured in the fogs of passion that had accumulated. Had the proposed war zone ever been seriously discussed, economic considerations must likewise have come into play, for it would have been obvious that the United States could not appear to sanction a free war upon a trade that promised the one means of escape from a serious depression. Actually, few seem to have supposed that the submarines could materially affect our exports, and the issue was met upon a more emotional plane. The President did not attempt to defend the great bulk of the war-supply business that was carried under foreign flags. He did commit himself irrevocably to the demand that the Germans desist from the destruction either of American-flag ships or the lives of American citizens on the high seas.

A war situation had thus been prepared, for ultimately there was no peaceful issue from this demand except acquiescence by Germany or its withdrawal by the United States. A war situation does not, of course, inevitably produce a war; accident, however, was again to play a part in intensifying the crisis. The submarine campaign might have developed gradually, in a slow crescendo of incidents, permitting both statesmanship and opinion to work out some peaceful adjustment to the problem. Instead, from February until May the campaign proceeded almost unnoticed, confirming the view that the whole matter was of small consequence, only to explode on May 7, with the torpedoing of the *Lusitania,* in an incident so shocking and so unexpected as to render any dispassionate treatment of the broad question very nearly impossible. The *Lusitania* did not bring the United States into the War; it did not even convince any decisive majority of the American people that war was desirable. It did have the important psychological effect of surrounding the President's position on the submarine campaign with an intense emotional field which added to the natural difficulties of retreat and constantly impeded any attempt to remove the war danger that had been created.

The war propaganda continued to operate to bring the public mind to a point at which it would support, if not clamor for, participation in the conflict. The preparedness agitation — in which patriotism seems so inextricably interwoven with less attractive motives that it is now useless even to try to disentangle them — undoubtedly contributed to the same end. The original sympathy with the Entente had been refined and deepened, through the operation of many factors, into an influential belief that permanent world peace might be erected upon an Entente victory; and this supplied a high and impressive reason for bringing the United States into the struggle to assure the victory and participate in the peace system. The growing dependence of our domestic prosperity upon the Entente war orders exerted its far-reaching, if perhaps somewhat subtle, influence. The more closely we became a partner of the Entente, the more genuine a menace, both politically and economically, did the prospect of German victory become. If at any time the Entente had actually seemed to be on the verge of defeat, the economic factor might have appeared more plainly as a positive force driving us into the war; as it was, its influence was rather the negative one of hindering any attempt to restore the country to a position of more genuine neutrality. The actual declaration was precipitated in another way; and in spite of all these forces working in the direction of our entanglement, it is still not inconceivable that the United States might have remained technically at peace.

It is fair to say that in one sense the United States had entered the European War by the middle of 1915. We were an intimate part of the war complex. Our economic power was wholly enlisted upon one side, and we were no longer neutral either in sentiment or in policy. Even so, a military participation, though likely, was hardly inevitable. In considering a future war there is the question of whether the development of this kind of one-sided relationship to the struggle can be avoided; but there is also the narrower question of whether, once it was established, an astute statesmanship might not still manage to retain a legal neutrality.

What actually effected the transition from legal neutrality to practical belligerence in 1917 was the war situation, prepared by Mr. Wilson with his first stand on the submarine and set, as it were, by the emotional shock of the *Lusitania*. The President was able to postpone the crisis for some two years by forcing upon the Germans a long series of compromises and partial surrenders. Although the submarines managed to torpedo many vessels and kill a considerable number of American citizens in the course of this correspondence, the Germans never forced the President to abandon his fundamental position. From the *Lusitania* crisis until the declaration of unrestricted submarine warfare on February 1, 1917, Mr. Wilson emerged substantially successful from each incident that arose. It was in this way that he avoided war. But each success only made a subsequent retreat more difficult for him; as time went on he became more and more the prisoner of his own victories.

The final victory came in May 1916, when to surmount the *Sussex* crisis he compelled the Germans to agree formally to use their submarines only in accordance with the rules of visit and search. In doing so, however, he posed an issue of American rights upon the high seas in such a form that there was no possible future escape from it. This would have been a satisfactory method of keeping us out of war had Mr. Wilson possessed any threat powerful enough to compel the Germans to live up to the engagement. Unfortunately, he did not; for it requires a very powerful threat indeed to compel a power fighting for its life to leave untouched a weapon it believes to be the key to victory. In January 1917, the Germans took it up again. They had done what the President had declared would be a *casus belli,* and what every shade of influential opinion, including his political opponents as well as many of his supporters, had agreed with him would be a *casus belli.* President Wilson found himself almost automatically at war.

This, in brief, is more or less what actually happened. Yet to recount it leaves one with a sense of dissatisfaction. Even at the time the specific issue of the right of certain American citizens to travel through a war zone seemed inadequate to explain why the people of the United States should be going down into the most frightful and most exhausting war in history. Many of those who urged us on at the time (including the President) were careful to explain that it was not really because of the ship question that we should take up the sword—but in the interests of peace and civilization, or the Monroe Doctrine or international law. Since then, many quite different reasons have been advanced to resolve the conundrum that unquestionably remains. Why did not the United States modify its position on the submarine when the issue was presented with the Gore-McLemore resolutions in February 1916? We might have warned Americans not to travel in the war zone, left the question of ship sinkings to post-war adjudication (as we left the questions of Entente interference with our cargoes) and allowed the belligerents to decide the issue of the sea war themselves. Why did Mr. Wilson in February 1917, at once break off diplomatic relations instead of accepting the German action and making the best of it? Why did Congress pass the war resolution, when there was no passionate demand for war in the country and when many of the members themselves probably preferred not to?

For the answer it is necessary to seek among the factors that have already been mentioned – the propaganda, the economic relationships, the personalities of statesmen, the exigencies of domestic politics, the fears and hatreds (whether well founded or not) of German imperialism, the altruistic dreams of world peace. These, however, are all elusive and insubstantial quantities, one shading into another in a baffling fashion and each presenting, when the attempt is made to isolate it as the primarily significant factor, certain difficulties. The influence of "Allied propaganda" for instance is today very generally misconceived. The effective propaganda for the Entente cause was that generated in the United States and by the Americans; undoubtedly it was powerfully reinforced by the spontaneous outpourings from all sources of Entente opinion, but the conscious use of censorship and official propaganda bureaus hardly did more than give precision and effect to forces that could never have been created in that way.

"The bankers" present a similar difficulty. J. P. Morgan and Company, and the other houses that participated in the Entente financing, appear to have been much more the channels than the generators of the forces they are supposed to have wielded. In the early days they assisted greatly in setting up the machinery that connected the American need for markets with the Entente need for supplies, but they could never themselves have established the tremendous potential they thus helped to discharge. Their machinery at first ran almost entirely upon cash. It was not until the late summer of 1916 that it was necessary to resort to credit upon a significant scale, and by that time domestic prosperity had become so intimately dependent upon the war-supply business that credit must almost certainly have been forthcoming even had the bankers been less eager to supply the facilities. Finally, the private loans floated from that time onward were in general fully secured. The financial crisis that appeared with the beginning of 1917 arose from the fact that the Allies' security was beginning to run out. The point of Mr. Page's famous telegram of March 5, 1917, urging the President to enter the war to save the war-supply business was not that the government should bail out the bankers, but that it should replace them. Here again one must set down the role of the specifically banking interest as at most an indirect one.

One may broaden the charge to cover the whole complex of profit-making business of which the bankers were an essential part.

No doubt the "profit motive," as a generalized concept, may be held responsible for almost anything in a profit-making society. More narrowly, there were quite probably many individual businessmen who perceived that their bread was buttered on the side of belligerency. It is difficult to detect any specific intrigue, however, in which such men selfishly applied pressure to influence the critical decisions of the President or the Congress in regard to the submarine. The profit motive may have helped to get us into a war situation and hindered our attempts to get out, but it did not directly control the transition from formal neutrality to formal belligerence.

There is a similar elusiveness about each of the many other factors that have been cited by one or another commentator as the decisive one. Those who pin the major responsibility upon the vanity and irascibility of President Wilson seldom attempt to explain how another statesman might, in fact, have met the situation as it was abruptly presented to him in February 1917. Those who cling to the wartime view that the United States actually entered the struggle in order to preserve democratic institutions and the freedom of peoples from a German aggression must still meet many metaphysical difficulties in showing why there was so long a delay in taking up the issue, why so many in 1917 refused to accept this as the true issue and why the mass of the population was still hoping that war would be avoided at the moment it was finally declared upon a point that even at the time seemed to be of relatively minor importance.

The facts of the period from 1914 to 1917 are complex enough to support almost any theory of historical causation that one may apply to them, at the same time that they are obstinate enough to resist almost any theory of how the ultimate entanglement could have been prevented. An examination of the facts must remain as an essential foundation of any policy designed to control a similar situation in the future. Yet it is to be suspected that before the facts can be of much use there will have first to be agreement upon many profound issues as to the ends which the control should serve, the proper philosophy of international relations, the real character and objects of the state in the international and domestic complex — issues the very existence of which seems to be scarcely realized as yet by the most of those participating in the current debate. They have so far confined themselves to the problem of how the nation is to avoid entanglement in another foreign war. The far more important question of whether the nation (whatever they may conceive that to mean) will want to avoid entanglement has hardly even been raised.

Arthur S. Link

FOR WOODROW WILSON and the American people, who had a positive disinclination to play the game of power politics, events on the international stage intruded in an ironic if fateful way from 1914 to 1917. By the spring of 1915 the United States was the only great power not directly involved in the war then raging from western Europe to the Far East. Desiring only to deal fairly with both sides and to avoid military involvement, the President soon found that neutrality, as well as war, has its perplexities and perils.

The way in which Wilson met the challenges to America's peace and security raised by the death grapple between the opposing alliances has never been fully explained, notwithstanding scores of books and articles. Too often, historians, in company with public men, have looked for culprits instead of facts. Too often they have misunderstood the facts even when they found them. Too often they have written as if Wilson and his advisers made policy in a vacuum independent of the interplay of conflicting pressures. If we can see the President's policies of neutrality in the light of his convictions and objectives, the pressures and events (both domestic and foreign) that bore constantly upon him, and the alternatives between which he was often forced to choose — if we can do this, then perhaps we will see that his task in foreign policy at this juncture was not as simple as it has sometimes been described.

Among the most pervasive pressures controlling Wilson's decisions throughout the period 1914–1917 were the attitudes and opinions of the American people concerning the war and America's proper relation to it. . . .

The dominant American sentiment throughout the period of nonintervention can be summarily characterized by the single ad-

From Arthur S. Link, *Wilson the Diplomatist* (Baltimore: Johns Hopkins Press, 1957), pp. 31–33, 35–50, 73–74, 76–80, 82, 85–90. Reprinted by permission of the Johns Hopkins University Press.

ARTHUR S. LINK (1920–) is Edwards Professor of American History at Princeton University. He is the author of many books on the Wilsonian era; his major work is a multi-volume biography of Woodrow Wilson.

jective "neutral." This is not to say that Americans had no opinions on the merits of the war and the claims of the opposing alliances, or that there were no differences among the popular reactions. It is simply to state the fairly obvious fact that the preponderant majority, whose opinions played a decisive role in shaping Wilson's policies, did not believe that their interests and security were vitally involved in the outcome of the war and desired to avoid participation if that were possible without sacrificing rights that should not be yielded. The prevalence and astounding vitality of neutralism, in spite of the severest provocations and all the efforts of propagandists on both sides, formed at once the unifying principle of American politics and the compelling reality with which Wilson had to deal from 1914 to 1917.

On the other hand, it would be a large error to imply that Wilson was a prisoner of the public opinion of the majority, and that his will to adopt sterner policies toward one group of belligerents or the other was paralyzed by the stronger counterforce of neutralism. Actually, the evidence points overwhelmingly to the conclusion that Wilson personally shared the opinions of the majority, in brief, that he was substantially neutral in attitude and that his policies were controlled as much by his own convictions as by the obvious wishes of the people. . . .

All authorities, whether friendly or hostile to Wilson, would agree that the acid tests of his neutrality were the policies that he worked out and applied vis-à-vis the British from 1914 to 1917. He has been most condemned by that group of historians highly censorious of his policies, generally known as revisionists, on this score — for becoming the captive of pro-Allied influences within his administration, for condoning such sweeping British control of neutral commerce that the Germans were forced to resort to drastic countermeasures, for permitting American prosperity to become dependent upon loans and exports to the Allies, in short, for permitting a situation to develop that made it inevitable that the United States would go to war if the success of Allied arms was ever seriously threatened.

Like most fallacious arguments, this one contains a certain element of plausibility. Wilson did condone a far-reaching British maritime system. American neutrality did work greatly to the benefit of the Allies. The error arises in saying that these things occurred because Wilson and his advisers necessarily wanted them to occur. . . .

In view of the prevailing American sentiment at the outbreak of the war, a policy of strict official neutrality was the only possible course for the United States government. This fact prompted the President's official proclamations of neutrality, supplemented by his appeal to the American people for impartiality in thought; the subsequent working out by the State Department of the elaborate technical rules to preserve American neutrality; and the establishment of a Joint State and Navy Neutrality Board to advise the various departments upon the correct interpretation of international law.

One cannot read the records revealing how these policies were formulated without being convinced that their authors were high-minded in their determination to be fair to both sides. Indeed, Wilson and the man who chiefly influenced him in the formulation of the rules of neutrality, Secretary of State Bryan, were so intent upon being fair to the Germans that they adopted policies during the first months of the war that were highly disadvantageous to the British, if not unneutral. One was to prevent the sale of submarine parts, and hence parts for any naval craft, by a private American firm to the British government, on the ground that such a sale would be "contrary to . . . strict neutrality." Wilson persisted in supporting Bryan in this matter, in spite of advice from Counselor Lansing and the Joint Neutrality Board to the effect that their position was contrary to international law.

Infinitely more damaging to the Allies was the administration's second effort to lean over backward in being "strictly" neutral — the ban of loans by American bankers to the belligerent governments that the President permitted Bryan to impose in August, 1914. From a technical viewpoint, the ban was not unneutral, but it was highly prejudicial to the Allies because its effect was potentially to deny them their otherwise legal right to purchase supplies in the American market. These two incidents are not to be understood as revealing any anti-British bias on the part of Wilson and Bryan, although British officials at the time were convinced that they did. I mention them only to show what an important role the administration's desire to be impartial played in the formation of policies vis-à-vis the British during the early period of American neutrality.

The other pressure shaping American policies at this time was the force of combined demands at home for the virtually free transit of American ships and goods to the European neutrals and the belligerent Central Powers. So powerful were these demands, especially from cotton growers and exporters and their spokesmen in Congress, that Wilson personally sponsored two measures highly disadvantageous to the British and unneutral in fact as well as in spirit. One was a change in the ship registry law, put into effect by an act approved August 18, 1914, which made it easy for German or other foreign shipping firms to take out American registry for their vessels. The other was a plan to establish a federal corporation to purchase German ships in American ports and to use them to carry supplies to the belligerents, particularly to Germany. Wilson applied heavy pressure to obtain congressional approval of this, the so-called ship-purchase bill, during the short term from December, 1914, to March, 1915; he failed only because of a stout senatorial filibuster.

In negotiations with the British government during the early months of the war, Wilson fought hard in response to domestic pressures to keep the channels of international commerce open to American ships and goods. He did not go as far in defense of neutral rights as some of his predecessors, but he did suggest a code so sweeping that an enforcement of it would have meant almost total destruction of the British system of maritime controls. Specifically, the President first proposed on August 6, 1914, that the belligerents adopt the rules of naval warfare laid down in the Declaration of London of 1909, a convention never ratified by Great Britain or the United States, which permitted the free transit of all goods except those obviously contraband. When the British rejected this suggestion, the President came back on October 16, proposing a compromise that would have still seriously impaired the effectiveness of British sea power. When this effort also failed, Wilson then announced that his government would assert and defend all its rights under international law and treaties.

I have described these policies and proposals because they so clearly reveal Wilson's neutral intentions and what he would have done in matters of trade had he been able to make the rules himself. But he obviously could not follow his personal preferences alone or respond only to domestic pressures. In seeking to assert and defend American neutral rights he ran head-on into a reality as important as the reality of the pressures at home. It was the British determination to use sea power to prevent American ships and goods from going to the sustenance of the German economy and military forces.

British assumption of a nearly absolute control of the seas washing western Europe began with relatively mild measures in August, 1914, and culminated in the suppression of virtually all commerce to the Central Powers in March, 1915. For the British, this was not a question of adhering to the laws of blockade or of violating them, or of doing things merely to be nice to American friends. It was a question of achieving their supreme objective, to deprive their enemies of vital raw materials and goods, without risking the alienation of the United States. The controlling fact for the British was the necessity of preserving American friendship, in order to assure the uninterrupted rhythm of the North Atlantic trade. . . .

The crucial question all along, therefore, was whether the United States, the only neutral power strong enough successfully to challenge the British measures, would acquiesce or resist to the point of threatening or using force. The American response during the formative period of neutrality was, in brief, to accept the British system and to limit action against it to a vigorous assertion of American legal rights for future adjudication. All this is too well known to require any further exposition. What is not so well understood are the reasons why Wilson and his advisers acquiesced in a solution that denied the objectives that they and a large segment of the American public demanded. These reasons may be briefly summarized, as follows:

First, the British maritime system, in spite of American allegations to the contrary, enjoyed the advantage of being legitimate and usually legal, or nearly so, by traditional criteria. It was legitimate rather than fraudulent, and legal rather than capricious or terroristic, in its major aspects because the British did in fact hold undisputed sea supremacy and were therefore able to execute their controls in an orderly fashion. In asserting their own rights, the

Americans could not well deny the advantages that accrued to the British by virtue of their sea power. The British, for example, had an undoubted right to establish a blockade of the Central Powers, and the American attempt to persuade the London government to use techniques effective only in the days of the sailing ship did not have much cogency in the twentieth century.

Second, much of the success of the British in establishing their control depended upon the way in which they went about it. Had they instituted their total blockade at the outset of the war, the American reaction would undoubtedly have been violent. Instead, the British applied their controls gradually, with a careful eye upon American opinion, using the opportunities provided by recurrent crises in German-American relations to institute their severest measures.

Third, the British were careful never to offend so many American interests at one time that retaliation would have been inevitable, or any single interest powerful enough by itself to compel retaliation. . . .

Fourth, there was great significance in the language and symbolism that the British Foreign Office used in defending the measures of the Admiralty and Ministry of Blockade. By justifying their maritime system in terms of international law and the right of retaliation, and (at least before the summer of 1916) by making an honest effort to meet American objections half way when possible, the British made it almost inevitable that the Washington authorities would have to reply in the same language, thus giving a purely *legal* character to the issues involved and for the most part avoiding raising the issues of sovereignty and inherent national rights. The significance of this achievement can be seen in the conviction of Wilson and the majority of Americans that the Anglo-American disputes did involve only property rights, which should be vindicated only by an appeal to much-controverted international law. Moreover, by appealing to the American government and people in the name of friendship and by always professing their devotion to the cause of humanity, the British succeeded in evoking strong feelings of sympathy and understanding on the other side of the water.

Finally, the British were able partially to justify their own blockade measures as legitimate adaptations to a changing technology by pointing to precedents established by the Washington government itself during the American Civil War. To be sure, the British drew some incorrect analogies (as Lansing pointed out) between American and British practice; even so, their main contention — that the American government had also stretched the rules of blockade to allow for technological changes — was essentially correct.

Wilson's refusal to challenge the British maritime system, in short, to break the British blockade, was almost inevitable in view of the facts we have just reviewed, *if the President's objective was simply to maintain as best he could the neutral position of the United States.* An absolute neutrality was in any event impossible because of the total character of the war and America's importance in the world economy. It often happened that any action by the United States inevitably conferred a benefit on one side and thereby injured the other, at least indirectly. In these circumstances, neutrality often consisted of doing the things that would give the least unwarranted or undeserved advantages.

By this standard, it would have been more unneutral than neutral for Wilson to have broken the British maritime system by enforcing highly doubtful technical rights under international law. Judged by practical standards rather than by the often conflicting criteria of neutrality, Wilson's acceptance of the British system seems realistic and wise — indeed, the only choice that he could have made in the circumstances. This is true because the results of destroying the British blockade would have been the wrecking of American friendship with the two great European democracies and the probable victory of the Central Powers, without a single compensating gain for the interests and security of the United States. Only the sure achievement of some great political objective like a secure peace settlement, certainly not the winning of a commercial advantage or the defense of doubtful neutral rights, would have justified Wilson in undertaking a determined challenge to British sea power.

The second stage in Anglo-American relations, lasting from the summer of 1915 to the late spring of 1916, saw the development of the natural economic consequence of the American adjustment to tightening British control of the seas. That consequence was the burgeoning of an enormous war trade between the United States and the Allies. The United States became the storehouse and armory of the Allies neither because there was any conspiracy on the part of certain pro-Allied leaders in Washington to make American prosperity dependent upon an Allied victory, nor because American businessmen and bankers were willing to incur the risks of war in order to increase their profits. The United States became the storehouse of the Allies for the simple reason that Great Britain and not Germany controlled the seas.

The war trade itself was entirely neutral. Indeed, any action by the United States government to impede it, unless undertaken for overriding political motives, would have been grossly prejudicial and unneutral. If it had been permitted to develop in a normal way, this commerce would have raised no important problems in the relations of the United States with the Allies. A problem of the first magnitude did arise, however, because the President, in the summer of 1914, had permitted Secretary Bryan to enforce his own private moral views by imposing a ban on loans by American bankers to the belligerents. . . .

Bryan's ban could not survive the development of the war trade on a large scale because, in the first place, it (like the Embargo of 1808) was potentially nearly as disastrous to the United States as to the Allies. American material well-being was in large measure dependent upon foreign trade, and particularly upon trade with the Allied world. Such trade was possible during wartime only if American businessmen were willing to do for the Allies what they always did for solvent customers in temporary straits, namely, sell them goods on credit.

The most important reason that Bryan's embargo could not survive, however, was that it was an essentially unneutral policy that impeded the growth of the chief economic consequence of American neutrality, the legitimate war trade. The credit embargo and the war trade could not both survive. The former gave way because Wilson finally realized that it would be as unneutral to interfere with the extension of credit as it would be to stop the flow of goods. Bryan's ban was in a sense, therefore, a casualty chiefly of American neutrality. . . .

The second stage in Anglo-American relations also witnessed

the apparent convergence of the diplomatic policies of the two countries on the high level. During the summer and autumn of 1915 Colonel Edward M. House, Wilson's confidant and principal adviser on foreign policy, conceived a plan by which the American and British leaders would join hands to press for an end to the war through Wilson's mediation. The British Foreign Secretary, Sir Edward Grey, replied that his government would co-operate only if the Washington administration were willing to go beyond simple mediation and would agree to join a postwar international organization established for the purpose of effecting disarmament, maintaining freedom of the seas, and preserving peace. Wilson hopefully consented, and House went to Berlin, Paris, and London in January, 1916, to lay the diplomatic basis of mediation.

In London, House worked out in documentary form with Grey and the other members of the British Cabinet the specific terms of Anglo-American co-operation. Initialed by House and Grey on February 22, 1916, and known as the House-Grey Memorandum or Agreement, this document declared that President Wilson was ready, upon hearing from England and France that the time was ripe, to propose that a conference be called to end the war. Should the Allies accept and Germany refuse the invitation, the United States would "probably" enter the war against Germany. Should the conference meet and Germany refuse to accept a reasonable settlement, then the United States would also "probably" enter the war on the Allied side.

To the so-called revisionists the conclusion of the House-Grey Agreement is irrefutable proof that Wilson had abandoned neutrality and meant to take the country into war at the first opportunity. . . .

The revisionists are correct in asserting that the conclusion of the House-Grey Agreement marked the beginning of a new and epochal phase in Wilson's policies toward the belligerents. Otherwise they have missed the entire meaning of the affair, for the House-Grey Agreement was in Wilson's purpose *not an instrument of intervention, but a means of averting American involvement.* The truth of this important generalization will perhaps become evident when we recall the realities of the American diplomatic situation during late 1915 and early 1916, and when we understand Wilson's motives and intentions in devising a solution.

The overshadowing reality confronting the makers of American foreign policy at this time was the grave possibility of war with Germany over the submarine issue. It caused Wilson and Lansing, for example, to abandon ambitious plans for further intervention in Mexico. It speeded the American acquiescence in the British maritime system. Most important, it prompted the President and his advisers to search for ways to avert the rupture that might draw the United States into the maelstrom.

One way out of the predicament was to come to a full understanding with the German government over the issues involved in the submarine controversy. This is what Lansing attempted to do and almost succeeded in accomplishing during his negotiations over the *Lusitania* affair. Another way out and a surer means of averting the peril of American involvement in the future was to bring the war itself to an end through Wilson's mediation. It seemed at the time that the best hope of peace lay in Anglo-American co-operation for a peace of compromise, specifically in the kind of co-operation detailed in the House-Grey Agreement.

Thus Wilson approved this plan of mediation, but with a full realization that certain obligations and risks were involved. There was the necessity of giving positive assurances to the Allies, for they would have been at a fatal disadvantage in a peace conference without American support, in view of the strategic advantages that the Germans then enjoyed on the Continent of Europe. There was, moreover, the risk of war if the Germans refused to approve an armistice or proved to be unreasonable at a peace conference after agreeing to end the fighting. However, Wilson gave the necessary assurances in the belief that the risk of war involved was insignificant as compared to the greater danger of hostilities with Germany if he could not somehow bring the war to an end. This, then, was his dominant motive in sending House to Europe in January, 1916, and in approving the House-Grey Agreement at the cost of Lansing's proposed compromise for submarine warfare.

In the final analysis, our judgment of Wilson's mediation plans must depend upon the kind of settlement that he had in mind and for which he was willing to run the risk of war in order to achieve peace. It is clear that Wilson envisaged a "reasonable" settlement based upon recognition that the war was a stalemate and upon a return for the most part of the *status quo ante bellum.* It meant, Wilson also hoped, the kind of settlement in which all the belligerents would forego annexations and indemnities, put aside past differences, and join hands with the United States to create a new international order. In his final discussions with the British Cabinet, Colonel House made it clear that this, and this only, was the kind of settlement that Wilson was prepared to use the House-Grey Agreement to achieve. In other words, as House told the British leaders, the President would "throw the weight of the United States on the side of those wanting a just settlement — a settlement which would make another such war impossible." . . .

In the circumstances prevailing during the late autumn and early winter of 1916–1917, the Germans had three possible choices of policy. These were, first, to join hands with Wilson in a drive for peace generally on the President's terms; second, to make a limited bid for victory by intensifying the submarine war at the risk of alienating the United States; and, third, to make a supreme bid for victory by instituting a total blockade of all commerce to the British Isles. The situation from the German point of view was such that this choice would not depend upon anything that Wilson did or said, unless, of course, the President could be used as a German pawn or was willing openly to support Germany's war objectives. The German decision would depend entirely upon a realistic evaluation of the possibilities of the military situation, that is, upon whether the Imperial army and navy were capable of imposing terms upon the enemies of the Reich.

Discussions of these possibilities had begun in Germany in earnest in mid-August, 1916, as a consequence of the urgent demand of the Admiralty for permission to resume unrestricted submarine attacks in the near future. The civilian and military leaders rejected the demand at a conference at Pless Castle on August 31, 1916, on the ground that the navy did not have enough submarines to enforce a blockade and that it would obviously be foolhardy to risk American retaliation at this time. Actually, it was the new commanders of the army, Generals Paul von Hindenburg and Erich von Ludendorff, who made this decision. The military situation, they said, was too menacing to justify assuming the risk of war with America. There was heavy Allied pressure on the western front; above all, there was the grave danger of an Allied invasion of the Balkans, which might cause the collapse of Austria-Hungary.

Events of the late summer and early autumn combined inexorably to create a new situation in which a different decision would be made. First, the great British offensive on the Somme, aimed at tearing a huge hole in the German lines and a thrust into Belgium, failed; as a result, the German position in the West was again secure. Second, after dawdling in the matter for nearly two years, the Admiralty had finally launched a large program of submarine construction and the training of crews; by the end of the year it would be possible to talk in terms of dealing England a deathblow underseas. Finally, the army's counteroffensive against the Russians and its smashing victory over Rumania removed all cause for concern about the security of Austria-Hungary and the Balkans. . . .

Almost formless at the outset of the war, German war objectives had grown in a direct ratio to the progress of the Imperial armies in the field. By the late autumn of 1916 the military situation was so favorable and the potentialities of an effective submarine blockade were so great that the German leaders inevitably abandoned thought of a compromise peace and began to plan for a settlement that would remove all threats to future German security. As drawn up by Bethmann-Hollweg, amended by Hindenburg, and approved by the German and Austrian governments, the German peace terms were breathtaking in scope. They included, in the East, the establishment of a Polish kingdom under German control and German annexation of Lithuania and Courland on the Baltic; in the West, destruction of British naval supremacy, an indemnity from England and France, the annexation of strategic parts of France and Belgium, and the reconstruction of Belgium as a German vassal; and, overseas, the annexation of all or part of the Belgian Congo. To be sure, these were the maximum German objectives at the time; a realization of even part of them, however, would have secured German domination of Europe for years to come.

This was the kind of settlement that the German leaders were determined to obtain through peace negotiations. They knew that they could never obtain such terms, or even a large part of them, through Wilson's mediation. They knew that Wilson would demand, among other things, the restitution of a free and independent Belgium and perhaps the return of Alsace-Lorraine to France. Acceptance of Wilson's mediation and a compromise peace, even one based entirely upon the *status quo ante bellum,* would, in German eyes, be tantamount to defeat, for it would mean the frustration of everything for which so much German blood had been shed. As a consequence, no German leader, civilian or military, ever seriously considered accepting Wilson's *mediation.* During all the high-level discussions about peace plans, no German leader ever seriously mentioned such a possibility. On the contrary, all German diplomatic efforts were concentrated upon the goal of preventing Wilson's mediation, or "meddling," as the Germans called it.

This statement needs some clarification. The Germans were eager, almost desperately eager, to win the President's support for their peace plans. They wanted Wilson's help in forcing the Allies to the peace table at a time when all the odds favored the winning of a German peace. They were willing to give pledges of postwar disarmament and membership in a League of Nations, if this were necessary to win the President's support. But they did not want, indeed, they would not permit, Wilson's mediation or even his presence at the peace conference.

Wilson did not know these facts during the first stages of the peace discussions, but the truth finally came out in January, 1917, when the President begged the Foreign Office in Berlin to come out frankly and fully in acceptance of his mediation. Then the German leaders had to say that they would welcome Wilson's cooperation only after the peace treaty had been signed, not at the conference of belligerents itself. Shrewdly perceiving the German intentions, Wilson refused to be a pawn in Berlin's game.

Wilson's refusal meant that the German leaders would now proceed to consider means of achieving through force what they had failed to win by their inept diplomacy. The High Command had already made the decision by late December; it was confirmed by a conference of all leaders at Pless Castle on January 9, 1917. That decision was, in brief, to begin unrestricted submarine warfare against all shipping, belligerent and neutral, in the approaches to the British Isles and the eastern Mediterranean after January 31.

It was easily the most fateful decision made by any government during the course of the war, and the German records fully reveal the reasons for its adoption. It now seemed beyond all doubt that the navy had sufficient power to establish an effective submarine blockade of the British Isles, for it could send between twenty-five and thirty submarines into western waters by February 1, 1917, and a growing number after that date. Moreover, other circumstances, particularly a short wheat crop in the New World, augured well for the success of the blockade. Indeed, on a basis of elaborate calculations the Admiralty spokesmen guaranteed absolutely to reduce the British to actual starvation within five months after the submarine blockade began. If this were possible, then Germany had it within her power to win a total victory and a settlement that would establish the Reich in an unassailable position. To the military leaders, who had despaired of winning the war in the trenches, it was an opportunity that could not be refused.

Fear of American belligerency no longer had any effect on German policy in such an atmosphere of confident expectation. The German leaders all assumed that a wholesale attack on American maritime commerce would drive the United States into the war. These same leaders also concluded that American belligerency would not make any difference. On the contrary, American participation would have certain positive advantages, for it would mean the diversion of huge quantities of food and matériel to an American army in training during the very period when the U-boats would be winning the war on the seas. But in any event, American participation was in the circumstances necessary to the success of the German plans, because the submarine blockade could succeed only if it were total, that is, only if American as well as British ships were prevented from carrying life-giving supplies to the beleaguered British Isles. Of course, no German leader wanted recklessly to provoke an American declaration of war; all Germans, however, were prepared to incur American belligerency if they could win the war by so doing.

It was the only decision that seemed possible to the Imperial military commanders. No nation involved in a desperate war for survival will fail to use a weapon, whether it be the submarine or the atomic bomb, when that weapon promises to bring quick and overwhelming victory. But the submarine campaign brought catastrophic defeat to Germany and misfortunes unnumbered to the world because it destroyed all possibility of a peace of reconciliation. For this outcome, the political leaders in Berlin, particularly Chancellor Bethmann-Hollweg, were primarily responsible. Not once during the critical months of 1916 did they attempt to organize any movement for peace on a basis that could succeed. Not once did the Foreign Office make any serious effort to understand Wilson's motives and objectives. Not once during the final debates over submarine policy did the Chancellor attempt to subject the Admiralty's dubious promises to any really searching scrutiny, to determine in a realistic way what the effect of American participation would be, or to inform the Reichstag of the consequences of failure of unlimited underseas warfare. It is true that the Supreme High Command, which now had the constitutional right to override the Chancellor on submarine policy, might have proceeded as it did in any event. None the less, the fact remains that Bethmann-Hollweg simply made no serious effort to influence what was the most fateful decision confronting Germany's leaders since the formation of the Empire. . . .

There was, however, only one decision that Wilson could now make. No great power could continue to maintain diplomatic intercourse with a government that promised to destroy its shipping and slaughter its citizens in violation of national and treaty rights and solemn pledges. Small neutral states like Holland and Norway had no choice but to suffer under protest, but a great nation like the United States had responsibilities commensurate with its power and influence. Continuing to maintain relations with Berlin after the issuance of the blockade proclamation of January 31 would have meant nothing less than Wilson's condoning of the German assault upon American rights and lives. The remarkable thing is not that Wilson severed diplomatic relations as he did on February 3, but that he hesitated at all. . . .

By the middle of March, therefore, it seemed that Wilson had made his decision in favor of a limited defensive war on the seas. "We stand firm in armed neutrality," he declared, for example, in his second inaugural address on March 5, "since it seems that in no other way we can demonstrate what it is we insist upon and cannot forego." Yet on April 2 (he had meanwhile convened Congress for this earlier date), scarcely more than a month after he had uttered these words, he stood before Congress and asked for a declaration of full-fledged war. What events occurred, what forces were at work, what pressures were applied during this brief interval to cause Wilson to make the decision that he had been trying so desperately to avoid? We should perhaps put the question in a less positive way, as follows: What caused the President to abandon armed neutrality and to *accept* the decision for war?

There was first the fact that from the end of February to the end of March the Germans gave full evidence of their determination to press a relentless, total attack against all ships passing through the war zones that enveloped western Europe. The sinking of the British liner *Laconia* without warning on February 25 and with loss of American life, the ruthless destruction of three American merchantmen (*City of Memphis, Illinois,* and *Vigilancia*) on March 18, and the relentless attacks against the vessels of other neutral nations, to say nothing of the slashing attacks against Allied merchant shipping, removed all doubt in Wilson's mind about the deadly seriousness of the German intention to conduct total warfare against all commerce and human life within the broad war zones.

The more the character of the submarine blockade became apparent, the stronger the conviction grew in the President's mind that armed neutrality was neither a sufficient response physically, nor a proper or legally possible one. . . . It was simply that the German assault upon American lives and property was so overwhelming and so flagrant that the only possible way to cope with it was to claim the status of a belligerent in order to strike at the sources of German power. "I would be inclined to adopt . . . [armed neutrality]," the President wrote only two days before he delivered his war message,

> indeed, as you know, I had already adopted it, but this is the difficulty: . . . To make even the measures of defense legitimate we must obtain the status of belligerents.

Certainly Wilson had convinced himself that this was true, but I have a strong suspicion that he would have stood doggedly by his first decision to limit American action to a defense of rights on the seas if this decision had not been overridden by convictions, events, pressures, and ambitions that were themselves decisive in Wilson's final shift from armed neutrality to war, in forcing him to the conclusion that the *immediate* circumstances left the United States with no choice but full-scale participation.

One of the most important of these factors was the subtlest and the one for which the least direct evidence can be adduced. It was Wilson's apparent fear that the threat of a German victory imperiled the balance of power and all his hopes for the future reconstruction of the world community. We must be careful here not to misinterpret his thoughts and motives. There is little evidence that he accepted the decision for war because he thought that a German victory would seriously endanger American security, because he wanted to preserve Anglo-American control of the North Atlantic sea lanes, or because he desired to maintain the traditional balance of European power because it served American interests. Nor is there any convincing evidence that Wilson's attitude toward the objectives of the rival alliances had changed by the time that he made his final decision.

On the other hand, there was now a great and decisive difference in the relative position of the belligerents: The Allies seemed about to lose the war and the Central Powers about to win it. This, almost certainly, was a governing factor in Wilson's willingness to think in terms of war. Germany, he told Colonel House, was a madman who must be curbed. A German victory meant a peace of domination and conquest; it meant the end of all of Wilson's dreams of helping to build a secure future.

As the President pondered America's duty at this juncture in history, the answer must have seemed obvious to him — to accept belligerency, because now only through belligerency could the United States fulfill its mission to insure a just and lasting peace of reconciliation. This could be accomplished only by preventing a German victory and only by the assertion of such power and influence among the Allies as would come to the United States by virtue of its sacrifice of blood and treasure. . . .

The combined weight of official and public opinion was another pressure meanwhile driving Wilson toward acceptance of the decision for war. It was a fact of no little consequence that by the end of March every important member of the administration, including those members of the Cabinet who had heretofore opposed any bellicose measures, urged the President to admit that a state of war with Germany in fact existed. Public opinion had remained stubbornly pacific until near the end of February, 1917. Then the publication of the Zimmermann telegram, in which the German government proposed to Mexico a war alliance against the United States, the sinking of the *Laconia,* and, above all, the destruction of American ships in the war zones after mid-March generated a demand for war that grew with mounting crescendo in all sections and among all classes, until it seemed beyond doubt to be a national and a majority demand. . . .

All this is said without any intention of implying that Wilson ever *wanted* war. The agony of his soul was great as he moved through the dark valley of his doubts. He had no illusions about the merits of the conflict into which he and his people were being drawn. He saw the risks of intervention, both to his own nation and to the world, with remarkable clarity. But he could devise no alternative; and he set aside his doubts in the hope that acting now as a belligerent, with all the power and idealism of the American people sustaining him, he could achieve objectives to justify the misery of mankind.

6

The 1920's

Decade of Decline or Destiny?

THE DECADE OF THE 1920's occupies an ambiguous position in American history. Sandwiched between two exciting eras – the Progressive era and World War I on the one side and the New Deal on the other – the 1920's appear almost out of place. Certainly the presidents – Harding, Coolidge, Hoover – were not of the stature of men like the two Roosevelts and Woodrow Wilson. Few legislative landmarks or creative social experiments emerged from the decade of the postwar era. Indeed, one important attempt at reform – prohibition – came close to being a fiasco. For these reasons, popular writers, movies, and television in recent years have depicted the decade in terms of a decline in morality, an orgy of financial speculation, a reaction against authority, an increase in organized crime, and a withdrawal from world affairs; in short, a time when established institutions and standards were in the process of disintegration. The popular designation of these years – the Roaring Twenties – sums up the traditional view.

Upon closer examination, however, the 1920's become far more complex than the picture presented in the popular stereotype. While Americans in later years looked back at the postwar era with distaste – even hostility – partly because it ended in the worst depression in American history – contemporaries viewed the period in a quite different light. One group in American society, the businessmen, felt that they were living in a new era. To them the twenties were marked not by conservatism but by change and innovation. The application of scientific procedures and new measures of efficiency in industry, businessmen believed, would bring about a level of prosperity that would eliminate poverty from the country completely. Under an enlightened and informed business leadership and a government sympathetic to business ideals, they predicted a new golden age for America.

The optimistic outlook on the part of businessmen was expressed in a variety of ways. Spokesmen of industry never tired of proclaiming that the nation's greatness resulted from the labors of individual entrepreneurs who had raised America to a level of prosperity hitherto unmatched in history. Perhaps the most spectacular glorification of business values and ideals was exemplified in a biography of Jesus by Bruce Barton in 1925. Barton's book was ostensibly an effort to write about the career of Jesus in a popular vein. But Barton's conclusion was cast in business terms that were simple to understand: Jesus was the greatest organizer and promoter in history because he had succeeded in "selling" Christianity to millions of persons over the centuries. As Barton put it in his preface to the book:

> A physical weakling! Where did they get that idea? Jesus pushed a plane and swung an adze; he was a successful carpenter. He slept outdoors and spent his days walking around his favorite lake. His muscles were so strong that when he drove the moneychangers out, nobody dared to oppose him!
>
> A kill-joy! He was the most popular dinner guest in Jerusalem! The criticism which proper people made was that he spent too much time with publicans and sinners (very good fellows, on the whole, the man thought) and enjoyed society too much. They called him a "wine bibber and a gluttonous man."
>
> A failure! He picked up twelve men from the bottom ranks

> of business and forged them into an organization that conquered the world. . . . [For the story of Jesus is] the story of the founder of modern business.[1]

Confidence in the 1920's was by no means confined to businessmen. Even American historians, who were traditionally hostile to business because of their liberal sympathies, saw much to praise. Charles and Mary Beard, for example, were not particularly impressed with either the Harding or Coolidge administrations when they published *The Rise of American Civilization* in 1927. Yet they did not view the twenties as a decade of reaction. Although the Beards admitted that Harding and Coolidge were dealing with complex problems in much the same manner as William McKinley and Marcus A. Hanna of bygone days, they noted that a large group of rebels in Congress fought the Republican presidents and occasionally won an issue. But the outstanding development of the 1920's to the Beards was not the political battles; it was rather the rapid growth of industry and mechanization in this era which left its imprint on virtually every phase of American life. "The most common note of assurance," they concluded in their work, "was belief in unlimited progress. . . . Concretely it meant an invulnerable faith in democracy, in the ability of the undistinguished masses, as contrasted with heroes and classes, to meet by reasonably competent methods the issues raised in the flow of time – a faith in the efficacy of that new and mysterious instrument of the modern mind, 'the invention of invention,' moving from one technological triumph to another, overcoming the exhaustion of crude natural resources and energies, effecting an even wider distribution of the blessings of civilization – health, security, material goods, knowledge, leisure, and aesthetic appreciation, and through the cumulative forces of intellectual and aesthetic reactions, conjuring from the vasty deeps of the nameless and unknown creative imagination of the noblest order, subduing physical things to the empire of the spirit – doubting not the capacity of the Power that had summoned into being all patterns of the past and present, living and dead, to fulfill its endless destiny."[2]

1. Bruce Barton, *The Man Nobody Knows: A Discovery of the Real Jesus* (Indianapolis, 1925), Preface.
2. Charles A. and Mary R. Beard, *The Rise of American Civilization* (2 vols.: New York, 1927), II, 800.

The sociologists, like the historians, also found much to be optimistic about during the decade. Although they were critical of many aspects of American life, most sociologists were confident that existing defects could be remedied. In the past, they argued, few statesmen or political leaders had possessed an adequate understanding of how American society functioned and judgments were often made on the basis of inadequate or misleading information. Only rarely had scientific methods been applied to social problems. What was required now, claimed the sociologists, was the gathering of quantitative and objective data that would enable leaders to define factors that governed society. Armed with the knowledge provided by sociologists, future statesmen would be able to make decisions in a truly enlightened manner.

As a general rule, sociologists during the 1920's were fond of emphasizing what they called a "cultural lag," that is, the condition wherein the institutions of a given society lagged behind the advances in technological and scientific knowledge. Such a lag was responsible for the internal tensions and difficulties in America, they maintained. The solution was obvious: existing institutions had to be brought up to date to conform to the findings of science. Once they caught up, the American millennium would begin. If American society would only accept the findings and recommendations of the social scientists, the sociologists claimed, a new utopia lay just ahead.

Sociologists, therefore, asserted with confidence that the 1920's represented the beginnings of a new era in American history. Even Thorstein Veblen, one of the most devastating commentators on the irrationality of the capitalistic profit system, seemed to think that most of society's pressing problems could be solved. All that was required, he concluded in *The Engineers and the Price System* (1921), was a transference of power and authority from the businessman — who viewed industry in terms of profits rather than efficiency and social utility — to the engineer — an individual to whom productivity and efficiency were ends in themselves. Although Veblen had little confidence that America's leaders would seize upon opportunities presented to them, he did imply that possible solutions to America's major problems lay close at hand.

One serious note of dissent in this chorus of optimism and self-congratulation was struck by the literary intellectuals of the 1920's.

Many of them saw a decade of decline and degradation in America rather than one of destiny. They pictured Americans as being caught up in an irresistible surge of materialism — a people who had failed to grasp the meaning and significance of life. American society as a result lacked depth and was noted for the superficiality of its cultural, artistic, and intellectual achievements.

Among the earliest indictments by intellectuals was the symposium edited by Harold E. Stearns. Published in 1922 under the title *Civilization in the United States,* the book was a biting commentary on the superficial quality of American life. Stearns pointed out in his preface that each of the thirty contributors was a native American who had written his piece independently of the others, but that all had reached virtually the same conclusions. First, that hypocrisy was a major characteristic of American life; to most Americans the cardinal sin was not the immoral or dishonest act itself, but rather being found out or caught. Second, that America lacked a genuine sense of nationalistic self-consciousness — a fact that prevented the country from living up to its promise. Third — and most important — that America's social life was one of "emotional and aesthetic starvation," one in which "the mania for petty regulation, the driving, regimentating, and drilling, the secret society and its grotesque regalia, the firm grasp on the unessentials of material organization of our pleasures and gaieties are all eloquent stigmata." Could America be changed, asked Stearns? The answer was "yes." "There must be an entirely new deal of the cards in one sense; we must change our hearts. For only so, unless through the humbling of calamity or scourge, can true art and true religion and true personality . . . grow up in America to exorcise these painted devils we have created to frighten us away from the acknowledgement of our spiritual poverty." [3]

Most of Stearns' contributors agreed with his general indictment. To Lewis Mumford the American city was both an index of the nation's material success and a symbol of its spiritual failure. To H. L. Mencken the American politician was a cowardly and frightened individual whose primary concern was holding fast to his office. To Harold E. Stearns America's intellectuals were confined in a spiritual prison by a regimented and standardized society.

3. Harold E. Stearns, *Civilization in the United States: An Inquiry by Thirty Americans* (New York, 1922), pp. vi–vii.

To John May the press was controlled by advertising and the public was gullible and uncritical in accepting at face value whatever appeared in their newspapers. The other chapters in *Civilization in the United States* included discussions of art, law, education, radicalism, business, advertising, and other aspects of American life, and all were equally critical in their approach. Most of the writers left the impression that America was a cultural wasteland and an intellectual desert with few redeeming features. So widespread was deception and hypocrisy, they concluded, that democracy itself seemed threatened.

Although many of the literary intellectuals were critical of American society in the twenties, few could agree upon a specific remedy, let alone a general diagnosis of its malaise. Some writers migrated to Paris in order to find an environment conducive to their art. Other artists congregated in Greenwich Village, in New York City, where they could remain aloof from the sordid materialism that seemed to permeate every nook and corner of American life. Still others related the decline in American civilization to the breakdown of Western civilization as a whole. Led by Irving Babbitt and Paul Elmer More, these "New Humanists," as they were called, insisted upon the necessity of man's "inner check" to control his desires and impulses. They emphasized the need for a "natural aristocracy" and scoffed at the idea of progress that was generally accepted by most Americans. Yet many of these alienated intellectuals – a group that included such outstanding figures as F. Scott Fitzgerald, Sinclair Lewis, Ernest Hemingway, John Dos Passos, and William Faulkner – were capable of creating a rich and enduring literature in the twenties and providing a cultural renaissance in America that perhaps had had no equal since the transcendentalist era of nearly a century before.

The great depression of the 1930's that began with the stock market crash in 1929, however, provided a new perspective from which to judge the previous decade. Now the optimistic outlook of the twenties seemed erroneous if for no other reason than the fact that America's prosperity had culminated in the worst economic disaster that the nation had ever known. With the seemingly imminent collapse of the capitalist system, business values and ideals were cast into disrepute. Businessmen who had been the heroes of the 1920's became the villains of the 1930's in the popular mind.

The view of the 1920's by the social scientists was less affected by the depression than was that of the businessmen. Having emphasized the application of intelligence and science to social problems in a period of prosperity, sociologists were even more adamant about taking such an approach during the depression. However, there was a growing realization among the social scientists that certain difficulties would impede the realization of their technocratic and scientific utopia. The famous report by the President's Committee on Social Trends in 1933, a project commissioned in 1929, came to the conclusion that the task of social understanding and control was far more complex than had been previously imagined. There were elements in American life to which concepts and projects involving mechanization, efficiency, and change simply could not be applied. What was required was not an outright rejection of older approaches to social problems, but a careful analysis of modern society that struck a correct balance between tradition and change.

The interpretation of the twenties by historians was much more influenced by the depression than was that of the sociologists. However, this change in outlook was hardly surprising. Those historians who had written about the 1920's earlier had done so in a rather casual and superficial manner. For one thing, many of the sources required for an understanding of the so-called era of "normalcy" were only just becoming available by the end of the decade. But a much more basic reason for the shift in emphasis lay in the intellectual orientation of the profession itself. Having been reared in the liberal ideology of Progressivism, many historians of the Progressive school tended to interpret American history within the framework of a continuous class conflict that resulted in alternating periods of reform and reaction. Each era of liberal reform, they believed, was succeeded by a period of conservative consolidation or reaction. Caught up in the maelstrom of New Deal reform, these historians looked back at the 1920's as a time of reaction — a decade dominated by ultra-conservative presidents who reflected the selfish and narrow desires of the business community. In many respects such historians accepted at face value the claim by Franklin Delano Roosevelt that the New Deal was simply a continuation of America's traditional liberal values that had been momentarily subverted by the First World War and the ensuing era of disillusionment in the postwar period.

The typical interpretation of the twenties by such Progressive historians ran along the following lines. By 1920 the American people had tired of the moralistic fervor that had been characteristic of the Progressive era and of Wilsonian idealism. Having lived through two crusades lasting for over two decades – one for domestic reform and the other to make the world safe for democracy – the American people were ripe for a return to "normalcy," to use the word coined by Warren G. Harding during the presidential campaign of 1920. But "normalcy" turned out to be anything but normal. In contrast to both the Progressive and New Deal periods, which were exciting ones – if only because the American people and their leaders recognized and attempted to cope with the problems facing them and set out in a resolute and imaginative manner to come to grips with them – the twenties had a decidedly negative atmosphere. Under the conservative, and at times reactionary, Republican leadership, the American people abdicated their responsibilities. They withdrew from the efforts on the part of other nations to ensure lasting peace; they rejected Progressive attempts to grapple with the problems of an increasingly complex industrial society and retreated instead into an outdated idea of individualism; and they turned the affairs of state over to the business community which was interested only in the pursuit of the almighty dollar.

Given this negative interpretation, it is not difficult to understand the events and developments that Progressive historians chose to document their case. Generally speaking, they were prone to write about the suppression of dissent, the near prostration of the labor movement, and the relative decline in the economic position of the farmer and worker in American society. In their eyes the twenties was a period of bigotry marked by the rise of the Ku Klux Klan, the abandonment of the ideal of America as a haven for the oppressed peoples of the world, and the resurgence of anti-Catholicism and anti-Semitism. It was a time of corruption, symbolized by the scandals of the Harding administration; even the restoration of "honesty" under Coolidge simply meant a policy whereby the federal government turned many of its functions over to business. But worst of all, it was a time when idealism seemed sadly out of date – when the youth of America were alienated from their society and the homogeneity of the nation seemed threatened by competing group loyalties. If any one theme stood out in the writings of Progressive historians, it was their assumption that the 1920's had been an irresponsible decade.

The picture of the "Roaring Twenties" or the "Jazz Age," to use designations that later became popular, was evident in the work of many historians. Vernon L. Parrington, writing within the Progressive tradition, sharply criticized the literary figures of the 1920's for throwing away their democratic-liberal heritage to emulate Europe's radical writers. To those historians writing within a Marxian framework – such as Lewis Corey or John Chamberlain – the decade was an exercise in futility – a period marked by the triumph of monopolistic capitalism which inevitably concluded with the worst depression in American history. Perhaps the most savage indictment of the decade appeared in John Dos Passos's brilliant trilogy, *U.S.A.* In this literary masterpiece, Dos Passos drew an unforgettable picture of the era. Using a variety of literary techniques to create an impressionistic view of a period, he emphasized the corrupting nature of materialism upon potentially "good" individuals.

The critical approach to the 1920's continued to hold the allegiance of some leading contemporary historians writing within the Progressive tradition down to the 1950's and 1960's. Arthur M. Schlesinger, Jr., in *The Crisis of the Old Order 1919–1933* (1957), spelled out in great detail the failure of that period. Unlike other historians who had dealt with the 1920's before him, Schlesinger was in a position to write in an authoritative manner because of the greater mass of source materials that were available. Although Schlesinger took note of the intellectual and technological advances in the twenties, his picture of the period remained a relatively hostile one. In his view the 1920's were but a prelude to the New Deal.

Similarly, John D. Hicks, in *Republican Ascendancy 1921–1933* (1960), a volume in the New American Nation series, took much the same approach as Schlesinger. "It is not unfair," wrote Hicks in another essay, "to characterize the period . . . as an age of disillusionment. The high hopes with which the United States had entered World War I had been shattered; neither the League of Nations, nor the World Court, nor the disarmament program, nor the outlawry of war provided adequate guarantees of peace.

. . . Politically speaking, the swing to conservatism had brought little comfort. The Harding scandals had left an ugly smell that even the puritanical Coolidge had found it difficult to eradicate; but for the ills of the times the Progressives under LaFollette could suggest only shopworn remedies of little relevance to the new age. American society was on the loose. . . . Then, despite business control of every aspect of American economic and political life, including a successful businessman in the White House, business had gone broke. Small wonder that the very bottom had fallen out of American confidence." [4]

The first selection in this chapter, by John Kenneth Galbraith, a Harvard economist, discusses the state of the American economy during the twenties. In presenting his argument, Galbraith makes a distinction between the stock market crash in October, 1929, and the ensuing depression because the first did not automatically cause the second. The depression of the 1930's, he writes, followed the stock market crash because the American economy had been unsound. Being in a vulnerable position, the economy was unable to withstand the blow it received from Wall Street. Although Galbraith is by no means completely hostile toward the 1920's, his interpretation falls largely within the Progressive tradition of American historiography because of the picture it presents of a maldistribution of income and unsound corporate and banking structure, and a generally weakened economy in the world at large during the decade. Given these conditions, Galbraith concludes, the depression was a logical outgrowth of the economic developments that took place in the twenties.

The popular stereotype of the 1920's, however, had already begun to undergo a reevaluation in the late 1930's, and this changing view gained momentum in the 1940's. During the drab days of the depression, many persons and especially the youth of America looked back upon the gaiety and irresponsibility of the twenties with a strange fascination and even a longing as they contemplated the bleak present and uncertain future. But the major shift in interpretation came during the Second World War. Concerned with maintaining the nation's morale during the war, certain critics began to denigrate the literature of the 1920's for its negative out-

4. John D. Hicks, *Normalcy and Reaction 1921–1933: An Age of Disillusionment* (Washington, D.C., 1960), p. 21.

look and its blanket condemnation of American society. In 1944 Bernard De Voto, the famous historian and literary critic, argued that American civilization had not been bankrupt in the twenties; the bankruptcy lay in the negative literary interpretation of that decade. Indeed, De Voto found much that was appealing as well as constructive during the 1920's.

While De Voto was condemning the literary rebels of the twenties for their negative and irresponsible outlook, other literary historians were beginning to approach the decade with a more appreciative eye. In 1955 Frederick J. Hoffman published his work *The Twenties: American Writing in the Postwar Decade.* After a thorough examination of the subject, Hoffman concluded that the writers of the 1920's had lived in a world that appeared to be cut loose from the past and therefore had sought to discover new ways of expressing the human condition. These literary artists, he continued, "had to invent new combinations of spirit and matter and new forms of expressing the human drama. They were not aided by any secure ordering of social or religious systems. . . . Their restless desire for the new was always motivated by their distrust of the old. . . . the 1920's were an opportunity and a challenge offered to a group of persons who were freshly and naively talented, anxious to learn *how* to restate and redramatize the human condition, morally preoccupied with the basic problem of communicating their insights into their present world." [5]

Although De Voto and Hoffman came to sharply divergent judgments about the literature of the 1920's, they were not very far apart in their general view of the period as a whole; both found much that was constructive and exciting during those years. Their break with the prevailing critical approach was soon echoed by other scholars. Indeed, shortly after the end of World War II, the pendulum began to swing away from the Progressive interpretation of the twenties. Rejecting the older and more critical view of the period, historians as well as other social scientists took a fresh look at the twenties, and in doing so offered a new perspective for understanding the events that transpired between 1921 to 1933.

The new view of the twenties was actually the joint product of scholars in a number of disciplines. George Soule, for example, an

5. Frederick J. Hoffman, *The Twenties: American Writing in the Postwar Decade* (Second edition: New York, 1962), pp. 434–436.

economic historian, concluded in his *Prosperity Decade* (1947) that the economic picture traditionally drawn of the period was an erroneous one. It was true that the rich became richer in the 1920's, Soule wrote, but at the same time the poor were also getting richer – albeit at a slower rate. In his view the depression that began in 1929 had much more deeply-rooted causes than those previously advanced. To Soule the depression grew out of a fundamental maladjustment of productivity and purchasing power – a maladjustment that was not indigenous to the 1920's but whose origins stretched back into American history for many decades.

Other historians in the post-World War II era joined in the growing chorus of praise that celebrated the achievements of American capitalism rather than emphasizing its defects. They argued that it was America's productive capacity, after all, that had made possible the Allied victory during World War II and provided the free world with the means to resist the Soviet challenge after 1945. At the same time, American capitalism had given to the American people an affluent society hitherto unattainable and did so without resorting to a government-owned or managed economy. This new perspective was particularly evident in David M. Potter's challenging book, *People of Plenty: Economic Abundance and the American Character,* published in 1954. In this work Potter maintained that economic abundance had been the most important determinant in the shaping of the American character. Although Potter was not writing in terms of specific time periods, his interpretation placed the 1920's squarely within the mainstream of American history. In this context, the depression of the 1930's became the exception to the general rule of American prosperity. To put it another way, there was nothing unique or different about the twenties from an economic point of view.

The changing picture of the 1920's was reflected too in the ways that historians began to look at the politics of that period. In the second selection, Arthur S. Link questions whether the portrayal of the twenties as a reactionary decade actually fits the known facts. Link argues that historians for a long time accepted uncritically the hypothesis that Progressivism had disintegrated at the end of the World War I. Progressive ideals and leadership supposedly were submerged by the rising tide of reaction and bigotry in the postwar era. This was not so, says Link. Progressivism, after all, had not been a single national movement; it had been composed of a number of diverse reform movements operating at different levels in society. The war had shattered the coalition of Progressive reformers, but many of the individual reform efforts continued in the postwar period — albeit with less vigor. There were still many Progressive leaders in the Congress in the twenties, Link maintains. This fact was often obscured by the reactionary and conservative figures who were elected as presidents or dominated the executive branch of the government and thus concealed from public view continued existence of Progressive ideals that later reasserted themselves in the New Deal era. Link implicitly rejects the Progressive historiography of the twenties; his picture of the decade is far less critical because of his desire to redress the balance by pointing to the achievements as well as the failures of that era.

As historians examined the 1920's in greater detail, the reputations of some men who had been vilified by earlier scholars were rehabilitated. Herbert Hoover, for example, had been savagely attacked by writers in the 1930's and early 1940's for holding on to an outdated philosophy of individualism that prevented him from taking appropriate governmental measures to combat the destructive effects of the great depression. Many scholars in the post World War II era, on the other hand, were more prone to praise Hoover than to condemn him.

In the third selection, written in the 1950's, Carl Degler examines the "ordeal" of Herbert Hoover. To Degler the picture of Hoover as a cold-hearted individual and inept politician who was incapable of acting in the face of a national calamity simply has no basis in fact. Hoover, according to Degler, always retained close ties with both Democratic and Republican Progressives; in this respect he was quite unlike his two predecessors in the White House. After becoming President he signed a number of Progressive measures into law, including the Norris–La Guardia Act of 1932, which forbade the use of the injunction against labor unions where such a device might be used to prevent picketing, strikes, and boycotts. Hoover also adopted a number of measures designed to combat the effects of the depression. In Degler's eyes, Hoover was no Social Darwinist arguing for the survival of the fittest; he was a true activist, but one who operated within a very rigid ideology.

Hoover, above all, was committed to a philosophy of individualism; he abhorred the thought of the government's competing with or becoming a substitute for private enterprise. As a result he was completely opposed to the idea of an unbalanced budget. Hoover's difficulty, writes Degler, was not that he did nothing, but that he found it difficult to compromise his political principles or admit that he was wrong. From Degler's evaluation, Hoover emerges as an able though unfortunate president who anticipated to a large degree many of the measures that emerged during the New Deal.

By the mid-1950's, other historians were well along in their task of reevaluating the older points of view about the 1920's. Rather than a strange interruption of the normal course of American history, the twenties had become in the eyes of many scholars a continuation of the Progressive era and a prelude to the New Deal. While this controversial decade had many unique characteristics of its own, it also had much in common with both America's past and its future. To Henry F. May, for example, the period was one in which "common values and common beliefs were replaced by separate and conflicting loyalties." Prior to 1910, claimed May, American culture had been unified more or less under the leadership of a Protestant upper-middle-class aristocracy. After the first decade of the twentieth century, May continued, the position of this elite began to decline as other groups, including the rising new middle class, laboring class, and the ethnic minorities, achieved a new-found maturity and gained greater power within American society. The cultural disintegration of the 1920's – a movement synonymous with the decline of the old Protestant literary and moral tradition – was a complex development. To divine the true nature of the decade, May concluded, would require an examination not only of the politics, economics, literature, and science of the period, but also of the relationship between each of these elements.[6]

Surprisingly enough, the 1920's have generated far less controversy among historians than either the Progressive or New Deal era. One reason for this relative lack of interest may lie in the fact that the twenties appear to be an unexciting and uneventful decade in contrast to those that preceded and succeeded it. Nevertheless,

6. Henry F. May, "Shifting Perspectives on the 1920's," *Mississippi Valley Historical Review,* XLIII (December, 1956), 424–427.

an understanding of the basic nature of this decade is crucial, because it often conditions the particular interpretation the historian takes in evaluating the Progressive and New Deal movements. If the Progressive period is assumed to be a liberal one, then the 1920's often becomes by comparison one of conservatism and reaction. If, on the other hand, the Progressive era is considered to be less liberal than commonly supposed, then the 1920's appear less reactionary and more closely related to Progressivism. Similarly, if the New Deal is assumed to be a radical movement, then the twenties seem to present a picture of conservatism. But if the Democratic response to the depression is assumed to have been a conservative one, then the preceding years — particularly those of the Hoover regime — appear to be important ones because many of the New Deal reforms emerged from them.

It should be noted, in conclusion, that historians have usually looked on the 1920's as a decade with certain distinct and unifying characteristics. One may question whether this approach to the period is a correct one. Is it meaningful, for example, to speak about the economic developments in the twenties in terms of presidential administrations? Indeed, can important economic developments be studied within such a restricted time span? Would it not be more accurate for historians to study the emergence of a complex industrial economy in the twentieth century as a whole? Such an approach might preclude a specific discussion of the twenties apart from nearly a century of economic history. To put it another way, is it possible — or even desirable — to periodize the twenties as a decade apart, giving it a uniqueness that it may not have possessed? These are only a few questions that students must deal with if the true nature of the 1920's is to be clearly assessed.

John Kenneth Galbraith

AFTER THE Great Crash came the Great Depression which lasted, with varying severity, for ten years. In 1933, Gross National Product (total production of the economy) was nearly a third less than in 1929. Not until 1937 did the physical volume of production recover to the levels of 1929, and then it promptly slipped back again. Until 1941 the dollar value of production remained below 1929. Between 1930 and 1940 only once, in 1937, did the average number unemployed during the year drop below eight million. In 1933 nearly thirteen million were out of work, or about one in every four in the labor force. In 1938 one person in five was still out of work.

It was during this dreary time that 1929 became a year of myth. People hoped that the country might get back to twenty-nine; in some industries or towns when business was phenomenally good it was almost as good as in twenty-nine; men of outstanding vision, on occasions of exceptional solemnity, were heard to say that 1929 "was no better than Americans deserve."

On the whole, the great stock market crash can be much more readily explained than the depression that followed it. And among the problems involved in assessing the causes of depression none is more intractable than the responsibility to be assigned to the stock market crash. Economics still does not allow final answers on these matters. But, as usual, something can be said.

[II]

As already so often emphasized, the collapse in the stock market in the autumn of 1929 was implicit in the speculation that went

JOHN K. GALBRAITH is Professor of Economics at Harvard University and served as Ambassador to India under President John F. Kennedy. He has written a number of widely read and controversial works, including *American Capitalism* (1952) and *The Affluent Society* (1958).

before. The only question concerning that speculation was how long it would last. Sometime, sooner or later, confidence in the short-run reality of increasing common stock values would weaken. When this happened, some people would sell, and this would destroy the reality of increasing values. Holding for an increase would now become meaningless; the new reality would be falling prices. There would be a rush, pellmell, to unload. This was the way past speculative orgies had ended. It was the way the end came in 1929. It is the way speculation will end in the future.

We do not know why a great speculative orgy occurred in 1928 and 1929. The long accepted explanation that credit was easy and so people were impelled to borrow money to buy common stocks on margin is obviously nonsense. On numerous occasions before and since credit has been easy, and there has been no speculation whatever. Furthermore, much of the 1928 and 1929 speculation occurred on money borrowed at interest rates which for years before, and in any period since, would have been considered exceptionally astringent. Money, by the ordinary tests, was tight in the late twenties.

Far more important than rate of interest and the supply of credit is the mood. Speculation on a large scale requires a pervasive sense of confidence and optimism and conviction that ordinary people were meant to be rich. People must also have faith in the good intentions and even in the benevolence of others, for it is by the agency of others that they will get rich. In 1929 Professor Dice observed: "The common folks believe in their leaders. We no longer look upon the captains of industry as magnified crooks. Have we not heard their voices over the radio? Are we not familiar with their thoughts, ambitions, and ideals as they have expressed them to us almost as a man talks to his friend?" Such a feeling of trust is essential for a boom. When people are cautious, questioning, misanthropic, suspicious, or mean, they are immune to speculative enthusiasms.

Savings must also be plentiful. Speculation, however it may rely on borrowed funds, must be nourished in part by those who participate. If savings are growing rapidly, people will place a lower marginal value on their accumulation; they will be willing to risk some of it against the prospect of a greatly enhanced return. Speculation, accordingly, is most likely to break out after a substantial period of prosperity, rather than in the early phases of recovery from a depression. Macaulay noted that between the Restoration and the Glorious Revolution Englishmen were at loss to know what to do with their savings and that the "natural effect of this state of things was that a crowd of projectors, ingenious and absurd, honest and knavish, employed themselves in devising new schemes for the employment of redundant capital." Bagehot and others have attributed the South Sea Bubble to roughly the same causes. In 1720 England had enjoyed a long period of prosperity, enhanced in part by war expenditures, and during this time private savings are believed to have grown at an unprecedented rate. Investment outlets were also few and returns low. Accordingly, Englishmen were anxious to place their savings at the disposal of the new enterprises and were quick to believe that the prospects were not fantastic. So it was in 1928 and 1929.

Finally, a speculative outbreak has a greater or less immunizing effect. The ensuing collapse automatically destroys the very mood speculation requires. It follows that an outbreak of speculation provides a reasonable assurance that another outbreak will not immediately occur. With time and the dimming of memory, the immunity wears off. A recurrence becomes possible. Nothing would have induced Americans to launch a speculative adventure in the stock market in 1935. By 1955 the chances are very much better.

[III]

As noted, it is easier to account for the boom and crash in the market than to explain their bearing on the depression which followed. The causes of the Great Depression are still far from certain. A lack of certainty, it may also be observed, is not evident in the contemporary writing on the subject. Much of it tells what went wrong and why with marked firmness. However, this paradoxically can itself be an indication of uncertainty. When people are least sure they are often most dogmatic. We do not know what the Russians intend, so we state with great assurance what they will do. We compensate for our inability to foretell the consequences of, say, rearming Germany by asserting positively just what the consequences will be. So it is in economics. Yet, in explaining what happened in 1929 and after, one can distinguish between explanations that might be right and those that are clearly wrong.

A great many people have always felt that a depression was inevitable in the thirties. There had been (at least) seven good years; now by an occult or biblical law of compensation there would have to be seven bad ones. Perhaps, consciously or unconsciously, an argument that was valid for the stock market was brought to bear on the economy in general. Because the market took leave of reality in 1928 and 1929, it had at some time to make a return to reality. The disenchantment was bound to be as painful as the illusions were beguiling. Similarly, the New Era prosperity would some day evaporate; in its wake would come the compensating hardship.

There is also the slightly more subtle conviction that economic life is governed by an inevitable rhythm. After a certain time prosperity destroys itself and depression corrects itself. In 1929 prosperity, in accordance with the dictates of the business cycle, had run its course. This was the faith confessed by the members of the Harvard Economic Society in the spring of 1929 when they concluded that a recession was somehow overdue.

Neither of these beliefs can be seriously supported. The twenties by being comparatively prosperous established no imperative that the thirties be depressed. In the past, good times have given way to less good times and less good or bad to good. But change is normal in a capitalist economy. The degree of regularity in such movements is not great, though often thought to be. No inevitable rhythm required the collapse and stagnation of 1930–40.

Nor was the economy of the United States in 1929 subject to such physical pressure or strain as the result of its past level of performance that a depression was bound to come. The notion that the economy requires occasional rest and resuscitation has a measure of plausibility and also a marked viability. During the summer of 1954 a professional economist on President Eisenhower's personal staff explained the then current recession by saying that the economy was enjoying a brief (and presumably well-merited) rest after the exceptional exertions of preceding years. In 1929 the labor force was not tired; it could have continued to produce indefinitely at the best 1929 rate. The capital plant of the country was not depleted. In the preceding years of prosperity, plant had been renewed and improved. In fact, depletion of the capital plant occurred during the ensuing years of idleness when new investment was sharply curtailed. Raw materials in 1929 were ample for the current rate of production. Entrepreneurs were never more eupeptic. Obviously if men, materials, plant, and management were all capable of continued and even enlarged exertions a refreshing pause was not necessary.

Finally, the high production of the twenties did not, as some have suggested, outrun the wants of the people. During these years people were indeed being supplied with an increasing volume of goods. But there is no evidence that their desire for automobiles, clothing, travel, recreation, or even food was sated. On the contrary, all subsequent evidence showed (given the income to spend) a capacity for a large further increase in consumption. A depression was not needed so that people's wants could catch up with their capacity to produce.

[IV]

What, then, are the plausible causes of the depression? The task of answering can be simplified somewhat by dividing the problem into two parts. First there is the question of why economic activity turned down in 1929. Second there is the vastly more important question of why, having started down, on this unhappy occasion it went down and down and down and remained low for a full decade.

As noted, the Federal Reserve indexes of industrial activity and of factory production, the most comprehensive monthly measures of economic activity then available, reached a peak in June. They then turned down and continued to decline throughout the rest of the year. The turning point in other indicators — factory payrolls, freight-car loadings, and department store sales — came later, and it was October or after before the trend in all of them was clearly down. Still, as economists have generally insisted, and the matter has the high authority of the National Bureau of Economic Research, the economy had weakened in the early summer well before the crash.

This weakening can be variously explained. Production of industrial products, for the moment, had outrun consumer and investment demand for them. The most likely reason is that business concerns, in the characteristic enthusiasm of good times, misjudged the prospective increase in demand and acquired larger inventories than they later found they needed. As a result they curtailed their buying, and this led to a cutback in production. In short, the summer of 1929 marked the beginning of the familiar inventory recession. The proof is not conclusive from the (by present standards) limited figures available. Department store inventories, for which figures are available, seem not to have been out of line early in the year. But a mild slump in department store sales in April could have been a signal for curtailment.

Also there is a chance — one that students of the period have generally favored — that more deep-seated factors were at work and made themselves seriously evident for the first time during that summer. Throughout the twenties production and productivity per worker grew steadily: between 1919 and 1929, output per worker in manufacturing industries increased by about 43 per cent. Wages, salaries, and prices all remained comparatively stable, or in any case underwent no comparable increase. Accordingly, costs fell and with prices the same, profits increased. These profits sustained the spending of the well-to-do, and they also nourished at least some of the expectations behind the stock market boom. Most of all they encouraged a very high level of capital investment. During the twenties, the production of capital goods increased at an average annual rate of 6.4 per cent a year; non-durable consumers' goods, a category which includes such objects of mass consumption as food and clothing, increased at a rate of only 2.8 per cent. (The rate of increase for durable consumers' goods such as cars, dwellings, home furnishings, and the like, much of it representing expenditures of the well-off to well-to-do, was 5.9 per cent.) A large and increasing investment in capital goods was, in other words, a principal device by which the profits were being spent. It follows that anything that interrupted the investment outlays — anything, indeed, which kept them from showing the necessary rate of increase — could cause trouble. When this occurred, compensation through an increase in consumer spending could not automatically be expected. The effect, therefore, of insufficient investment — investment that failed to keep pace with the steady increase in profits — could be falling total demand reflected in turn in falling orders and output. Again there is no final proof of this point, for unfortunately we do not know how rapidly investment had to grow to keep abreast of the current increase in profits. However, the explanation is broadly consistent with the facts.

There are other possible explanations of the downturn. Back of the insufficient advance in investment may have been the high interest rates. Perhaps, although less probably, trouble was transmitted to the economy as a whole from some weak sector like agriculture. Further explanations could be offered. But one thing about this experience is clear. Until well along in the autumn of 1929 the downturn was limited. The recession in business activity was modest and underemployment relatively slight. Up to November it was possible to argue that not much of anything had happened. On other occasions, as noted – in 1924 and 1927 and of late in 1949 – the economy has undergone similar recession. But, unlike these other occasions, in 1929 the recession continued and continued and got violently worse. This is the unique feature of the 1929 experience. This is what we need really to understand.

[V]

There seems little question that in 1929, modifying a famous cliché, the economy was fundamentally unsound. This is a circumstance of first-rate importance. Many things were wrong, but five weaknesses seem to have had an especially intimate bearing on the ensuing disaster. They are:

THE BAD DISTRIBUTION OF INCOME. In 1929 the rich were indubitably rich. The figures are not entirely satisfactory, but it seems certain that the 5 per cent of the population with the highest incomes in that year received approximately one third of all personal income. The proportion of personal income received in the form of interest, dividends, and rent – the income, broadly speaking, of the well-to-do – was about twice as great as in the years following the Second World War.

This highly unequal income distribution meant that the economy was dependent on a high level of investment or a high level of luxury consumer spending or both. The rich cannot buy great quantities of bread. If they are to dispose of what they receive it must be on luxuries or by way of investment in new plants and new projects. Both investment and luxury spending are subject, inevitably, to more erratic influences and to wider fluctuations than the bread and rent outlays of the $25-a-week workman. This high-bracket spending and investment was especially susceptible, one may assume, to the crushing news from the stock market in October of 1929.

THE BAD CORPORATE STRUCTURE. In November 1929, a few weeks after the crash, the Harvard Economic Society gave as a principal reason why a depression need not be feared its reasoned judgment that "business in most lines has been conducted with prudence and conservatism." The fact was that American enterprise in the twenties had opened its hospitable arms to an exceptional number of promoters, grafters, swindlers, impostors, and frauds. This, in the long history of such activities, was a kind of flood tide of corporate larcency.

The most important corporate weakness was inherent in the vast new structure of holding companies and investment trusts. The holding companies controlled large segments of the utility, railroad, and entertainment business. Here, as with the investment trusts, was the constant danger of devastation by reverse leverage. In particular, dividends from the operating companies paid the interest on the bonds of upstream holding companies. The interruption of the dividends meant default on the bonds, bankruptcy, and the collapse of the structure. Under these circumstances, the temptation to curtail investment in operating plant in order to continue dividends was obviously strong. This added to deflationary pressures. The latter, in turn, curtailed earnings and helped bring down the corporate pyramids. When this happened, even more retrenchment was inevitable. Income was earmarked for debt repayment. Borrowing for new investment became impossible. It would be hard to imagine a corporate system better designed to continue and accentuate a deflationary spiral.

THE BAD BANKING STRUCTURE. Since the early thirties, a generation of Americans has been told, sometimes with amusement, sometimes with indignation, often with outrage, of the banking practices of the late twenties. In fact, many of these practices were made ludicrous only by the depression. Loans which would have been perfectly good were made perfectly foolish by the collapse of the borrower's prices or the markets for his goods or the value of the collateral he had posted. The most responsible bankers — those who saw that their debtors were victims of circumstances far beyond their control and sought to help — were often made to look the worst. The bankers yielded, as did others, to the blithe, optimistic, and immoral mood of the times but probably not more so. A depression such as that of 1929–32, were it to begin as this is written, would also be damaging to many currently impeccable banking reputations.

However, although the bankers were not unusually foolish in 1929, the banking structure was inherently weak. The weakness was implicit in the large numbers of independent units. When one bank failed, the assets of others were frozen while depositors elsewhere had a pregnant warning to go and ask for their money. Thus one failure led to other failures, and these spread with a domino effect. Even in the best of times local misfortune or isolated mismanagement could start such a chain reaction. (In the first six months of 1929, 346 banks failed in various parts of the country with aggregate deposits of nearly $115 million.) When income, employment, and values fell as the result of a depression bank failures could quickly become epidemic. This happened after 1929. Again it would be hard to imagine a better arrangement for magnifying the effects of fear. The weak destroyed not only the other weak, but weakened the strong. People everywhere, rich and poor, were made aware of the disaster by the persuasive intelligence that their savings had been destroyed.

Needless to say, such a banking system, once in the convulsions of failure, had a uniquely repressive effect on the spending of its depositors and the investment of its clients.

THE DUBIOUS STATE OF THE FOREIGN BALANCE. This is a familiar story. During the First World War, the United States became a creditor on international account. In the decade following, the surplus of exports over imports which once had paid the interest and principal on loans from Europe continued. The high tariffs, which restricted imports and helped to create this surplus of exports remained. However, history and traditional trading habits also accounted for the persistence of the favorable balance, so called.

Before, payments on interest and principal had in effect been deducted from the trade balance. Now that the United States was a creditor, they were added to this balance. The latter, it should be said, was not huge. In only one year (1928) did the excess of exports over imports come to as much as a billion dollars; in 1923 and 1926 it was only about $375,000,000. However, large or small, this difference had to be covered. Other countries which were buying more than they sold, and had debt payments to make in addition, had somehow to find the means for making up the deficit in their transactions with the United States.

During most of the twenties the difference was covered by cash – i.e., gold payments to the United States – and by new private loans by the United States to other countries. Most of the loans were to governments – national, state, or municipal bodies – and a large proportion were to Germany and Central and South America. The underwriters' margins in handling these loans were generous; the public took them up with enthusiasm; competition for the business was keen. If unfortunately corruption and bribery were required as competitive instruments, these were used. In late 1927 Juan Leguia, the son of the President of Peru, was paid $450,000 by J. and W. Seligman and Company and the National City Company (the security affiliate of the National City Bank) for his services in connection with a $50,000,000 loan which these houses marketed for Peru. Juan's services, according to later testimony, were of a rather negative sort. He was paid for not blocking the deal. The Chase extended President Machado of Cuba, a dictator with a marked predisposition toward murder, a generous personal line of credit which at one time reached $200,000. Machado's son-in-law was employed by the Chase. The bank did a large business in Cuban bonds. In contemplating these loans, there was a tendency to pass quickly over anything that might appear to the disadvantage of the creditor. Mr. Victor Schoepperle, a vice-president of the National City Company with the responsibility for Latin American loans, made the following appraisal of Peru as a credit prospect:

> Peru: Bad debt record, adverse moral and political risk, bad internal debt situation, trade situation about as satisfactory as that of Chile in the past three years. Natural resources more varied. On economic showing Peru should go ahead rapidly in the next 10 years.

On such showing the National City Company floated a $15,000,000 loan for Peru, followed a few months later by a $50,000,000 loan, and some ten months thereafter by a $25,000,000 issue. (Peru did prove a highly adverse political risk. President Leguia, who negotiated the loans, was thrown violently out of office, and the loans went into default.)

In all respects these operations were as much a part of the New Era as Shenandoah and Blue Ridge. They were also just as fragile, and once the illusions of the New Era were dissipated they came as abruptly to an end. This, in turn, forced a fundamental revision in the foreign economic position of the United States. Countries could not cover their adverse trade balance with the United States with increased payments of gold, at least not for long. This meant that they had either to increase their exports to the United States or reduce their imports or default on their past loans. President Hoover and the Congress moved promptly to eliminate the first possibility — that the accounts would be balanced by larger imports — by sharply increasing the tariff. Accordingly, debts, including war debts, went into default and there was a precipitate fall in American exports. The reduction was not vast in relation to total output of the American economy, but it contributed to the general distress and was especially hard on farmers.

THE POOR STATE OF ECONOMIC INTELLIGENCE. To regard the people of any time as particularly obtuse seems vaguely improper, and it also establishes a precedent which members of this generation might regret. Yet it seems certain that the economists and those who offered economic counsel in the late twenties and early thirties were almost uniquely perverse. In the months and years following the stock market crash, the burden of reputable economic advice was invariably on the side of measures that would make things worse. In November of 1929, Mr. Hoover announced a cut in taxes; in the great no-business conferences that followed he asked business firms to keep up their capital investment and to maintain wages. Both of these measures were on the side of increasing spendable income, though unfortunately they were largely without effect. The tax reductions were negligible except in the higher income brackets; businessmen who promised to maintain investment and wages, in accordance with a well-understood convention, considered the promise binding only for the period within which it was not financially disadvantageous to do so. As a result investment outlays and wages were not reduced until circumstances would in any case have brought their reduction.

Still, the effort was in the right direction. Thereafter policy was almost entirely on the side of making things worse. Asked how the government could best advance recovery, the sound and responsible adviser urged that the budget be balanced. Both parties agreed on this. For Republicans the balanced budget was, as ever, high doctrine. But the Democratic Party platform of 1932, with an explicitness which politicians rarely advise, also called for a "federal budget annually balanced on the basis of accurate executive estimates within revenues . . ."

A commitment to a balanced budget is always comprehensive. It then meant there could be no increase in government outlays to expand purchasing power and relieve distress. It meant there could be no further tax reduction. But taken literally it meant much more. From 1930 on the budget was far out of balance, and balance, therefore, meant an increase in taxes, a reduction in spending, or both. The Democratic platform in 1932 called for an "immediate and drastic reduction of governmental expenditures" to accomplish at least a 25 per cent decrease in the cost of government.

The balanced budget was not a subject of thought. Nor was it, as often asserted, precisely a matter of faith. Rather it was a formula. For centuries avoidance of borrowing had protected people from slovenly or reckless public housekeeping. Slovenly or reckless keepers of the public purse had often composed complicated arguments to show why balance of income and outlay was not a mark of virtue. Experience had shown that however convenient this belief might seem in the short run, discomfort or disaster followed in the long run. Those simple precepts of a simple world did not hold amid the growing complexities of the early thirties. Mass unemployment in particular had altered the rules. Events had played a very bad trick on people, but almost no one tried to think out the problem anew.

The balanced budget was not the only strait jacket on policy. There was also the bogey of "going off" the gold standard and, most surprisingly, of risking inflation. Until 1932 the United States added formidably to its gold reserves, and instead of inflation the country was experiencing the most violent deflation in the nation's history. Yet every sober adviser saw dangers here, including the danger of runaway price increases. Americans, though in years now well in the past, had shown a penchant for tinkering with the money supply and enjoying the brief but heady joys of a boom in prices. In 1931 or 1932, the danger or even the feasibility of such a boom was nil. The advisers and counselors were not, however, analyzing the danger or even the possibility. They were serving only as the custodians of bad memories.

The fear of inflation reinforced the demand for the balanced budget. It also limited efforts to make interest rates low, credit plentiful (or at least redundant) and borrowing as easy as possible under the circumstances. Devaluation of the dollar was, of course, flatly ruled out. This directly violated the gold standard rules. At best, in such depression times, monetary policy is a feeble reed on which to lean. The current economic clichés did not allow even the use of that frail weapon. And again, these attitudes were above party. Though himself singularly open-minded, Roosevelt was careful not to offend or disturb his followers. In a speech in Brooklyn toward the close of the 1932 campaign, he said:

> The Democratic platform specifically declares, "We advocate a sound currency to be preserved at all hazards." That is plain English. In discussing this platform on July 30, I said, "Sound money is an international necessity, not a domestic consideration for one nation alone." Far up in the Northwest, at Butte, I repeated the pledge . . . In Seattle I reaffirmed my attitude . . .

The following February, Mr. Hoover set forth his view, as often before, in a famous letter to the President-elect:

> It would steady the country greatly if there could be prompt assurance that there will be no tampering or inflation of the currency; that the budget will be unquestionably balanced even if further taxation is necessary; that the Government credit will be maintained by refusal to exhaust it in the issue of securities.

The rejection of both fiscal (tax and expenditure) and monetary policy amounted precisely to a rejection of all affirmative government economic policy. The economic advisers of the day had both the unanimity and the authority to force the leaders of both parties to disavow all the available steps to check deflation and depression. In its own way this was a marked achievement – a triumph of dogma over thought. The consequences were profound.

[VI]

It is in light of the above weaknesses of the economy that the role of the stock market crash in the great tragedy of the thirties must be seen. The years of self-depreciation by Wall Street to the contrary, the role is one of respectable importance. The collapse in securities values affected in the first instance the wealthy and the well-to-do. But we see that in the world of 1929 this was a vital group. The members disposed of a large proportion of the consumer income; they were the source of a lion's share of personal saving and investment. Anything that struck at the spending or investment by this group would of necessity have broad effects on expenditure and income in the economy at large. Precisely such a blow was struck by the stock market crash. In addition, the crash promptly removed from the economy the support that it had been deriving from the spending of stock market gains.

The stock market crash was also an exceptionally effective way of exploiting the weaknesses of the corporate structure. Operating companies at the end of the holding-company chain were forced by the crash to retrench. The subsequent collapse of these systems and also of the investment trusts effectively destroyed both the ability to borrow and the willingness to lend for investment. What have long looked like purely fiduciary effects were, in fact, quickly translated into declining orders and increasing unemployment.

The crash was also effective in bringing to an end the foreign lending by which the international accounts had been balanced. Now the accounts had, in the main, to be balanced by reduced exports. This put prompt and heavy pressure on export markets for wheat, cotton, and tobacco. Perhaps the foreign loans had only delayed an adjustment in the balance which had one day to come. The stock market crash served nonetheless to precipitate the adjustment with great suddenness at a most unpropitious time. The instinct of farmers who traced their troubles to the stock market was not totally misguided.

Finally, when the misfortune had struck, the attitudes of the time kept anything from being done about it. This, perhaps, was the most disconcerting feature of all. Some people were hungry in 1930 and 1931 and 1932. Others were tortured by the fear that they might go hungry. Yet others suffered the agony of the descent from the honor and respectability that goes with income into poverty. And still others feared that they would be next. Meanwhile everyone suffered from a sense of utter hopelessness. Nothing, it seemed, could be done. And given the ideas which controlled policy, nothing could be done.

Had the economy been fundamentally sound in 1929 the effect of the great stock market crash might have been small. Alternatively, the shock to confidence and the loss of spending by those who were caught in the market might soon have worn off. But business in 1929 was not sound; on the contrary it was exceedingly fragile. It was vulnerable to the kind of blow it received from Wall Street. Those who have emphasized this vulnerability are obviously on strong ground. Yet when a greenhouse succumbs to a hailstorm something more than a purely passive role is normally attributed to the storm. One must accord similar significance to the typhoon which blew out of lower Manhattan in October 1929.

Arthur S. Link

IF THE DAY has not yet arrived when we can make a definite synthesis of political developments between the Armistice and the Great Depression, it is surely high time for historians to begin to clear away the accumulated heap of mistaken and half-mistaken hypotheses about this important transitional period. Writing often without fear or much research (to paraphrase Carl Becker's remark), we recent American historians have gone on indefatigably to perpetuate hypotheses that either reflected the disillusionment and despair of contemporaries, or once served their purpose in exposing the alleged hiatus in the great continuum of twentieth-century reform.

Stated briefly, the following are what might be called the governing hypotheses of the period under discussion: The 1920's were a period made almost unique by an extraordinary reaction against idealism and reform. They were a time when the political representatives of big business and Wall Street executed a relentless and successful campaign in state and nation to subvert the regulatory structure that had been built at the cost of so much toil and sweat since the 1870's, and to restore a Hanna-like reign of special privilege to benefit business, industry, and finance. The surging tides of nationalism and mass hatreds generated by World War I continued to engulf the land and were manifested, among other things, in fear of communism, suppression of civil liberties, revival of nativism and anti-Semitism most crudely exemplified by the Ku Klux Klan, and in the triumph of racism and prejudice in immigration legislation. The 1920's were an era when great traditions and ideals were repudiated or forgotten, when the American people, propelled by a crass materialism in their scramble for wealth,

"What Happened to the Progressive Movement in the 1920's," *American Historical Review,* LXIV (July, 1959), 833–851. Reprinted by permission of the American Historical Association and Arthur S. Link.

ARTHUR S. LINK (1920–) is Edwards Professor of American History at Princeton University. He is the author of many books on the Wilsonian era; his major work is a multi-volume biography of Woodrow Wilson.

uttered a curse on twenty-five years of reform endeavor. As a result, progressives were stunned and everywhere in retreat along the entire political front, their forces disorganized and leaderless, their movement shattered, their dreams of a new America turned into agonizing nightmares.

To be sure, the total picture that emerges from these generalizations is overdrawn. Yet it seems fair to say that leading historians have advanced each of these generalizations, that the total picture is the one that most of us younger historians saw during the years of our training, and that these hypotheses to a greater or lesser degree still control the way in which we write and teach about the 1920's, as a reading of textbooks and general works will quickly show.

This paper has not been written, however, to quarrel with anyone or to make an indictment. Its purposes are, first, to attempt to determine the degree to which the governing hypotheses, as stated, are adequate or inadequate to explain the political phenomena of the period, and, second, to discover whether any new and sounder hypotheses might be suggested. Such an effort, of course, must be tentative and above all imperfect in view of the absence of sufficient foundations for a synthesis.

Happily, however, we do not have to proceed entirely in the dark. Historians young and old, but mostly young, have already discovered that the period of the 1920's is the exciting new frontier of American historical research and that its opportunities are almost limitless in view of the mass of manuscript materials that are becoming available. Thus we have (the following examples are mentioned only at random) excellent recent studies of agrarian discontent and farm movements by Theodore Saloutos, John D. Hicks, Gilbert C. Fite, Robert L. Morlan, and James H. Shideler; of nativism and problems of immigration and assimilation by John Higham, Oscar Handlin, Robert A. Devine, and Edmund D. Cronon; of intellectual currents, the social gospel, and religious controversies by Henry F. May, Paul A. Carter, Robert M. Miller, and Norman F. Furniss; of left-wing politics and labor developments by Theodore Draper, David A. Shannon, Daniel Bell, Paul M. Angle, and Matthew Josephson; of the campaign of 1928 by Edmund A. Moore; and of political and judicial leaders by Alpheus T. Mason, Frank Freidel, Arthur M. Schlesinger, Jr.,

Merlo J. Pusey, and Joel F. Paschal.[1] Moreover, we can look forward to the early publication of studies that will be equally illuminating for the period, like the biographies of George W. Norris, Thomas J. Walsh, and Albert B. Fall now being prepared by Richard Lowitt, Leonard Bates, and David Stratton, respectively, and the recently completed study of the campaign and election of 1920 by Wesley M. Bagby.[2]

Obviously, we are not only at a point in the progress of our research into the political history of the 1920's when we can begin to generalize, but we have reached the time when we should

1. Theodore Saloutos and John D. Hicks, *Agrarian Discontent in the Middle West, 1900–1939* (Madison, Wis., 1951); Gilbert C. Fite, *Peter Norbeck: Prairie Statesman* (Columbia, Mo., 1948), and *George N. Peek and the Fight for Farm Parity* (Norman, Okla., 1954); Robert L. Morlan, *Political Prairie Fire: The Nonpartisan League, 1915–1922* (Minneapolis, Minn., 1955); James H. Shideler, *Farm Crisis, 1919–1923* (Berkeley, Calif., 1957); John Higham, *Strangers in the Land: Patterns of American Nativism, 1860–1925* (New Brunswick, N. J., 1955); Oscar Handlin, *The American People in the Twentieth Century* (Cambridge, Mass., 1954); Robert A. Devine, *American Immigration Policy, 1924–1952* (New Haven, Conn., 1957); Edmund D. Cronon, *Black Moses: The Story of Marcus Garvey and the Universal Negro Improvement Association* (Madison, Wis., 1955); Henry F. May, "Shifting Perspectives on the 1920's," *Mississippi Valley Historical Review,* XLIII (Dec., 1956), 405–27; Paul A. Carter, *The Decline and Revival of the Social Gospel* (Ithaca, N. Y., 1956); Robert M. Miller, "An Inquiry into the Social Attitudes of American Protestantism, 1919–1939," doctoral dissertation, Northwestern University, 1955; Norman F. Furniss, *The Fundamentalist Controversy, 1918–1931* (New Haven, Conn., 1954); Theodore Draper, *The Roots of American Communism* (New York, 1957); David A. Shannon, *The Socialist Party of America: A History* (New York, 1955); Daniel Bell, "The Background and Development of Marxian Socialism in the United States," *Socialism and American Life,* ed. Donald D. Egbert and Stow Persons (2 vols., Princeton, N. J., 1952), I, 215–405; Paul M. Angle, *Bloody Williamson* (New York, 1952); Matthew Josephson, *Sidney Hillman: Statesman of American Labor* (New York, 1952); Edmund A. Moore, *A Catholic Runs for President: The Campaign of 1928* (New York, 1956); Alpheus Thomas Mason, *Brandeis: A Free Man's Life* (New York, 1946), and *Harlan Fiske Stone: Pillar of the Law* (New York, 1956); Frank Freidel, *Franklin D. Roosevelt: The Ordeal* (Boston, 1954); Arthur M. Schlesinger, Jr., *The Age of Roosevelt: The Crisis of the Old Order* (Boston, 1957); Merlo J. Pusey, *Charles Evans Hughes* (2 vols., New York, 1951); Joel Francis Paschal, *Mr. Justice Sutherland: A Man against the State* (Princeton, N. J., 1951).

2. Wesley M. Bagby, "Woodrow Wilson and the Great Debacle of 1920," MS in the possession of Professor Bagby; see also his "The 'Smoked-Filled Room' and the Nomination of Warren G. Harding," *Mississippi Valley Historical Review,* XLI (Mar., 1955), 657–74, and "Woodrow Wilson, a Third Term, and the Solemn Referendum," *American Historical Review,* LX (Apr., 1955), 567–75.

attempt to find some consensus, however tentative it must now be, concerning the larger political dimensions and meanings of the period.

In answering the question of what happened to the progressive movement in the 1920's, we should begin by looking briefly at some fundamental facts about the movement before 1918, facts that in large measure predetermined its fate in the 1920's, given the political climate and circumstances that prevailed.

The first of these was the elementary fact that the progressive movement never really existed as a recognizable organization with common goals and a political machinery geared to achieve them. Generally speaking (and for the purposes of this paper), progressivism might be defined as the popular effort, which began convulsively in the 1890's and waxed and waned afterward to our own time, to insure the survival of democracy in the United States by the enlargement of governmental power to control and offset the power of private economic groups over the nation's institutions and life. Actually, of course, from the 1890's on there were many "progressive" movements on many levels seeking sometimes contradictory objectives. Not all, but most of these campaigns were the work of special interest groups or classes seeking greater political status and economic security. This was true from the beginning of the progressive movement in the 1890's; by 1913 it was that movement's most important characteristic.

The second fundamental fact — that the progressive movements were often largely middle class in constituency and orientation — is of course well known, but an important corollary has often been ignored. It was that several of the most important reform movements were inspired, staffed, and led by businessmen with very specific or special-interest objectives in view. Because they hated waste, mismanagement, and high taxes, they, together with their friends in the legal profession, often furnished the leadership of good government campaigns. Because they feared industrial monopoly, abuse of power by railroads, and the growth of financial oligarchy, they were the backbone of the movements that culminated in the adoption of the Hepburn and later acts for railroad regulation, the Federal Reserve Act, and the Federal Trade Commission Act. Among the many consequences of their participation in the progressive movement, two should be mentioned because of their significance for developments in the 1920's: First, the strong identification of businessmen with good government and economic reforms for which the general public also had a lively concern helped preserve the good reputation of the middle-class business community (as opposed to its alleged natural enemies, monopolists, malefactors of great wealth, and railroad barons) and helped to direct the energies of the progressive movement toward the strengthening instead of the shackling of the business community. Second, their activities and influence served to intensify the tensions within the broad reform movement, because they often opposed the demands of farm groups, labor unions, and advocates of social justice.

The third remark to be made about the progressive movement before 1918 is that despite its actual diversity and inner tensions it did seem to have unity; that is, it seemed to share common ideals and objectives. This was true in part because much of the motivation even of the special-interest groups was altruistic (at least they succeeded in convincing themselves that they sought the welfare of society rather than their own interests primarily); in part because political leadership generally succeeded in subordinating inner tensions. It was true, above all, because there were in fact important idealistic elements in the progressive ranks – social gospel leaders, social justice elements, and intellectuals and philosophers – who worked hard at the task of defining and elevating common principles and goals.

Fourth and finally, the substantial progressive achievements before 1918 had been gained, at least on the federal level, only because of the temporary dislocations of the national political structure caused by successive popular uprisings, not because progressives had found or created a viable organization for perpetuating their control. Or, to put the matter another way, before 1918 the various progressive elements had failed to destroy the existing party structure by organizing a national party of their own that could survive. They, or at least many of them, tried in 1912; and it seemed for a time in 1916 that Woodrow Wilson had succeeded in drawing the important progressive groups permanently into the Democratic party. But Wilson's accomplishment did not survive even to the end of the war, and by 1920 traditional partisan loyalties were reasserting themselves with extraordinary vigor.

With this introduction, we can now ask what happened to the progressive movement or movements in the 1920's. Surely no one would contend that after 1916 the political scene did not change significantly, both on the state and national levels. There was the seemingly obvious fact that the Wilsonian coalition had been wrecked by the election of 1920, and that the progressive elements were divided and afterward unable to agree upon a program or to control the national government. There was the even more "obvious" fact that conservative Republican presidents and their cabinets controlled the executive branch throughout the period. There was Congress, as Eric F. Goldman had said, allegedly whooping through procorporation legislation, and the Supreme Court interpreting the New Freedom laws in a way that harassed unions and encouraged trusts.[3] There were, to outraged idealists and intellectuals, the more disgusting spectacles of Red hunts, mass arrests and deportations, the survival deep into the 1920's of arrogant nationalism, crusades against the teaching of evolution, the attempted suppression of the right to drink, and myriad other manifestations of what would now be called a repressive reaction.[4]

Like the hypotheses suggested at the beginning, this picture is overdrawn in some particulars. But it is accurate in part, for progressivism was certainly on the downgrade if not in decay after 1918. This is an obvious fact that needs explanation and understanding rather than elaborate proof. We can go a long way toward answering our question if we can explain, at least partially, the extraordinary complex developments that converge to produce the "obvious" result.

For this explanation we must begin by looking at the several progressive elements and their relation to each other and to the two major parties after 1916. Since national progressivism was never an organized or independent movement (except imperfectly and then only temporarily in 1912), it could succeed only when its constituent elements formed a coalition strong enough to control one of the major parties. This had happened in 1916, when southern and western farmers, organized labor, the social justice elements, and a large part of the independent radicals who had here-

3. Eric F. Goldman, *Rendezvous with Destiny* (New York, 1953), 284. The "allegedly" in this sentence is mine, not Professor Goldman's.

4. H. C. Peterson and Gilbert C. Fite, *Opponents of War, 1917–1918* (Norman, Okla., 1957); Robert K. Murray, *Red Scare: A Study in National Hysteria, 1919–1920* (Minneapolis, Minn., 1955).

tofore voted the Socialist ticket coalesced to continue the control of Wilson and the Democratic party.

The important fact about the progressive coalition of 1916, however, was not its strength but its weakness. It was not a new party but a temporary alliance, welded in the heat of the most extraordinary domestic and external events. To be sure, it functioned for the most part successfully during the war, in providing the necessary support for a program of heavy taxation, relatively stringent controls over business and industry, and extensive new benefits to labor. Surviving in a crippled way even in the months following the Armistice, it put across a program that constituted a sizable triumph for the progressive movement — continued heavy taxation, the Transportation Act of 1920, the culmination of the long fight for railroad regulation, a new child labor act, amendments for prohibition and woman suffrage, immigration restriction, and water power and conservation legislation.

Even so, the progressive coalition of 1916 was inherently unstable. Indeed, it was so wracked by inner tensions that it could not survive, and destruction came inexorably, it seemed systematically, from 1917 to 1920. Why was this true?

First, the independent radicals and antiwar agrarians were alienated by the war declaration and the government's suppression of dissent and civil liberties during the war and the Red scare. Organized labor was disaffected by the administration's coercion of the coal miners in 1919, its lukewarm if not hostile attitude during the great strikes of 1919 and 1920, and its failure to support the Plumb Plan for nationalization of the railroads. Isolationists and idealists were outraged by what they thought was the President's betrayal of American traditions or the liberal peace program at Paris. These tensions were strong enough to disrupt the coalition, but a final one would have been fatal even if the others had never existed. This was the alienation of farmers in the Plains and western states produced by the administration's refusal to impose price controls on cotton while it maintained ceilings on the prices of other agricultural commodities,[5] and especially by the administration's failure to do anything decisive to stem the downward plunge

5. On this point, see Seward W. Livermore, "The Sectional Issue in the 1918 Congressional Elections," *Mississippi Valley Historical Review,* XXXV (June, 1948), 29–60.

of farm prices that began in the summer of 1920.[6] Under the impact of all these stresses, the Wilsonian coalition gradually disintegrated from 1917 to 1920 and disappeared entirely during the campaign of 1920.

The progressive coalition was thus destroyed, but the components of a potential movement remained. As we will see, these elements were neither inactive nor entirely unsuccessful in the 1920's. But they obviously failed to find common principles and a program, much less to unite effectively for political action on a national scale. I suggest that this was true, in part at least, for the following reasons:

First, the progressive elements could never create or gain control of a political organization capable of carrying them into national office. The Republican party was patently an impossible instrument because control of the GOP was too much in the hands of the eastern and midwestern industrial, oil, and financial interests, as it had been since about 1910. There was always the hope of a third party. Several progressive groups — insurgent midwestern Republicans, the railroad brotherhoods, a segment of the AF of L, and the moderate Socialists under Robert M. La Follette — tried to realize this goal in 1924, only to discover that third party movements in the United States are doomed to failure except in periods of enormous national turmoil, and that the 1920's were not such a time. Thus the Democratic party remained the only vehicle that conceivably could have been used by a new progressive coalition. But that party was simply not capable of such service in the 1920's. It was so torn by conflicts between its eastern, big city wing and its southern and western rural majority that it literally ceased to be a national party. It remained strong in its sectional and metropolitan components, but it was so divided that it barely succeeded in nominating a presidential candidate at all in 1924 and nominated one in 1928 only at the cost of temporary disruption.[7]

6. Arthur S. Link, "The Federal Reserve Policy and the Agricultural Depression of 1920–1921," *Agricultural History,* XX (July, 1946), 166–75; and Herbert F. Margulies, "The Election of 1920 in Wisconsin: The Return to 'Normalcy' Reappraised," *Wisconsin Magazine of History,* XXXVIII (Autumn, 1954), 15–22.

7. For a highly partisan account of these events see Karl Schriftgiesser, *This Was Normalcy* (Boston, 1948). More balanced are the already cited Freidel, *Franklin D. Roosevelt: The Ordeal,* and Schlesinger, *The Age of Roosevelt: The Crisis of the Old Order.*

Progressivism declined in the 1920's, in the second place, because, as has been suggested, the tensions that had wrecked the coalition of 1916 not only persisted but actually grew in number and intensity. The two most numerous progressive elements, the southern and western farmers, strongly supported the Eighteenth Amendment, were heavily tinged with nativism and therefore supported immigration restriction, were either members of, friendly to, or politically afraid of the Ku Klux Klan, and demanded as the principal plank in their platform legislation to guarantee them a larger share of the national income. On all these points and issues the lower and lower middle classes in the large cities stood in direct and often violent opposition to their potential allies in the rural areas. Moreover, the liaison between the farm groups and organized labor, which had been productive of much significant legislation during the Wilson period, virtually ceased to exist in the 1920's. There were many reasons for this development, and I mention only one — the fact that the preeminent spokesmen of farmers in the 1920's, the new Farm Bureau Federation, represented the larger commercial farmers who (in contrast to the members of the leading farm organization in Wilson's day, the National Farmers' Union) were often employers themselves and felt no identification with the rank and file of labor.

It was little wonder, therefore (and this is a third reason for the weakness of progressivism in the 1920's), that the tension-ridden progressive groups were never able to agree upon a program that, like the Democratic platform of 1916, could provide the basis for a revived coalition. So long as progressive groups fought one another more fiercely than they fought their natural opponents, such agreement was impossible; and so long as common goals were impossible to achieve, a national progressive movement could not take effective form. Nothing illustrates this better than the failure of the Democratic conventions of 1924 and 1928 to adopt platforms that could rally and unite the discontented elements. One result, among others, was that southern farmers voted as Democrats and western farmers as Republicans. And, as Professor Frank Freidel once commented to the author, much of the failure of progressivism in the 1920's can be explained by this elementary fact.

A deeper reason for the failure of progressives to unite ideologically in the 1920's was what might be called a substantial paralysis of the progressive mind. This was partly the result of the repudiation of progressive ideals by many intellectuals and the defection from the progressive movement of the urban middle classes and professional groups, as will be demonstrated. It was the result, even more importantly, of the fact that progressivism as an organized body of political thought found itself at a crossroads in the 1920's, like progressivism today, and did not know which way to turn. The major objectives of the progressive movement of the prewar years had in fact been largely achieved by 1920. In what direction should progressivism now move? Should it remain in the channels already deeply cut by its own traditions, and, while giving sincere allegiance to the ideal of democratic capitalism, work for more comprehensive programs of business regulation and assistance to disadvantaged classes like farmers and submerged industrial workers? Should it abandon these traditions and, like most similar European movements, take the road toward a moderate socialism with a predominantly labor orientation? Should it attempt merely to revive the goals of more democracy through changes in the political machinery? Or should it become mainly an agrarian movement with purely agrarian goals?

These were real dilemmas, not academic ones, and one can see numerous examples of how they confused and almost paralyzed progressives in the 1920's. The platform of La Follette's Progressive party of 1924 offers one revealing illustration. It embodied much that was old and meaningless by this time (the direct election of the president and a national referendum before the adoption of a war resolution, for example) and little that had any real significance for the future.[8] And yet it was the best that a vigorous and idealistic movement could offer. A second example was the plight of the agrarians and insurgents in Congress who fought so hard all through the 1920's against Andrew Mellon's proposals to abolish the inheritance tax and to make drastic reductions in the taxes on large incomes. In view of the rapid reduction of the federal debt, the progressives were hard pressed to justify the continuation of

8. For a different picture see Belle C. La Follette and Fola La Follette, *Robert M. La Follette* (2 vols., New York, 1953); and Russel B. Nye, *Midwestern Progressive Politics, 1870–1950* (East Lansing, Mich., 1951). Both works contribute to an understanding of progressive politics in the 1920's.

nearly confiscatory tax levels, simply because few of them realized the wide social and economic uses to which the income tax could be put. Lacking any programs for the redistribution of the national income (except to farmers), they were plagued and overwhelmed by the surpluses in the federal Treasury until, for want of any good arguments, they finally gave Secretary Andrew Mellon the legislation he had been demanding.[9] A third and final example of this virtual paralysis of the progressive mind was perhaps the most revealing of all. It was the attempt that Woodrow Wilson, Louis D. Brandeis, and other Democratic leaders made from 1921 to 1924 to draft a new charter for progressivism. Except for its inevitable proposals for an idealistic world leadership, the document that emerged from this interchange included little or nothing that would have sounded new to a western progressive in 1912.

A fourth reason for the disintegration and decline of the progressive movement in the 1920's was the lack of any effective leadership. Given the political temper and circumstances of the 1920's it is possible that such leadership could not have operated successfully in any event. Perhaps the various progressive elements were so mutually hostile and so self-centered in interests and objectives that even a Theodore Roosevelt or a Woodrow Wilson, had they been at the zenith of their powers in the 1920's, could not have drawn them together in a common front. We will never know what a strong national leader might have done because by a trick of fate no such leader emerged before Franklin D. Roosevelt.

Four factors, then, contributed to the failure of the progressive components to unite successfully after 1918 and, as things turned out, before 1932: the lack of a suitable political vehicle, the severity of the tensions that kept progressives apart, the failure of progressives to agree upon a common program, and the absence of a national leadership, without which a united movement could never be created and sustained. These were all weaknesses that stemmed to a large degree from the instability and failures of the progressive movement itself.

There were, besides, a number of what might be called external causes for the movement's decline. In considering them one must begin with what was seemingly the most important — the alleged

9. Here indebtedness is acknowledged to Sidney Ratner, *American Taxation: Its History as a Social Force in Democracy* (New York, 1942).

fact that the 1920's were a very unpropitious time for any new progressive revolt because of the ever-increasing level of economic prosperity, the materialism, and the general contentment of the decade 1919 to 1929. Part of this generalization is valid when applied to specific elements in the population. For example, the rapid rise in the real wages of industrial workers, coupled with generally full employment and the spread of so-called welfare practices among management, certainly did much to weaken and avert the further spread of organized labor, and thus to debilitate one of the important progressive components. But to say that it was prosperity per se that created a climate unfriendly to progressive ideals would be inaccurate. There was little prosperity and much depression during the 1920's for the single largest economic group, the farmers, as well as for numerous other groups. Progressivism, moreover, can flourish as much during periods of prosperity as during periods of discontent, as the history of the development of the progressive movement from 1901 to 1917 and of its triumph from 1945 to 1956 prove.

Vastly more important among the external factors in the decline of progressivism was the widespread, almost wholesale, defection from its ranks of the middle classes – the middling businessmen, bankers, and manufacturers, and the professional people closely associated with them in ideals and habits – in American cities large and small. For an understanding of this phenomenon no simple explanations like "prosperity" or the "temper of the times" will suffice, although they give some insight. The important fact was that these groups found a new economic and social status as a consequence of the flowering of American enterprise under the impact of the technological, financial, and other revolutions of the 1920's. If, as Professor Richard Hofstadter had claimed,[10] the urban middle classes were progressive (that is, they demanded governmental relief from various anxieties) in the early 1900's because they resented their loss of social prestige to the *nouveaux riches* and feared being ground under by monopolists in industry, banking, and labor – if this is true, then the urban middle classes were not progressive in the 1920's for inverse reasons. Their temper was dynamic, expansive, and supremely confident. They knew that

10. Richard Hofstader, *The Age of Reform: From Bryan to F.D.R.* (New York, 1955), 131 ff.

they were building a new America, a business civilization based not upon monopoly and restriction but upon a whole new set of business values — mass production and consumption, short hours and high wages, full employment, welfare capitalism. And what was more important, virtually the entire country (at least the journalists, writers in popular magazines, and many preachers and professors) acknowledged that the nation's destiny was in good hands. It was little wonder, therefore, that the whole complex of groups constituting the urban middle classes, whether in New York, Zenith, or Middletown, had little interest in rebellion or even in mild reform proposals that seemed to imperil their leadership and control.

Other important factors, of course, contributed to the contentment of the urban middle classes. The professionalization of business and the full-blown emergence of a large managerial class had a profound impact upon social and political ideals. The acceleration of mass advertising played its role, as did also the beginning disintegration of the great cities with the spread of middle- and upper-middle-class suburbs, a factor that diffused the remaining reform energies among the urban leaders.

A second external factor in the decline of the progressive movement after 1918 was the desertion from its ranks of a good part of the intellectual leadership of the country. Indeed, more than simple desertion was involved here; it was often a matter of a cynical repudiation of the ideals from which progressivism derived its strength. I do not mean to imply too much by this generalization. I know that what has been called intellectual progressivism not only survived in the 1920's but actually flourished in many fields.[11] I know that the intellectual foundations of our present quasi-welfare state were either being laid or reinforced during the decade. Even so, one cannot evade the conclusion that the intellectual-political climate of the 1920's was vastly different from the one that had prevailed in the preceding two decades.

During the years of the great progressive revolt, intellectuals — novelists, journalists, political thinkers, social scientists, histori-

11. *Ibid.*, 5, 131, 135 ff. For a recent excellent survey, previously cited, see Henry F. May, "Shifting Perspectives on the 1920's." Schlesinger's previously cited *Age of Roosevelt* sheds much new light on the economic thought of the 1920's.

ans, and the like – had made a deeply personal commitment to to the cause of democracy, first in domestic and then in foreign affairs. Their leadership in and impact on many phases of the progressive movement had been profound. By contrast, in the 1920's a large body of this intellectual phalanx turned against the very ideals they had once deified. One could cite, for example, the reaction of the idealists against the Versailles settlement; the disenchantment of the intellectuals with the extension of government authority when it could be used to justify the Eighteenth Amendment or the suppression of free speech; or the inevitable loss of faith in the "people" when en masse they hounded so-called radicals, joined Bryan's crusade against evolution, or regaled themselves as Knights of the Ku Klux Klan. Whatever the cause, many alienated intellectuals simply withdrew or repudiated any identification with the groups they had once helped to lead. The result was not fatal to progressivism, but it was serious. The spark plugs had been removed from the engine of reform.

The progressive movement, then, unquestionably declined, but was it defunct in the 1920's? Much, of course, depends upon the definition of terms. If we accept the usual definition for "defunct" as "dead" or "ceasing to have any life or strength," we must recognize that the progressive movement was certainly not defunct in the 1920's; that on the contrary at least important parts of it were very much alive; and that it is just as important to know how and why progressivism survived as it is to know how and why it declined.

To state the matter briefly, progressivism survived in the 1920's because several important elements of the movement remained either in full vigor or in only slightly diminished strength. These were the farmers, after 1918 better organized and more powerful than during the high tide of the progressive revolt; the politically conscious elements among organized labor, particularly the railroad brotherhoods, who wielded a power all out of proportion to their numbers; the Democratic organizations in the large cities, usually vitally concerned with the welfare of the so-called lower classes; a remnant of independent radicals, social workers, and social gospel writers and preachers; and finally, an emerging new vocal element, the champions of public power and regional developments.

Although they never united effectively enough to capture a

major party and the national government before 1932, these progressive elements controlled Congress from 1921 to about 1927 and continued to exercise a near control during the period of their greatest weakness in the legislative branch, from 1927 to about 1930.

Indeed, the single most powerful and consistently successful group in Congress during the entire decade from 1919 to 1929 were the spokesmen of the farmers. Spurred by an unrest in the country areas more intense than at any time since the 1890's,[12] in 1920 and 1921 southern Democrats and midwestern and western insurgents, nominally Republican, joined forces in an alliance called the Farm Bloc. By maintaining a common front from 1921 to 1924 they succeeded in enacting the most advanced agricultural legislation to that date, legislation that completed the program begun under Wilsonian auspices. It included measures for high tariffs on agricultural products, thoroughgoing federal regulation of stockyards, packing houses, and grain exchanges, the exemption of agricultural cooperatives from the application of the antitrust laws, stimulation of the export of agricultural commodities, and the establishment of an entirely new federal system of intermediate rural credit.

When prosperity failed to return to the countryside, rural leaders in Congress espoused a new and bolder plan for relief — the proposal made by George N. Peek and Hugh S. Johnson in 1922 to use the federal power to obtain "fair exchange" or "parity" prices for farm products. Embodied in the McNary-Haugen bill in 1924, this measure was approved by Congress in 1927 and 1928, only to encounter vetoes by President Calvin Coolidge.

In spite of its momentary failure, the McNary-Haugen bill had a momentous significance for the American progressive movement. Its wholesale espousal by the great mass of farm leaders and spokesmen meant that the politically most powerful class in the country had come full scale to the conviction that the taxing power should be used directly and specifically for the purpose of underwriting (some persons called it subsidizing) agriculture. It was a milestone in the development of a comprehensive political doctrine

12. It derived from the fact that farm prices plummeted in 1920 and 1921, and remained so low that farmers, generally speaking, operated at a net capital loss throughout the balance of the decade.

that it was government's duty to protect the economic security of all classes and particularly depressed ones. McNary-Haugenism can be seen in its proper perspective if it is remembered that it would have been considered almost absurd in the Wilson period, that it was regarded as radical by non-farm elements in the 1920's, and that it, or at any rate its fundamental objective, was incorporated almost as a matter of course into basic federal policy in the 1930's.

A second significant manifestation of the survival of progressivism in the 1920's came during the long controversey over public ownership or regulation of the burgeoning electric power industry. In this, as in most of the conflicts that eventually culminated on Capitol Hill, the agrarian element constituted the core of progressive strength. At the same time a sizable and well-organized independent movement developed that emanated from urban centers and was vigorous on the municipal and state levels. Throughout the decade this relatively new progressive group fought with mounting success to expose the propaganda of the private utilities, to strengthen state and federal regulatory agencies, and to win municipal ownership for distributive facilities. Like the advocates of railroad regulation in an earlier period, these proponents of regulation or ownership of a great new natural monopoly failed almost as much as they had succeeded in the 1920's. But their activities and exposures (the Federal Trade Commission's devastating investigation of the electric power industry in the late 1920's and early 1930's was the prime example) laid secure foundations for movements that in the 1930's would reach various culminations.

Even more significant for the future of American progressivism was the emergence in the 1920's of a new objective, that of committing the federal government to plans for large hydroelectric projects in the Tennessee Valley, the Columbia River watershed, the Southwest, and the St. Lawrence Valley for the purpose, some progressives said, of establishing "yardsticks" for rates, or for the further purpose, as other progressives declared, of beginning a movement for the eventual nationalization of the entire electric power industry. The development of this movement in its emerging stages affords a good case study in the natural history of American progressivism. It began when the Harding and Coolidge administrations attempted to dispose of the government's hydroelectric and nitrate facilities at Muscle Shoals, Alabama, to private interests. In the first stage of the controversy, the progressive objective was merely federal operation of these facilities for the production of cheap fertilizer — a reflection of its exclusive special-interest orientation. Then, as new groups joined the fight to save Muscle Shoals, the objective of public production of cheap electric power came to the fore. Finally, by the end of the 1920's, the objective of a multipurpose regional development in the Tennessee Valley and in other areas as well had taken firm shape.

In addition, by 1928 the agrarians in Congress led by Senator George W. Norris had found enough allies in the two houses and enough support in the country at large to adopt a bill for limited federal development of the Tennessee Valley. Thwarted by President Coolidge's pocket veto, the progressives tried again in 1931, only to meet a second rebuff at the hands of President Herbert Hoover.

All this might be regarded as another milestone in the maturing of American progressivism. It signified a deviation from the older traditions of mere regulation, as President Hoover had said in his veto of the second Muscle Shoals bill, and the triumph of new concepts of direct federal leadership in large-scale development of resources. If progressives had not won their goal by the end of the 1920's, they had at least succeeded in writing what would become perhaps the most important plank in their program for the future.

The maturing of an advanced farm program and the formulation of plans for public power and regional developments may be termed the two most significant progressive achievements on the national level in the 1920's. Others merit only brief consideration. One was the final winning of the old progressive goal of immigration restriction through limited and selective admission. The fact that this movement was motivated in part by racism, nativism, and anti-Semitism (with which, incidentally, a great many if not a majority of progressives were imbued in the 1920's) should not blind us to the fact that it was also progressive. It sought to substitute a so-called scientific and a planned policy for a policy of laissez faire. Its purpose was admittedly to disturb the free operation of the international labor market. Organized labor and social workers had long supported it against the opposition of large employers. And there was prohibition, the most ambitious and revealing progressive experiment of the twentieth century. Even the contemned anti-evolution crusade of Bryan and the fundamentalists and the surging drives for conformity of thought and action in other fields should be mentioned. All these movements stemmed from the conviction that organized public power could and should be used purposefully to achieve fundamental social and so-called moral change. The fact that they were potentially or actively repressive does not mean that they were not progressive. On the contrary, they superbly illustrated the repressive tendencies that inhered in progressivism precisely because it was grounded so much upon majoritarian principles.

Three other developments on the national level that have often been cited as evidences of the failure of progressivism in the 1920's appear in a somewhat different light at second glance. The first was the reversal of the tariff-for-revenue-only tendencies of the Underwood Act with the enactment of the Emergency Tariff Act of 1921 and the Fordney-McCumber Act of 1922. Actually, the adoption of these measures signified, on the whole, not a repudiation but a revival of progressive principles in the realm of federal fiscal policy. A revenue tariff had never been an authentic progressive objective. Indeed, at least by 1913, many progressives, except for some southern agrarians, had concluded that it was retrogressive and had agreed that the tariff laws should be used deliberately to achieve certain national objectives — for example, the crippling of noncompetitive big business by the free admission of articles manufactured by so-called trusts, or benefits to farmers by the free entry of farm implements. Wilson himself had been at least partially converted to these principles by 1916, as his insistence upon the creation of the Federal Tariff Commission and his promise of protection to the domestic chemical industry revealed. As for the tariff legislation of the early 1920's, its only important changes were increased protection for aluminum, chemical products, and agricultural commodities. It left the Underwood rates on the great mass of raw materials and manufactured goods largely undisturbed. It may have been economically shortsighted and a bad example for the rest of the world, but for the most part it was progressive in principle and was the handiwork of the progressive coalition in Congress.

Another development that has often been misunderstood in its relation to the progressive movement was the policies of consistent support that the Harding and Coolidge administrations adopted for business enterprise, particularly the policy of the Federal Trade Commission in encouraging the formation of trade associations and the diminution of certain traditional competitive practices. The significance of all this can easily be overrated. Such policies as these two administrations executed had substantial justification in progressive theory and in precedents clearly established by the Wilson administration.

A third challenge to usual interpretations concerns implications to be drawn from the election of Harding and Coolidge in 1920 and 1924. These elections seem to indicate the triumph of reaction among the mass of American voters. Yet one could argue that both Harding and Coolidge were political accidents, the beneficiaries of grave defects in the American political and constitutional systems. The rank and file of Republican voters demonstrated during the preconvention campaign that they wanted vigorous leadership and a moderately progressive candidate in 1920. They got Harding instead, not because they wanted him, but because unusual circumstances permitted a small clique to thwart the will of the majority.[13] They took Coolidge as their candidate in 1924 simply because Harding died in the middle of his term and there seemed to be no alternative to nominating the man who had succeeded him in the White House. Further, an analysis of the election returns in 1920 and 1924 will show that the really decisive factor in the victories of Harding and Coolidge was the fragmentation of the progressive movement and the fact that an opposition strong enough to rally and unite the progressive majority simply did not exist.

There remains, finally, a vast area of progressive activity about which we yet know very little. One could mention the continuation of old reform movements and the development of new ones in the cities and states during the years following the Armistice: For example, the steady spread of the city manager form of government, the beginning of zoning and planning movements, and the efforts

13. Much that is new on the Republican preconvention campaign and convention of 1920 may be found in William T. Hutchinson, *Lowden of Illinois: The Life of Frank O. Lowden* (2 vols., Chicago, 1957).

of the great cities to keep abreast of the transportation revolution then in full swing. Throughout the country the educational and welfare activities of the cities and states steadily increased. Factory legislation matured, while social insurance had its experimental beginnings. Whether such reform impulses were generally weak or strong, one cannot say; but what we do know about developments in cities like Cincinnati and states like New York, Wisconsin, and Louisiana[14] justifies a challenge to the assumption that municipal and state reform energies were dead after 1918 and, incidentally, a plea to young scholars to plow this unworked field of recent American history.

Let us, then, suggest a tentative synthesis as an explanation of what happened to the progressive movement after 1918:

First, the national progressive movement, which had found its most effective embodiment in the coalition of forces that reelected Woodrow Wilson in 1916, was shattered by certain policies that the administration pursued from 1917 to 1920, and by some developments over which the administration had no or only slight control. The collapse that occurred in 1920 was not inevitable and cannot be explained by merely saying that "the war killed the progressive movement."

Second, large and aggressive components of a potential new progressive coalition remained after 1920. These elements never succeeded in uniting effectively before the end of the decade, not because they did not exist, but because they were divided by conflicts among themselves. National leadership, which in any event did not emerge in the 1920's, perhaps could not have succeeded in subduing these tensions and in creating a new common front.

Third, as a result of the foregoing, progressivism as an organized national force suffered a serious decline in the 1920's. This decline was heightened by the defection of large elements among the urban middle classes and the intellectuals, a desertion induced by technological, economic, and demographic changes, and by the outcropping of certain repressive tendencies in progressivism after 1917.

Fourth, in spite of reversals and failures, important components of the national progressive movement survived in considerable vigor

14. See e.g., Allan P. Sindler, *Huey Long's Louisiana: State Politics, 1920–1952* (Baltimore, Md., 1956).

and succeeded to a varying degree, not merely in keeping the movement alive, but even in broadening its horizons. This was true particularly of the farm groups and of the coalition concerned with public regulation or ownership of electric power resources. These two groups laid the groundwork in the 1920's for significant new programs in the 1930's and beyond.

Fifth, various progressive coalitions controlled Congress for the greater part of the 1920's and were always a serious threat to the conservative administrations that controlled the executive branch. Because this was true, most of the legislation adopted by Congress during this period, including many measures that historians have inaccurately called reactionary, was progressive in character.

Sixth, the progressive movement in the cities and states was far from dead in the 1920's, although we do not have sufficient evidence to justify any generalizations about the degree of its vigor.

If this tentative and imperfect synthesis has any value, perhaps it is high time that we discard the sweeping generalizations, false hypotheses, and clichés that we have so often used in explaining and characterizing political developments from 1918 to 1929. Perhaps we should try to see these developments for what they were — the normal and ordinary political behavior of groups and classes caught up in a swirl of social and economic change. When we do this we will no longer ask whether the progressive movement was defunct in the 1920's. We will ask only what happened to it and why.

Carl N. Degler

IN 1958 HERBERT HOOVER published a book about his old chief entitled *The Ordeal of Woodrow Wilson*. Wilson's struggle for the League was short and his part in it has gained lustre with passing years. Not so with the ordeal of Herbert Hoover. The Great Depression was considerably longer and his reputation has never been free from the memory of that ordeal. Today, in fact, there are two Hoovers. The first is the living man, the former President who has unstintingly and very capably served Democratic and Republican Administrations alike. He is the Hoover of nation-wide birthday celebrations, of rhapsodic editorials, of admiring Republican national conventions. That conception bears almost no relation to the second, the historical Hoover. In the history books his Administration is usually depicted as cold-hearted, when not pictured as totally devoid of heart, inept, or actionless in the face of the Great Depression. Simply because of the wide gulf between the two Hoovers it is time to try to answer the question William Allen White posed over thirty years ago. Writing an evaluation of Hoover's Administration in the *Saturday Evening Post* of March 4, 1933, White closed his piece with the following words: "So history stands hesitant waiting for time to tell whether Herbert Hoover . . . by pointing the way to social recovery . . . is the first of the new Presidents . . . or whether . . . he is the last of the old."

The notion of two Hoovers should never have grown up; his life and views were too consistent for that. During Hoover's tenure of office, Theodore Joslin, his press secretary, undertook to examine closely all the President's utterances and writings of the preceding ten or eleven years. "In all of those million-odd words, dealing

"The Ordeal of Herbert Hoover," *The Yale Review*, LII (June, 1963), 563–583, copyright Yale University Press. Reprinted by permission of *The Yale Review*.

CARL N. DEGLER (1921–) is Professor of History at Vassar College. He has written numerous articles and essays on various phases of our history as well as an interpretive study *Out of Our Past* (1959).

with every important subject," Joslin reported in 1934, "the number of times he reversed himself or modified an important position could be counted on the fingers of one hand." And so it has remained even after March 4, 1933.

Nor were those principles, to which Hoover held so consistently, simply conservative ones, as has so often been assumed. In 1920, for example, when Hoover's political career began, he was the darling of the progressives who still clustered about the figure of the fallen Wilson. College and university faculties were calling upon Hoover to run for president that year – on either ticket. Indeed, his silence as to which party he belonged to, for a time caused his name to figure as prominently in Democratic primaries as in Republican. For example, he received the most votes by far in the Michigan Democratic primary that year. That year, too, Franklin Roosevelt, who was also a member of Woodrow Wilson's Administration, wrote Josephus Daniels that Herbert Hoover "is certainly a wonder, and I wish we could make him President of the United States. There could not be a better one." (Nor did Roosevelt's enthusiasm cool until much later. In 1928 he refused to write an article against Hoover's candidacy because Hoover was "an old personal friend.")

Hoover's principles were distinctly and publicly progressive. In 1920, for example, he defended the principle of collective bargaining and the right to strike – two very unpopular principles at that date – before a frosty Chamber of Commerce in Boston. As Secretary of Commerce in the Harding Administration he opposed the sweeping federal injunction against the railroad strikers and worked with Harding to have the steel industry abandon the twelve-hour day. In his book of guiding principles, *American Individualism,* which he published in 1922, he was careful to distinguish his views from laissez-faire capitalism. The American way, he insisted, "is not capitalism, or socialism, or syndicalism, nor a cross breed of them." It did include, though, government regulation in order to preserve equality of opportunity and individual rights. "This regulation is itself," he pointed out, "proof that we have gone a long way toward the abandonment of the 'capitalism' of Adam Smith. . . ." While Secretary of Commerce in the 1920's he instituted much needed regulations for the burgeoning radio and airplane industries. It was Herbert Hoover who said in 1922 at the first conference on radio that "the ether is a public medium and its use must be for the public benefit. The use of radio channels is justified only if there is public benefit. The dominant element of consideration in the radio field is, and always will be, the great body of the listening public, millions in number, country-wide in distribution." In the same address, he said, "It is inconceivable that we should allow so great a possibility for service to be drowned in advertising chatter." In 1928 he was recommending that a three billion dollar reserve of public works be built up to serve as an economic stabilizer in times of recession.

In short, though he served both Harding and Coolidge, Herbert Hoover was not of their stripe. As he himself said later in his memoirs, "Mr. Coolidge was a real conservative, probably the equal of Benjamin Harrison. . . . He was a fundamentalist in religion, in the economic and social order, and in fishing." (The last because Coolidge, the fishing tyro, used worms for bait.) Moreover, unlike Coolidge, Hoover did not publicly ignore the scandals that rocked the Harding Administration. In June 1931, while dedicating the Harding Memorial at Marion, Ohio, Hoover went out of his way to speak of the tragedy of Warren Harding and of the enormity of the betrayal of a public trust by Harding's friends.

Hoover's record as president contains a number of truly progressive achievements. Although he cannot take credit for initiating the Norris-La Guardia Act of 1932, the fact remains that one of the most important prolabor acts in the whole history of American labor was signed by Herbert Hoover. Like other progressives, he sponsored legislation for conservation like the giant Boulder Dam project and the St. Lawrence Seaway.

But perhaps the most striking example of Hoover's willingness to recognize the new role of government in dealing with the complexities of an industrial economy was his breaking precedent to grapple directly with the Depression. From the outset Hoover rejected the advice of his Secretary of the Treasury, Andrew Mellon, who, as Hoover himself said, was a country-banker of narrow social vision. Mellon believed the crash should be permitted to run its course unmolested. His simple formula in a depression, as he told Hoover, was "Liquidate labor, liquidate stocks, liquidate farms, liquidate real estate." A panic, he told the President, was not so bad. "It will purge the rottenness out of the system. High costs of living and high living will come down. People will work harder, live more moral lives. Values will be adjusted, and enterprising people will pick up the wrecks from less competent people."

In contrast, Hoover's anti-depression action was swift in coming. Within a matter of weeks after the great crash of the stock market at the end of October, Hoover called a meeting of prominent business, labor, and farm leaders to work out plans for preventing the market crash from adversely affecting the rest of the economy. A week later he met for the same purpose with railway presidents. The economic leaders agreed to his plan of holding the line on wages and encouraging industrial expansion. In his annual message to Congress in December 1929, Hoover proudly told of these and other efforts his Administration had made to stem the economic decline. These efforts, he said, "must be vigorously pursued until normal conditions are restored." In January he continued to expand public works on Boulder Dam and on highway construction. By the end of July 1930, the Administration had got underway $800 million in public works, and the President called upon the states and local units of government to follow the national government's example in order to provide as much employment as possible.

The President was well aware of the unprecedented character of his swift anti-depression action. He said as much in his message to Congress in December 1929; he made the same point more explicitly at the Gridiron dinner in April 1930. The country, he said, had avoided the dole and other unsatisfactory devices to meet unemployment by "voluntary cooperation of industry with the Government in maintaining wages against reductions, and the intensification of construction work. Thereby we have inaugurated one of the greatest economic experiments in history on a basis of nation-wide cooperation not charity."

At first Hoover was optimistic about the effects of his program. Several times during the first year he compared the economic decline with that of 1921–22, usually with the observation that the earlier one was the more difficult. As he told the Chamber of Commerce in May 1930, the amount of public works contracted for was already three times the amount in the corresponding period of the previous "great depression."

Yet his optimism did not keep him from action. One thing he

emphasized was the necessity of learning from this Depression about the prevention of future ones. He advocated better statistical measures and reform of the banking structure to prevent the drain of credit from productive to speculative enterprise, such as had led to the stock market boom and crash. Moreover, although he emphasized from the beginning that the Depression was "worldwide" and that its "causes and its effects lie only partly in the United States," he did not use this as an excuse for inactivity. There was no need simply to wait for the rest of the world to recover, he said. "We can make a very large degree of recovery independently of what may happen elsewhere." In October 1930 he told the American Bankers Association that depressions were not simply to be borne uncomplainingly. "The economic fatalist believes that these crises are inevitable and bound to be recurrent. I would remind these pessimists that exactly the same thing was once said of typhoid, cholera, and smallpox." But instead of being pessimistic, medical science went to work and conquered those diseases. "That should be our attitude toward these economic pestilences. They are not dispensations of Providence. I am confident in the faith that their control, so far as the cause lies within our own boundaries, is within the genius of modern business."

Hoover also told the bankers that he could not condone the argument which had been reported from some of them that the people would have to accept a lower standard of living in order to get through the Depression. Such a suggestion, he said, could not be countenanced either on idealistic or on practical grounds. To accept it would mean a "retreat into perpetual unemployment and the acceptance of a cesspool of poverty for some large part of our people." Several times during the Depression Hoover made it clear that the government had a responsibility to employ as many as possible as its contribution to the mitigation of the unemployment which was growing alarmingly.

The failure of the economy to respond to treatment and the loss of many Republican seats in the elections of 1930 caused Hoover for a while to place new emphasis upon the foreign sources of the Depression. At the end of 1930 he told the Congress that the "major forces of the depression now lie outside of the United States." In fact, though, the real collapse of the European economy was still almost six months away. Hoover was most fearful that the growing Congressional demands for new expenditures would throw the budget out of balance. His concern about the budget and his hostility toward the Congress were both measured in his tactless remark at a press conference in May 1931 that "I know of nothing that would so disturb the healing process now undoubtedly going on in the economic situation" as a special session of Congress. "We cannot legislate ourselves out of a world economic depression; we can and will work ourselves out."

The last sentence, because it was obviously too sweeping to be accurate, was to plague him for years. More important, he quite clearly did not believe it himself, since he later advocated legislation for just the purposes he said it could not serve. In the very next month, for example, he explained at some length to a group of Republican editors just how much the Administration had been doing to extricate the country from the Depression. "For the first time in history the Federal Government has taken an extensive and positive part in mitigating the effects of depression and expediting recovery. I have conceived that if we would preserve our democracy this leadership must take the part not of attempted dictatorship but of organizing cooperation in the constructive forces of the community and of stimulating every element of initiative and self-reliance in the country. There is no sudden stroke of either governmental or private action which can dissolve these world difficulties; patient, constructive action in a multitude of directions is the strategy of success. This battle is upon a thousand fronts." Unlike previous administrations, he continued, his had expanded, instead of curtailing, public works during a depression. Public works expenditures, both by the federal and state governments, he said, continued to increase. Some two billion dollars were being spent, and a million men were employed on these projects. Aid was also being given to farmers in the drought areas of the South and Middle West.

That Hoover truly favored action over patient waiting for the storm to lift was further shown in his elaborate twelve-point program for recovery presented in his annual message in December 1931. Among his recommendations was the Reconstruction Finance Corporation, which would become one of the major agencies of his Administration and of the New Deal for stabilizing banks and aiding recovery. At a press conference the same month he emphasized anew the desirability of domestic action. "The major steps we must take are domestic. The action needed is in the home field and it is urgent. While reestablishment of stability abroad is helpful to us and to the world, and I am convinced that it is in progress, yet we must depend upon ourselves. If we devote ourselves to these urgent domestic questions we can make a very large measure of recovery irrespective of foreign influences." By early February 1932 the Reconstruction Finance Corporation was in operation. That same month he persuaded the Congress to enact the Glass-Steagall banking bill, which increased the bases for Federal Reserve bank reserves and thus expanded credit and conserved gold. The purpose of the RFC was to shore up failing banks and other financial institutions caught in runs upon their deposits. With the permission of the Interstate Commerce Commission, the RFC could also extend financial aid to railroads.

Beyond these operations, though, the President would not let the lending agency go. Especially did he resist federal aid to the unemployed, although the demands for it were growing monthly. He even opposed Congressional appropriations to the Red Cross on the ground that they would dry up private sources of relief funds. A dole, he said in 1931, must be avoided at all costs because "the net results of governmental doles are to lower wages toward the bare subsistence level and to endow the slacker." He did urge the citizenry generously to support, as he did himself, private charities, like the Red Cross, which were carrying so much of the burden of unemployment relief. At no time, of course, did Hoover object to helping the unemployed; he was no Social Darwinist arguing for the survival of only the fittest. Again and again, using the most idealistic language, he called upon Americans to extend a hand to those fellow citizens in need. But as much as he publicly and privately deplored the suffering which the economic crisis brought, he feared and deplored even more the effects which would be sure to follow if the federal government provided relief to the unemployed. Nowhere was the rigidity of Hoover's highly trained, agile, and well-stocked intellect more apparent than in this matter. Throughout his years as president, despite the cruelest of sarcastic barbs in the press and from the public platform, he held to his position.

Yet surprising as it may seem today, for a long time the country was with him. This was true even during 1931 and early 1932 when it was becoming increasingly evident that private charities, municipal relief funds, and even the resources of the states were inadequate to meet the costs of providing for ten or eleven million unemployed. Already in August 1931 Governor Franklin Roosevent had told the New York legislature that unemployment relief "must be extended by government – not as a matter of charity but as a matter of social duty." Yet, as late as February 1932 the country was still following Hoover's view of relief and not Roosevelt's. This was shown by the fate of a bill sponsored by liberal Senators Robert M. La Follette, Jr. of Wisconsin and Edward F. Costigan of Colorado to provide federal money to the states for relief. The bill was defeated by a vote of 48 to 35. Democratic Senators made up some forty percent of the votes which killed the measure.

By May 1932, though, the pressure for some federal assistance in relief matters was building up fast. The National Conference of Social Workers, which in the previous year had refused to endorse the principle of federal relief, now switched to supporting it. More important from Hoover's standpoint was the announcement by Senator Joseph Robinson, the conservative Democratic leader in the Senate, that he was joining the liberals in favoring federal relief. Within two days the President announced, after consultation with Robinson, that the RFC would hereafter lend money to the states if their resources for relief were exhausted. The next day the President defended the extraordinary powers of the RFC as necessitated by the economic emergency. In words which sound in retrospect like those of his successor, he said, "We used such emergency powers to win the war; we can use them to fight the depression, the misery and suffering from which are equally great."

Soon thereafter, though, the President demonstrated that he would not take another step toward putting the federal government into the relief field. Two bills by Democrats which went beyond his limits were successfully vetoed. After Congress had adjourned in July 1932, he issued a nine-point program for economic recovery, but most of the items on it were old and the rest were only recommendations for exploratory conferences. By the summer of 1932, then, the Hoover program for recovery had been completed; his principles would permit him to go no further.

As one reviews the actions which Hoover took it is impossible to describe him as a do-nothing president. He was unquestionably one of the truly activist presidents of our history. But he was an activist within a very rigid framework of ideology. Of all American presidents, Herbert Hoover was probably the most singlemindedly committed to a system of beliefs. His pragmatism was well hidden and what there was of it emerged only after great prodding from events. To a remarkable degree, one can observe in his acts as president those principles of individualism which he set forth so simply in his book ten years before. The very same principle, for example, which prevented his sanctioning federal relief to the unemployed, dictated the tone and content of his veto of the bill to create a government corporation to operate Muscle Shoals. The government, he said, should not compete with private enterprise. Moreover, such a project, by being run by the federal government, abrogated the basic principle that all such enterprises should be "administrated by the people upon the ground, responsible to their own communities, directing them solely for the benefit of their communities and not for the purposes of social theories or national politics. Any other course deprives them of liberty." It was this same belief in individual freedom and cooperation which kept him from accepting a governmental system of old age and unemployment insurance. He advocated such measures only when undertaken voluntarily and through private insurance companies.

Even the Reconstruction Finance Corporation, perhaps his most enduring anti-depression agency, was created to assist private business, not to supplant it. True, it was a credit agency in competition with private enterprise, but it was designed to perform tasks which no private institution dared risk; the competition was therefore minimal if not nonexistent. Moreover, although it has been frequently alleged that the RFC lent money to corporations while the Administration denied relief to the unemployed, in Hoover's mind the distinction was crucial and real. The RFC was making loans which would be repaid – and most were – when the banks got back on their feet; it was not making grants. Even when Hoover did permit the RFC to lend money to the states for relief purposes he still insisted that no grants of federal funds be made.

But there was an even more important social justification for agencies like the RFC and the Federal Home Loan Board, which

Congress created in July 1932 at the President's request. Hoover recognized as no president had before that the welfare of society was dependent upon business and that government, therefore, must step in. He did this, not because, as some critics said, he favored business over the common people, but because he recognized that if the banks failed the economy would collapse, savings would be lost, and jobs destroyed. The RFC and the Federal Home Loan Board, in effect, socialized the losses of financial institutions by using government to spread their obligations through society. Hoover was not prepared, though, to socialize the losses of the unemployed. That step in ameliorating the impact of the Depression was undertaken by the New Deal through the WPA and other relief agencies. In this respect Hoover was a transitional figure in the development of the government as an active force in the economy in times of depression. He was the first to smash the old shibboleth of government unconcern and impotence.

Perhaps his long-term role was even greater. In the face of great opposition and much outright hostility, he made a determined and even courageous effort to give the business community and voluntary private agencies a chance to show whether they could bring the nation out of a depression. Their failure to do so gave a moral as well as a political impetus to the New Deal. Just as after Munich no one could say the West had not done its utmost to meet Hitler halfway, so after Hoover's Administration no one could say that government had rushed in before other social or economic agencies had been given a try. That this was so goes a long way toward explaining the remarkable consensus among Americans ever since the 1930's that government has the prime responsibility for averting or cushioning the effects of a depression.

A second principle which stopped Hoover from permitting the federal government to provide relief was his conviction that the budget must not be unbalanced. As early as February 1930 he warned the Congress against extravagance and told of his own efforts to economize. Economy was essential, he emphasized, in order to avoid increasing taxes. But as decreasing revenues began to fall behind expenditures, Hoover's concern to keep the budget in balance overcame his reluctance to increase taxes. On July 1, 1931 the deficit was almost $500 million — an astronomical figure in those days when the total federal budget was less than $4 billion.

In December of that same year Hoover recommended an increase in taxes. When Congress proved dilatory he told a press conference in March 1932 that a balanced budget "is the very keystone of recovery. It must be done." Anything less would undo all the recovery measures. "The Government," he warned, "no more than individual families can continue to expend more than it receives without inviting serious consequences."

Hoover recommended a manufacturers' sales tax as the chief new revenue device, in which suggestion he was joined by the new Democratic Speaker of the House, John Nance Garner of Texas. Garner enjoyed a reputation for being hostile to business and something of a radical in the old Populist tradition, but in the matter of bringing the budget into balance he stood four-square with the President. Congress did not pass the sales tax, but it did pass one of the largest peacetime tax increases in American history.

Today it seems incredible that in a time of economic slump when consumer purchasing power was the principal requirement for recovery, the nation should elect to take money out of the hands of consumers. Yet this was precisely what the bill, recommended and signed by the Republican President and passed by the Democratic House, entailed. In fact, when in the course of the debate the House seemed hesitant about increasing taxes, the Democratic Speaker, John Garner, could not contain his anxiety. Conspicuously forsaking the Speaker's chair, Garner advanced to the well of the House to make an earnest plea for more taxes. At the conclusion of his speech, he asked "every man and every woman in this House who . . . is willing to try to balance the budget to rise in their seats." Almost the whole House, with its majority of Democrats, rose to its feet, to a growing round of applause. When he asked those who did not want to balance the budget to rise, no one did. The overwhelming majority of the newspapers of the country strongly commended the Congress in June 1932 for its efforts to balance the budget through increased taxes.

During the campaign of 1932 the Democrats continued to equal or even outdo Hoover in their slavish adherence to the ideal of a balanced budget. Franklin Roosevelt, for example, unmercifully attacked the Administration for its extravagance and its unbalanced budget, calling the fifty percent increase in expenditures since 1927 "the most reckless and extravagant past that I have been able to discover in the statistical record of any peacetime government anywhere, any time." He promised a cut of 25 percent in the budget if he were elected. Nor was this simply campaign oratory. As Frank Freidel has observed in his biography, Roosevelt was perfectly sincere in his dismay at the Hoover deficit and he would continue to be regretful about deficits until well after 1933.

From the record, then, it is evident that Democrats were in no better theoretical position to deal with the Depression than Hoover. Leaders of both parties thought of the government as a large household whose accounts must be balanced if national bankruptcy were to be avoided. Neither party could conceive of the central role which government must play in the economy in an industrial society in time of depression. It would take the whole decade of the New Deal and the continuance of the Depression before that fact would be learned by leaders and people alike.

Despite his fixation on the question of the budget, Hoover's conception of the Depression was sophisticated, rational, and coherent; the remedies he suggested were equally so, given his assumptions. In trying to find a way out, Hoover placed most reliance on what modern economists would call "expectations" of businessmen. If businessmen feel that times are good or at least that they are getting better, they will invest in new plant and equipment, which in turn will employ men and create purchasing power. In substance, the remedies Hoover offered were designed to raise the expectations of businessmen and to maintain purchasing power until the economy picked up again. His first step was securing agreement among businessmen to hold the line on wages in order to keep purchasing power from falling. (And, by and large, as a result of his efforts, wage rates did not fall until the middle of 1931, but employment did, with, unfortunately, the same effect.) A second step in his program was to use government to help out with public work projects and, when private agencies proved inadequate, to provide credit through agencies like the RFC and the Home Loan Board. Finally, as a third arrow in his anti-depression quiver, Hoover sought, through the prestige of his office, to create that sense of confidence and approaching good times which would encourage businessmen to invest. As it turned out, though, he gambled and lost. For with each successive ineffectual statement, the value of his words dropped, until, like the worthless coins of a profligate monarch who debases his own coinage, they were hurled back at his head by a disenchanted press and people.

The Hoover recovery program failed, but probably no government program then thought permissible could have been any more successful. Certainly the New Deal with its more massive injection of government money into the economy succeeded little better. It ended the decade with 9.5 million still unemployed, and industrial production remained below the 1929 level throughout the 1930's except for a brief period in late 1936 and early 1937. On the other hand, most of the countries of Western and Central Europe regained the 1929 level of production by early 1935.

Part of Hoover's ordeal during the Great Depression undoubtedly derived from his personality, which, for a president, was unusual. Indeed, until he became President he had rarely been connected with government other than in an office which was nonpartisan or which he soon made so. Outwardly, at least, he was far removed from the stereotype of the politician; he could not slap a back or utter a guffaw. He appeared shy in public, though stolid was a more accurate description. A bulky man of over 200 pounds, standing almost six feet when he entered the White House, he gave a paradoxical impression of conservative solidity and beaming youth at the same time. His public speech, like his writing, was formal, often stiff, and sometimes bordered on the pedantic. Early in Hoover's Administration, soon after the stock market crash, William Allen White, a Hoover supporter, spotted the new President's weakness. "The President has great capacity to convince intellectuals," he wrote. "He has small capacity to stir people emotionally and through the emotions one gets to the will, not through the intellect." Even Hoover's press secretary recognized that he "experienced the greatest difficulty in interpreting himself and his acts to the public." Indeed, it was characteristic of Hoover that though he found speech writing one of the most laborious of his tasks, he insisted upon writing all his own speeches. The compulsion could be at least enervating, and at worst dangerous to his health. Often he traded sleep for time to work on his speeches and at least once, at St. Paul in the campaign of 1932, he was on the verge of collapse from fatigue. His method of writing was tedious and incredibly time-consuming, involving innumerable drafts, meticulously gone over by himself, only to have still further proofs run off for more rewriting. Yet, after all this effort, his final draft usually was dry, too long, and ponderous.

In view of his poor public image, it is not surprising that for most of his presidency, Hoover's relations with the press were strained when not downright painful. Although he continued the press conferences which Wilson had begun, they were formal affairs with written questions; many reporters were convinced that the President concealed more than he revealed in the meetings. But it was probably Hoover's sensitivity to criticism that worked the real damage. His annual addresses to newspapermen at the Gridiron Club, which, as was customary, mercilessly lampooned his administration, often carried an edge, betraying his sensitivity to the press corps' jibes. Only occasionally did his private wit break through in public. At the Gridiron Club dinner in December 1932, after his defeat for reelection, he puckishly said, "You will expect me to discuss the late election. Well, as nearly as I can learn, we did not have enough votes on our side. During the campaign I remarked that this Administration had been fighting on a thousand fronts; I learned since the campaign that we were fighting on 21 million fronts." (The size of the Democratic vote.) This was one of the rare times that Hoover poked fun at himself in public.

Yet, despite his difficulties as a public figure, in private Hoover was neither phlegmatic nor shy. In fact he was extremely convivial, seeking constant company, whether at the White House or at his retreat on the Rapidan in the Blue Ridge Mountains. His wife told Joslin that the President could not be happy without numbers of people around him. His friends cherished his constant flow of stories and he delighted in his cigars and pipe. He was an outdoor type of man, reveling in fishing and hiking. Although he liked a joke, he rarely laughed out loud, though his friends knew well his soft chuckle. His own brand of humor could be heavy-handed. Thus in January 1931, when addressing the National Automobile Chamber of Commerce, he observed, with a smile, that 3.5 million cars had been sold in the first year of the depression and that consumption of gasoline was up five percent. "This certainly means," he twitted, "that we have been cheerful in the use of automobiles; I do not assume they are being used for transportation to the poorhouse. While I am aware that many people are using the old automobile a little longer it is obvious that they are still using it and it is being worn out. Altogether the future for the industry does not warrant any despondency." Will Rogers was not so sure. Some months later in a radio broadcast, he drawled, "We are the first nation in the history of the world to go to the poorhouse in an automobile."

Part of the reason Hoover resented the barbed comments of the press was that he worked so hard. It was as characteristic of Herbert Hoover that he was the first president to have a telephone on his desk as it was characteristic of Calvin Coolidge that he refused to have one. Hoover rose at 6 a.m. each morning, joined a group of his friends for a brisk half-hour session with a five pound medicine ball on an improvised court on the White House grounds, then went in to breakfast. He was at his desk by 8:30. He worked steadily all day, smoking incessantly, and usually well into the night. Often he would wake up in the middle of the night and pore over papers or write for an hour or two before going back to sleep. Nevertheless, he rose at the same early hour. Subordinates were not always able to keep up with his pace; some had to be dispatched to rest, but Hoover, miraculously, never succumbed to his self-imposed regimen. His secretary reports that he was not sick a single day of the four years he spent in the White House. A few days at the camp on the Rapidan or a short trip usually sufficed to restore his energies and his will to work. But toward the end of his tenure, even the optimism and strength of a Hoover faltered, at least once. He told his secretary, "All the money in the world could not induce me to live over the last nine months. The conditions we have experienced make this office a compound hell."

Aside from the circumstances in which he found himself as President, one of the reasons the office was "hell' was that Hoover was a poor politician. Often it is said that he did not like politics, or even that he was above politics. Both statements describe the image he held of himself, but many of Hoover's actions while in office are clearly partisan and political. If, for example, he could objectively recognize the weaknesses of the Harding Administration once he was elected president, he could also say during the campaign of 1928 that "the record of the seven and one years" of Coolidge and Harding "constitutes a period of rare courage in leadership and constructive action. Never has a political party been able to look back upon a similar period with more satisfaction." In December 1931, when some voices were calling for a coalition government to deal with the worsening depression, Hoover made it clear that he would have nothing to do with Democrats. "The day that we begin coalition government you may know that our democracy has broken down," he told newspapermen at a Gridiron Club dinner. On the other hand, he could appoint Democrats to office, as he did former Senator Atlee Pomerene to head the RFC when he wanted that office to win support from Democrats. Nor was he devoid of political dramatics. In September 1931 he made a quick descent upon the American Legion Convention in Detroit in a successful effort to stop the Legion from going on record in favor of a bonus for veterans. By going all the way to Detroit, speaking for eleven minutes, and then immediately leaving for Washington again, he demonstrated the importance of his message and the weight of the schedule of work he pursued in Washington. Moreover, as the account written by his Press Secretary Joslin makes clear, he was no more above benefiting from parliamentary trickery in Congress than the next politically-minded president. As Joslin wrote, "It was characteristic of the President to hit back when attacked." Hoover suffered deeply when attacked, and he did not turn the other cheek. As William Allen White, who supported and admired the President, wrote in 1933, "he was no plaster saint politically. He had, during his three years, rather consistently and with a nice instinct chosen to honor in public office men of a conservative type of mind." Moreover, the behind-the-scenes circumstances of his nomination in 1928 and his renomination in 1932, both of which were steam-roller operations, should remove any doubts about his willingness and ability to use devices and tactics quite customary in politics.

No, it was not that he was above politics or that he really despised the operations of politicians. His difficulty was that he was temperamentally incapable of doing what a politician has to do — namely, to admit he could be wrong and to compromise. In the whole volume of his memoirs devoted to the Depression there is not a single mention of a major error on his part, though his opponents are taxed with errors in every chapter. Over a hundred pages of the volume are devoted to the answering of every charge of Franklin Roosevelt in 1932. Nowhere, though, does he notice that in 1932, he himself in his speech at Detroit incorrectly quoted Roosevelt and then proceeded to criticize at length his opponent for something he never said. This inability to admit error, to compromise, William Allen White recognized in 1931 as Hoover's undoing. After all, White wrote, "Politics . . . is one of the minor branches of harlotry, and Hoover's frigid desire to live a virtuous life and not follow the Pauline maxim and be all things to all men, is one of the things that has reduced the oil in his machinery and shot a bearing. . . ." Hoover's inability to admit error and the seriousness with which he viewed himself are both illustrated in another incident during the campaign of 1932. One of the Democrats' favorite sports that year was recalling, with appropriate sounds of derision, Hoover's remarks in 1928 to the effect that the United States was well on the way to abolishing poverty. Hoover, instead of admitting he had been somewhat optimistic, once again donned his hair shirt and stolidly endorsed the earlier statement because, as he said, it expressed the ideals for which Americans stood. Yet this was in the middle of the Depression and he was running for reelection.

In good times, Herbert Hoover's humble birth might have been an asset, but in the Great Depression it was not. Left an almost penniless orphan at nine, Hoover became a world figure and a millionaire before he was forty-five. With such spectacular success behind him it was understandable that he should think, albeit mistakenly, that anyone could achieve at least half as much as he. Undoubtedly his own experience fostered his insistence, throughout his life, that individual initiative was the prime motive force in a good society. What to other men appear as obstacles or handicaps, to the self-made man appear, at least in retrospect, as goads or incentives. Like most such men, Hoover attributed his success to will. When Theodore Joslin once asked him what had been his boyhood ambition, he replied without hesitation, "to be able to earn my own living without the help of anybody, anywhere." To such a man individual effort seems capable of moving mountains unaided; he is loath to see it shunted aside by collective action even in times of economic dislocation. The self-made man can indeed be the wrong man at such times.

Nor was it an accident that the other prominent self-made

politician of the time, Alfred E. Smith, was also doubtful about the virtues of government aid to the unemployed, that he should attack Franklin Roosevelt for accusing the Hoover Administration of aiding the corporations and ignoring the poor. "I will take off my coat and vest," Smith vowed in the spring of 1932, "and fight to the end against any candidate who persists in any demagogic appeal to the masses of the working people of this country to destroy themselves by setting class against class and rich against poor." In a short time, Smith's views, like Hoover's, would bring him to outright opposition to the New Deal. It is not without significance in this respect that Roosevelt, who came to represent government benevolence toward the unemployed, was no self-made man, but lived securely and unadventurously on inherited wealth.

The differences in social origins of Roosevelt and Hoover, of course, are only one facet of the divergence between the Hoover Administration and the New Deal. Indeed, since the 1930's it has become commonplace to see Hoover and Roosevelt as opposites. Certainly there are differences — and important ones — between the administrations of the two Presidents, but we are now far enough removed from both to recognize also the real continuity between them that William Allen White was prescient enough to foresee dimly. When the two administrations are seen against the backdrop of previous administrations and earlier social attitudes, the gulf between them shrinks appreciably. Both men, it is worth recalling, were protégés of Woodrow Wilson; both of them, therefore, accepted a role for government in the economy which added up to a sharp departure from laissez-faire. Both, in the course of their respective administrations, drew upon their experiences in the First World War, where they had seen government intervening in the economy. Hoover's RFC, for example, was frankly modeled, as he said, after the War Finance Corporation. Both saw big business standing in need of controls, and, for a while, both believed that cooperation between business and government was the best way to achieve that control. Hoover, for instance, cited the Federal Reserve System as the ideal kind of business and government cooperation for purposes of regulating the economy; Roosevelt in the NRA also placed his trust in controls worked out through business and government cooperation.

Moreover, both Roosevelt and Hoover took the view that it was government's responsibility to do something about a depression; neither man was willing to subscribe to the view which prevailed before 1929 – namely, that economic declines were simply natural phenomena through which the nation struggled as best it could and that government could not be expected to do much about them.

Finally, it is also worth noticing that the temperament of the two men, their conceptions of America and of its future are much closer than the conventional picture paints them. (It was Roosevelt, during the campaign of 1932, who created the erroneous image of Hoover as the man without faith or hope in the future.) All through the Depression, Hoover's unvarying theme was that all this would pass and the essential vigor of the American economy would reassert itself. Undoubtedly he counted too heavily on the influence of his words to overcome the lack of business confidence, but there is no question of his optimistic outlook. One measure of it was the shock he received when he read Roosevelt's address to the Commonwealth Club in San Francisco. That was the speech in which Roosevelt talked about the frontier being ended and opportunities for economic growth being limited. Hoover took up the challenge, denying "the whole idea that we have ended the advance of America, that this country has reached the zenith of its power, the height of its development. That is the counsel of despair for the future of America. That is not the spirit by which we shall emerge from this depression." The important point is that such pessimism was really not expressive of Roosevelt's thought, either. Although historians have frequently referred to the Commonwealth Club address as the one clear indication during the campaign of 1932 of the philosophy behind the New Deal, we now know that the speech was neither written by Roosevelt, nor read by him before he appeared before his audience. As Rexford Tugwell has pointed out, the Commonwealth Club address, which Berle and he wrote, did not reflect Roosevelt's true attitude toward the American economic future. Indeed, its very singularity among Roosevelt's campaign speeches demonstrates how foreign it was to Roosevelt's feelings and convictions. The speech belied his abundant enthusiasm for the future, and his deep faith in the country and its capacities. Moreover, he soon contradicted its import in his Inaugural Address, when he electrified the country with the cry, "All we have to fear is fear itself."

How ironical that these words of Roosevelt should be so well known, when it was Herbert Hoover who all along had been saying the same thing – in less graphic and less credible language, to be sure – but saying it nonetheless. That fact, too, contributed to the ordeal of Herbert Hoover.

7

The New Deal

Revolutionary or Conservative?

FRANKLIN DELANO ROOSEVELT was perhaps the most controversial president ever to occupy the White House. For over twelve years he led the American people, first through the worst depression in their history and then through a war that encompassed virtually the entire globe. To his admirers he was an individual of heroic stature, a leader who firmly believed that it was possible to preserve free and democratic institutions by internal reforms without adopting authoritarian or totalitarian methods and overturning the basic structure of American society. To his enemies he was a misguided, even immoral, individual who mistakenly believed that he could save American democracy by taking the people down the road to the welfare state — a road that would eventually end in socialism and therefore the negation of individual freedom. Unlike some other presidents, Roosevelt had the uncanny ability to arouse strong passions. He was a person who was either loved or hated; few remained neutral toward him or reacted blandly to his personality or accomplishments.

Why did Roosevelt arouse such strong passions? The answer to this ostensibly simple question is anything but simple. Certainly there was little in his background or his accomplishments prior to 1933 that would explain the controversial nature of his presidential tenure. Even those friends and associates who worked closely with Roosevelt during his dozen years in the White House were not always able to grasp his many-sided personality or understand why he acted as he did. Frances Perkins, his long-time Secretary of Labor, described him as "the most complicated human being I ever knew," a comment that was echoed by others such as Henry Morgenthau and Robert E. Sherwood.

The controversy that surrounded Roosevelt's years in the White House has almost been matched by the quantity and quality of books written about him by friends, associates, and enemies. Unlike other presidents whose careers were not chronicled until decades after their death, Roosevelt has already been the subject of literally hundreds of books and articles. Part of the reason for this situation undoubtedly lies in the fact that much of the source material left by Roosevelt [1] and his associates was opened up to scholars within a surprisingly short time after his death in 1945. But part of the reason surely lies in the fascination with the New Deal and the changes that American society underwent during the years from 1933 to 1945. However the Roosevelt years are interpreted, it is difficult to avoid the conclusion that the United States was a very different nation in 1945 as compared with 1933.

It was the sheer magnitude of the New Deal innovations early in his presidential career that caused Roosevelt to become such a highly controversial figure. Although his victory in 1932 was relatively broad-based, he soon alienated many businessmen as well as other powerful interest groups. As a result, he came under increasingly harsh attacks as the 1930's progressed. Some accused him of subverting traditional American ideals of individualism and liberty by moving toward a welfare state that could end only in socialism and an omnipotent state. Such a staunch Democrat as Al Smith, for example, hotly argued during the presidential campaign of 1936 that Roosevelt was indeed taking the American people down the road to socialism. "It is all right with me if they [the Roosevelt Administration] want to disguise themselves as

1. It has been estimated that Roosevelt's personal papers occupy more than 9,000 cubic feet at the Hyde Park Library; this figure does not include the papers of other important New Deal officials.

Norman Thomas or Karl Marx, or Lenin, or any of the rest of that bunch," Smith shouted, "but what I won't stand for is allowing them to march under the banner of Jefferson, Jackson and Cleveland."

The attack on Roosevelt's New Deal from the right was echoed also by the critics of the left. There were many who felt that the traditional American attachment to individualistic values had been rendered obsolete by the nation's industrial and technological advances. Rexford G. Tugwell, a professor of economics and one of the early New Deal "brain trusters" was one such critic. He was convinced that America's competitive economy had never worked well; to attempt to reform it with minor changes would prove hopelessly inadequate. What was required, Tugwell concluded, was thorough and effective governmental planning for all aspects of the economic system; only in this way could the economy be stabilized and future depressions avoided. Much to his disappointment, the New Deal seemed too pragmatic. Roosevelt, he finally concluded, was either unwilling or unable to plan in a rational and systematic manner. To the left of men like Tugwell stood the Socialist and Communist groups in America. Their criticism was that the New Deal was too conservative; the only proper approach to the depression was a complete overhaul of America's social and economic system and the establishment of a socialist state.

Thus, during the depression years the New Deal was attacked from many points of view. To some it was too radical; to others it was too conservative or reactionary. Still others viewed Roosevelt's policies as a series of pragmatic and expedient moves in response to specific events and deplored the fact that the President never seemed to give much thought to the overall dimensions of the crisis facing the American people. To be sure, many of these critics were reflecting to a large extent the passions and emotions of the age in which they were living. Faced with the problem of coming to grips with the greatest depression the country had ever known, they did not have the perspective nor the dispassionate attitude required to view the issues at stake in a detached or objective manner. Their criticisms, nevertheless, helped to establish the framework of reference with which later writers were to approach the New Deal. In brief, the question usually raised by contemporary commentators and later historians revolved around the role of the New Deal in American life. Was the New Deal simply an extension of the Progressive tradition, or did it involve a radical departure from the mainstream of American history?

For historians reared in the tradition of the Progressive school there was little doubt about the basic nature of the New Deal. Viewing America's past in terms of a conflict between liberalism and conservatism and the people versus the vested interests, they saw the New Deal as simply another phase in the struggle against monopoly, privilege, and special interests. To them the New Deal was related to earlier reform movements, including Jeffersonian and Jacksonian Democracy, Populism, and Progressivism, all of which has represented the people in their continuing struggle to achieve a greater measure of political, economic, and social equality. While they often referred to the revolutionary character of the New Deal, their use of the term "revolutionary" did not necessarily imply a sharp break with the past. Louis Hacker, although not squarely in the Progressive tradition, referred to the New Deal as the "Third American Revolution" in the mid-1940's. His description of the New Deal, however, was anything but revolutionary. Some of its policies, he wrote, were improvisations; some were descended from Populism and Progressivism; but always "there existed the thought that the responsibility of public authority for the welfare of the people was clear and that the intervention of the state was justifiable." [2] Hacker's last point, while by no means acceptable to all Americans, was hardly novel; reformers and intellectuals had been urging government-sponsored reforms since the mid-nineteenth century.

To Henry Steele Commager, one of America's most distinguished historians, the relationship between the New Deal and earlier reform movements was obvious. Writing at the time of Roosevelt's death, Commager explicitly denied the revolutionary character of the New Deal. What was simply a new deal of old cards appeared radical for two reasons: the rapidity with which the New Deal program was enacted into law; and the fact that the movement contrasted so sharply with the do-nothing attitude of the Harding-Coolidge-Hoover administrations. If the New Deal

2. Louis M. Hacker, *The Shaping of the American Tradition* (New York, 1947), p. 1125–1126.

was compared with the Progressive era rather than the 1920's, Commager maintained, "the contrast would have been less striking than the similarities. . . . [For] precedent for the major part of New Deal legislation was to be found in these earlier periods." The achievements of Roosevelt — the restoration of self-confidence, the reassertion of faith in democracy, and the rehabilitation of the nation's human and natural resources — all demonstrated the affinity of the New Deal to the earlier reform movements in American history.[3]

Perhaps the fullest and most eloquent argument favoring the idea that the New Deal was a continuation and extension of America's liberal past was advanced by the outstanding historian writing in the Progressive tradition, Arthur M. Schlesinger, Jr. A former professor at Harvard University, Schlesinger has been the most persuasive and brilliant historian writing within and in defense of America's liberal tradition. He was, of course, much more than a historian. A leading intellectual, important member of the Kennedy Administration, and shrewd commentator on current affairs, Schlesinger has been an activist as well as a scholar. As a historian, Schlesinger since the close of World War II has championed a modified brand of American liberalism whose roots, he believed, go far back into the nation's history. Thus, his Pulitzer-prize winning study, *The Age of Jackson* (1945), argued that Jacksonian Democracy was a liberal political movement based on a coalition of urban workers and other democratic groups in American society. Schlesinger attempted also to rebuild the intellectual foundations of the liberal ideology in his writings. His book, *The Vital Center* (1948), incorporated Niebuhrian theology into the corpus of American liberalism so as to give the latter a more realistic and viable character. Taking cognizance of the reaction against liberal ideas since the 1940's, Schlesinger borrowed Reinhold Niebuhr's emphasis on original sin and reinterpreted the liberal ideology in order to purge that ideology of the charge that its utopian optimism had been unrealistic and its adherents had been incapable of meeting the challenge of totalitarianism since the 1930's.

All of American history, according to Schlesinger, was char-

3. Henry Steele Commager, "Twelve Years of Roosevelt," *American Mercury*, LX (April, 1945), 391–401.

acterized by a cyclical movement which saw periods of liberal reform followed by alternate periods of conservative consolidation. In his eyes Jacksonian Democracy followed the decline of Jeffersonian Democracy, the Progressive era followed the age of the Robber Barons, and the New Deal came after the sterile conservatism of the 1920's. Indeed, Schlesinger argued, the New Frontier of John F. Kennedy and the Great Society of Lyndon B. Johnson were themselves reactions to the inaction of the Eisenhower years. The generative force behind this cycle was social conflict — conflict which arose from a constant accumulation of disquietude and discontent within American society. Schlesinger spelled out his thesis in a series of books and articles, one of which was *The Age of Roosevelt,* a multi-volumed study of the New Deal.

In the first selection Schlesinger discusses the origins of the New Deal. To him the New Deal represented much more than a mere response to the depression. On the contrary, the New Deal was an integral part of the history of American liberalism; it was another phase of the liberal-conservative cycle in American history. By the 1920's, Schlesinger claimed, the nation had tired of the Progressive crusade. National disinterest in politics meant that power gravitated inevitably toward powerful economic interests, and government increasingly came under the control and influence of the business community. As a result of this shift in power, there was a progressive alienation of various groups from American society, including the farmers, workers, minority ethnic groups, and disenchanted intellectuals. Even without a depression, Schlesinger suggested, the New Deal was bound to have happened in one form or another. What the depression did was to give the New Deal its particular character — a political movement responding to the immediate problem of an impending economic collapse. The New Deal, he concluded, rejected the dogmatic absolutes and the simplistic dichotomies posed in contemporary ideologies such as communism and fascism. To Schlesinger the New Deal was a practical, energetic, and pragmatic movement based on the assumption that a "managed and modified capitalist order achieved by piecemeal experiment could combine personal freedom and economic growth."

Schlesinger's approach to the New Deal was echoed by other historians. Frank Freidel, author of what appears to be the most definitive multi-volumed biography of Roosevelt, wrote in much the same historiographical tradition as that of Schlesinger. Freidel, however, posed the discussion in quite different terms. To him the New Deal was basically the work of a number of persons who had grown to maturity during the Progressive era and who still shared the moral fervor of that period. Like Roosevelt, they were conservative men whose primary goal was to save rather than to destroy the free enterprise system. These humanitarian reformers were willing to use the machinery and authority of government to improve the lot of the common man. Taken as a whole, the New Deal was based on "American objectives and experience in the Progressive Era and during the first World War." [4] To put it another way, Roosevelt's program was squarely within the American tradition; his goals were essentially to conserve the existing economic and social system by eliminating obvious defects rather than changing it by radical programs.

Historians such as Commager, Schlesinger, and Freidel were all favorably disposed to the New Deal because they identified themselves with the American liberal or Progressive tradition. This is not to imply that they were uncritical toward Roosevelt and the New Deal; in many instances they found much that was inadequate, wrong, or misleading about the goals, program, and administration of many New Deal experiments. Generally speaking, however, they wrote with approval of Roosevelt's pragmatism, his faith in American democracy, and his obvious distaste for totalitarian methods. The alternative to the New Deal, they hinted, might very well have been a dictatorship of the right or left if the nation had continued to drift along as it had under Hoover.

While such historians who identified themselves in the Progressive tradition were interpreting the New Deal in a favorable light, others, particularly those adhering to a conservative ideology, were writing in quite a different vein. Conceiving of individual freedom and competition in almost absolutist terms, they saw the New Deal as a violent departure from traditional American values. To them the New Deal was anything but a continuation of America's political tradition; it represented rather an outright rejection

4. Frank Freidel, *The New Deal in Historical Perspective* (2nd ed.: Washington, D.C., 1965), p. 6.

of everything that was good and desirable within that tradition. During the decade of the thirties, many critics, especially spokesmen of conservative social groups and businessmen, took this position on the New Deal. Former President Hoover, for example, sounded a note of warning in 1934 when he condemned the expansion of the federal government's role and the subsequent regimentation of American life. "It is a vast shift," he wrote, "from the American concept of human rights which even the government may not infringe to those social philosophies where men are wholly subjective to the state. It is a vast casualty to Liberty if it shall be continued." [5]

Hoover's hostility was matched by other writers like John T. Flynn, a former liberal who had become progressively disillusioned by America's liberal tradition. Author of several books on Roosevelt, Flynn's antagonism against the New Deal reached a peak in his work *The Roosevelt Myth.* Specifically denying the achievements that liberal historians had credited to the New Deal, he argued that Roosevelt had substituted for the free enterprise system one that operated upon "permanent crises and an armament economy." In the process of implementing New Deal programs, the vigor of state governments had been sapped, the authority of Congress had been eroded, and unprecedented power had been concentrated in the hands of the president. One result of Roosevelt's New Deal policies was the appearance of a staggering federal debt; "a debt that can never be paid and which can be taken off our shoulders only by a great and devastating inflation." [6]

The charge by conservative writers that the New Deal represented a break with the past, interestingly enough, was echoed by some Progressive historians. One of these was Richard Hofstadter who, although writing within a liberal framework, was among the severest critics of America's liberal tradition. American liberalism, Hofstadter argued, had failed because of its moralizing tendencies and its inability to come to grips with the fundamental issues of the day. In *The Age of Reform: From Bryan to F.D.R.,* he insisted that the New Deal could not under any circumstances be interpreted as a continuation of the liberal-Progressive tradition.

5. Herbert Hoover, *The Challenge to Liberty* (New York, 1934), p. 103.
6. John T. Flynn, *The Roosevelt Myth* (rev. ed.: New York, 1956), pp. 414, 445.

The section in his book devoted to the New Deal was appropriately entitled "The New Departure."

To Hofstadter the New Deal was markedly different from any other indigenous American political movement. Past reform movements, Hofstadter noted, had generally operated under the assumption that their purpose was to clear the way for new enterprises and new men – to smash established privilege and monopoly and to provide all Americans with an equal opportunity in life. Within this context, the national government was considered to be either negative in its nature or an obstacle in the way of success. Earlier reform movements had taken it for granted that American society was essentially a healthy society but one that needed further democratization to reach its full potential.

The New Deal, according to Hofstadter, was based on entirely different premises. Instead of viewing American society as healthy, New Deal reformers saw it as a sick society in need of changes that could only be instituted through federal action. Thus the New Deal accepted the idea of federal responsibility for the relief of the unemployed, supported legislation for social security, unemployment insurance, wages and hours, and public housing, and did not fear massive expenditures that resulted in deficit spending. Many of the traditional aims of past reform movements – to restore government to the people and to destroy big business and monopolies – were simply bypassed or ignored by Roosevelt. Considering the nature and magnitude of New Deal programs, Hofstadter concluded, the movement had to be considered a new departure in American life. "The New Deal, and the thinking it engendered," wrote Hofstadter, "represented the triumph of economic emergency and human needs over inherited notions and inhibitions. . . . At the core of the New Deal, then, was not a philosophy (F.D.R. could identify himself philosophically only as a Christian and democrat), but an attitude, suitable for practical politicians, administrators, and technicians, but uncongenial to the moralism that the Progressives had for the most part shared with their opponents." [7]

The New Deal, Hofstadter pointed out with an ironic touch, represented a reversal of the usual ideological roles of American

7. Richard Hofstadter, *The Age of Reform: From Bryan to F.D.R.* (New York, 1955), pp. 314, 323.

conservatives and reformers. The conservatives had traditionally prided themselves on their sense of realism, their distrust of abstract plans for remaking society, and their belief in the necessity for institutional continuity. Reformers, on the other hand, had invariably appealed to moral sentiments, denounced existing injustices, and aroused the indignation of the community. By the 1930's, however, the traditional roles of the two had become reversed. Reformers appealed not to moral abstractions, but to concrete grievances of specific groups — farmers without markets, unemployed men without bread, laborers seeking to organize in unions of their own choosing, and to those groups concerned with the soundness of banks, investment markets, and manufacturing enterprises. Conservatives were now in the position of moral critics — they denounced the New Deal precisely because of its violation of traditional rules, its abandonment of the nation's moral heritage, its departure from sound principles, and its imposition of a federal tyranny upon the American people.

Oddly enough, Hofstadter was unhappy with the efforts of both conservatives and reformers. The reformers from the New Deal on, according to him, had refused to think in terms of rational planning and remained content to respond in a pragmatic way to individual pressures and situations as they arose. The criticisms of the conservatives, on the other hand, were "hollow and cliche-ridden," the complaints of a class increasingly cut off from the world of reality. But all that Hofstadter could do — at least in his role as historian and contemporary critic — was to hope that a better understanding of America's past political tradition might help future politicians to formulate a more realistic philosophy.

The second selection, by Rexford G. Tugwell, one of Roosevelt's economic advisers, represents the judgment of a liberal like Hofstadter who was critical of the New Deal. When Tugwell first joined the administration in the early 1930's, he was a firm believer in governmental planning in economic affairs. The old faith in a self-regulating market, he maintained, had never been justified; it was part of the American mythology of a free enterprise system. Distrustful of business and businessmen, Tugwell felt that only the federal government was in a position to control the economy in such a way as to make it run smoothly and efficiently.

After leaving government service to return to the academic

world, Tugwell set out to write a biography of Roosevelt, which was finally published in 1957. The picture Tugwell draws of Roosevelt and the New Deal in this selection is a friendly one, but one marked with a sense of disappointment. According to Tugwell, the productive capacity of the American economy by the late 1920's had far outrun purchasing power, thus giving rise to a fundamental maladjustment which resulted in the depression. The Republicans under Hoover initially denied that the economic situation was serious. Later they adopted half-way measures and encouraged private rather than public relief. When Roosevelt came to power, he was faced with a grave emergency but one which gave him an unprecedented opportunity such as no other president had had. Although he was a master improviser and politician, Roosevelt never conceived of New Deal measures in terms of rational planning. Many of the New Deal innovations, indeed, resulted from careful balancing between the claims of various competing pressure groups. Roosevelt, Tugwell concluded, was a political pragmatist with a progressive bent. Despite his essential greatness, he was unable or unwilling to seize the opportunity and institute far-reaching reform measures. Whether future historians would continue to look upon the New Deal in this manner, Tugwell admitted, was an open question.

Both Hofstadter and Tugwell were critical of Roosevelt because of his political opportunism and his pragmatic approach to serious problems. Implicit in their writings was the belief that the New Deal could not be interpreted as a part of America's liberal tradition. Oddly enough, they were in agreement with recent neo-conservative historians who had also rejected the thesis that American history could be understood in terms of class and ideological conflict. In the eyes of these more recent historians, American history had been marked not by conflict and divisions, but by stability and unity. Domestic struggles in the United States, they maintained, were over means, never over ends. To look upon the politics of the 1930's as an expression of fundamental divisions among the American people, they concluded, was a mistake.

But if the New Deal did not reflect fundamental class and ideological divisions, what did it reflect? This question is dealt with by Heinz Eulau, a political scientist at Stanford University writing in essentially a neo-conservative vein, in the third selection in this chapter. The New Deal, Eulau insists, defies ideological classification. It is true, he admits, that many individuals associated with Roosevelt had their own particular blueprints for the reconstruction of American society. Taken as a whole, however, the New Deal had many sides, and for this reason was not the product of a cohesive and rational ideology. Nor did the New Deal articulate a faith in a better tomorrow; it did not call upon people to join a crusade to remake their society or to experiment with new and untried schemes. But if the New Deal was not an ideology, a faith, a crusade, an experiment, a revolt, or a charisma, what was it? To Eulau the answer to this question is clear. The New Deal, he suggests, was "both a symbol and evidence of the nation's political maturity"; it represented an effort to solve problems "through politics rather than through ideology or violence." In Eulau's eyes a mature politics involves adjustment, compromise, and integration. By this standard the New Deal symbolized a mature politics because it was seeking solutions to problems rather than imposing preconceived solutions on problems.

By implication Eulau was agreeing with those neo-conservative historians who rejected class and ideological interpretations of American history in favor of an approach that emphasized the stability of American institutions and the pragmatism of American culture. The distinguishing characteristic of American history, therefore, was a rejection of the unrealistic intellectual and ideological characteristics of European thought and the substitution in their place of common sense. To writers like Eulau the New Deal must be understood as part of the basic common-sense approach of most Americans and their rejection of the world of ideology. In this sense the New Deal was not comparable to earlier liberal movements; the New Deal was simply an attempt to cope with unique problems in a simple and sensible manner.

Considering, then, the many ways historians have written about the New Deal, is it possible to come to any sort of definitive conclusions about its essential nature? Can Roosevelt and the New Deal be positioned precisely in terms of their place within the American political tradition? In dealing with this question, it should be emphasized that many of the apparent differences between students writing about the New Deal are partly semantical in nature. When describing the operation of specific New Deal programs, for example, the differences of opinion between historians tend to narrow sharply. Thus, what the W.P.A., N.R.A., and other federal agencies *did* is often not a subject of dispute. The issue that invariably leads to conflict is the *intent* of the participants involved. The controversy involves not the relief activities of the 1930's, to cite one instance, but whether or not the concept of federal relief undermined the cherished American ideals of individualism and liberty.

The semantic difficulty may be seen in the various ways historians have used the word "pragmatic." When Roosevelt was described as a "pragmatic leader," what did this mean? Actually the term was used in at least three different ways. Edgar E. Robinson, for example, has described Roosevelt's personal leadership as "pragmatic — an individual playing by ear." What Robinson meant by his characterization was that Roosevelt, in order to gain an immediate political advantage, never considered the long-range effects of his policies. "Roosevelt's failure," Robinson concluded, "lay in his unsuccessful attempt to justify the means or establish the ends he had in view." Underlying Robinson's thesis was the criticism that the New Deal resulted in an almost fatal concentration of power in the hands of the executive — a "power that could destroy the world or build it in the image of an entirely new scientific perspective." [8]

A second use of the term "pragmatic," as we have already seen in Tugwell's case, involved the criticism that Roosevelt never even understood the need for long-range economic planning. Roosevelt limited himself to immediate problems and tended to neglect more fundamental issues. Consequently, he never took advantage of the unparalleled opportunity for reform that arose out of the greatest single economic crisis that the American people had ever faced. While New Deal measures were important in giving status and material benefits to groups in American society that had been hitherto neglected, relatively speaking, these reforms fell short of their real potential. This view of Roosevelt, which has been echoed by many writers, is based on the underlying assumption that New Deal pragmatism and rational governmental planning were incompatible.

8. Edgar Eugene Robinson, *The Roosevelt Leadership 1933–1945* (Philadelphia, 1955), pp. 393, 397, 408.

The term "pragmatic" has been used in a third way to describe a mental attitude and frame of mind that rejected the dogmatic thinking of the 1930's and remained open and receptive to new ideas. William E. Leuchtenberg, a Columbia University historian, has argued that the "pragmatism" of the New Deal seemed striking only because the period as a whole was characterized by rigid ideological thinking. The New Deal was pragmatic, Leuchtenberg maintained, "only in contrast to the rigidity of Hoover and of the Left." Moreover, the movement was pragmatic in the sense that reformers themselves remained skeptical about final utopias and ultimate solutions and were always open to experimentation. To Leuchtenberg the New Deal was more than a movement to experiment or to improvise; it was a movement led by men who were committed to the proposition that it was possible to make human life more tolerable, that depressions were by no means inevitable events, and that human affairs were not necessarily guided by inexorable deterministic laws.[9]

The problem of understanding and assessing the achievements of the New Deal and its place in American history, therefore, is one whose answer will largely be determined by a series of prior assumptions about the nature of the American past and the nation's ideals in both the present and the future. To those historians whose view is that America is founded upon an atomistic philosophy — that the nation's greatness arose from the achievements of talented and ambitious individuals and was not related to the activities of the government — the New Deal will always appear as a movement alien and hostile to traditional values. In this context the New Deal represents a new departure in American history that will end perhaps in a collectivistic and authoritarian government. On the other hand, to those scholars who adhere to a corporate philosophy — that society is more than a mere aggregate of private individuals and that a modern complex industrial economy requires a certain amount of public regulation as well as government-sponsored reform — the New Deal becomes a political movement inspired by proper ideals. Instead of being an aberration in terms of the American political tradition, the New Deal was a movement consonant with previous struggles for justice and equality.

9. William E. Leuchtenberg, *Franklin D. Roosevelt and the New Deal 1932–1940* (New York, 1963), pp. 344–345.

The problem of judging the nature and accomplishments of the New Deal is, then, a difficult one, for it involves the entire fabric of the American past. Indeed, to avoid any broad judgments is in effect to render a judgment, albeit on an unconscious rather than a conscious level. In the final analysis, therefore, historians will continue to grapple with the place of the New Deal in American life. Was the New Deal a continuation of America's liberal tradition or was it a repudiation of that tradition? Can the New Deal be understood in ideological terms or should it be viewed as a political movement characterized by an underlying pragmatism? These are only some of the broad questions that must be answered in order to assess the nature and significance of the New Deal.

Arthur M. Schlesinger, Jr.

IN THE BACKGROUND of any historical episode lies all previous history. The strands which a historian may select as vital to an understanding of the particular episode will vary widely according to his interest, his temperament, his faith and his time. Each man must unravel the seamless web in his own way. I do not propose here any definitive assessment of the sources of the New Deal. I doubt whether a final assessment is possible. I want rather to call attention to certain possible sources which may not have figured extensively in the conventional accounts, including my own – to the relation of the New Deal to the ebb and flow of American national politics and then its relation to the international dilemma of free society in this century.

Such relationships are speculative; nonetheless, an attempt to see them may perhaps cast light on some of the less discussed impulses behind the New Deal itself. To begin – and in order to make a sharp issue – let me ask this question: would there have been a New Deal if there had been no depression? Without a depression, would we have had nothing but a placid continuation, so long as prosperity itself continued, of the New Era of the Twenties?

I would answer that there would very likely have been some sort of New Deal in the Thirties even without the Depression. I think perhaps our contemporary thinking has come too unreflectively to assume depression as the necessary preliminary for any era of reform. Students of American history know better. The fight against depression was, to be sure, the heart of the New Deal, but it has not been the central issue of traditional American reform:

"Sources of the New Deal: Reflections on the Temper of a Time," *Columbia University Forum,* II (Fall, 1959), 4–12.

ARTHUR M. SCHLESINGER, JR. (1917–) is a former Professor of History at Harvard University. He was also a Special Assistant to President John F. Kennedy. Among his published works are *The Age of Jackson* (1945), *The Age of Roosevelt* (1956–), and *A Thousand Days: John F. Kennedy in the White House* (1965).

it was not the heart of Jeffersonian democracy nor of Jacksonian democracy nor of the anti-slavery movement nor of the Progressive movement.

What preceded these other epochs of reform was an accumulation of disquietudes and discontents in American society, often non-economic in character, and producing a general susceptibility to appeals for change — this and the existence within society of able men or groups who felt themselves cramped by the status quo and who were capable of exploiting mounting dissatisfaction to advance policies and purposes of their own. This combination of outsiders striving for status and power and a people wearying of the existing leadership and the existing ideals has been the real archetype of American reform.

The official order in the Twenties presented perhaps the nearest we ever came in our history to the identification of the national interest with the interests, values and goals of a specific class — in this case, of course, the American business community. During the generation before Harding, the political leaders who had commanded the loyalties and the energies of the American people — Theodore Roosevelt and Woodrow Wilson — expressed strains in American life distinct from and often opposed to the dominant values of business. They represented a fusion of patrician and intellectual attitudes which saw in public policy an outlet for creative energy — in Lippmann's phrase, they stood for mastery as against drift. In the service of this conception, they led the people into great national efforts of various sorts, culminating in the convulsive and terrible experience of war. Two decades of this — two decades under the glittering eyes of such leaders as Roosevelt and Wilson, Bryan and La Follette — left the nation in a state of exhaustion.

By 1920 the nation was tired of public crisis. It was tired of discipline and sacrifice. It was tired of abstract and intangible objectives. It could gird itself no longer for heroic moral or intellectual effort. Its instinct for idealism was spent. "It is only once in a generation," Wilson himself had said, "that a people can be lifted above material things. That is why conservative government is in the saddle two-thirds of the time." And the junior official to whom he made this remark, the young Assistant Secretary of the Navy, also noted soon after his unsuccessful try for the Vice-Presidency in 1920, "Every war brings after it a period of materialism and conservatism; people tire quickly of ideals and we are now repeating history." John W. Davis, the Democratic candidate in 1924, said a few years later: "The people usually know what they want at a particular time . . . In 1924 when I was a candidate what they wanted was repose."

A nation fatigued with ideals and longing for repose was ready for "normalcy." As popular attention receded from public policy, as values and aspirations became private again, people stopped caring about politics, which meant that political power inevitably gravitated to society's powerful economic interests — the government of the exhausted nation quite naturally fell to the businessmen. And for nearly a decade the business government reigned over a prosperous and expanding country.

Yet, for all the material contentment of the Twenties, the decade was also marked by mounting spiritual and psychological discontent. One could detect abundant and multiplying symptoms of what Josiah Royce, after Hegel, used to call a self-estranged social order. The official creed began to encounter growing skepticism, and even opposition and ridicule, in the community at large. Able and ambitious groups, denied what they considered fitting recognition or opportunity, began to turn against the Establishment.

If the economic crash of 1929 astonished the experts, a spiritual crash was diagnosed well in advance. "By 1927," reported Scott Fitzgerald, "a widespread neurosis began to be evident, faintly signalled, like a nervous beating of the feet, by the popularity of crossword puzzles." In the same year Walter Lippmann pointed more soberly to the growing discrepancy between the nominal political issues of the day and the actual emotions of the people. If politics took up these real issues, Lippmann said, it would revolutionize the existing party system. "It is not surprising, then, that our political leaders are greatly occupied in dampening down interest, in obscuring issues, and in attempting to distract attention from the realities of American life."

What was wrong with the New Era was not (as yet) evidence of incompetence or stupidity in public policy. Rather, there was a profound discontent with the monopoly of power and prestige by a single class and the resulting indifference of the national government to deeper tensions. Those excluded from the magic circle suffered boredom, resentment, irritation and eventually indignation over what seemed the intolerable pretensions and irrelevances of their masters. Now it is the gravest error to underrate the power of boredom as a factor in social change. Our political scientists have pointed out convincingly how the human tendency toward inertia sets limits on liberalism; I wish they would spend equal time showing how the human capacity for boredom sets limits on conservatism. The dominant official society — the Establishment — of the Twenties was an exceedingly boring one, neither bright nor witty nor picturesque nor even handsome, and this prodded the human impulse to redress the balance by kicking up heels in back streets.

All this encouraged the defection of specific groups from a social order which ignored their needs and snubbed their ambitions. Within the business community itself there were dissident individuals, especially in the underdeveloped areas of the country, who considered that opportunities for local growth were unduly restrained by Wall Street's control of the money market. The farmers felt themselves shut out from the prevailing prosperity. Elements in the labor movement resented their evident second-class citizenship. Members of foreign nationality groups, especially the newer immigration and its children, chafed under the prevalent assumption that the real America was Anglo-Saxon, Protestant, middle-class and white. In time some of the younger people of the nation began to grow restless before the ideals held out to them; while others, in accepting these ideals, acquired a smug mediocrity which even depressed some of their elders.

Gravest among the symptoms was the defection of the intellectuals: writers, educators, newspapermen, editors — those who manned the machinery of opinion and who transmitted ideas. The fact of their particular estrangement and discontent guaranteed the articulation, and thus, to a degree, the coordination of the larger unrest. The intellectuals put the ruling class in its place by substituting for its own admiring picture of itself a set of disrespectful images, which an increasing number of people found delightful and persuasive; the insiders, who had before been seen in the reverent terms of Bruce Barton and the *American Magazine,* were now to be seen less reverently through the eyes of H. L. Mencken and Sinclair Lewis. Satire liberated people from the illusion of business infallibility and opened their minds to other visions of

American possibility. The next function of the intellectuals was precisely to explore and substantiate those other visions. They did so with zest and ingenuity; and the result was that, beneath the official crust, the Twenties billowed with agitation, criticism and hope. Dewey affirmed man's capability for social invention and management; Beard argued that intelligent national planning was the irresistible next phase in history; Parrington insisted that Jeffersonian idealism had a sound basis in the American past, and indeed, expressed a truer Americanism than did materialism. Together the satirists and the prophets drew a new portrait of America – both of the American present and of the American promise – and the increasingly visible discrepancy between what was and what might be in America armed the spreading discontent.

The well of idealism was rising again; energies were being replenished, batteries recharged. Outsiders were preparing to hammer on the gates of the citadel. The 1928 election, in which an Irish Catholic challenged Yankee Protestant supremacy, illustrated the gathering revolt against the Establishment. And, though Hoover won the election, Samuel Lubell has pointed out that "Smith split not only the Solid South but the Republican North as well." Smith carried counties which had long been traditionally Republican; he smashed the Republican hold on the cities; he mobilized the new immigrants. In losing, he polled nearly as many votes as Calvin Coolidge had polled in winning four years before. He stood for the vital new tendencies of politics; and it is likely that the prolongation of these tendencies would have assured a national Democratic victory, without a depression, in 1932 or certainly by 1936. And such a Democratic victory would surely have meant the discharge into public life of able and ambitious people denied preference under a business administration – much the same sort of people, indeed, who eventually came to power with the New Deal; and it would have meant new opportunities for groups that had seen the door slammed in their faces in the Twenties – labor, the farmers, the ethnic minorities, the intellectuals.

The suspicion that a political overturn was due even without a depression is fortified, I think, by the calculations of my father in his essay of some years back "The Tides of National Politics." In this essay he proposed that liberal and conservative periods in our national life succeed themselves at intervals of about fifteen or sixteen years; this alternation takes place, he wrote, without any apparent correlation with economic circumstances or, indeed, with anything else, except the ebb and flow of national political psychology. By this argument, a liberal epoch was due in America around 1934 or 1935, depression or no.

In short, the New Deal was, among other things, an expression of what would seem – to use a currently unfashionable concept – an inherent cyclical rhythm in American politics. The Depression did not cause the cycle: what the Depression did was to increase its intensity and deepen its impact by superimposing on the normal cycle the peculiar and unprecedented urgencies arising from economic despair. One might even argue – though I do not think I would – that the Depression coming at another stage in the cycle would not necessarily have produced a New Deal. It is certainly true, as I said, that depressions did not induce epochs of reform in 1873 or in 1893. I think myself, however, that the magnitude of the shock made a political recoil almost certain after 1929. Still, the fact that this recoil took a liberal rather than a reactionary turn may well be due to the accident that the economic shock coincided with a liberal turn in the political cycle.

In any event, the fact remains that the historical New Deal, whether or not something like it might have come along anyway, was after all brought into being by the Depression. It assumed its particular character as it sought to respond to the challenge of economic collapse. And, in confronting this challenge, it was confronting a good deal more than merely an American problem. Mass unemployment touched the very roots of free institutions everywhere. "This problem of unemployment," as Winston Churchill said in England in 1930, "is the most torturing that can be presented to civilized society." The problem was more than torturing; it was something civilized society had to solve if it were to survive. And the issue presented with particular urgency was whether representative democracy could ever deal effectively with it.

Churchill, in the same Romanes lecture at Oxford in 1930, qustioned whether it could: democratic governments, he said, drifted along the lines of least resistance, took short views, smoothed their path with platitudes, and paid their way with sops and doles. Parliaments, he suggested, could deal with political problems, but not with economic. "One may even be pardoned," Churchill said, "for doubting whether institutions based on adult suffrage could possibly arrive at the right decisions upon the intricate propositions of modern business and finance." These were delicate problems requiring specialist treatment. "You cannot cure cancer by a majority. What is wanted is a remedy."

The drift of discussion in the United States as well as in Britain in the early Thirties revealed an increasingly dour sense of existing alternatives; on the one hand, it seemed, was parliamentary democracy with economic chaos; on the other, economic authoritarianism with political tyranny. Even more dour was the sense that history had already made the choice — that the democratic impulse was drained of vitality, that liberalism was spent as a means of organizing human action. Consider a selection of statements from American writers at the time, and their mortuary resonance:

> The rejection of democracy is nowadays regarded as evidence of superior wisdom. (Ralph Barton Perry)
>
> The moral and intellectual bankruptcy of liberalism in our time needs no demonstration. It is as obvious as rain and as taken for granted. (Nathaniel Peffer)
>
> To attempt a defense of democracy these days is a little like defending paganism in 313 or the divine right of kings in 1793. It is taken for granted that democracy is bad and that it is dying. (George Boas)
>
> 'Liberalism is dead.' So many people who seem to agree upon nothing else have agreed to accept these three sweeping words. (Joseph Wood Krutch)
>
> Modern Western civilization is a failure. That theory is now generally accepted. (Louise Maunsell Fields)
>
> Why is it that democracy has fallen so rapidly from the high prestige which it had at the Armistice? . . . Why is it that in America itself — in the very temple and citadel of democracy — self-government has been held up to every ridicule, and many observers count it already dead? (Will Durant)

Only the most venerable among us can remember the creeping fear of a quarter of a century ago that the free system itself had run out of energy, that we had reached, in a phrase Reinhold Niebuhr used as a part of the title of a book in 1934, the "end of an era." What this pessimism implied for the realm of public policy was that democracy had exhausted its intellectual and moral resources, its bag of tricks was played out, and salvation now lay in moving over to a system of total control.

In affirming that there was no alternative between laissez-faire and tyranny, the pessimists were endorsing a passionate conviction held both by the proponents of individualism and the proponents of collectivism. Ogden Mills spoke with precision for American conservatives: "We can have a free country or a socialistic one. We cannot have both. Our economic system cannot be half free and half socialistic . . . There is no middle ground between governing and being governed, between absolute sovereignty and liberty, between tyranny and freedom." Herbert Hoover was equally vehement: "Even partial regimentation cannot be made to work and still maintain live democratic institutions." In such sentiments, Hoover and Mills would have commanded the enthusiastic assent of Stalin and Mussolini. The critical question was whether a middle way was possible – a mixed system which might give the state more power than conservatives would like, enough power, indeed, to assure economic and social security, but still not to much as to create dictatorship. To this question the Hoovers, no less than the Stalins and Mussolinis, had long since returned categorical answers. They all agreed on this, if on nothing else: no.

As I have said, economic planning was not just an American problem. Great Britain, for example, was confronting mass unemployment and economic stagnation; moreover, she had had since 1929 a Labor government. In a sense, it would have been hard to select a better place to test the possibilities of a tranquil advance from laissez-faire capitalism to a managed society. Here was a Labor leadership, sustained by a faith in the "inevitability of gradualness," ruling a nation committed by tradition and instinct to the acceptance of empirical change. How did the British Labor government visualize its problem and opportunity?

The central figures in the Labor government of 1929 were Ramsay MacDonald, now Prime Minister for the second time, and Philip Snowden, his sharp and dominating Chancellor of the Exchequer. Both were classical Socialists who saw in the nationalization of basic industry the answer to all economic riddles. Yet in the existing political situation, with a slim Labor majority, nationalization was out of the question. With socialism excluded, MacDonald and Snowden — indeed, nearly all the Labor party leaders — could see no alternative to all-out socialism but nearly all-out laissez-faire. A capitalist order had to be operated on capitalist principles. The economic policy of the Labor government was thus consecrated as faithfully as that of Herbert Hoover's Republican administration in the United States to the balanced budget and the gold standard — and, far more faithfully than American Republicanism, to free trade.

Socialism across the Channel was hardly more resourceful. As the German Social Democrat Fritz Naphtali put it in 1930, "I don't believe that we can do very much, nor anything very decisive, from the point of view of economic policy, to overcome the crisis until it has run its course." In this spirit of impotence, the democratic Socialists of Europe (until Léon Blum came to power some years later) denied the possibility of a middle way and concluded that, short of full socialization, they had no alternative but to accept the logic of laissez-faire.

The assumption that there were two absolutely distinct economic orders, socialism and capitalism, expressed, of course, an unconscious Platonism — a conviction that the true reality lay in the theoretical essences of which any working economy, with its compromises and confusions, could only be an imperfect copy. If in the realm of essences socialism and capitalism were separate phenomena based on separate principles, then they must be kept rigorously apart on earth. Nor was this use of Platonism — this curious belief that the abstraction was somehow more real than the reality, which Whitehead so well called the "fallacy of misplaced concreteness" — confined to doctrinaire capitalists and doctrinaire socialists. The eminent Liberal economist Sir William Beveridge, director of the London School of Economics, braintruster for the Lloyd George welfare reforms before the First World War, spoke for enlightened economic opinion when he identified the "inescapable fatal danger" confronting public policy in the Depression as "the danger of mixing freedom and control. We have to decide either to let production be guided by the free play of prices or to plan it socialistically from beginning to end . . . Control and freedom do not mix." Beveridge, encountering Donald Richberg in Washington in the glowing days of 1933, asked a bit patronizingly whether Richberg really believed that there was "a half-way between Wall Street and Moscow." As for Britain, "there is not much that anyone can do now to help us," Beveridge said. "We must plan to avoid another crisis later. We shall not by conscious effort escape this one."

So dogma denied the possibility of a managed capitalism. But could dogma hold out in Britain against the urgencies of depression? Some Englishmen dissented from the either/or philosophy. In the general election of 1929, for example, John Maynard Keynes and Hubert Henderson had provided the Liberal party with the rudiments of an expansionist policy, based on national spending and public works. As unemployment increased in 1930, so too did the pressure for positive government action. That year Sir Oswald Mosley, a member of the Labor government, proposed to a cabinet committee on unemployment an active program of government spending, accompanied by controls over banking, industry and foreign trade. But he could make no impression on the capitalist orthodoxy of the Socialist leaders; Snowden rejected the Mosley memorandum. Another minister suggested leaving the gold standard; Snowden covered him with scorn. To the party conference of 1930, MacDonald said, "I appeal to you to go back to your Socialist faith. Do not mix that up with pettifogging patching, either of a Poor Law kind or Relief Work kind." In other words, socialism meant all or – in this case – nothing!

As economic pressure increased, more and more had to be sacrificed to the balancing of the budget; and the implacable retrenchment meant more governmental economy, reduction in salaries, reduction in normal public works, until, in time, the frenzy for economy threatened the social services and especially the system of unemployment payments on which many British workers relied to keep alive. The summer crisis of 1931, after the failure of *Kreditanstalt,* weakened the pound; and to Snowden and the Labor government nothing now seemed more essential than staying on the gold standard. To keep Britain on gold required American loans; American loans would not be forthcoming unless satisfactory evidence existed of a determination to balance the budget; and the evidence most likely to satisfy J. P. Morgan and Company, which was arranging the American credit, was a cut in unemployment benefits.

In August 1931, MacDonald and Snowden confronted the cabinet with this dismal logic. Arthur Henderson made it clear that the whole cabinet absolutely accepted Snowden's economic theory: "We ought to do everything in our power to balance the Budget." But MacDonald's proposal for a cut in the dole seemed downright wrong; the Labor government fell. MacDonald soon returned to office as head of a National government. The new government, slightly more adventurous than its predecessors, took Britain off gold in a few weeks. Sidney Webb, Labor's senior intellectual, provided the Labor government its obituary: "No one ever told *us* we could do that!"

The Labor government having immobolized itself by its intellectual conviction that there was no room for maneuver, no middle way, now succeeded through its collapse in documenting its major premise. Then the experience of 1931 displayed the Right as too hardboiled ever to acquiesce in even the most gradual democratic change. "The attempt to give a social bias to capitalism, while leaving it master of the house," wrote R. H. Tawney, "appears to have failed."

If piecemeal reforms were beyond the power of the Labor government, as they were beyond the desire of a Tory government, then the only hope lay in the rapid achievement of full socialism; the only way socialism could be achieved seemed to be through ruthlessness on the Left as great as that on the Right. Such reasoning was responsible for the lust for catastrophic change that suffused the British Left and infected a part of the American Left in the early Thirties. No one drew more facile and sweeping conclusions than Harold Laski. The fate of the MacDonald government, Laski wrote, was "tantamount to an insistence that if socialists wish to secure a state built upon the principles of their faith, they can only do so by revolutionary means."

From this perspective Laski and those like him quite naturally looked with derision on the advocate of the middle way. In December 1934, for the perhaps somewhat baffled readers of *Redbook* magazine, Laski debated with Maynard Keynes whether America could spend its way to recovery. Public spending, Laski said with horror, would lead to inflation or heavy taxation or waste; it would mean, he solemnly wrote, "an unbalanced budget with the disturbance of confidence (an essential condition of recovery) which this implies": it would bequeath a "bill of staggering dimensions" to future generations. "Government spending as anything more than a temporary and limited expedient," he concluded, "will necessarily do harm in a capitalist society." This was, of course, not only the argument of Ramsay MacDonald but of Herbert Hoover; Laski's novelty was to use it to defend, not a balanced budget and the gold standard, but – socialist revolution.

One way or another, the British Left began to vote against liberal democracy. Sir Oswald Mosley, who had championed the most constructive economic program considered within the MacDonald government, indicated the new direction when, with John Strachey and others, he founded the authoritarian-minded New Party in 1931. Mosley's excesses soon led him toward fascism and discredit; but plenty of others were reaching similar conclusions about the impossibility of reform under capitalism. Sidney and Beatrice Webb abandoned Fabianism for the mirage of a new civilization in the Soviet Union. All peaceful roads to progress seemed blocked. After a visit with Roosevelt in Washington, Cripps wrote, "My whole impression is of an honest anxious man faced by an impossible task – humanizing capitalism and making it work." "The one thing that is not inevitable now," said Cripps, "is gradualness."

Both Right and Left – Hoover and Stalin, John W. Davis and Mussolini, Ogden Mills and Stafford Cripps – thus rejected the notion of a socially directed and managed capitalism, of a mixed economy, of something in between classical free enterprise and classical socialism. And the either/or demonstration commanded considerable respect in the United States – self-evidently on the American Right; and to some degree on the American Left. So Laski had made clear in *Democracy in Crisis* that the American ruling class would be as tough and hopeless as any other:

> What evidence is there, among the class which controls the destiny of America, of a will to make the necessary concessions? Is not the execution of Sacco and Vanzetti, the long indefensible imprisonment of Mooney, the grim history of American strikes, the root of the answer to that question?

In 1932 both Right and Left thus stood with fierce intransigence on the solid ground of dogma. In so doing, they were challenging an essential part of the American liberal tradition. When Professor Rexford G. Tugwell of the Columbia University economics department, on leave in Washington, revisited his campus in 1933, he rashly bragged of the New Deal's freedom from "blind doctrine," and the *Columbia Spectator,* then edited by a brilliant young undergraduate named James Wechsler, seized on this boast as the fatal weakness of Tugwell's argument and of the whole New Deal. "This is the crux of the problem," the *Spectator* said; "the blind stumbling in the most chaotic fashion — experimenting from day to day — without any anchor except a few idealistic phrases — is worthless. It is merely political pragmatism."

Merely political pragmatism — to ideologists, whether of Right or of Left, this seemed conclusive evidence of intellectual bankruptcy. As the conservatives had said that any attempt to modify the capitalist system must mean socialism, so the radicals now said that any attempt to maintain the capitalist system must mean fascism. "Roosevelt's policies can be welded into a consistent whole," wrote I. F. Stone, "only on the basis of one hypothesis . . . that Mr. Roosevelt intends to move toward fascism." "The essential logic of the New Deal," wrote Max Lerner, "is increasingly the naked fist of the capitalist state."

Convinced of the fragility of the system, the radicals saw themselves as the forerunners of apocalypse. "American commercial agriculture is doomed," wrote Louis Hacker; capitalism was doomed, too, and the party system, and the traditional American way of life. In 1934 Sidney Hook, James Burnham, Louis Budenz, V. F. Calverton, James Rorty and others addressed "An Open Letter to American Intellectuals." "We cannot by some clever Rooseveltian trick," the letter warned,

> evade the unfolding of basic economic and political developments under capitalism . . . Let us not deceive ourselves that we shall not have to face here also the choice between reaction, on the one hand, and a truly scientific economy under a genuine workers' democracy on the other.

In 1935 *The New Republic* stated with magisterial simplicity the argument of the radicals against the New Dealers, of New York against Washington, of the Marxists against the pragmatists.

> Either the nation must put up with the confusions and miseries of an essentially unregulated capitalism, or it must prepare to supersede capitalism with socialism. *There is no longer a feasible middle course.*

Both radicalism and conservatism thus ended in the domain of either/or. The contradictions of actuality which so stimulated the pragmatists of Washington, only violated the proprieties and offended the illusions of the ideologists. While they all saw themselves as hardheaded realists, in fact they were Platonists, preferring essence to existence and considering abstractions the only reality.

The great central source of the New Deal, in my judgment, lay precisely in the instinctive response of practical, energetic, and compassionate people to those dogmatic absolutes. This passion to sacrifice reality to doctrine presented a profound challenge to the pragmatic nerve. Many Americans, refusing to be intimidated by abstractions or to be overawed by ideology, responded by doing things. The whole point of the New Deal lay in its belief in activism, its faith in gradualness, its rejection of catastrophism, its indifference to ideology, its conviction that a managed and modified capitalist order achieved by piecemeal experiment could combine personal freedom and economic growth. "In a world in which revolutions just now are coming easily," said Adolf Berle, "the New Deal chose the more difficult course of moderation and rebuilding." "The course that the new Administration did take," said Harold Ickes, "was the hardest course. It conformed to no theory, but it did fit into the American system — a system of taking action step by step, a system of regulation only to meet concrete needs, a system of courageous recognition of change." Tugwell, rejecting laissez-faire and communism, spoke of the "third course."

Roosevelt himself, of course, was the liberal pragmatist *par excellence*. His aim was to steer between the extremes of chaos and tyranny by moving always, in his phrase, "slightly to the left of center." "Unrestrained individualism" he wrote, had proved a failure; yet "any paternalistic system which tries to provide for security for everyone from above only calls for an impossible task and a regimentation utterly uncongenial to the spirit of our people." He constantly repeated Macaulay's injunction to reform if you wished to preserve.

Roosevelt had no illusions about revolution. Mussolini and Stalin seemed to him, in his phrase, "not mere distant relatives" but "blood brothers." When Emil Ludwig asked him his "political motive," he replied, "My desire is to obviate revolution . . . I work in a contrary sense to Rome and Moscow." He said during the 1932 campaign:

> Say that civilization is a tree which, as it grows, continually produces rot and dead wood. The radical says: 'Cut it down.' The conservative says: 'Don't touch it.' The liberal compromises: 'Let's prune, so that we lose neither the old trunk nor the new branches.' This campaign is waged to teach the country to march upon its appointed course, the way of change, in an orderly march, avoiding alike the revolution of radicalism and the revolution of conservatism.

I think it would be a mistake to underestimate the extent to which this pragmatic attitude was itself a major source of New Deal vitality. The exaltation of the middle way seems banal and obvious enough today. Yet the tyranny of dogma was such in the early years of the Great Depression that infatuation with ideology blocked and smothered the instinctive efforts of free men to work their own salvation. In a world intoxicated with abstractions, Roosevelt and the New Dealers stood almost alone in a stubborn faith in rational experiment, in trial and error. No one understood this more keenly than the great English critic of absolutes; Keynes, in an open letter to Roosevelt at the end of 1933, stated the hopes generated by the New Deal with precision and eloquence. "You have made yourself," Keynes told Roosevelt,

> the trustee for those in every country who seek to mend the evils of our condition by reasoned experiment within the framework of the existing social system. If you fail, rational choice will be gravely prejudiced throughout the world, leaving orthodoxy and revolution to fight it out. But, if you succeed, new and bolder methods will be tried everywhere, and we may date the first chapter of a new economic era from your accession to office.

The question remains: why did the New Deal itself have the pragmatic commitment? Why, under the impact of depression, was it not overborne by dogma as were most other governments and leaders in the world? The answer to this lies, I suspect, in the point I proposed earlier – in the suggestion that the New Deal represented, not just a response to depression, but also a response to pent-up frustration and needs in American society – frustrations and needs which would have operated had there been no depression at all. The periodic demand for forward motion in American politics, the periodic break-through of new leadership – these were already in the works before the Depression. Depression, therefore, instead of catching a nation wholly unprepared, merely accelerated tendencies toward change already visible in the national community. The response to depression, in short, was controlled and tempered by the values of traditional American experimentalism, rather than those of rigid ideology. The New Deal was thus able to approach the agony of mass unemployment and depression in the pragmatic spirit, in the spirit which guaranteed the survival rather than the extinction of freedom, in the spirit which in time rekindled hope across the world that free men could manage their own economic destiny.

Rexford G. Tugwell

[I]

IT MAY seem strange — incongruous — to speak of President Roosevelt as in direct descent, politically, from Ignatius Donnelly, Pitchfork Ben Tillman, Tom Watson, Sockless Jerry Simpson and Mary Elizabeth Lease, that wild-eyed agrarian female radical who shouted up and down America in 1890 that farmers ought to raise less corn and more hell. It is nevertheless true that President Roosevelt owed his election largely — not, of course, wholly — to the movement, long gathering force, long frustrated, which was headed by Donnelly and others of the Farmers' Alliance, the Grangers, and the Populists in the Midwest and the South of the last century. It would be more accurate to say that President Roosevelt was in direct descent from Bryan, and that Bryan had been the inheritor of all the agrarian unrest. That he won, as Bryan could not, was because the depression of 1929 was worse than that of 1893, and because the number of those who were shaken in their Republicanism was greater in proportion to the whole.

It is possible that this overemphasizes the agricultural influence on the election of 1932. But on the whole I do not think so. There never has been a time, since the opening and settlement of the West, when a union of the West with the South — the traditional marriage of corn with cotton — was not an irresistible political combination. Since the Civil War, because Republican reconstruction alienated the defeated States, a combination had been available only to the Democrats. The Republicans had had to depend on the somewhat less solid Northeast for a combination with the West.

"The New Deal in Retrospect," *Western Political Quarterly,* I (December, 1948), 373–385. Reprinted by permission of the University of Utah, copyright owners.

REXFORD G. TUGWELL (1891–   ) taught at Columbia University and the University of Chicago and served in Washington under Franklin Delano Roosevelt during the 1930's. In addition to many economic works, he has also written *The Democratic Roosevelt* (1957).

And usually the Republican alliance with big business had been difficult, to say the least, to sell to the farmers. During the Harrison and McKinley days, and even during the Roosevelt and Taft administrations, to say nothing of the Harding-Coolidge-Hoover era, the Republicans were the party of respectability and responsibility; they were conservative, sound, devoted to the interests of business, in favor of high tariffs, suspicious of labor, and against currency manipulation. They were the party of the creditors. They were, also, all the time, a majority party, notwithstanding the Wilsonian interlude from 1912 to 1920. Wilson was a minority President for at least four years; and possibly, in one sense, eight, since issues were so greatly confused by war as hardly to be separable, and he may have squeezed through in 1916 for other than domestic reasons.

Bryan, of course, in 1896, and afterward in 1900 and 1908, was the first of the *national* political leaders to represent in a formidable way the interests of the agrarian West against the East. The campaign of 1896 was one of the most thrilling in all American history. Almost half a century of agrarian unrest and resentment found its embodiment in the silver-tongued boy-orator of the Platte. But Hanna, with the impeccably respectable McKinley as his candidate, managed to defeat him. That was the high tide. Never again would the Populist movement have so much support. For America was on the make. Farmers might feel ill-used and exploited; labor might be more resentful as the attempt was made to unionize and bargain collectively for the alleviation of long hours, low wages and execrable working conditions, and as courts and legislatures hampered progress; but that part of America which was on the make was still a majority — or could be made to seem so. But in 1932, the great bubble of prosperity had burst, and a decade-long depression in agriculture was registering at last in appropriate political terms.

On the whole, with minor setbacks, the increase in productivity in America, together with the exploitation of a continent still largely unexhausted by soil erosion and the depletion of other resources, had kept the challenging critics of things-as-they-are from becoming a majority until 1932. The situation which existed after World War I was one in which complacency, conservatism, loyal mutual support between government and business, together with isolation, seemed to a majority of the electorate to be a sufficient policy for the times. People wanted normalcy after their adventure abroad. Mr. Hoover, however, inheriting what had now become a tradition fixed by Harding and Coolidge, found himself unable to overcome a fast-developing crisis in economic life which began in the late '20's. And he was, of course, humiliatingly defeated by President Roosevelt in 1932, after serving for one term. He had won, it will be remembered, from Smith in 1928. But that campaign had been less dramatic than the concurrent phenomena of the bull market. The economic issue was not yet ready for political exploitation. There was still prosperity for almost everyone but the farmers.

What was the economic crisis? And how far had it gone by 1932? It had begun — and here is the connection with the agrarians and the long western disaffection which had been so brilliantly personified by Bryan — by a disastrous fall of farm prices in 1920–21. There had begun, then, one of those unbalanced deflationary movements which so often have occurred in American economic life as a result of the unplanned and uncontrolled actions of economic groups in pursuit of private interests. The world had wanted farm products in great quantity during the war; after it was over, an expanded agriculture found its markets failing and its prices going down. But prices of manufactured goods (which the farmer must buy) stayed high. It took more unprocessed wheat, hogs, cotton, or corn to buy farm machinery, or even processed food and fibre, than ever before. Presently it took almost twice as much, and farmers felt that not only natural causes were at fault. They were certain that the deflation was the result of policies originated in Washington by those who were unfriendly.

Farmers can always withstand a certain amount of this kind of thing by refusing to buy, and by becoming temporarily more self-sufficient. But there is a limit to the time the old tractor or harvester, the barn roof, or the milking machine will last without replacement. And when farmers do not buy, moreover, industry feels the loss of customers. Ultimately workers lose their jobs. The inescapable mutuality of economic groups in the American economy is thus demonstrated.

Moreover, farms have mortgages which represent what the farmer borrowed to pay for them. If the farm was bought at a time of high prices for farm-products, a high price was probably paid for the land — and with a high interest rate on the mortgages. When prices fall, it becomes harder to meet the interest and practically impossible to meet payments of principal. This in turn has an effect on all the financial institutions which loan to farmers, or deal in mortgages or other farm credits. And eventually the effect is felt in other institutions with which *they* deal. This may — and did by 1929 — go all the way back to Wall Street itself.

The farm price decline had begun in 1920. City people — industrialists, bankers, and even workers — are not much inclined to be concerned with farmers' woes — at least they had not been in the '20's. And otherwhere than in agriculture a great boom had been going on. It had been a peculiarity of this boom that prices had not gone up. In fact, non-farm commodity prices had been remarkably stable from 1920 to 1928. The publicity men of the industrialists had exploited this fact by talking about "profitless prosperity." But, of course, it had not actually been profitless. What had been happening as a result of the many technical advances during the war could now be understood; efficiency was greater and costs were coming down. Profits, in spite of stable prices, were going up and up.

It is one of the unalterable conditions for the successful continuation of large-scale industry that purchasing power among consumers must be sufficient to carry off the volume produced. In order to maintain purchasing power in volume, consumers' incomes and the total of prices attached to goods and services for sale must be roughly equal. They cannot be equal unless prices come down as costs come down; otherwise, the increasing profits go into more factories and increased production. In the long run warehouses fill with goods for which there is no demand. This is a very short and, because short, inaccurate account of the basic trouble in 1929. It leaves out, for instance, the effect of the vast pools of sterile savings, and also those which financed the wild speculation after 1927. But it does emphasize the fact that, by 1929, productive power *had* far outrun purchasing power. The farmers had first been priced out of the market; then other consumers had followed; and all the time vast increases in plant were being made. Also vast speculations were taking place with the ever-growing surpluses of business. Suddenly it was seen that the huge debts contracted at the inflated levels of speculation could not be paid. All creditors tried to force payment of debts to them at once. There was panic.

[II]

The Republican answer to the spreading depression after 1928 had been, first to deny its seriousness, and then to encourage the raising of private relief funds. Mr. Hoover was reluctant to admit that the government had any responsibility at all. But he did consent to the setting up of the Reconstruction Finance Corporation for business relief, and this was one phase of the famous "trickle" theory which was afterward emphasized by the Democrats. The R.F.C. was finally authorized, also, to loan $300,000,000 to the states for relief; and a farm aid program, which offered more succor for processors than for farmers, was begun. But that was Mr. Hoover's limit. He would not admit, any more than Coolidge had, that the federal government had a direct responsibility to the people for their welfare.

The campaign of 1932 came after almost four years of grinding deflation, succeeding almost a decade of agricultural depression. There were idle factories, unemployment, hunger — all the phenomena of industrial paralysis. During this time Mr. Roosevelt was governor of New York where the miseries of depression were felt to their utmost. Toward the end of Mr. Hoover's administration it became quite obvious that the time was coming for a new man and a new program; he had lost practically all his popular support. What could be more logical than that the Governor of the Empire State, a life-long liberal, an experienced and popular public figure, should succeed to the Presidency.

It was one of those times, which come occasionally in the life of the nation, when the nomination for the Presidency is especially valuable, because, unless mistakes are made, winning is a foregone conclusion. Mr. Roosevelt was a professional politician. He was well aware of the possibilities. There had been, in fact, two most astute agents at work for years — Louis McHenry Howe and James A. Farley — rounding up delegates: or rather, preparing to round them up when the time should arrive. There was opposition to be expected. The conservative wing of the party had the choice of Byrd of Virginia and Ritchie of Maryland; and Smith naturally felt himself entitled to another chance since he had sacrificed himself in 1928. Developing events, however, favored President Roosevelt rather than an outright conservative. The depression deepened. Disillusionment with Republicanism extended itself to the normally Republican middle classes; and the Republican farmers were awaiting the word of hope to abandon their political leaders if not their party.

There was drama in the nomination of 1932 in Chicago. Not until President Roosevelt's own forces had worked out a modus operandi with a substantial section of the Southern Democracy could the business be concluded. In this it was arranged for Mr. Garner of Texas to be Vice-President. This, it might be said, added to the fact that some seventeen chairmanships of committees in the new Congress were to be held by Southerners, would present President Roosevelt with a sectional problem which would torment him throughout his more than twelve years in the Presidency. For the West, the South, and the big city machines would make a difficult team to handle. And often compromises and trades would be necessary which would emasculate what it was proposed to do. Nevertheless, it was a condition of nomination that such a compromise should take place. And President Roosevelt, an Easterner, did join the South and the West more successfully than any politician had been able to do since the Civil War. This was where his happiest faculties had their fullest scope.

The election was less dramatic. The campaign, because its outcome became so favorable in prospect, turned into a cautious statement of progressive hopes and beliefs, the items of which had been familiar since the times of Bryan, T. Roosevelt, and Wilson. Nevertheless, it was a statement, however tame, of progressive intentions. Perhaps the fact that a *progressive* was to succeed Hoover, after Harding and Coolidge, intensified the fears of Wall Street. When a *Roosevelt* administration became a certainty, it became equally certain that new forces would come into control. Perhaps this may have caused the deflation to run deeper than it otherwise might. Everyone was trying to become liquid — free of debt — at once. And everyone distrusted the shaky institutions of finance, which were suspected of having made vast loans abroad and to industrialists at home, with depositors' funds, which would never be repaid. Their struggles to collect, and the unwillingness of depositors to trust them further, brought President Roosevelt to his inauguration day in the midst of complete economic paralysis, with banks closing, Governors declaring bank holidays – that is, moratoria – unemployment at twelve or thirteen millions, hardship and misery everywhere. The great new post-war factories were now closed, transportation systems were bankrupt and idle. Only soup kitchens and what were called "Hoovervilles" – shack villages on dump heaps – were busy.

To a nation thus paralyzed and sunk in despair, a golden voice proclaimed in the First Inaugural that Americans had nothing to fear but fear itself. It seemed as though a great sleeper awoke at that call and found that, after all, he had a useful strength. He stretched and looked for ways to use it. No less than 460,000 citizens wrote personally to their President as a result of this one speech. It swamped the White House facilities, but it showed what a welcome change Roosevelt was after Hoover. The people had a man.

The first measures had to be emergency ones: to assuage fears, to relieve suffering, and to set up more equal exchange among those who made various kinds of goods and provided various kinds of services. Measures looking to longer-run social security could await a measure of recovery. So, in fact, could the reforms still holding over, remaining to be done, from older progressive regimes – notably the Wilsonian, though some of that program had been achieved then.[1]

Theoretically the Wilsonian measures should have prevented what had happened in 1929 and subsequently. And Democrats really had the choice of saying that their reforms had been sabotaged by Republican administrations or admitting frankly what they had done had not been enough. In the Roosevelt campaign the candidate practically admitted the deficiency by way of redefining progressivism. He called it the New Deal.

The A.A.A. was devised to restore agriculture to "parity"[2] in the national community and bring farmers again into the concert

1. A Federal Trade Commission for fair trade practices; the Underwood Tariff Act, which reduced duties some ten per cent; an income tax to provide revenues lost by tariff reduction – a constitutional amendment having now made the tax possible; and the Federal Reserve Act to decentralize the "money power."

2. That is, to bring the prices of farm products into such relationship with industrial goods that they would buy as much as they had before the agricultural depression.

of economic interests. And the N.R.A. was provided to encourage the immediate resumption of industrial activity — the President's re-employment agreement, of which the well-remembered symbol was the Blue Eagle. And along with this, the financial system was bolstered by emergency loans to banks by the R.F.C. which amounted to a guarantee of deposits,[3] gold was made a government monopoly, and the dollar devalued so that debts could be paid in cheaper money. This was inflation. In an instant, people's savings, insurance policies, bank deposits, etc., lost about one-third of their value. But hardly anyone even noticed this; they were worth very little anyway in a national debacle. But the American competitive situation in foreign markets was improved.

This fiscal program disrupted the London Economic Conference of that spring because the President would not give other nations the advantage of currencies cheaper than ours. And international agreement on economic matters would make no progress for years to come. But Americans could sell again because foreigners could buy, and domestic debtors felt better because they could resume paying their debts — so, it is to be presumed, did the creditors, except that what was owing to them was being paid in dollars with diminished value. Also the whole international scene was overshadowed by negotiations about the payment of the debts holding over from World War I. It was so widely believed that these ought to be collected that the impossibility of collecting them made a real political problem for President Roosevelt.

[III]

The administration of the new measures was necessarily ragged. For relief, for instance, there was no organization at all and one had to be devised offhand by Hopkins and his helpers — Williams, Gill, Hunter, Baker and others — and long chances had to be taken "in getting the money out." The same was true of the A.A.A. Scores of thousands of employees had to be engaged and trained on the job to do things which were just the reverse of all accepted bureaucratic rules and practices. And as for the N.R.A. — under General Johnson its administration immediately became a caricature of decent procedure.[4]

3. Made permanent later in the Federal Deposit Insurance Corporation.
4. There were businessmen running that show. The others were being managed by professors, editors, bureaucrats and social workers.

Impromptu organization and freehand administration brought criticism even from those who were benefiting most; the sharpest dissent came from the business community, which was smarting from its own failure and from the humiliating need to be bailed out and set on its feet again. During the subsequent period, when it came to putting through certain reforms, business, again fairly prosperous, was about as vigorous in its opposition as though it had not been prostrate a year or two before. Nevertheless, a Securities and Exchange Act was passed and the Anti-Trust Division of the Department of Justice was given new life under Mr. Thurman Arnold. These will be recognized as theretofore unfinished business on the progressive agenda.

It can be imagined, even by those who belong to a generation which has no recollection of the incidents of those years, what life was like in the United States during the Great Depression following 1929 and also during the years of recovery, beginning in 1933. The years between the crash and the Roosevelt inauguration, when the nation was finally told that recovery was not hopeless but waited only for effort of the people themselves, were drab and miserable. There was shame, lost pride and broken initiative as well as hunger, cold and sickness. Perhaps the deflation had run its course by March of '33. It was said afterward by the President's enemies that this was so and that his measures had rather retarded than assisted. But no one thought so then. His voice came to them over the radio in the cultivated accents of Groton and Harvard; but it was warm and reassuring. What he said to do was done, even by the Congress. For the moment the Southern reactionaries were willing to give their support; and the business community which might have objected was hopelessly discredited.

[IV]

There will always be question, I suppose, whether, when the policies of reaction were bankrupt and even the most pushing private interests were frightened for once into considering the state of the nation, more might not have been done. For the genuinely constructive part of the New Deal would consist, not in relieving the miseries and anxieties of depression, and not even in reforms which had been long delayed, but in taking at least the minimum measures to insure that depression might not recur. It is often said, for instance — and as often denied — that in that spring of 1933 a genuine national banking, credit, and currency-issuing system might have been set up. The sanctity of banking and bankers of the old sort had certainly evaporated. Merely to belong to a profession which had taken people's funds for safekeeping and failed to keep them safe at all was to be under suspicion. And to this there were added the doubtful investment of depositors' funds, and speculations in the money market and in brokers' loans, to say nothing of proved participation in the orgiastic bull-market itself. And perhaps the public in general was the more severe for feeling guilty itself. For participation in stock gambling had been incredibly widespread. Perhaps no one would have objected much to any suggestion for change which would have made such activities impossible in the future. And the Federal Reserve System — which had itself been devised in the liberal times of Wilson, although those who had studied its history knew it to be a compromise — had utterly failed to do what its authors and defenders had claimed for it: control speculation, prevent misuse of funds, and decentralize the money power. It seemed rather to have contributed to than to have checked the fatal succession of events which had led to the crash.

Mr. Laski, a shrewd observer of the American scene, in his *The American Presidency,* says flatly that President Roosevelt went as fas as he could have gone, and he mentions specifically the criticism that the situation in 1933 was not seized on to nationalize the financial system. People who hold such views, he says, do not understand the American system. A President cannot seize occasions to establish institutions which outrun people's understanding of what is appropriate. He must wait for opinion to precede any such action.

The answer might be made to this, that opinion was ready enough, but that President Roosevelt was not — that there was no one who knew how to set up a better system, and, especially, no one available to President Roosevelt. As a matter of fact, Wall Street — people like Thomas Lamont, Russell Leffingwell, Walter W. Stewart, and others — had, together with such orthodox university authorities as H. Parker Willis, B. M. Anderson, E. W. Kemmerer, et al., a monopoly of knowledge and competence in the field of money and banking. And they, all of them, had vested interests in the Federal Reserve System. There was no one in the United States, like Keynes in Britain, who represented a genuinely alternative opinion and who could have carried out a reform.

At any rate, what President Roosevelt chose to do was to take such measures as would relieve stress – segregation of gold, devaluation of the dollar, reopening of the banks with reassurance to depositors, extension of more liberal credits to farmers and home owners, expansion of loans to banks and other businesses by the already existing R.F.C. All these were intended to renew confidence in old institutions as an alternative to creating new ones.

As to Mr. Laski's dictum that American Presidents may not get ahead of established opinion, it may be ventured that the great ones among them always have – which is one characteristic of their greatness. Jefferson made the Louisiana purchase, Monroe issued a famous hands-off warning to other powers, Lincoln appointed Grant and freed the slaves, Theodore Roosevelt created a Panama to contain the Canal, Wilson committed us to the League of Nations (it was only an error in method which prevented ratification), and President Roosevelt himself certainly took chances of the same sort, some successful, some not. Passamaquoddy, the Florida ship canal, and the subsistence homestead programs were not successes; nor was the N.R.A. But the T.V.A., the Civilian Conservation Corps, the A.A.A. and several others, were. It is too much to say that our President cannot assume a position of leadership. That there are limits no one would deny. The real question here is whether President Roosevelt did not miss a great opportunity which a Wilson, for instance, would have exploited to the limit.

Certainly the Federal Reserve System had failed; and certainly we still have it – with, of course, some added features, such as the F.D.I.C. A new system might have been mismanaged by the old hands; but that is always a risk.

[V]

What is involved here is the Roosevelt method. He did seek not only relief from the crisis of those years, but the means of preventing new ones. He chose to do it, however, by political finesse rather than by coups of the sort by which Jefferson took Louisiana or even by the bolder kind of leadership which he showed later with respect to the coming war. He preferred to manipulate interests against one another until the weight was on the side he wanted it to be on and was sufficient for the purpose. In this, his method is reminiscent of that of Lincoln, who also was a great improviser and knew the uses of compromise. He encouraged this group, discouraged or ignored that one, meted out discreet punishment, gave rewards — and, because he had a long time in which to do it, came out with something. It was not usually something new and neatly shaped to its purpose; but rather something misshaped by compromise and reluctant agreement, awkward, hard to operate, completely satisfactory to no one. But it did get a measure of the necessary result.

He utilized the potential strength of the farm lobby and its Congressional bloc, together with the temporary weakness of the industrial lobbies and their representatives, to establish agriculture in a new and very much improved bargaining position. It is true that, in administration, it would turn out to be about as favorable to the processors of farm products, to financial institutions dependent on agriculture and to the vast bureaucracy of the Farm Bureau and the state colleges as to the farmers themselves, and that it would pretty much exclude from its benefits share-croppers and farm labor. But it was, undoubtedly, something. And it would probably offer enormous resistance to any such deflation as had happened in 1920–21.

A similar attempt to establish good businesses in a strong competitive position in the economy vis-a-vis those which were not good — that is, businesses which would be fair to labor, would bargain collectively, and would adhere to fair standards of competition against those which would not — completely broke down from maladministration amid the wholesale welter of sharp practice, selfishness and greed which characterized the N.R.A. in its later stages. But by then business was on its feet anyway; and business, good or bad, was not likely to suffer generally in the American economy.

Aside from this, a succession of laws, and continuing favoritism in their administration, established labor in such a bargaining position as it had never occupied before. It is sometimes said that the New Deal ended in 1936 with the Wagner-Steagall Housing Act;

but the consolidation of labor's position as a favored claimant for a share in the national income continued at least until 1938, when the Fair Labor Standards Act was passed. This more or less completed a system, rather incoherent and rickety, which had begun with the 7A clauses in the N.R.A. Act, the labor provisions, and had continued through the National Labor Relations Act in 1935.

Certain other measures provided limits to future deflations. After the Social Security System was set up, however awkward and insufficient it may have been, the kind of ultimate, squalid misery which had been so prevalent from 1929 to 1933 would not be possible again so long as we had any national income to distribute. There was nothing bold about this and other similar measures; they had been commonplace in Germany, the United Kingdom and elsewhere for two generations; but American businessmen seemed to think – or at least said – that they led straight to Communism. And they required characteristic Roosevelt maneuvering to achieve.

What could save and justify the Roosevelt New Deal was not, however, its minima, its bulwarks against renewed deflations and unbalance. These were good for what they were. But what was needed much more was an increase in the national income through renewed and intensified production. President Roosevelt had to cure a paralysis of the social organism brought about by the coiling constrictions of a *laissez faire* in the last stages of its logical development from individual enterprise to price-controlling and production-reducing monopoly. One way to attack this was through government spending, which was desirable for other reasons as well – relief of poverty, the building up of resources such as water power and reclamation projects, and the rehabilitation of farms, neglected forests and parks, and blighted urban areas. The difficulty with this was that it had to precede the collection of taxes on the income it might generate, and that an annual and balanced budget was a fetish which had survived even the depression. People with savings and insurance and people on salary knew well enough what happened when the budget was unbalanced. It made their dollars less valuable. And they were against it, along with the larger financiers. President Roosevelt always had trouble with this. And he was always reluctant to do as much as was necessary to get the result of a productivity which would have buried the investment in spending in an avalanche of goods. Not until he learned to trust Keynes did he understand what had to be done, in realistic magnitudes, if the result was to be got in that way. Perhaps he did not actually learn it until the magnificent outpouring of goods for war began after the New Deal days were over.

There was another way, of course, than that of public spending, devaluation of the dollar and inflation. That was the way of control and, indeed, of strict public management of the price structure, of production programs, and of the whole system of distribution, together with severe taxation to achieve a balanced budget. This would have required a discipline which would perhaps have been regarded as overheroic for Americans, although it was used in a limited way when they went to war a few years later; at any rate, the President studied and rejected it. He was a reluctant and inconsistent Keynesian in this matter until the program was several years old and was no longer so urgently necessary. The first $3,300 million in 1933 did something, together with successive appropriations of similar magnitude, but never enough. A national income of 75 or 80 billions achieved within a few years seemed magnificent after the 37 billions of Mr. Hoover's last year. But what could have been done at any time only became apparent when war preparations began and the national income really rose, passing 150 billions, with no signs of strain whatever.

[VI]

To the backward look, President Roosevelt and his New Deal have a pattern and a meaning which, in the midst of the maneuverings and compromises of the time, was often lost sight of — by everyone but President Roosevelt himself. Inconsistency did not bother him greatly, provided there was an advantage — even if only a slight one — for the policy he wanted. It did not worry him overmuch to live in turmoil. And the constant attacks to which he was subjected by the press, even if unpleasant, were rather favorable than otherwise for what he expected to accomplish. It did not decrease the confidence common folk had in him to have constantly on view the hatred borne their champion by those whom they mistrusted.

There were few who ever saw him with the mask of confidence removed. The gaiety of his laughter in time of fear echoed not only through the unaccustomed rooms of the White House, but symbolically in every home in the land. And if he was often uncertain, that was, as he said, because he was the quarterback of a team which had to be directed on the field, and it was not a fundamental uncertainty, only a tentativeness about tactic. There was necessarily improvisation, because there had been no planning. There would be failures. But the team would ultimately win. Its members might seem ill-assorted. They might be zealous to carry the ball over often; and they might even indulge in some sabotage, if they thought they could get away with it, in favor of friends or in their own political interest. But he was the captain as well as the quarterback. It was his game; and on the whole it was his victory. Looking back from the fourth year of life in America since his death, men know how much poorer they are without him. Perhaps one test of the New Deal's worth was the great grief of common folk everywhere when the news of his death came to them so suddenly in April of 1945. They knew, even if more analytical critics did not, that they had lost a champion, even a friend. Their judgment must always temper that of objective historians.

The New Deal may have been a progressive interlude in an America predominantly reactionary. That still remains to be seen. The personality of Roosevelt, like that of Lincoln, who, in spite of superficial difference, he so much resembles, confuses the judgment. His maneuverings, his continual trading of what he thought were small advantages for what he thought were large ones, his ability to make the most incongruous assistants work together as a team, the fact that he had a scheme in mind (as can be seen by rereading the Campaign Speeches of 1932), and that he saw most of it carried out – all this must be taken into account. He spent all his days in office working not only, as during the war, for his nation's survival, but for the strengthening in it of those groups and forces which he judged to be needful, creative, democratic, tolerant and kindly. Whether and to what extent he succeeded will become clearer as time passes. It seems to me that we have gained some parity or balance among economic groups, that we approach clearer designs of what we must do, and that we have clearly established the minima of social security – and this was what Roosevelt meant by "New Deal." The critical judgment as to all these matters and as to others will no doubt become sharper and more rational; but those who have the advantage of distance and reflection will not have the memorial treasure of his presence. That, to those who knew him, will always be among the most precious of their possessions and the most illuminating of their guides.

Heinz Eulau

THE NEW DEAL of Franklin D. Roosevelt, just as the New Freedom of Woodrow Wilson before, and the Fair Deal of Harry Truman later, had its quota of ideologues, but was not an ideology; it had its following of true believers, but was not a chiliastic faith; it produced far-ranging reforms, but was not a crusade; it was rich in inventions, but was not an experiment; it mobilized huge majorities, but was not a revolt of the masses; it generated forceful national leadership, but was not a charismatic surrender. It is possible to see the New Deal as the fulfillment of the promise of American life – Herbert Croly's dream in the years before the first World War; or as an exercise in instrumental pragmatism which John Dewey had celebrated in the years following that war. But if it was the realization of the liberal promise or the application of the pragmatic philosophy, it was so by way of improvisation rather than design. All of these elements were present, but they do not express the dynamics of the New Deal. If it was anything, the New Deal between 1932 and 1940 was, simply and foremost, evidence of the viability of democratic politics in an age of crisis.

Ardently defended by its admirers, and bitterly denounced by its enemies, the New Deal came to make a lasting impression on the American experience – an impression, I venture to say, which in the long run can only be compared with the birth of the nation itself and the fratricidal blood-letting of the Civil War. The New Deal fascinated and continues to fascinate the national consciousness, not only because it was an intense and dramatic political episode, but also because it was, like the birth of the United States and the Civil War, a national event. By comparison, the earlier

"Neither Ideology Nor Utopia: The New Deal in Retrospect," *The Antioch Review,* XIX (Winter, 1959–1960), 523–37. Reprinted by permission of the *Antioch Review.*

HEINZ EULAU (1915–) is Professor of Political Science at Stanford University. He was formerly an editor of *The New Republic.* Among his published works is *Class and Party in the Eisenhower Years* (1962).

New Freedom and the later Fair Deal were merely incidents — the former a pale prospectus, the latter a faded postscript, to the politically most exciting period in American history.

NOT AN IDEOLOGY

Though the New Deal was non-ideological, this does not mean that it was anti-ideological. In fact, it was shot through with ideologies, or utopias, whichever emphasis one may prefer. Total planners and piecemeal planners, budget-balancers and deficit-spenders, trust-regulators and trust-busters, protectionists and free traders, "sound money" proponents and inflationists — all vied with each other under the hospitable tent that was the New Deal. Wall Street bankers, Midwest farmers, Harvard economists, Columbia lawyers, labor intellectuals, old-time progressives, new liberals, social workers — men of the Right, Left, and Middle — supplied ideas and programs, if not panaceas. Theories were welcome as they had never been welcome before; and never before, or thereafter, did so many blueprints of a better order reach the citadel of influence. Ideas were, indeed, the true coins of the realm.

But, for precisely these reasons, there was little of the ideological in the New Deal — if by ideology one means a coherent and consistent set of beliefs, values, opinions, and aspirations. To attempt to construct out of the welter of these beliefs and values, opinions and aspirations an internally congruent system of thought is to do violence to history and to the meaning of the New Deal. Not that such attempts have not been made, or will not be made in the future. But they can be made only at the risk of great distortion. For the New Deal was an ideologically much too elusive phenomenon to be squeezed into the convenient categories of ideological analysis. In fact, insofar as it responded to ideological pressures at all, the New Deal was engaged in a continuous effort to disengage itself from ideological commitments.

The difficulty of ideological analysis is that it cannot easily free itself from the Aristotelian mode of thinking, with its neat and even aesthetically satisfying dichotomies. This is the mode of thought which pitches liberty against security, private property against public ownership, national regulation against decentralization, monopoly against competition. Granted, the New Deal emphasized the positive role of national government and strong federal action. But, granted too, the consequences of such action, as in the federal grants-in-aid programs, were an enormous expansion and strengthening of both state and municipal activities. Granted, the Tennessee Valley Authority represented as "socialist" an undertaking as had ever been devised in the United States. But, granted too, one of its consequences was the flowering of private enterprise in an area where previously it had great trouble flowering. Granted, the New Deal promoted social and economic security in manifold ways. But, granted too, it did not do so at the expense of liberty: there was hardly a period in American history in which public discussion of public issues and the freedom to speak freely had been practiced with as much abandon as under the New Deal. The New Deal simply defies ideological classification.

All this does not mean that the New Deal was not anchored in a cultural milieu of attitudes and predispositions which was congenial to its operation. This milieu was the liberal tradition in America. As Louis Hartz has suggested, in one sense the whole American political tradition is liberal. In this perspective, the New Deal, non-ideological though it was, was clearly an indication, if not a vindication, of liberalism. Without this tradition, there would have been no New Deal. But, in the American context, the liberal tradition as such has rarely been experienced as an ideology. Rather, it appears as a cultural fact which, like the air we breathe, is so close, so natural, so much a part of our daily life that we fail to notice it. The liberal tradition explains, I suspect, why its many contradictions and inconsistencies were "built in" New Deal programs, plans, and policies. For liberalism, unlike other isms, has never been a set of dogmas, but a state of mind. It represents an attitude which insists on questioning self-evident propositions, partly to find out what evidence there is to support them, partly to discover possible alternatives. It follows that liberalism is not bound to any particular social or economic system. No wonder that so many different ideologues, theoreticians, administrators, and politicians could find the New Deal a congenial environment in which to work. Indeed, they shaped that environment. And the New Deal reflected, in varying degrees and at varying times, the varying enthusiasm and different approaches to the national problems.

NOT A FAITH

That the New Deal gave new hope to millions, that it brought new confidence into government, that it ultimately became a testament of national courage, there is little doubt. Where there had been drift, the New Deal offered mastery. Just as Hoover's "we are at the end of our string" had symbolized the old order, Roosevelt's "firm belief that the only thing we have to fear is fear itself" symbolized the new approach. But at no time did the New Deal assume that man does not live by bread alone. It generated fresh expectations in the hearts of people who had recently experienced little but misery, and a new spirit came about the land. But it was a hope and a spirit nourished not by promises and good intentions, but by governmental action. The New Deal was a reconfirmation of the old American assumption that action is its own reward. What the New Deal articulated was not a faith in a better morrow, but a call for action now.

And the people were captivated, not because they were asked to be true believers, but because action gave them a new sense of dignity. The dole had given them the minimum means of subsistence, and charity had made them loathe a humility to which they were not accustomed. Now they found their way into public works, conservation corps, rural settlements, and, as the economy began to grind again, back into jobs in industry, transportation, and commerce. They were grateful. But even if the New Deal had tried to take the role of the savior, it is doubtful that it could have saved many souls. What generated the new spirit that made the thirties so exciting was not government action alone. True, the government played a role it had never played in the lives of Americans before. But what sustained the popular drive and confidence that came with the New Deal was the old faith that man can control his destiny – given the conditions that make action and self-help possible.

Much nonsense has been written to the effect that the New Deal made of Americans unthinking and faithful dependents of a "welfare state," so-called – a people which has lost initiative and entrusts its fate to the benevolence of an all-powerful government. The welfare state, it is alleged, is the new dispensation – man's reward on this earth for conformity and compliance based on faith and political suicide. But the New Deal was not a sacred mission; it was a most secular, indeed profane, manifestation of modern man's quest for security — not the security that comes from an anticipation of heavenly bliss, but the security that comes from an ability to make this earth one's home.

The New Deal, then, was not an "escape from freedom," a surrender of the intellectual faculties. Rather than calling for faith, it was an enormous educational effort. Perhaps never before in the history of the republic was it necessary to re-educate the preferences and redirect the energies of the people. Whatever one may wish to call it — propaganda or education — the American people were exposed to a flow of information about the activities of the government unexcelled in the past. And the people responded. There was new understanding of the difficulties besetting the nation, a new tolerance of innovations, and a new commitment to creative intelligence in politics. Rarely has there been so much knowledgeable participation of the people in public affairs. Letters poured into Washington, and the newspaper columns reflected popular interest. Rather than escaping from freedom, people once more had a genuine sense of being part of the governmental enterprise. Not submission to authority, but a lively feeling of one's efficacy, one's ability to influence the course of events, characterized the popular response. It has sometimes been said that if the New Deal had wanted to assume totalitarian forms, it could have done so without much difficulty — for people were ready to accept almost anything that would give them a better deal. Nothing could be further from reality. The New Deal was what it was and became what it became precisely because it did not promise a millennium, but confronted the American people with the harsh realities of the present, first at home, and then abroad.

NOT A CRUSADE

To think of the New Deal as a unified program, a plan, or a policy is as mistaken as to think of it as a movement or a crusade. There were many programs and policies, and there was more than a movement. What made the New Deal the phenomenon it was — a new deal in American life, a fresh start — was not a zest for reform, but the need to respond to national problems as they were dictated by the exigencies of the moment, not as they may have been preconceived by reformers. Whatever preferences for reform may have motivated individual New Dealers as they found themselves in the seats of power and influence after the politically lean years of normalcy, the task at hand was to revive the economy, not to translate long-cherished proposals for reform into reality.

Reforms, of course, there were. Some were successful and became permanent features of American life. Industrial violence, long the scourge of labor-management relations, gave way to the peaceful method of collective bargaining. Unemployment and old-age insurance programs remedied long-standing ills among the socially and economically most disadvantaged sector of the population. Securities legislation brought discipline and responsibility into the disorderly state of banking and investment practices. But other reforms were doomed to failure. Rural resettlement was a temporary stop-gap and fell victim to its own idealism. The National Resources Planning Board never got off the ground. Other programs were conceived as self-liquidating and were liquidated, though some of them, like the Civilian Conservation Corps or Public Works Administration, left a rich heritage of national accomplishment. Still other programs represented *ad hoc* inventions to cope with pressing problems which had hardly been envisaged by the reformers. They were, in fact, determined efforts by the government to maintain the *status quo*. Programs such as agricultural adjustment or bank deposit insurance were acts not so much of reform as of preservation.

The one attempt made to conduct a crusade – the National Recovery Administration under Hugh Johnson – resembled more an Alice-in-Wonderland grotesque than a viable governmental structure and policy. NRA had important successes – abolishing child labor, setting maximum hours and minimum wages, removing unfair trade practices, and so forth – which, once re-enacted after NRA's demise, became monuments of social progress. But, on the whole, NRA was a fiasco because it tried to do too much in too little time within a single institutional setting which, at its roots, sought to reconcile business regulation by business itself with protection of free-market mechanisms by the government. The effort often led to an atmosphere of histrionics much at variance with that kind of earnestness that is the hallmark of reform. The Blue Eagle campaign was more a circus, really, than a crusade, and few tears were shed when the whole enterprise was declared unconstitutional.

It is only in the perspective of history that the New Deal can possibly be conceived as a political or social movement. But even in this perspective, it was only a new phase, a most intensive phase, perhaps, forced by the great depression to heroic exertion, in the long-range national development which is the promise of American life. It was directly related — not only in ideas it shared, but also in some of its older personnel — to both the Square Deal and the New Freedom, to the historical trend to achieve Jeffersonian ends by Hamiltonian means. That the Square Deal had been Republican and the New Freedom Democratic made the national character of the New Deal all the more poignant. Of all the movements, so-called, in American history, the New Deal was truly national in scope, liberal in purpose, and effective in action.

NOT AN EXPERIMENT

The New Deal has come to be cited as the prize exhibit of the success of the experimental method in the making of public policy and the development of administrative techniques. The New Deal's willingness and capacity to chart new social and political paths is seen as an expression of John Dewey's philosophy of instrumentalism. But this interpretation represents a tendency to over-intellectualize the political process. It is more often in the nature of an apologia than of analysis. By calling anything new an "experiment," success of the experiment is heralded as proof of the uses of experimentation, while failure is explained away as inconsequential. The analogy between social efforts to create new alternatives and scientific experimentation ignores more than it explains. In fact, when the metaphor becomes a myth, it may be detrimental to a genuine understanding of the New Deal.

Roosevelt himself gave credence to the experimental metaphor when he declared that what the country needed was "bold, persistent experimentation." Yet one may doubt that his call for experimentation was intended to make experimental pragmatism into a political formula. His notion hardly included the scientist's image of the carefully designed and controlled experiment. As he suggested, "it is common sense to take a method and try it; if it fails, admit it frankly and try another. But above all, try something." But an experiment is the very opposite of common sense. Quite clearly, Roosevelt's accent was less on the nature of the method used than on the injunction to "try something." Roosevelt was prepared to try things, not to test theoretical propositions or to follow hunches – his mind was much too untheoretical for that – but to meet urgent social needs and pressures. Indeed, many potential New Deal proposals never left the drafting boards, not because they might not have worked, but because they were politically unfeasible. And not a few others were prematurely terminated long before their success or failure could have been demonstrated.

Though the New Deal was not an experiment or a series of experiments, it was admittedly an experience in social inventiveness. There was, again in Roosevelt's words, no room for "foolish traditions." Innovation, not experiment, was the trade-mark of the New Deal. The proliferation of administrative agencies came with the suspicion that the old-line departments would not or could not aggressively pursue the new policies; balancing the budget no longer meant what it had traditionally meant – social values defied accounting in terms of dollars and cents, and it was the national economy, not the government budget, that was thought to be at stake; an agriculture of abundance was to be realized, paradoxically, through promoting programs of scarcity, like killing pigs and plowing under the crops which could not be marketed at adequate prices; and on the political front, from Roosevelt's personal appearance at the 1932 Chicago convention to his breaking of the two-term tradition eight years later, the New Deal defied conventions. Yet, it is interesting to note that in politics proper this proved most difficult, as the ill-fated "court-packing plan" or the President's aborted attempt to influence the 1938 Democratic primaries demonstrated.

But, paradoxically too, the New Deal with all its inventions was in the great American political and social tradition. For that tradition meant innovation: free public lands, free religious worship, free public education, a chance at economic betterment and social mobility, a broad democratic franchise, and many other social gains had at first been innovations – inventions which at one time had made the difference between the Old World and the New. The New Deal was in the mainstream of that tradition, but again with a difference.

NOT A REVOLT

Easy comparison can be made between the New Deal's success in mobilizing great electoral majorities and the plebiscitary mirages performed by totalitarian regimes. Both, it has been claimed, represented that revolt of the masses which José Ortega y Gasset had so somberly described only a few years earlier. Increased popular participation in the most far-reaching decision a national community can make – the election of its government – has been said to be a sign not of social health, but of social tension; an index of cleavage rather than consensus; evidence of despair rather than creative involvement.

Whatever the veracity of this argument in regard to totalitarian mass behavior, it lacks relevance to the New Deal as a political event. The New Deal elections were not plebiscites, but hard-fought, free battles of the ballot. Even in the landslide election of 1936, almost seventeen million people, or about 38 per cent of the total electorate, voted for the Republican candidate. In spite of the personal attractiveness of the Democratic candidate, few campaigns in twentieth century America have been as genuinely democratic as the early New Deal elections. Although the press was predominantly anti-New Deal, rarely has there been so much discussion of the real issues facing the nation. What moved the New Deal majorities was not a sense of revolt, but a renewed spirit of confidence in the willingness and ability of the government to carry out the popular mandate.

In organizing its electoral majorities, the New Deal restructured the political map. Its political techniques were anything but the contrived plebiscitarian technology of mass manipulation. That the New Deal succeeded in harnessing to its wagon the forces of labor, the young as well as the old, the socially underprivileged ethnic groups, farmers as well as urbanites, former Republicans as well as former Socialists, was not the result of hidden persuasion or silent threat, but of its sensitivity to popular needs and demands. In doing so, the New Deal was an almost perfect system of political feedback. Rarely in a modern democracy has the politics of democracy been equally conducive to the strengthening of democracy as a viable political system.

Had the New Deal been an ideology, a faith, or a crusade, it might have been otherwise. But because it was none of these things, the New Deal could engage in its support the great electoral majorities which it needed in order to cope forcefully with the tasks of the nation. Nevertheless, impressive as the New Deal majorities were, it would be to simplify the situation if one elevated the New Deal into a flowering of the majoritarian principle as a "general will." The New Deal majority was, above all, a product of the political process as it had developed its particular flavor in the American culture. In the abstract, one might say that the majority demanded "something be done," or that it approved of what was done. Yet, that something was invariably done, sooner or later, does not mean that the majority, so-called, was agreed on what should be done, or that it endorsed what was done for the same reasons. To assume that the New Deal majorities were united in purposes and goals is not only naive, but incorrect. The New Deal majorities were, in reality, only evidence of the complex processes of group adjustment and compromise that had preceded the electoral majorities; proof that these processes were reasonably efficient in generating the electoral power that was needed to continue the processes of adjustment and compromise. Like all American majorities, the New Deal majorities were the products of a salient coalition politics, only more so. No ideological or militant politics, no revolt of the masses, could have been equally successful — at least not in a free democracy.

NOT A CHARISMA

If ever the right man came to occupy the right office at the right time, Franklin D. Roosevelt was that man. Indeed, so close was the contemporary identification of New Deal and FDR, and so close does it continue to be in the perspective of history, that it is difficult to think of the one without the other. Both FDR's most devoted supporters and his most vociferous critics, as well as the historians of whatever persuasion, are agreed that it was the President who symbolized the New Deal. But to acknowledge that FDR was the chief architect of the New Deal, its most convincing spokesman, its forceful leader and also its most tangible target, is not to imply that he was a charismatic personality. Undoubtedly, there were people who ascribed to him the qualities of charisma – infallibility, omniscience, omnipotence. And some of his most bitter opponents were equally intent on seeing in him the very incarnation of the charismatic opportunist. But neither orientation is correct. FDR was unduly loved by some and unduly hated by others, but to the vast majority of the American people he was Mr. President – the legally chosen head of a government whose function it was to represent and execute the power of the nation in time of crisis. This role FDR was superbly fitted and able to carry out.

While it is facile to interpret the New Deal in terms of the President's role and personality, one wonders what FDR would have been like as chief executive without the New Deal? Was it because FDR was not an ideologue, a reformer, or a prophet that the New Deal was not an ideology, a faith, or a crusade for reform? Or was it because the New Deal was none of these things that FDR came to play the role he did? A categorical answer is impossible. The President's personality and the character of the New Deal, if it is permissible to speak of character, were admirably blended to produce the kind of strong governmental leadership which the nation required in the moment of crisis. But this makes it all the more necessary not to exaggerate, yet also not to minimize, the role of the President in the total configuration of the New Deal. Because the tendency to exaggerate has probably been the dominant one, it seems desirable to point to some less frequently noticed features of the New Deal's personnel.

While Roosevelt never allowed the impression to prevail that he was not boss and master of the situation, his effectiveness as a leader did not derive from an unqualified loyalty that he may have been able to exact from his "subordinates." Rather, it derived from his ability to allow his lieutenants enough free-wheeling initiative to work out programs and policies – and it was one of his favorite images to see himself as the quarterback who was merely called upon to call the signals. The forceful leadership provided by the New Deal was not just Roosevelt's, but truly the product of teamwork. Leadership under the New Deal was both concentrated, in the White House, and decentralized, in the many departments and agencies of the federal government, most of them headed by able men who themselves were leaders, not henchmen or yes-men.

Moreover, the spirit of leadership under the New Deal was not only pervasive in the executive branch, but also in the legislative branch, and, after the mandate of 1936, in the judicial branch as well. There has been a tendency to neglect the part played by Congress in providing political leadership. There were the "Hundred Days," it is true, when the new Congress had little choice but to go along with the President's "must" programs. But the New Deal Congresses were not simply "rubber-stamp" legislatures. They included men of vision, wisdom, and sagacity, progressives who often succeeded in moving the White House in directions in which it would not have moved on its own initiatve. Similarly, once the Supreme Court — or rather two of its members, including the Chief Justice — had realized that it could not set itself up against the wishes of the great majority of the people and the popular President, it produced decisions which themselves were important ingredients of New Deal policies.

It is in this larger context of "collective leadership" shared by all the branches of the federal government that the President's role must be located. Economic policies and social programs came from many sources — braintrusters, interest groups, administrators, Congressmen, and Justices. It was Roosevelt's genius that he could pick men with ideas, and it was his glory that he encouraged ideas; it was his skill that he could articulate both popular needs and governmental responses; it was his confidence that he could transmit similar confidence to his associates; it was his power that he could humor, persuade, and, if necessary, threaten those who sat on the sidelines; it was his personality that he could make charm and courage instruments of government; above all, it was his spirit that he could convey his own idealism to the people as well as those who worked with him and for him.

But Roosevelt was not an ideologue — for he did not work with theoretical preconceptions, but with presuppositions. He was not a prophet — for his faith was terrestrial, not celestial. He was not a crusader — for he did not do many things he might have done by way of reform. He was not an agitator — for he was not driven by frustration, but committed to the proposition that common problems are best solved by common efforts. He was not a charismatic leader – for his own self-image as a politician forbade a charismatic image to be held by others. Roosevelt was a politician who saw that the business of government was politics, and who came to the business of government as a politician.

A MATURE POLITICS

If the New Deal was not an ideology, a faith, a crusade, an experiment, a revolt, or a charisma, what was it? In retrospect, what makes the New Deal so memorable, so significant an event in the history of the United States is that it is both a symbol and evidence of the nation's political maturity: its ability to solve its problems through politics rather than through ideology or violence. Politicians though they were, the Founding Fathers essentially distrusted politics. Whatever their real commitments, they believed in the cult of reason and natural law. In the Civil War, ideological intransigence – Lincoln, who came too late and passed away too early, excepted – underlined the poverty of politics, so largely responsible for both the violence and its unfortunate aftermath. By way of contrast, the New Deal was neither distrustful of politics nor poor in political strategies. If a commitment there was, it was a commitment to a mature politics.

A mature politics cannot afford to be either ideological or utopian. Ideologists and utopians are essentially apolitical. They are, in many respects, like children who are preoccupied almost exclusively with what they want when they want it, for whom their little selves are the center of the cosmos. Preoccupied with their own diagnoses and therapies, ideologists and utopians are, paradoxically, "thoughtless" in the literal sense of the word – blind to the needs of others and unconcerned with the consequences of their self-centered aspirations for others. Responsibility is a concept alien to both children and ideologues alike. Maturity, on the other hand, is the capacity to respond to others without making the demands of the self the sole criterion of perception or behavior. Real and necessary as the demands of the mature person are, maturity involves recognition of the legitimate interests of others. A mature politics involves adjustment, compromise, integration. It can never be a purely ideological politics which exaggerates the importance of the self at the expense of the other, or which may even mean the destruction of the other.

The New Deal was a politics of maturity in this sense, for it brought to the problems it faced political, not ideological, solutions. This is often not understood by its ideological critics or ideological defenders. The very debate which the New Deal aroused, and continues to arouse, is the best evidence. The New Deal is "incomprehensible" to the ideologues of the Right and Left because it was so unideological, because it was not a "scheme" but a "deal" so different from the political solitaire which the ideologue likes to play. The New Deal was a search for acceptable solutions to problems rather than an imposition of preconceived solutions on problems. The ideologues and theoreticians were necessary to the New Deal, vital in its growth and development, but they could not be its conductors. Some were disgusted, others despaired, unable to fathom the rationale of a program which was no program and had no rationale that fitted their ideological preconceptions. Those who stayed with the New Deal — men as different in their interest as Harold Ickes, the old progressive, or Jesse Jones, the financier, or Henry Wallace, the Republican farmer — served the New Deal for what it was: not a return to an ideological yesteryear, or a road to a utopian tomorrow, but a political enterprise which harnessed political forces in the spirit of political maturity.

It was not so much a characteristic of the New Deal's political maturity that many ideas and interests found expression in the hurly-burly of politics, but that politics took these ideas and interests seriously, that it encouraged their expression, that it took it for granted that these ideas and interests would clash, and that it was ready to give, but also to take away. The New Deal represented, on the level of national politics, a tough-mindedness that allowed for little ideological self-indulgence. Ideological thinking, however camouflaged, is tender-minded because it is self-indulgent. But in politics self-indulgence means bargaining from a position of weakness rather than strength. It represents an escape from a politics of maturity, not a recognition of the potentialities as well as limitations of political life. The New Deal was politically tough and mature, for it accepted the limits of the possible.

Too much emphasis has been placed on the role of the "brain trust" and the intellectuals who joined the New Deal. That they played an enormous and desirable role in orienting the public policies of the New Deal cannot be denied. But to assume that they operated with the single-mindedness of an idealized high command is to ignore the great diversity of backgrounds and opinions that they brought to bear on the common effort. Rarely did New Deal measures represent a clear-cut ideological preference. Programs were proposed, adjustments were made, compromises were negotiated, and the new syntheses only remotely resembled the original proposals. The New Deal was a governmental process which reflected the necessities and obstacles of a mature democratic politics.

Only when the shadow of war had become a spectre worse than depression, and when the New Deal had remedied much of what sickened American life, did politics give way to defense and apologia as well as to surrender of the political imagination. There appeared the bandwagon mentality — what Morris Cohen has called "the vile habit of thinking that the latest is always the best" — and the convenient belief that present trends will continue indefinitely into the future. It was then that the New Deal tended to become an affair of pronunciamento and magic formula. But this, in fact, meant the end of the New Deal. Yet it is against this later phase that the New Deal can be best assessed — as a flowering of sensitivity to the paradoxes, ambiguities, complications, compromises, and adventures of politics. To live with these characteristics, not only to tolerate them but to thrive on them, was the mark of that political maturity which distinguished the New Deal as a national event.

8

The Coming of World War II

Avoidable or Inevitable?

DURING THE GREAT DEPRESSION of the 1930's the American people and their leaders remained preoccupied for much of the period with a myriad of domestic concerns. Concentrating on solving the problems of unemployment, underproduction, agricultural distress, and an economy that seemed to be on the verge of collapse, most individuals gave relatively little thought to events on the international scene. With a few notable exceptions, the aim of Americans was to solve their internal problems; foreign relations were important only to the extent that they threatened to involve the nation in another world holocaust similar to the one that began in 1914 and ended tragically four years later. Indeed, the desire to remain isolated from developments on the international scene was so pervasive that between 1934 and 1937 the Congress enacted and the President signed a series of acts designed precisely to prevent a repetition of the events from 1914 to 1917 that eventually ended in America's participation in World War I.

The outbreak of World War II in Europe in 1939 proved to be an important turning point in the development of American foreign policy. Domestic concerns such as the great depression and mass unemployment receded into the background as the fear of war swept over the country. Unlike Wodrow Wilson, Roosevelt refused to ask his countrymen to remain neutral in thought as well as action. "This nation," he told the American people in a fireside chat in September, 1939, "will remain a neutral nation, but I cannot ask that every American remain neutral in thought as well." From the very beginning of hostilities, Roosevelt's hope was to offer as much military aid to the Allies as he could without going to war. Upon presidential urging, Congress repealed the arms embargo that was then in effect because the two year cash-and-carry clause of the neutrality act of 1937 had expired. The fall of France in the spring of 1940 intensified Roosevelt's desire to rebuild America's military forces and to give England all aid short of war. In 1941 the program of military aid to the Allied cause was expanded considerably by the Lend-Lease Act that was passed in March. By the summer of that year, the United States was involved in an undeclared naval war with Germany as American naval forces assumed the responsibility of protecting shipping in the western half of the North Atlantic. The most dramatic gesture of American sympathy for the British cause came in August of 1941, when Roosevelt and Churchill met off the coast of Newfoundland and agreed to a joint statement on mutual war aims. Known as the Atlantic Charter, the document not only spelled out the hopes of the two leaders for a better world, but referred specifically to "the final destruction of the Nazi tyranny" as a war aim.

The situation in Asia was equally explosive. Beginning in 1937 Japan renewed her attack upon the Nationalist regime of Chiang Kai Shek. The United States, having long been committed to the preservation of the territorial integrity and independence of China, found itself facing a diplomatic crisis. Nazi victories in Europe had the effect of stimulating Japanese ambitions even further; after the fall of France, Japan occupied northern Indo-China and signified its desire to establish a "co-prosperity sphere" throughout eastern Asia – a euphemism for Japanese hegemony.

Roosevelt responded slowly to these developments in Asia. First, the American government adopted various forms of economic pressure. After Japan occupied southern Indo-China in July of 1941, Roosevelt took the decisive step of imposing all-inclusive economic sanctions. At this point Japan faced the choice of curtailing its ambitions, particularly in China, or breaking the restrictions by resorting to armed conflict. During the remainder of the year, Japan and the United States remained on a collision course that finally culminated in the fateful attack on Pearl Harbor on December 7, 1941.

Throughout the course of World War II, few Americans expressed any doubts over the issue of war guilt or their own involvement. Faced by totalitarian regimes in Germany, Italy, and Japan — regimes committed to the goal of world domination — the United States, it was felt, had no choice but to defend itself and become the champion of the free world. Roosevelt tried his best to avoid war and the use of American troops overseas, but the march of events seemed to destroy his hopes. The Japanese attack on Pearl Harbor had settled the issue of going to war in a conclusive manner. From this point on, America had committed its industrial and military might against the forces of aggression. Such was the position taken by most contemporary scholars and writers who dealt with American diplomacy from 1937 to 1941.

The first criticisms concerning America's foreign policies in the years prior to 1941 came toward the end of World War II. Not until after the war was over, however, did the revisionists — as those critical of Roosevelt came to be known — spell out their case in great detail. The reaction against Roosevelt's policies after 1945 was not a totally unexpected or surprising development. After each of America's past wars, a debate had taken place over the question of whether the nation ought to have become involved in overt hostilities. More important in explaining the criticisms of Roosevelt's diplomacy, however, was the widespread disillusionment in the United States with the results of World War II. America had gone to war in 1941 to destroy the forces of totalitarianism and then found itself faced with an even greater menace — the Soviet Union. Germany was divided, half of Europe lay under Russian domination, and the United States and the Soviet Union entered upon a period of strained diplomatic relations in the postwar era called the "cold war." When Soviet scientists developed their own atomic bomb in 1949, America felt its physical security threatened for the first time since 1783. America's wartime allies, Britain and France, could no longer be considered first-rate powers, and the British Commonwealth was facing a severe crisis as a result of the rise of Asian and African nationalism. In the Far East the situation looked equally as black: the destruction of Japanese power left a vacuum that was quickly filled by the Chinese Communist regime; India, gaining its independence, was weak; and Korea was left divided. At home the coming of the cold war posed problems of internal security as some persons feared that the nation was being threatened by subversives and Communists. The result was a period of repression in the early 1950's that seriously hampered the civil rights that American citizens had traditionally enjoyed under the Constitution. All of these developments raised serious doubts over the wisdom of America's participation in World War II.

Many of the major critics of Roosevelt's foreign policies, interestingly enough, had taken an isolationist position as regards America's foreign policy in the 1930's and some even had been associated with the school of revisionist writers who opposed America's entry into World War I. Harry Elmer Barnes, the father of World War I revisionism, had consistently opposed the course of Roosevelt's diplomacy and addressed meetings of the America First Committee — an isolationist organization of the 1930's and early 1940's. Charles A. Beard had spoken out against any American entanglements in the 1930's and testified before the Senate Foreign Relations Committee in opposition to the idea of a lend-lease program. And Charles C. Tansill, who had published the leading study in the 1930's critical of Wilson's foreign policies between 1914 and 1917, also played a key role in attacking New Deal diplomacy.

One of the first scholarly attempts to discredit Roosevelt's diplomacy came in 1946 and 1948, when Charles A. Beard published *American Foreign Policy, 1932–1940,* and *President Roosevelt and the Coming of the War, 1941,* respectively. Beard's works, receiving a good deal of attention because of the eminent reputation of their author, were quickly followed by a series of other books. Although the positions they took varied markedly, all the revisionists were in basic agreement on certain fundamental points. Moreover, most of them had nothing but contempt for historians who refused to accept their anti-Roosevelt thesis. Harry Elmer Barnes, for example, characterized those who disagreed with him as "court historians," thereby implying that they had sacrificed their scholarly integrity to gain favor in government circles.

The revisionist hypothesis was based on a number of assumptions. First, the revisionists denied that the Axis powers had threatened America's vital interests. Germany had no plans to attack the Western Hemisphere, they claimed, and the Japanese were concerned only about Asia. Roosevelt's charge that the American people were being directly threatened from abroad, therefore, had little or no substance. Secondly, Roosevelt's foreign policy was one that he knew would inevitably lead to war in Europe and Asia. Indeed, some revisionists went so far as to suggest that Roosevelt deliberately maneuvered Japan into declaring war. Thirdly, Roosevelt deliberately misled the American people by telling them that he was working for peace while, in reality, he was laying the foundation for war. His famous speech in Boston during the presidential campaign of 1940 in which he promised that American boys would not fight on foreign soil was simply one example of his cupidity. Finally, the revisionists emphasized that the long-term results of America's involvement in World War II were largely negative — if not disastrous; the United States, by upsetting the European balance of power and creating a power vacuum, made possible the emergence of the Soviet Union — a nation that presented a far more serious threat to American security than did Nazi Germany.

Many, though not all, of the revisionists looked upon Roosevelt as a leader who deliberately misled and lied to the American people. In his critical study of New Deal diplomacy, Charles A. Beard made this point quite explicit. Roosevelt, Beard wrote, kept reassuring the American people that he was doing everything he could to avoid war and maintain a neutral position. Yet every action that he took belied his statements. He gave military aid and assistance to Britain, first through the destroyer-base exchange, then through the Lend-Lease program, and finally by ordering American naval vessels to escort convoys. All of these steps were undertaken consciously; they were not forced upon a reluctant or unwilling president by events beyond his control. Roosevelt, claimed Beard, acted on the assumption that he was wiser than the American people and consequently did not feel that he had to tell them the truth. The

American people, Beard concluded, were faced with the fact "that the President of the United States possesses limitless authority publicly to misrepresent and secretly to control foreign policy, foreign affairs, and the war power." [1] Beard's thesis was echoed by other revisionists. As William Henry Chamberlain put it in 1953: "One is left, therefore, with the inescapable conclusion that the promises to 'keep America out of foreign wars' were a deliberate hoax on the American people, perpetrated for the purpose of insuring Roosevelt's re-election and thereby enabling him to proceed with his plan of gradually edging the United States into war." [2]

Although the revisionists were critical of Roosevelt's European diplomacy, they usually reserved their heaviest ammunition for his Far Eastern policy. Indeed, most of the criticism of Roosevelt centered around his dealings with Japan in the period from 1937 to 1941. Reduced to its simplest form, the revisionist indictment boiled down to the fact that Roosevelt had deliberately provoked the Japanese into attacking Pearl Harbor. At that point the President was able to take the American people into a war that he secretly wanted, but had not desired to ask for publicly.

Such a thesis, of course, operated on the assumption that the Japanese leaders wanted peace — but that Roosevelt's maneuverings had forced them into an untenable position that could be resolved only by war. Although not all revisionists argued along precisely the same lines, their general arguments were remarkably similar. They maintained that Japan's desire for peace was sincere and that she wished to end her four-year old war in China. Facing a crucial shortage of oil and other resources, the Japanese hoped to end the conflict on the Asiatic mainland in order to assure themselves continued access to those materials that were indispensable to the economic well-being of the nation. To achieve these objectives, the Japanese leaders did everything within their power to arrive at a satisfactory *modus vivendi* with the United States.

President Roosevelt, according to the revisionists, was not interested in peace; he wanted war. Instead of dealing with Japan on the basis of justice and equity, he pursued a policy that he knew

1. Charles A. Beard, *President Roosevelt and the Coming of the War, 1941: A Study in Appearances and Realities* (New Haven, 1948), p. 598.
2. William Henry Chamberlain, "The Bankruptcy of a Policy," in *Perpetual War for Perpetual Peace*, ed. Harry Elmer Barnes (Caldwell, 1953), p. 491.

would ultimately provoke Japanese retaliation. During 1941 the United States increased its economic pressures upon Japan by curtailing the shipments of oil and other raw materials. At the same time, America refused to agree to any concessions to Japan regarding China. By mid-1941 all Japanese assets in the United States had been frozen and in August Roosevelt sent a strong warning to Japan to abandon her expansionist policies. All of these moves, the revisionists claimed, were deliberately designed to provoke Japan into some form of retaliation.

The final step, said the revisionist writers, was taken in late November, 1941, when Secretary of State Cordell Hull submitted a ten-point proposal to Japan. This document demanded that Japan pull out of China and Indo-China. To the revisionists the document represented an American "ultimatum" and not one that could serve as the basis for diplomatic discussions. The perfidy of American leaders became even clearer in the days preceding the attack on Pearl Harbor. Some time earlier, the United States had broken Japan's secret code. Roosevelt and his advisers, therefore, knew that Japan really desired peace, but that she was ready to take military action if the American government persisted in its unyielding course. High American officials, including the President, even knew that a Japanese attack on the military and naval installations at Pearl Harbor was imminent. According to the revisionists, the desire of the Roosevelt Administration for war was so strong that government officials did not inform the military commanders in Hawaii of the possibility of an attack. In the end, then, Roosevelt's harsh policies provoked the Japanese into an attack on the unprepared military at Pearl Harbor, and gave him the declaration of war that he had so ardently desired. To achieve his goal, some revisionists maintained, Roosevelt knowingly sacrificed American lives as well as a large part of the American fleet at Pearl Harbor. As Harry Elmer Barnes wrote in *Perpetual War for Perpetual Peace* — a volume in which a number of leading revisionists spelled out their case — "The net result of revisionist scholarship applied to Pearl Harbor boils down essentially to this: In order to promote Roosevelt's political ambitions and his mendacious foreign policy some three thousand American boys were quite needlessly butchered. Of course, they were only a drop in the bucket compared to those who were ultimately slain in the war that resulted, which was as needless, in terms of vital American interests, as the surprise attack on Pearl Harbor."[3]

For the most part, American historians have rejected this revisionist hypothesis. They have done so largely on the grounds that it rests upon a simplistic conspiracy theory of history. Human beings, they claim, are complex creatures who are affected by complex motives. To argue that Franklin Delano Roosevelt knew the precise results of his policies would be to credit him with an omniscience that no human could possibly possess. As a leading nonrevisionist historian pointed out, it is one thing to charge that the Roosevelt Administration misunderstood Japan's intentions and underestimated her military strength; it is quite another matter to conclude that the tragic disaster of December 7, 1941, was a matter of calculated diplomatic planning by a scheming American president.[4]

The revisionist argument – at least in a modified version – nevertheless offers a historical thesis that cannot be easily dismissed. In the first selection in this chapter, Paul W. Schroeder discusses America's policy toward Japan in the crucial months preceding Pearl Harbor. Schroeder raises a number of issues which cast some doubt upon the wisdom of America's diplomatic moves. The major point at stake was whether the United States had been well-advised in taking a "hard" line toward Japan. This issue raised two interesting questions: should the United States have made the liberation of China a central aim of its policy, thereby requiring the immediate evacuation of Japanese troops; and should Roosevelt have declined the invitation of the Japanese premier to a personal meeting between the two leaders to discuss their differences? To Schroeder the answer to both these questions is an emphatic "no." Until mid-1941 American planners had consistently sought two reasonable and rather limited objectives; that of splitting the three Axis powers and stopping Japan's advance in Asia. With these goals within its reach, the United States then added a third; the liberation of China. The last objective, however, was not a limited one, nor could it be attained short of war. Because of its misguided sympathy toward China, the American government drove Japan back

3. *Ibid.*, p. 651.
4. Robert H. Ferrell, "Pearl Harbor and the Revisionists," *The Historian,* XVII (Spring, 1955), 233.

into the arms of the Axis powers and made inevitable an armed confrontation between the two nations. American policy makers, Schroeder concluded, were not evil men determined to bring about war; they were instead men who were blinded by a sense of their own moral righteousness and had abandoned that pragmatism required of all human beings if differences between nations are not always to end in war.

Schroeder's thesis, in many respects, had already been anticipated by other writers on this subject. George F. Kennan, the former ambassador to Russia, State Department official, and historian, for example, had argued in 1951 that the United States erred grievously in the twentieth century when it committed itself to the Open Door and the preservation of the territorial and administrative integrity of China. Although a nation-state, Kennan wrote, China had many attributes which failed to coincide with the European national state that had evolved in the eighteenth and nineteenth centuries. Consequently, the Open Door policy was difficult to implement because it rested on the fallacious assumption that China was no different from other states. More important, Kennan insisted, the United States continuously "hacked away, year after year, decade after decade, at the positions of the other powers on the mainland of Asia, and above all the Japanese, in the unshakeable belief that, if our principles were commendable, their consequences could not be other than happy and acceptable. But rarely could we be lured into a discussion of the real quantities involved: of such problems as Japan's expanding population, or the weaknesses of government in China, or the ways in which the ambitions of other powers could be practicably countered. Remember that this struck a particularly sensitive nerve in the case of countries whose interests on the Asiatic mainland were far more important to them than our interests there were to us. . . . There was always a feeling, both among the Japanese and among the British, that we were inclined to be spendthrift with their diplomatic assets in China for the very reason that our own stake in China meant so much less to us than theirs did to them." [5] The result, he concluded, was that the United States never exploited the possibility of arriving at a mutually satisfactory compromise with

5. George F. Kennan, *American Diplomacy 1900–1950* (Chicago, 1951), p. 48.

Japan. Like Schroeder, however, Kennan vehemently denied that the failure to reach a meaningful compromise was a deliberate choice of evil and scheming leaders.

The majority of writers dealing with America's diplomacy in the years prior to Pearl Harbor, however, took an exactly opposite point of view from the revisionists. The internationalist or interventionist school — to differentiate it from the revisionist school — based its arguments upon an entirely different set of assumptions. Writers of the internationalist school began with the proposition that the Axis powers had, in fact, posed a very serious threat to America's security and national interests. By the summer of 1940, the Nazis had conquered most of Western and Central Europe and Britain seemed to be on the verge of surrender. When Hitler invaded the Soviet Union in June, 1941, a German victory appeared to be a certainty. The danger, according to the internationalist school, was that America might have to face the victorious Axis powers alone. German and Italian campaigns in North Africa created a fear that control of that continent might provide a springboard for an attack upon the Western hemisphere. Axis successes in Europe, meanwhile, had stimulated the Japanese to increase their aggressive moves in Asia on the theory that the Allies were too preoccupied in the West to divert any forces to the Far East.

Roosevelt, according to the internationalist school, believed that Germany represented the greatest threat to America's security. It was in the national interest, therefore, to follow a policy designed to bring about a German defeat. Thus, Roosevelt embarked upon a program of extending to England all aid short of war in the belief that such a policy might prevent a Nazi victory and contribute to the eventual downfall of Germany. Although renouncing impartial neutrality, Roosevelt hoped that aid to England would permit his nation to protect its security without committing American troops to a foreign conflict. The undeclared naval war in the North Atlantic against Germany represented the limit of America's involvement.

Roosevelt's primary interest lay in Europe, the internationalist interpretation continued, and his Far Eastern policy was designed to avert any showdown with Japan. The steps that he took in 1940 and 1941 were intended to check Japan by all means short of war. The embargo on oil and other resources, the freezing of Japanese assets in the United States, the aid to China, and the massing of the American fleet in the Pacific were aimed at deterring, not provoking, the Japanese. America's objective was to seek a peaceful settlement with Japan, but a settlement that would uphold American security and principles, protect China, and honor the British, French, and Dutch interests in the Far East. Japan's expansionist ambitions, however, proved to be too great and Roosevelt came to realize that an armed conflict between the two nations was inevitable. According to the international writers, his policy at this point became one of stalling for time in order to permit an American military build-up.

Although the internationalist school of historians by no means approved of all of Roosevelt's diplomatic policies, they believed that the fundamental causes for America's involvement in the war lay outside the United States and in the trend of world events over which this country had little, if any, control. Most of them were convinced that Roosevelt had sought the goal of peace with great sincerity. In fact, many argued that his desire for peace led him to overestimate the opposition to his internationalist policies, which he could have pursued even more vigorously than he did.

Almost all of the historians in the internationalist school violently rejected the revisionist point of view – particularly the insinuation that Roosevelt had plotted to provoke the Japanese assault on Pearl Harbor. While many admitted that there might have been some blundering in both Washington and Hawaii, there was general agreement that the sneak attack came as a genuine surprise. In Washington neither civilian nor military authorities had interpreted the decoded Japanese messages correctly; virtually everyone assumed that the Japanese were moving to attack British and Dutch installations in the Southwest Pacific. Although it was true that the army and navy commanders in Hawaii were not given all of the information gained from breaking the Japanese code, most internationalist historians believed that the military officials on the spot would have interpreted the messages in the same light as their superiors in Washington. Even if they had been able to divine Japanese intentions correctly, there is some doubt as to whether a military disaster could have been avoided; the American fleet was extremely vulnerable to air attack and there were insufficient land-based planes to ward off a Japanese raid. In retrospect, then, the internationalist historians looked upon Pearl Harbor as a tragic disaster that grew out of faulty military and diplomatic planning rather than part of a presidential conspiracy.

The second and third selections are by two writers who represent the internationalist school of scholars. The first is by Dexter Perkins, one of the deans of American diplomatic historians, and constitutes a vigorous attack upon the revisionist school. To Perkins historical revisionism at the close of a military conflict seems to be a common occurrence among Americans. In part, this response stems from the letdown or disillusionment that results from a failure to secure all of the goals for which the war was fought; it is related also to the inevitable reaction against the strong executive leadership that characterizes most wartime administrations. Whatever the reasons for its rise, Perkins defines such revisionism as "history by hypothesis"; it suggests that the world would have been a better place had the United States remained aloof from any involvement in World War II. Perkins goes on to argue that a victorious Germany would have been a very serious menace to America. Nor did Roosevelt deceive the American people, according to Perkins. The President was basically in accord with public opinion for even the Republican party nominated Wendell Willkie in 1940 and took an internationalist position on foreign affairs. Although Roosevelt may have been devious in his public statements from time to time, he accurately reflected the mood and thinking of his fellow countrymen. In the final analysis, Perkins ends up with a favorable, though by no means uncritical, appraisal of Roosevelt's foreign policy prior to the war.

The third selection by Herbert Feis argues strongly against the revisionist thesis that Roosevelt deliberately exposed the American fleet at Pearl Harbor in order to provoke a Japanese attack. To Feis Japan was bent on dominating Asia, thus threatening America's interests in that part of the world. Had the United States not placed an embargo on trade with Japan, it would have been in the strange position of having undertaken preparations for war while at the same time strengthening the opponent it might meet in battle. Feis denies that there is conclusive evidence that Prince Konoye's offer to meet with Roosevelt in the autumn of 1941 might have averted a conflict. He rejects also the thesis that Secretary of State Cordell Hull's note of November 26, 1941, was in any sense an ultimatum. The basic cause of war, Feis concludes, was Japan's insistence on becoming the dominant power in the Far East. Short of a complete surrender on America's part in the most important aspects of its foreign policy in the Far East, the chances of avoiding war by means of diplomatic negotiations had always been very remote.

It should be emphasized that there are many points of disagreement among individual historians of the internationalist school even though all of them rejected the revisionist hypothesis. The differences between internationalist historians frequently reflected the same divisions that existed among Roosevelt's advisers prior to December 7, 1941. For example, Secretary of State Cordell Hull was generally cautious in his approach; he favored limiting overt action to steps short of war. Secretary of War Henry L. Stimson, on the other hand, believed that the policy of all aid short of war would not result in the defeat of the Axis powers, and that America would have to intervene sooner or later. Indeed, Stimson believed that American people would have supported Roosevelt in a declaration of war even before Pearl Harbor. Similarly, some internationalist historians, including Herbert Feis and Basil Rauch, were sympathetic to Hull and Roosevelt, while others, notably William L. Langer and S. Everett Gleason, argued that Roosevelt overestimated isolationist opposition to his policies and that the President actually lagged behind public opinion on the desirability of taking strong measures against the Axis powers.[6]

To evaluate in a fair and objective manner the events leading up to the Pearl Harbor disaster is not a simple task for scholars. The complexity of this historical problem arises from many reasons: the tangled web of interrelated events in the period before December, 1941, which makes it difficult, if not impossible, to separate causes and to point to any particular one as "definitive"; the fact that some of the goals for which America went to war were not achieved by the end of the conflict; and the problem of ascertaining the precise motives of the national leaders of the period. Historical judgment, furthermore, rests to a large degree upon the starting

6. Herbert Feis, *The Road to Pearl Harbor: The Coming of War Between the United States and Japan* (Princeton, 1950); Basil Rauch, *Roosevelt: From Munich to Pearl Harbor* (New York, 1950); William L. Langer and S. Everett Gleason, *The Challenge to Isolation, 1937–1940* (New York, 1952) and *The Undeclared War, 1940–1941* (New York, 1953).

assumptions held by various scholars; different historians approach the problem with a different set of starting assumptions and hence reach conflicting conclusions.

In contrasting the revisionist with the international school of historians, several differences are clearly discernible. First, both deal in a very different way with the issue of whether or not the Axis powers represented an immediate threat to American security. The revisionists maintained that there is no evidence showing that Hitler hoped to move into the Western hemisphere. Even if he had, the revisionists held the best policy would have been for America to have waited until Germany and Russia had destroyed one another; such a policy would have avoided the power vacuum that developed in Europe in the postwar period that enabled the Soviet Union to expand without checks. In the Far East, America also made a mistake by pushing Japan into war by an inflexible policy and a refusal to offer any reasonable compromises. The internationalists, on the other hand, believed that a victorious Germany posed a serious threat to American security, especially if one considers the military prowess and scientific potential of the Third Reich. Given Hitler's past behavior, there was no reason to assume that his ambitions would have been satisfied after conquering England and the Soviet Union. Insofar as the Far East was concerned, the internationalists took the view that Japan's unwillingness to abandon its imperialist policy was the prime cause of the war.

A second question both schools dealt with is the motivation behind Roosevelt's foreign policy. Did Roosevelt deceive the American people by telling them that his policy would lead to peace when in reality he wanted war? To this question the revisionists answered in the affirmative and the internationalists in the negative. Both schools had a serious problem on this score, however, because the issue revolves about the motivation and intentions of one man. How can the historian gauge the motives of any individual, particularly when so few human beings ever record their innermost convictions or are completely honest with themselves?

In many respects the most important difference separating the two schools was their judgment concerning the results of the war. To the revisionists the outcome of the war was dramatic evidence of the blundering and evil policy followed by Roosevelt and his advisers. The United States, after all, had gone to war to destroy the menace of totalitarianism. Instead, it was confronted after 1945 with the Soviet Union, a far greater menace than Nazi Germany. On the continent Russia controlled all of Eastern and a good part of Central Europe; in the Far East the destruction of Japanese power created a situation that ultimately led to a Communist take-over in China. The internationalist school, by way of comparison, readily admitted that the results of the war were anything but desirable, but its adherents also argued that these results did not necessarily make Hitler the lesser of two evils. Moreover, history suggests a tragic view of human destiny; for each problem solved more arise in its place. To expect a final solution to all problems is to be unrealistic. While Roosevelt may have miscalculated in some of his policies, he did not do so knowingly or deliberately; his mistakes were due to the limitations that characterize all human beings.

In general, then, the differing interpretations of America's entry into World War II reflect the personal faith of the historians in the particular policy they are advocating. The internationalist school believed that the United States, as a world power, could not neglect its responsibilities nor ignore events in other parts of the world. The world is far too small a place for the provincial isolationism that characterized American diplomacy in the early years of the Republic. Consequently, they believed that Roosevelt was on the right track even though some of his specific moves may not have been correct ones. The revisionists, on the other hand, argued that America's national interest could have been best served by remaining aloof from conflicts that did not immediately threaten the United States. Roosevelt, therefore, made a grievous error when he committed his nation — against the will of its people — to a world conflict. The American people, the revisionists concluded, are still paying the price of that mistake.

Which of these two schools of thought is correct? Were the revisionists justified in their claim that the United States should have stayed out of World War II? Were they right in attributing evil and invidious motives to Roosevelt and his advisers? Or were the internationalist historians right in arguing that World War II involved vital American interests and that Roosevelt was simply trying to safeguard these interests even though it meant that the nation might eventually enter the war? These are the basic issues confronting the student who is attempting to understand the background and events that led up to Pearl Harbor.

Paul W. Schroeder

IN JUDGING American policy toward Japan in 1941, it might be well to separate what is still controversial from what is not. There is no longer any real doubt that the war came about over China. Even an administration stalwart like Henry L. Stimson and a sympathetic critic like Herbert Feis concur in this. Nor is it necessary to speculate any longer as to what could have induced Japan to launch such an incredible attack upon the United States and Great Britain as occurred at Pearl Harbor and in the south Pacific. One need not, as Winston Churchill did in wartime, characterize it as "an irrational act" incompatible "with prudence or even with sanity." The Japanese were realistic about their position throughout; they did not suddenly go insane. The attack was an act of desperation, not madness. Japan fought only when she had her back to the wall as a result of America's diplomatic and economic offensive.

The main point still at issue is whether the United States was wise in maintaining a "hard" program of diplomatic and economic pressure on Japan from July 1941 on. Along with this issue go two subsidiary questions: the first, whether it was wise to make the liberation of China the central aim of American policy and the immediate evacuation of Japanese troops a requirement for agreement; the second, whether it was wise to decline Premier Konoye's invitation to a meeting of leaders in the Pacific. On all these points, the policy which the United States carried out still has distinguished defenders. The paramount issue between Japan and the United States, they contend, always was the China problem. In her China policy, Japan showed that she was determined to secure domination

From *The Axis Alliance and Japanese-American Relations, 1941*, pp. 200–216.

PAUL W. SCHROEDER (1927–) is Professor of History at the University of Illinois. He is the author of several books on diplomatic history; the book from which the present selection is taken was the recipient of the Beveridge prize of the American Historical Association.

over a large area of East Asia by force. Apart from the legitimate American commercial interests which would be ruined or excluded by this Japanese action, the United States, for reasons of her own security and of world peace, had sufficient stake in Far Eastern questions to oppose such aggression. Finally, after ten years of Japanese expansion, it was only sensible and prudent for the United States to demand that it come to an end and that Japan retreat. In order to meet the Japanese threat, the United States had a perfect right to use the economic power she possessed in order to compel the Japanese to evacuate their conquered territory. If Japan chose to make this a cause for war, the United States could not be held responsible.

A similar defense is offered on the decision to turn down Konoye's Leaders' Conference. Historians may concede, as do Langer and Gleason, that Konoye was probably sincere in wanting peace and that he "envisaged making additional concessions to Washington, including concessions on the crucial issue of the withdrawal of Japanese troops from China." But, they point out, Konoye could never have carried the Army with him on any such concession. If the United States was right in requiring Japan to abandon the Co-Prosperity Sphere, then her leaders were equally right in declining to meet with a Japanese Premier who, however conciliatory he might have been personally, was bound by his own promises and the exigencies of Japanese politics to maintain this national aim. In addition, there was the serious possibility that much could be lost from such a meeting – the confidence of China, the cohesiveness of the coalition with Great Britain and Russia. In short, there was not enough prospect of gain to merit taking the chance.

This is a point of view which must be taken seriously. Any judgment on the wisdom or folly of the American policy, in fact, must be made with caution – there are no grounds for dogmatic certainty. The opinion here to be developed, nonetheless, is that the American policy from the end of July to December was a grave mistake. It should not be necessary to add that this does not make it treason. There is a "back door to war" theory, espoused in various forms by Charles A. Beard, George Morgenstern, Charles C. Tansill, and, most recently, Rear Admiral Robert A. Theobald, which holds that the President chose the Far East as a rear entrance to the war in Europe and to that end deliberately goaded the Japanese into an attack. This theory is quite different and quite incredible. It is as impossible to accept as the idea that Japan attacked the United States in a spirit of overconfidence or that Hitler pushed the Japanese into war. Roosevelt's fault, if any, was not that of deliberately provoking the Japanese to attack, but of allowing Hull and others to talk him out of impulses and ideas which, had he pursued them, might have averted the conflict. Moreover, the mistake (assuming that it was a mistake) of a too hard and rigid policy with Japan was, as has been pointed out, a mistake shared by the whole nation, with causes that were deeply organic. Behind it was not sinister design or warlike intent, but a sincere and uncompromising adherence to moral principles and liberal doctrines.

This is going ahead too fast, however; one needs first of all to define the mistake with which American policy is charged. Briefly, it was this. In the attempt to gain everything at once, the United States lost her opportunity to secure immediately her essential requirements in the Far East and to continue to work toward her long-range goals. She succeeded instead only in making inevitable an unnecessary and avoidable war — an outcome which constitutes the ultimate failure of diplomacy. Until July 1941, as already demonstrated, the United States consistently sought to attain two limited objectives in the Far East, those of splitting the Axis and of stopping Japan's advance southward. Both aims were in accordance with America's broad strategic interests; both were reasonable, attainable goals. Through a combination of favorable circumstance and forceful American action, the United States reached the position where the achievement of these two goals was within sight. At this very moment, on the verge of a major diplomatic victory, the United States abandoned her original goals and concentrated on a third, the liberation of China. This last aim was not in accord with American strategic interests, was not a limited objective, and, most important, was completely incapable of being achieved by peaceful means and doubtful of attainment even by war. Through her single-minded pursuit of this unattainable goal, the United States forfeited the diplomatic victory which she had already virtually won. The unrelenting application of extreme economic pressure on Japan, instead of compelling the evacuation of China, rendered war inevitable, drove Japan back into the arms of

Germany for better or for worse, and precipitated the wholesale plunge by Japan into the South Seas. As it ultimately turned out, the United States succeeded in liberating China only at great cost and when it was too late to do the cause of the Nationalist Chinese much real good.

This is not, of course, a new viewpoint. It is in the main simply that of Ambassador Grew, who has held and defended it since 1941. The arguments he advances seem cogent and sensible in the light of present knowledge. Briefly summarized, they are the following: First is his insistence on the necessity of distinguishing between long-range and immediate goals in foreign policy and on the folly of demanding the immediate realization of both. Second is his contention that governments are brought to abandon aggressive policies not by sudden conversion through moral lectures, but by the gradual recognition that the policy of aggression will not succeed. According to Grew, enough awareness of failure existed in the government of Japan in late 1941 to enable it to make a beginning in the process of reversal of policy — but not nearly enough to force Japan to a wholesale surrender of her conquests and aims. Third was his conviction that what was needed on both sides was time — time in which the United States could grow stronger and in which the tide of war in Europe could be turned definitely against Germany, time in which the sense of failure could grow in Japan and in which moderates could gain better control of the situation. A victory in Europe, Grew observed, would either automatically solve the problem of Japan or make that problem, if necessary, much easier to solve by force. Fourth was his belief that Japan would fight if backed to the wall (a view vindicated by events) and that a war at this time with Japan could not possibly serve the interests of the United States. Even if one considered war as the only final answer to Japanese militarism, still, Grew would answer, the United States stood to gain nothing by seeking a decision in 1941. The time factor was entirely in America's favor. Japan could not hope to gain as much from a limited relaxation of the embargo as the United States could from time gained for mobilization; Roosevelt and the military strategists were in fact anxious to gain time by a *modus vivendi.*

There is one real weakness in Grew's argument upon which his critics have always seized. This is his contention that Konoye, faced after July 26 with the two clear alternatives of war or a genuine peace move, which would of necessity include a settlement with China, had chosen the latter course and could have carried through a policy of peace had he been given the time. "We believed," he writes, "that Prince Konoye was in a position to carry the country with him in a program of peace" and to make commitments to the United States which would "eventually, if not immediately" meet the conditions of Hull's Four Points. The answer of critics is that, even if one credits Konoye's sincerity and takes his assurances at face value, there is still no reason to believe that he could have carried even his own cabinet, much less the whole nation, with him on any program approximating that of Hull. In particular, as events show, he could not have persuaded the Army to evacuate China.

The objection is well taken; Grew was undoubtedly over-optimistic about Konoye's capacity to carry through a peaceful policy. This one objection, however, does not ruin Grew's case. He countered it later with the argument that a settlement with Japan which allowed Japanese garrisons to remain in China on a temporary basis would not have been a bad idea. Although far from an ideal solution, it would have been better, for China as well, than the policy the United States actually followed. It would have brought China what was all-important – a cessation of fighting – without involving the United States, as many contended, in either a sacrifice of principle or a betrayal of China. The United States, Grew points out, had never committed herself to guaranteeing China's integrity. Further, it would not have been necessary to agree to anything other than temporary garrisons in North China which, in more favorable times, the United States could work to have removed. The great mistake was to allow American policy to be guided by a sentimental attitude toward China which in the long run could do neither the United States nor China any good. As Grew puts it:

> Japan's advance to the south, including her occupation of portions of China, constituted for us a real danger, and it was definitely in our national interest that it be stopped, by peaceful means if possible, by force of arms if necessary. American aid to China should have been regarded, as we believe it was regarded by our Government, as an indirect means to this end, and not from a sentimental viewpoint. The President's

> letter of January 21, 1941, shows that he then sensed the important issues in the Far East, and that he did not include China, purely for China's sake, among them. . . . The failure of the Washington Administration to seize the opportunity presented in August and September, 1941, to halt the southward advance by peaceful means, together with the paramount importance attached to the China question during the conversations in Washington, gives rise to the belief that not our Government but millions of quite understandably sympathetic but almost totally uninformed American citizens had assumed control of our Far Eastern policy.

There remains the obvious objection that Grew's solution, however plausible it may now seem, was politically impracticable in 1941. No American government could then have treated China as expendable, just as no Japanese government could have written off the China Affair as a dead loss. This is in good measure true and goes a long way to explain, if not to justify, the hard American policy. Yet it is not entirely certain that no solution could have been found which would both have averted war and have been accepted by the American people, had a determined effort been made to find one. As F. C. Jones points out, the United States and Japan were not faced in July 1941 with an absolute dilemma of peace or war, of complete settlement or open conflict. Hull believed that they were, of course; but his all-or-nothing attitude constituted one of his major shortcomings as a diplomat. Between the two extremes existed the possibility of a *modus vivendi,* an agreement settling some issues and leaving others in abeyance. Had Roosevelt and Konoye met, Jones argues, they might have been able to agree on a relaxation of the embargo in exchange for satisfactory assurances on the Tripartite Pact and southward expansion, with the China issue laid aside. The United States would not have had to cease aid, nor Japan to remove her troops. The final settlement of the Far Eastern question, Jones concludes,

> would then have depended upon the issues of the struggle in Europe. If Germany prevailed, then the United States would be in no position to oppose Japanese ambitions in Asia; if Germany were defeated, Japan would be in no position to persist in those ambitions in the face of the United States, the USSR, and the British Commonwealth.

Such an agreement, limited and temporary in nature, would have involved no sacrifice of principle for either nation, yet would have removed the immediate danger of war. As a temporary expedient and as an alternative to otherwise inevitable and useless conflict, it could have been sold by determined effort to the public on both sides. Nor would it have been impossible, in the writer's opinion, to have accompanied or followed such an agreement with a simple truce or standstill in the China conflict through American mediation.

This appraisal, to be sure, is one based on realism. Grew's criticism of Hull's policy and the alternative he offers to it are both characterized by fundamental attention to what is practical and expedient at a given time and to limited objectives within the scope of the national interest. In general, the writer agrees with this point of view, believing that, as William A. Orton points out, it is foolish and disastrous to treat nations as morally responsible persons, "because their nature falls far short of personality," and that, as George F. Kennan contends, the right role for moral considerations in foreign affairs is not to determine policy, but rather to soften and ameliorate actions necessarily based on the realities of world politics.

From this realistic standpoint, the policy of the State Department would seem to be open to other criticisms besides those of Grew. The criticisms, which may be briefly mentioned here, are those of inconsistency, blindness to reality, and futility. A notable example of the first would be the inconsistency of a strong no-compromise stand against Japan with the policy of broad accommodation to America's allies, especially Russia, both before and after the American entrance into the war. The inconsistency may perhaps best be seen by comparing the American stand in 1941 on such questions as free trade, the Open Door in China, the territorial and administrative integrity of China, the maintenance of the prewar *status quo* in the Far East, and the sanctity of international agreements with the position taken on the same questions at the Yalta Conference in 1945.

The blindness to reality may be seen in the apparent inability of American policy makers to take seriously into account the gravity of Japan's economic plight or the real exigencies of her military and strategic position, particularly as these factors would affect the

United States over the long run. Equally unrealistic and more fateful was the lack of appreciation on the part of many influential people and of wide sections of the public of the almost certain consequences to be expected from the pressure exerted on Japan — namely, American involvement in a war her military strategists considered highly undesirable. The attitude has been well termed by Robert Osgood, "this blind indifference toward the military and political consequences of a morally-inspired position."

The charge of futility, finally, could be laid to the practice of insisting on a literal subscription to principles which, however noble, had no chance of general acceptance or practical application. The best example is the persistent demand that the Japanese pledge themselves to carrying out nineteenth-century principles of free trade and equal access to raw materials in a twentieth-century world where economic nationalism and autarchy, trade barriers and restrictions were everywhere the order of the day, and not the least in the United States under the New Deal. Not one of America's major allies would have subscribed wholeheartedly to Hull's free-trade formula; what good it could have done to pin the Japanese down to it is hard to determine.

But these are all criticisms based on a realistic point of view, and to judge the American policy solely from this point of view is to judge it unfairly and by a standard inappropriate to it. The policy of the United States was avowedly not one of realism, but of principle. If then it is to be understood on its own grounds and judged by its own standards, the main question will be whether the policy was morally right — that is, in accord with principles of peace and international justice. Here, according to its defenders, the American policy stands vindicated. For any other policy, any settlement with Japan at the expense of China, would have meant a betrayal not only of China, but also of vital principles and of America's moral task in the world.

This, as we know, was the position of Hull and his co-workers. It has been stated more recently by Basil Rauch, who writes:

> No one but an absolute pacifist would argue that the danger of war is a greater evil than violation of principle. . . . The isolationist believes that appeasement of Japan without China's consent violated no principle worth a risk of war. The

internationalist must believe that the principle did justify a risk of war.

This is not an argument to be dismissed lightly. The contention that the United States had a duty to fulfill in 1941, and that this duty consisted in holding to justice and morality in a world given to international lawlessness and barbarism and in standing on principle against an unprincipled and ruthless aggressor, commands respect. It is not answered by dismissing it as unrealistic or by proscribing all moral considerations in foreign policy. An answer may be found, however, in a closer definition of America's moral duty in 1941. According to Hull, and apparently also Rauch, the task was primarily one of upholding principle. This is not the only possible definition. It may well be contended that the moral duty was rather one of doing the most practical good possible in a chaotic world situation and, further, that this was the main task President Roosevelt and the administration had in mind at least till the end of July 1941.

If the moral task of the United States in the Far East was to uphold a principle of absolute moral value, the principle of non-appeasement of aggressors, then the American policy was entirely successful in fulfilling it. The American diplomats proved that the United States was capable of holding to its position in disregard and even in defiance of national interests narrowly conceived. If, however, the task was one of doing concrete good and giving practical help where needed, especially to China, then the American policy falls fatally short. For it can easily be seen not only that the policy followed did not in practice help China, but also that it could not have been expected to. Although it was a pro-China and even a China-first policy in principle, it was not in practical fact designed to give China the kind of help needed.

What China required above all by late 1941 was clearly an end to the fighting, a chance to recoup her strength. Her chaotic financial condition, a disastrous inflation, civil strife with the Communists, severe hunger and privation, and falling morale all enfeebled and endangered her further resistance. Chiang Kai-shek, who knew this, could hope only for an end to the war through the massive intervention of American forces and the consequent liberation of China. It was in this hope that he pleaded so strongly for a hard American policy toward Japan. Chiang's hopes, however, were wholly unrealistic. For though the United States was willing to risk war for China's sake, and finally did incur it over the China issue, the Washington government never intended in case of war to throw America's full weight against Japan in order to liberate China. The American strategy always was to concentrate on Europe first, fighting a defensive naval war in the Far East and aiding China, as before, in order to keep the Japanese bogged down. The possibility was faced and accepted that the Chinese might have to go on fighting for some years before eventual liberation through the defeat of Japan. The vehement Chinese protests over this policy were unavailing, and the bitter disillusionment suffered by the Chinese only helped to bring on in 1942 the virtual collapse of the Chinese war effort during the latter years of the war.

As a realistic appraisal of America's military capabilities and of her world-wide strategic interests, the Europe-first policy has a great deal to recommend it. But the combination of this realistic strategy with a moralistic diplomacy led to the noteworthy paradox of a war incurred for the sake of China, which could not then be fought for the sake of China and whose practical value for China at the time was, to say the least, dubious. The plain fact is that the United States in 1941 was not capable of forcing Japan out of China by means short of war and was neither willing nor, under existing circumstances, able to throw the Japanese out by war. The American government could conceivably have told the Chinese this and tried to work out the best possible program of help for China under these limitations. Instead, it yielded to Chinese importunities and followed a policy almost sure to eventuate in war, knowing that if the Japanese did attack, China and her deliverance would have to take a back seat. It is difficult to conceive of such a policy as a program of practical aid to China.

The main, though not the only, reason why this policy was followed is clearly the overwhelming importance of principle in American diplomacy, particularly the principle of nonappeasement of aggressors. Once most leaders in the administration and wide sections of the public became convinced that it was America's prime moral duty to stand hard and fast against aggressors, whatever the consequences, and once this conviction became decisive in the formulation of policy, the end result was almost inevitable: a policy designed to uphold principle and to punish the aggressor, but not to save the victim.

It is this conviction as to America's moral duty, however sincere and understandable, which the writer believes constitutes a fundamental misreading of America's moral task. The policy it gave rise to was bad not simply because it was moralistic but because it was obsessed with the wrong kind of morality — with that abstract "Let justice be done though the heavens fall" kind which so often, when relentlessly pursued, does more harm than good. It would be interesting to investigate the role which this conception of America's moral task played in the formulation of the American war aims in the Far East, with their twin goals of unconditional surrender and the destruction of Japan as a major power, especially after the desire to vindicate American principles and to punish the aggressor was intensified a hundredfold by the attack on Pearl Harbor. To pursue the later implications of this kind of morality in foreign policy, with its attendant legalistic and vindictive overtones, would, however, be a task for another volume.

In contrast, the different kind of policy which Grew advocated and toward which Roosevelt so long inclined need not really be considered immoral or unprincipled, however much it undoubtedly would have been denounced as such. A limited *modus vivendi* agreement would not have required the United States in any way to sanction Japanese aggression or to abandon her stand on Chinese integrity and independence. It would have constituted only a recognition that the American government was not then in a position to enforce its principles, reserving for America full freedom of action at some later, more favorable time. Nor would it have meant the abandonment and betrayal of China. Rather it would have involved the frank recognition that the kind of help the Chinese wanted was impossible for the United States to give at that time. It would in no way have precluded giving China the best kind of help then possible — in the author's opinion, the offer of American mediation for a truce in the war and the grant of fuller economic aid to try to help the Chinese recover — and promising China greater assistance once the crucial European situation was settled. Only that kind of morality which sees every sort of dealing with an aggressor, every instance of accommodation or conciliation, as appeasement and therefore criminal would find the policy immoral.

What the practical results of such a policy, if attempted, would have been is of course a matter for conjecture. It would be rash to claim that it would have saved China, either from her wartime collapse or from the final victory of communism. It may well be that already in 1941 the situation in China was out of control. Nor can one assert with confidence that, had this policy enabled her to keep out of war with Japan, the United States would have been able to bring greater forces to bear in Europe much earlier, thus shortening the war and saving more of Europe from communism. Since the major part of the American armed forces were always concentrated in Europe and since in any case a certain proportion would have had to stand guard in the Pacific, it is possible that the avoidance of war with Japan, however desirable in itself, would not have made a decisive difference in the duration of the European conflict. The writer does, however, permit himself the modest conclusions that the kind of policy advocated by Grew presented real possibilities of success entirely closed to the policy actually followed and that it was by no means so immoral and unprincipled that it could not have been pursued by the United States with decency and honor.

Dexter Perkins

REVISIONISM MAY be defined as an after-the-event interpretation of American participation in war, with the accent on the errors and blunders that provoked the struggle and on the folly of the whole enterprise. If we accept this definition, we shall certainly agree that there has been plenty of revisionism in the course of our history. The war of 1812 has sometimes been judged to have been futile and sometimes described as a war of intended conquest. The Mexican War has come in for harsh treatment as a war of unnecessary aggression. James G. Randall, one of the foremost students of the Civil War period, suggests that a less passionate view of the sectional problem might have made the conflict avoidable. Again and again it has been stated by reputable historians that William McKinley might have prevented the war of 1898 had he stressed in his message to Congress the very large concessions that had been made by Spain. The First World War was brilliantly represented by Walter Millis as the product of a blundering diplomacy and of economic pressures not entirely creditable. And since 1945 we have had a crop of historians, headed by so eminent a member of his historical generation as Charles A. Beard, attempting to show that the maddest folly of all was our entry into the conflict that ended less than a decade ago. Clearly, revisionism is an American habit; though, in saying this, I do not mean to imply that it is unknown in other lands.

The roots of the revisionist tendency are worth speculating about. Such a point of view, I take it, is particularly apt to find expression in a country where peace is highly treasured and where the glorification of war is relatively uncommon. Just as many Americans easily put away the hates and resentment of war at the end

"Was Roosevelt Wrong?," *Virginia Quarterly Review,* XXX (Summer, 1954), 355–372. Reprinted with the permission of the *Virginia Quarterly Review* and Dexter Perkins.

DEXTER PERKINS (1889–   ) is Emeritus Professor of History at the University of Rochester. He is the author of many books on various phases of American diplomatic history, including three volumes on the Monroe Doctrine.

of the struggle and display a tendency towards reconciliation with the vanquished, so they tend to forget the passions that animated them and drove them into the conflict, and to view what at the time seemed reasonable and natural as something that with a little more forbearance or wisdom could have been avoided. And there are other factors that reinforce this point of view. Wars are apt to end in disillusionment. After the glorious hopes of the years 1917 and 1918 came the clash of national selfishnesses at Versailles, and a distraught and threatened world. In 1945 the defeat of Hitler and Japan was soon seen to have left grave problems ahead. In the East, the American defense of China and the hopes of a strong democratic nation in the Orient ended in the victory of the Chinese Reds. And in Europe, though the peril from the ambitions of Hitler was exorcised, the United States found itself face to face with a new totalitarianism, far-ranging in its ambitions like the old. In such a situation it was natural to forget the menace that had been defeated, and to ask whether there might not have been a better solution to the problems that ended with the capitulation ceremonies at Rheims and on the deck of the *Missouri*.

After every large-scale war, moreover, there is a reaction against that strong executive leadership which is almost inevitably associated with periods of crisis in the life of the nation. This was true in 1920; and it was true after 1945. During the conflict the personality of Mr. Roosevelt loomed large, and almost immune from attack. But under the surface there was hostility, and this was to take the form of criticism of his war policies. Sometimes this criticism came, as in the case of Frederic R. Sanborn in his "Design for War," from one who had a strong animus against the New Deal, and who approached the record of the administration in the field of foreign policy with this animus. Sometimes, on the other hand, as in the case of Charles A. Beard, it came from one who regarded the Roosevelt diplomacy as jeopardizing and perhaps wrecking far-reaching programs of internal reform. In these two cases, and in virtually every other, strong emotions entered into the account. It has been a satisfaction to the revisionists to tear down the President; and there has always been — and it was inevitable that there should be — a reading public to fall in with this point of view, either from personal dislike of Roosevelt or from partisan feeling.

Revisionism, then, has roots in the very nature of the case. But, if we analyze it coolly, what shall we think of it? This is the question I propose to examine in this essay.

It seems to me fair to say at the outset that it is impossible to avoid the conclusion that revisionism is essentially history by hypothesis. It suggests — indeed in some instances it almost claims — that the world would have been a better place, or that at any rate the present position of the United States would have been happier, if this country had not intervened in the Second World War. Such a proposition can be put forward, but it cannot be established like a theorem in geometry. We cannot go back to 1939 or 1941 and re-enact the events of those stirring and tumultuous years. In a sense, we are bound by the past.

None the less, it seems worth while, even though we are in the realm of speculation rather than scientific history, to state the revisionist point of view. First, with regard to Germany, the point of view is advanced that the United States was in no essential danger from Adolf Hitler, that he demonstrated no very great interest in the American continents, that he desired until almost the day of Pearl Harbor to keep out of trouble with the United States, that there is no reliable evidence that he meditated an assault upon the New World. It is possible for the revisionist to go further. The ambitions of Hitler, it would be maintained, would have been checked and contained within limits by the presence of the great totalitarian state to the East. The two colossi would act each as a restraint on the other. It needed not the intervention of the American government to preserve the safety of the New World. As to Asia, the argument runs somewhat differently. Less emphasis is placed on the question of national security and more on a certain interpretation of national interest. The United States, we are told, had only a meager interest in China; its trade and investments there were insignificant, and were likely to remain so. They were distinctly inferior to our trade and investments in Japan. The shift in the balance of the Far East that might come about through a Japanese victory over Great Britain was no real concern of the United States. As to the Philippines, they might have been left alone had we stayed out of the war, or conversely, they were not worth the sacrifice involved in maintaining our connection with them. Such are the assumptions, implied, if not always expressed, in the revisionist view of the problem of the Orient.

Now some of the assertions in this rationale are unchallengeable. It is true that Hitler desired to avoid a clash with the United States until just before Pearl Harbor. It is true that the economic interests of the United States in China were inferior to our interests in Japan. These are facts, and must be accepted as facts. But there still remain a good many questions about the revisionist assumptions. For example, was there in 1940 and 1941 no danger of the destruction of British naval power, and would that destruction have had no unhappy consequences for the United States? Granted that the documents show great reluctance on the part of the Fuehrer to challenge the United States, would this reluctance have outlasted the fall of Great Britain? Granted that the Kremlin might have exercised a restraining influence on the Germans, is it certain that the two powers might not have come to an understanding as they did in 1939, and had at other periods in the past? Just how comfortable a world would it have been if the psychopathic leader of Germany had emerged from the Second World War astride a large part of the Continent, with the resources of German science at his command? There are questions, too, that can be asked about the Orient. Did the United States have no responsibility for the Philippines, and would the islands have been safe for long if the Japanese had dominated the Far East? Could the United States divest itself of all concern for China, abandoning a policy of nearly forty years duration and a deep-seated American tradition? Was the destruction of British power in this part of the world a matter of no concern to this country? Could the defeat of Britain in the East be separated from the fate of Britain in the world at large? These are extremely large questions, and it is a bold man who will brush them aside as inconsequential or trivial, or who will reply to them with complete dogmatism. Indeed, it is because they raise so many problems cutting to the root of our feelings, as well as our opinions, that they arouse so much controversy. Nor is there any likelihood that we can ever arrive at a complete consensus with regard to them.

We must, I think, seek a somewhat narrower frame of reference if we are to answer the revisionists with facts, and not with speculations. One of the ways to answer them, and one particularly worth pursuing with regard to the war in Europe, is to analyze the policy of the Roosevelt administration in its relation to public sentiment.

Foreign policy, in the last analysis, depends, not upon some logical formula, but upon the opinion of the nation. No account of American diplomacy in 1940 and 1941 can pretend to authority which does not take into account the tides of sentiment which must always influence, and perhaps control, the course of government. It is not to be maintained that a President has no freedom of action whatsoever; he can, I think, accelerate or retard a popular trend. But he does not act independently of it; the whole history of American diplomacy attests the close relationship between the point of view of the masses and executive action. A peacefully-minded President like McKinley was driven to war with Spain; a President who set great store by increasing the physical power of the nation, like Theodore Roosevelt, was limited and confined in his action; and Franklin Roosevelt himself, when, in the quarantine speech of October, 1937, he sought to rouse the American people against aggression, was compelled to admit failure, and to trim his sails to the popular breeze. These things are of the essence; to fail to observe them is to fail to interpret the past in the true historical spirit.

Let us apply these conceptions to the period 1939 to 1941. It will hardly be denied that from the very beginning of the war public sentiment was definitely against Germany. Indeed, even before the invasion of Poland, the public opinion polls show a strong partiality for the democratic nations. As early as January, 1939, when asked the question whether we should do everything possible to help England and France in case of war, 69 per cent of the persons polled answered in the affirmative, and the same question in October produced a percentage of 62 per cent on the same side. No doubt this sentiment did not extend to the point of actual participation in the war, but it furnished a firm foundation for the action of the President in calling Congress in special session, and in asking of it the repeal of the arms embargo on shipments of war in the interest of the Allies. The measure to this effect was introduced in the Congress towards the end of September; and it was thoroughly debated. There are several things to be said in connection with its passage. The first is that after its introduction there was a consistent majority of around 60 per cent in the polls in favor of passage. The second is that, though there was a strong partisan flavor to the debate, the defections when they came were more numerous on the Republican than on the Democratic side. It is true that, without the leadership of the President, the repeal could not have been enacted. But also it did not fly in the face of public sentiment (so far as that can be measured), but on the contrary reflected it.

With the fall of France there took place a deep and significant development in public opinion. This change the revisionists usually do not mention. They prefer to treat of American policy as if it were formed in a vacuum without regard to the moving forces that have so much to do with the final decisions. Yet the evidences are ample that in June of 1940 the American people were deeply moved. Take, for example, the action of the Republican nominating convention. There were several outstanding professional politicians in the running in 1940, Senator Taft, Senator Vandenberg, Thomas E. Dewey. Each one of these men represented a policy of caution so far as Europe was concerned. Yet what did the convention do? It turned to a relatively unknown figure, to a novice in politics who had, however, more than once declared himself as advocating extensive assistance to the democracies. The choice of Wendell Willkie as the Republican candidate for the Presidency is a fact the importance of which cannot be denied. It is worth while calling attention to other like phenomena. One of these is the overwhelming majorities by which the Congress appropriated largely increased sums for the armed forces, not only for the navy but for the army and the air force as well. Perhaps the American people, or the representatives of the American people, ought not to have been perturbed at what was happening in Europe. But the fact is that they were perturbed. They were perturbed in a big way. And the votes in the legislative halls demonstrate that fact.

Or take another example. The movement for a conscription law in time of peace developed rapidly after June of 1940. It developed with very little assistance from the White House. It cut across party lines. And it resulted in a legislative enactment which reflected the excitement of the public mind. How can we interpret the measure otherwise? Was there not a substantial body of opinion in the United States that feared a German victory?

Another important factor to be noted is the formation in June of 1940 of the Committee to Defend America by Aiding the Allies. It is highly significant that this movement arose at all. It is doubly significant that it found a leader in a Kansan Republican such as

William Allen White. It is trebly significant that, once initiated, it spread like wild-fire, and that by September there were more than 650 chapters in the United States. And it is also to be noted that in New York there soon came into being a more advanced group, the so-called Century Group, which advocated war if necessary to check the aggressions of Germany.

And it is further to be observed that out of the Committee to Defend America came an agitation for what was eventually to be the bases-destroyer deal of September 2, 1940. This deal, by the way, was approved by 62 per cent of the persons polled on August 17, 1940, two weeks before it was actually consummated.

Let us go further. The next important step forward in American policy was the lend-lease enactment of the winter of 1941. This measure, it would appear from the polls, was based on a very distinct evolution of public sentiment. In July of 1940 59 per cent of the persons polled preferred to keep out rather than to help England at the risk of war, and 36 per cent took the contrary view. In October the percentages were exactly reversed: they were 36 to 59. By January of 1941 68 per cent of those interviewed thought it more important to assist Great Britain than to keep out of war. And the lend-lease enactment, when presented to the Congress, passed the Lower House by the impressive vote of 317 to 71 and the Senate by 60 to 31. As in the legislation of 1939, though the vote again had a partisan flavor, there were more defections from the Republicans in favor of the measure than of Democrats against it. And there is something more to be added to the account in this instance. By the winter of 1941 the America Firsters had appeared upon the scene. A counter-propaganda was now being organized against the administration. Yet this new group, despite its vigorous efforts, failed signally to rally majority opinion. And Senator Taft, who represented the most thoughtful opposition to the administration, himself proposed a measure of assistance to Great Britain.

I shall treat a little later of the various measures requiring no legislative sanction which the President took in the course of the year 1941. But it is important to observe that throughout the period there was a strong public sentiment that believed that it was more important to defeat Germany than to keep out of war. This view was held, according to the polls, by 62 per cent of those interrogated in May of 1941 and by 68 per cent in December of 1941.

As early as April, 1941, 68 per cent of the pollees believed it important to enter the war if British defeat was certain.

We should next examine the legislation of the fall of 1941. By this time the Congress was ready to authorize the arming of American merchant ships, and this by a heavy vote. The measure was passed by 259 to 138 in the House and the Senate amended it and passed it by 50 to 37. Congress was ready, more reluctantly, to repeal those provisions of the neutrality acts which excluded American vessels from the so-called war zones. It was moving in the direction of fuller and fuller engagement against Hitler. We shall never know, of course, what the next step would have been had not that step been taken by Germany. It was the dictator of the Reich who declared war on the United States, not the American national legislature that declared war on the Fuehrer and his minions. But in the period between 1939 and 1941 it seems safe to say that the foreign policy of the Roosevelt administration was in accord with the majority public opinion of the nation. It seems incontestable that the President was acting on assumptions which majority opinion accepted, and pursuing a course of action which majority opinion approved.

This circumstance is naturally either ignored or obscured in the revisionist literature. And what makes it easier to forget is the undeniable fact that Franklin Roosevelt was unhappily sometimes given to equivocation and shifty conversation. Very early, it is true, as early as the quarantine speech of October, 1937, he sounded the alarm against the totalitarians. Very often he stated his conviction that their continued progress presented a threat to the United States. On occasion he took his courage in his hands as, when at Charlottesville in June of 1940, in an election year, he came out frankly in favor of aid to the democracies, or in the declaration of unlimited emergency in the address of May 27, 1941. There is little doubt that he deemed the defeat of Hitler more important than the avoidance of war (as did many other Americans, as we have seen). Yet he was often less than frank in his approach, and the emphasis he laid on his devotion to peace was often excessive. He shocked even his ardent admirer, Robert Sherwood, in the election of 1940. His presentation of the case for lend-lease does not at all times suggest candor; indeed, the very phrase seems a bit of cajolery. With regard to the question of convoy, in the spring of 1941, he was clever and, though verbally correct, hardly wholly open in his approach to the problem. In the famous episode of the *Greer* (an attack by a German submarine on a vessel which was reporting its position to a British destroyer), he misrepresented the facts, or spoke without full knowledge of them. All this it is only right to admit. Yet we must not exaggerate the importance of these considerations. The country knew where it was going with regard to Germany. It accepted lend-lease as desirable. Of the patrolling of the ocean lanes which followed, the President spoke candidly in the speech of May 27, 1941. There was nothing clandestine about the occupation of Greenland or Iceland. The pattern in the fall of 1941 would most probably not have been much altered if Roosevelt had been more scrupulous with regard to the *Greer*. In the last analysis we come back to the essential fact that Roosevelt represented and expressed in action the mood of the country with regard to Germany.

The question is, I believe, more difficult when we come to examine American policy towards Japan. We can say with some assurance that the denunciation of the treaty of commerce of 1911, undertaken by the administration in July of 1939 as an indication of American displeasure with Japanese policy, was distinctly well received. Indeed, if the State Department had not acted, the legislature might have. We can also say that in August of 1939 there was an overwhelming feeling against sending war materials to Nippon. When in September of 1940, an embargo on the export of scrap iron was imposed, 59 per cent of the persons polled on this issue approved the step that had been taken. And in 1941 the number of persons who believed that some check should be put on Japan even at the risk of war rose from 51 per cent to 70 per cent between July and September, and stood at 69 per cent at the time of Pearl Harbor.

But we have fewer indications of the direction of public sentiment in the action of Congress, and no actual votes on which to base our estimate of how the representatives of the American people felt with regard to the important problem of our course of action in the Orient. We must, I think, speak less confidently on this question of public opinion than in the case of Germany. We must turn rather to an analysis of the policy of the administration, and to revisionist criticism of that policy.

First of all, let us look at some of the uncontroverted facts. We know that there were militarist elements in Japan. We know that as early as 1934 Japan proclaimed its doctrine of a Greater East Asia in the famous Amau statement. We know that in the same year it upset the naval arrangements made at Washington and London. We know that it set up a special régime in North China in 1935. We know that it became involved in a war with China in 1937. This, of course, was only prelude. The outbreak of the European conflict in Europe, and the collapse of France, offered to the sponsors of further aggressive action a great opportunity. The occupation of Northern Indo-China followed. In the summer of 1940, the impetuous and aggressive Matsuoka came to the Foreign Office. On September 27, 1940, there was signed a tripartite pact with Japan, which bound Nippon to come to the assistance of the Axis powers if they were attacked by a power then at peace with them. In other words, the Tokyo government sought to confine and limit American policy. In April of 1941 came a neutrality pact with Russia which freed the hands of the Japanese militarists for a policy of advance towards the South. In July came the occupation of the rest of Indo-China. The occupation of *northern* Indo-China made some sense from the point of view of blocking the supply route to the Chinese Nationalists. The occupation of *southern* Indo-China made no sense, except as the prelude to further acts of aggression. And in due course the aggression came.

Admittedly, this is only one side of the story. The question to be examined is, did these acts take place partly as a result of American provocation? Was it possible for a wiser and more prudent diplomacy to have avoided the rift that occurred in December, 1941? Revisionist criticism of our Oriental policy has been expressed in a variety of ways. In its most extreme form, it suggests that the President and his advisers actually plotted war with Japan. In its less extreme form, it directs its shafts at a variety of actions, of which I shall examine the most important. They are the conversations with the British as to the defense of the Far East, the commitments made to China, the severance of commercial relations, the failure to accept the proposals of Prince Konoye for direct conversations with the President, and the breakdown of the modus vivendi proposal of November, 1941. I shall examine each of these briefly, but let us first turn to the accusation that American policy was directed towards producing and not avoiding an armed conflict in the Orient.

It seems quite impossible to accept this view on the basis of the documentation. During the greater part of 1940 and 1941, it was certainly not the objective of the Roosevelt administration to bring about a clash in the Far East. On the contrary such a clash was regarded as likely to produce the greatest embarrassment in connection with the program of aid to Britain. The military and naval advisers of the President were opposed to it, and said so again and again. Even on the eve of Pearl Harbor this was the case. In addition, Secretary Hull was opposed to it. Ever the apostle of caution, he made his point of view quite clear almost up to the end. And as for the President, it is worth pointing out that on the occasion of the Japanese occupation of southern Indo-China he came forward with a proposal for the neutralization of that territory in the interests of peace, and that in August he frankly stated it to be his purpose to "baby the Japanese along." That he feared Japanese aggression is likely, almost certain; that he desired it is something that cannot be proved.

But let us look at the various specific actions which have awakened criticism on the part of the revisionists. In the first place I cannot see that staff conversations with the British were open to any objections whatsoever. If the object of the Roosevelt administration was to limit Japanese aggression in the Far East, then it seems wholly rational to take precautions against such aggression, and surely it could reasonably be expected that such precautions would serve as a deterrent rather than as an incitement to action. It is, in my judgment, rather distorted thinking that regards such action as provocation. This is precisely the point of view of the Kremlin today with regard to the North Atlantic treaty and the European defense pact, or, to take another example, very like the contention of the Germans when they invaded Belgium in 1914. Because the British had engaged in military conversations with the Belgians looking to the possible violation of the neutrality treaty of 1839, it was claimed by apologists for Germany that the violation of neutrality was defensible. Where is the possible justification for such reasoning?

There is more to be said with regard to the breaking off, by the United States, of commercial and financial relations with Japan on the heels of the Japanese occupation of southern Indo-China in the summer of 1941. Undoubtedly this created an extraordinarily difficult situation for the government in Tokyo. Undoubtedly the cutting off of the oil supply from the United States gave great additional force to the arguments of the militarists. Undoubtedly, in the absence of a far-reaching diplomatic arrangement, it presented a strong reason for "bursting out" of the circle, and going to war. If the administration put faith in this measure of economic coercion as a substitute for physical resistance, its faith was to turn out to be groundless. For myself, I have for a long time believed that economic coercion against a strong and determined power is more likely to produce war than to prevent it. But there are circumstances that ought to be mentioned in favor of the action of the administration. It is to be emphasized that the severance of commercial and financial relations resulted not in a breach of the negotiations with Japan but in a resumption of those negotiations. It is to be remembered that Prince Konoye's proposal for a personal conference with the President came after and not before the President's action. American policy by no means put an end to the efforts of those substantial elements in Japan who feared a clash with this country and who were laboring to prevent it. It must be pointed out, also, that the alternative was by no means a pleasant one. At a time when we were deeply engaged in the Atlantic, when we were being more and more deeply committed with regard to the war in Europe, when our domestic supply of oil might have to be substantially curtailed, the continuation of our exports to the Far East to assist Japan in possible projects of aggression was a very difficult policy to follow. It may even be that it would have proven to be totally impracticable from a political point of view.

We come in the third place to the efforts of Premier Konoye to establish direct contact with President Roosevelt. It is well known that Ambassador Grew believed at that time, and that he has more than once stated since, that a good deal was to be hoped from such a meeting. And it is by no means clear why, if the objective were the postponement of a crisis, the experiment should not have been tried. Secretary Hull brought to this problem, as it seems to me, a rigidity of mind which may properly be criticized. In insisting on a previous definition of the issues before the meeting was held, he was instrumental in preventing it. While we cannot know what the result of such a meeting would have been, we are entitled, I think, to wish that it had been held. All the more is this true since it would appear likely that Prince Konoye was sincere in the effort which he made to avoid war.

But there is another side to the matter. We cannot be absolutely sure of Konoye's good faith. We can be still less sure of the willingness of the Tokyo militarists to support him in the far-reaching concessions that would have been necessary. And in the final analysis we cannot be sure of the ability of the American government to make concessions on its own part.

And here we come, as it seems to me, to the crux of the matter. It was the American policy in China that created an impassable barrier in our negotiations with Japan. It is necessary to examine that policy. From one angle of vision the patience of the American government in dealing with the China incident seems quite remarkable. There was a good deal to complain of from 1935 onward, certainly from 1937 onward, if one were to think in terms of sympathy for an aggressed people and in terms of the traditional policy of the United States with regard to this populous nation. The Roosevelt administration moved very slowly in its opposition to Japan. It made its first loan to Chiang Kai-shek in the fall of 1938. It denounced the commercial treaty of 1911 with Nippon only in the summer of 1939. And it embarked upon a policy of really substantial aid to China only contemporaneously with the signing of the tripartite pact in the fall of 1940. Its increasing assistance to Chiang is intelligible on the ground that to keep the Japanese bogged down in China was one means of checking or preventing their aggressive action elsewhere.

The fact remains, however, that it was the Chinese question which was the great and central stumbling block in the long negotiations that took place in 1941. Though the Japanese had entered into an alliance with the Axis powers, it seems not unlikely that, in 1941, as the issue of peace or war defined itself more clearly, they would have been willing to construe away their obligations under that alliance had they been able to come to terms with the United States on the Chinese problem. But by 1941 the American government was so far committed to the cause of Chiang that it really had very little freedom of maneuver. The various Japanese proposals for a settlement of the China incident would have involved a betrayal of the Chinese Nationalist leader. The proposal for a coalition government, a government of the Nationalists and the puppet régime of Wang Ching-wei, could hardly have been accepted. The proposal that America put pressure on Chiang to negotiate, and cut off aid to him if he refused, was by this time equally impracticable. And the question of the withdrawal of the Japanese troops in China presented insuperable difficulties. True it is that in October of 1941 the idea of a total withdrawal seems to have been presented to Mr. Welles by Mr. Wakasugi, Admiral Nomura's associate in the negotiations. But the idea was emphatically rejected by the militarists in Tokyo, and perhaps there was never a time when they would have agreed to any proposal that at the same time would have been acceptable to Chungking. The American government had been brought, by its policy of association with the Chinese Nationalists, to the point where understanding with Japan was practically impossible.

This fact is dramatically illustrated by the negotiations over the *modus vivendi* in November, 1941. At this time, as is well known, proposals were brought forward for the maintenance of the *status quo,* and a gradual restoration of more normal relations through the lifting of the commercial restrictions, and through the withdrawal of the Japanese from southern Indo-China. At first it seemed as if there were a possibility of working out some such proposal. But the Chinese objected most violently, and Secretary Hull dropped the idea. In the face of Chinese pressure, and of the possible popular indignation which such a policy of concession might produce, and acting either under the orders or at least with the assent of the President, he backed down. We must not exaggerate the importance of this. There is no certainty that the *modus vivendi* would have been acceptable to Tokyo, and, judging by the Japanese proposals of November 20, there is indeed some reason to think otherwise. But the fact remains that our close association with Chiang was a fundamental factor in making the breach with Japan irreparable. And it seems fair to say in addition that our hopes with regard to Nationalist China were at all times, in 1941 as later, very far removed from political reality.

Let us not, however, jump to absolute conclusions with regard to questions that, in the nature of the case, ought not to be a matter of dogmatic judgment. If there was a party in Japan, and a substantial one, which feared war with the United States and earnestly sought for accommodation, there was also a party which regarded the course of events in Europe as a heaven-sent opportunity for national self-aggrandizement. That this party might in any case have prevailed, whatever the character of American policy, does not seem by any means unlikely. It is significant that in July of 1941 the fall of Matsuoka brought no change in policy in the Far East, and that the so-called moderate, Admiral Toyoda, gave the orders for the crucial and revealing occupation of southern Indo-China in the summer of 1941.

Let us not forget, either, that after all it was the Japanese who struck. The ruthless act of aggression at Pearl Harbor was no necessary consequence of the breakdown of negotiations with the United States. If new oil supplies were needed, they were, of course, to be secured by an attack on the Dutch East Indies, not by an attack on Hawaii. Though there were strategic arguments for including America in any war-like move, there were strong political reasons for not doing so. No greater miscalculation has perhaps ever been made than that made by the militarists at Tokyo in December, 1941. By their own act, they unified American opinion and made their own defeat inevitable. It will always remain doubtful when the decisive involvement would have come for the United States had the bombs not dropped on Pearl Harbor on the 7th of December of 1941.

What, in conclusion, shall we say of revisionist history? There is a sense in which it is stimulating to the historian, and useful to historical science, to have the presuppositions, the conventional presuppositions, of the so-called orthodox interpreters of our foreign policy, subjected to criticism. There is surely some reason to believe that the candid examination of the views of these critics will, in the long run, result in a more accurate and a more objective view of the great events of the prewar years and in a better balanced judgment of President Roosevelt himself.

But there is another side of the question which, of course, must be recognized. It is fair to say that virtually all revisionist history (like some orthodox history) is written with a *parti pris.* It is hardly possible to speak of it as dictated by a pure and disinterested search for truth. It is, on the contrary, shot through with passion and prejudice, with passion and prejudice that may spring from comprehensible or even good motives, but which are passion and prejudice none the less. It also rests upon hypotheses which, in the nature of the case, cannot be demonstrated, and assumptions that will, it is fair to say, never be generally, or perhaps even widely, accepted. As to its practical effects, there are no signs that the isolationism of the present era has important political effects, so far as foreign policy is concerned. Conceivably, it provides some reinforcement for partisan Republicanism. But even here it seems considerably less effective than the unscrupulous campaign of Senator McCarthy and his colleagues to represent the previous administration as one saturated with Communists. The urgency of present issues may make revisionism less of a force in our time than it was two decades ago. As to this, we shall have to see what the future unfolds.

Herbert Feis

TEN YEARS after victory, we look ruefully at the way the world has gone. It is right and natural to search out any errors of judgment or faults of character that have led us to our present pass. But such self-scrutiny can go awry if governed by a wish to revile rather than a wish to understand. Unless we are alert, that could happen as a result of the suspicions that have come to cluster around the way in which the United States became engaged in the Second World War – torch-lit by the Pearl Harbor disaster.

The more recently available sources have added but little to our knowledge of the events that led to our entry into the war. The books of memoirs written by Japanese witnesses have told us something more, especially about the struggle within the Japanese Government. But in my reading, while they may improve our knowledge of details, they do not change the fundamental view of this experience or its main features. In American and British records still kept secret there may be information or explanations that would do so. But even this I doubt. With no new great revealing facts to display, and no great new insights to impart, the most useful service would seem to be to act as caretaker of what is known, and in particular to deal with certain warped comments and inferences that seasonally must feel the straightening edge of evidence.

Of all the accusations made, the one most shocking to me is that Roosevelt and his chief advisers deliberately left the Pacific Fleet and base at Pearl Harbor exposed as a lure to bring about a direct Japanese attack upon us.

This has been diffused in the fact of the fact that the Japanese

"War Came at Pearl Harbor: Suspicions Considered," *The Yale Review,* XLV (Spring, 1956), 378–390. Copyright Yale University Press. Reprinted by permission of *The Yale Review.*

HERBERT FEIS (1893–) is a member of the Institute for Advanced Study, Princeton, New Jersey. In addition to having taught at several universities, he also held some positions in the federal government. He is the author of a multi-volume history of the diplomacy of the Second World War.

High Military Command conference before the Imperial Throne on September 6, 1941, resolved that "If by the early part of October there is no reasonable hope of having our demands agreed to in the diplomatic negotiations mentioned above, we will immediately make up our minds to get ready for war against America (And England and Holland)." This is September 6. The plan for the attack on Pearl Harbor was not approved and adopted until October; and Secret Operation Order #1, the execution of the plan, was not issued until November 5. The presence of the Pacific Fleet at Pearl Harbor was not a lure but an obstacle.

The literature of accusation ignores or rejects the real reasons why the Pacific Fleet was kept in Hawaii. It must do so, since one of the main reasons was the hope that its presence there would deter the Japanese from making so threatening a move south or north that American armed forces might have to join in the war. It scorns the fact that the American military plans — to be executed in the event that we became engaged in war — assigned vital tasks to this Pacific Fleet. A mind must indeed be distracted if it can believe that the American Government could, at one and the same time, use the Pacific Fleet as a target and count on having it as part of its main defending force.

A variant of this accusation, which at least does not require such a willingness to believe the worst, might also be noted — that despite ample knowledge that Pearl Harbor was about to be attacked, the American Government purposefully left it exposed and allowed the event to happen.

Those who do not find such an idea at odds with their view of the sense of duty and regard for human life of President Roosevelt and his chief advisers can find striking points about the occurrence that may be construed to correspond with this conception. How they glare out of the record in hindsight: Ambassador Grew's warnings; Secretary Hull's acute gleam put into words at least three times in Cabinet Councils in November that the Japanese attack might come "at any moment, anywhere"; the intercepted Japanese messages telling of the Japanese effort to secure minute information as to the location of the ships of our Pacific Fleet in the Harbor; carelessness in checking up on the protective measures taken by the local commanders; failure to use the chance to give an effective last-minute warning to Hawaii. How else, it is asked, can these be explained except in terms of secret and conscious purpose?

However, just as hindsight makes the failure of perception plain, so it also makes it understandable — but only by bringing back to mind the total circumstances. That can be done here only in the barest way. Up to then Japanese strategy had been wary, one small creeping step after another, from Manchuria to North China into China and down into Indo-China. American military circles came to take it for granted that it would go on that way. Then there was the fact that Japan's basic objectives lay to the south and southeast; there and there only it could get what it needed — raw materials, oil, and island bases to withstand the attack from the West. Expectation already set in that direction was kept there by impressive and accurate intelligence reports of movements under way. Against this flow of preconception, the signs pointing to Pearl Harbor were not heeded.

Such features of contemporary thinking within the American Government explain, though they do not excuse, the failure to discern that Pearl Harbor was going to be attacked. To think the contrary is to believe that the President and the heads of the American Army, Navy, and Air Force were given to deep deception, and in order to have us enter the war were ready to sacrifice not only the Pacific Fleet but the whole war plan for the Pacific. This, I think, is the difference between history and police court history.

I have taken note of these accusations that have been built about the disaster at Pearl Harbor because they appeal to the sense of the sinister which is so lively in our times. But I am glad to turn to ideas and interpretations of broader historical import.

The first of these is that Roosevelt and the Joint Chiefs of Staff were obligated by secret agreements with Churchill and their British colleagues to enter the war at some time or other, in one way or other. Therefore, it is further supposed, the American authors of this agreement had to cause either Germany or Japan, or both, to attack us.

This view derives encouragement from the fact that the American Government *did* enter into a secret agreement about strategy with the British. The accord, known as ABC-1 Staff Agreement, adopted at Washington in March, 1941, set down the respective missions of the British and American elements in the event that the

United States should be at war with Germany or Japan, or both; and subsequently the American basic joint war plan, Rainbow-5, was adjusted to fit this combined plan of operations. An attempt was made at a similar conference in Singapore soon after to work out a more detailed United States–British–Dutch operating plan for the Pacific. This attempt failed; but the discussion that took place there left a lasting mark on American official thinking, for the conferees defined the limits on land and sea beyond which Japanese forces could not be permitted to go without great risk to the defenders.

The ABC-1 agreement did not place the Roosevelt Administration under *political* obligation to enter the war against either Germany or Japan, not even if Japan attacked British or Dutch areas in the Far East. Nor did Roosevelt give a promise to this effect to Churchill when they met at Newfoundland in August, 1941. Up to the very eve of the Japanese assault the President refused to tell the British or Dutch what we would do. In short, the Government kept itself officially free from any obligation to enter the war, certainly free of any obligation to thrust itself into the war.

But I do think this accord conveyed responsibilities of a moral sort. After ABC-1 was adopted, production of weapons in the United States and the British Commonwealth took it into account; and the allocation of weapons, troops, ships, and planes as between threatened areas was based on the expectation that the United States would carry out the assignments set down in the plan.

Thus, it may be fairly thought, Roosevelt and his administration were obligated to try to gain the consent of Congress and the American people to play the part designated in the joint plans if Japanese assaults crossed the land and sea boundaries of resistance that were defined at these joint staff conferences. In the last November weeks when the end of the diplomatic talks with Japan came into sight, and General Marshall and Admiral Stark were asked what measures should be taken in face of the threatened Japanese advances, they advised the President to declare the limits defined at Singapore, and to warn the Japanese that we would fight if these were crossed. There is much reason to think this would have been done even had the Japanese not struck at Pearl Harbor and the Philippines, and this boundary would have been the line between peace and war. But this reaffirmation was made not as a measure required to carry out a secret accord, but because it was believed to be the best course.

A variant explanation of the way we dealt with Japan runs somewhat as follows: that Roosevelt was determined to get into the war against Germany; that he had to find a release from his public promises that the United States would not enter "foreign wars" unless attacked; that his efforts to do so by unneutral aid to Britain and the Soviet Union had failed because Hitler had refused to accept the challenge; and so he sought another door into war, a back door, by inviting or compelling the Japanese attack.

This interpretation, with its kick at the end, twists the record around its own preconception. The actions taken did not flow from a settled wish to get us into war. They trailed along the rim of necessity of the true purpose – which was to sustain resistance against the Axis. How many times the American Government refused to do what the British, French, Chinese, Russians, Dutch asked it to do, because it might involve us in actual combat!

This slant of reasoning about American action passes by the course of Japanese conduct which aroused our fears and stimulated our opposition: the way in which, despite all our pleas and warnings, Japan pressed on. By not recognizing that these Japanese actions called for American counteraction, it excuses them. Thus our resistance is made to appear as nothing else but a deceitful plot to plunge us into war. Furthermore, it dismisses as insincere the patient attempt to calm Japan by diplomatic talks, by offers to join in safeguarding its security.

There were influential individuals in the Roosevelt Administration who wanted to get into the war and indifferent as to how we got into it. Of these, Secretary of the Interior Ickes was, I believe, the most candid, at any rate in his diary entries. Secretary of the Treasury Morgenthau and his staff also had a positive wish that we should engage in war – but against Germany, not against Japan, for that might have brought a diversion of forces to the Pacific. Secretary of War Stimson thought that it would not be possible for Great Britain to sustain the fight unless we entered it; but toward the very end, particularly as it was becoming plain that the Soviet Union was going to survive the Nazi assault, he began to wish for delay. However, time and time again the memoirs and diaries record the impatience of these officials, and those who thought like them, with Hull's caution and Roosevelt's watchful indirection.

The most genuine point made by those who dissent, one that merits thorough analysis, is that the American Government, in conjunction with the British and Dutch, refused to continue to supply Japan with machines and materials vital to it – especially oil. It is contended that they thereby compelled Japan to resort to war, or at least fixed a time period in which Japan was faced with the need of deciding to yield to our terms or go to war.

In reflecting upon this action, the reasons for it must not be confused with the Japanese response to it. Japan showed no signs of curbing its aggressive course. It paid no heed to repeated and friendly warnings that unless it did, the threatened countries would have to take counter-measures. As when on February 14, 1941, while the Lend-Lease Act was being argued in Congress, Dooman, Counsellor of the American Embassy in Japan and known to be a firm and straightforward friend of that country, carried back from Washington the message for the Vice-Minister for Foreign Affairs: that the American people were determined to support Britain even at the risk of war; that if Japan or any other country menaced that effort "it would have to expect to come in conflict with the United States"; and that the United States had abstained from an oil embargo in order not to impel Japan to create a situation that could only lead to the most serious outcome. Japan's answer over the following months had been to force its way further into Indo-China and threaten the Dutch East Indies.

This sustained proof that Japan was going on with its effort to dominate Asia, and the alliance pledging it to stand by Germany if that country got into war with the United States, made a continuation of trade with Japan an act of meekness on our part. Japan was concentrating its foreign purchases on products needed for war, while reducing civilian use by every means, and was thus accumulating great reserve stocks. These were enabling it to maintain its invasion of China without much strain, while continuing to expand its war-making power. Had *effective* restraints – note that I do not say *total* restraints – not been imposed, the American Government would have been in the strange position of having declared an unlimited national emergency, of calling upon the American people to strengthen their army, navy, and air force in great urgency, while at the same time nourishing the opponent that might have to be met in battle. This was a grave, if not intolerable, responsibility.

It is hard to tell how squarely the American and British Governments faced the possible consequence of their restrictive measures. My impression is that they knew the danger of war with Japan was being increased; that Japan might try to get by force the means denied it. The Japanese Government served plain warnings that this game of thrust and counterthrust might so end. These were soberly regarded, but did not weaken the will that Japan was not to have its way by threat.

Mingled with the anxiety lest these restrictive measures would make war more likely, there was a real hope that they might be a deterrent to war. Conceivably they would bring home to the Japanese people that if it came to war, they might soon run out of the means for combat, while the rapid growth of American military strength would make it clear that they could not in the end win. And, as evidence of these probabilities became plain, the conciliatory elements in the Japanese Government would prevail over the more militant ones.

This almost happened. But the reckless ones, those who would rather court fatality than accept frustration, managed to retain control of Japanese decision. The pressure applied by us did not prevent war, and may have brought the time of decision for war closer. The valid question, however, is not whether the American Government resorted to these restrictions *in order* to drive Japan to attack; it is whether the American Government failed to grasp a real chance, after the restraints had begun to leave their mark in Japanese official circles, to arrive at a satisfactory understanding that would have averted war. Twice, in the opinion of some qualified students of the subject, such a chance emerged, or at least appeared on the horizon of diplomacy. Were they real opportunities or merely mirages or decoys?

The first of these was the occasion when in the autumn of 1941, the Japanese Prime Minister, Prince Konoye, sought a personal meeting with the President. It is averred that the President's failure to respond lost a chance to avert the war without yielding any American principle or purpose. Some think the reason was that American diplomacy was inflexible, dull in its insight, and too soaked in mistrust. Others, more accusatory, explain the decision by a lack of desire for an agreement that would have thwarted the design for war.

Since there is no conclusive evidence of what Konoye intended to propose or could have achieved, comment on this subject must enter into "the boggy ground of what-might-have-been." Some observers, including Ambassador Grew, believe that Konoye could have made a real, and an irreversible, start toward meeting American terms. It will always be possible to think that this is so. But to the Americans in authority, the chance seemed small. Konoye was a man who in every past crisis had allowed himself to flounder between criss-crossed promises; hence there was good reason to fear an attempt at deception. Such glimpses as we have of what he might have proposed do not support the view that he could have offered a suspension or end of the fight against China. His freedom to negotiate would have been subject to the conditions stated by those who had controlled Japan's course up to then – their price for allowing him to go to meet the President.

Even so, to repeat, it is possible that skilled and more daring American diplomacy might have handled the meeting so as to get a satisfactory accord; or, failing that – and this is the more likely chance – to bring about so deep a division within the Japanese circle of decision as to have prevented warlike action. These alluring historical queries will continue to roam in the land of might-have-been.

But the risks were great. The echoes of Munich and its aftermath were still loud. The American Government might have found itself forced to make a miserable choice: either to accept an accord which would have left Japan free to complete its conquest of China and menace the rest of Asia, or to face a deep division among the American people. Any understanding with Japan that was not clear and decisive would have had unpredictable consequences. The Chinese Government might have felt justified in making a deal following our own. The Soviet Union, at this time just managing with the greatest effort and agony to prevent German victory, might also have chosen to compromise with Hitler rather than to fight it out. Speculations such as these must leave the subject unsettled. But in any case I think it clear that the American decision was one of judgment, not of secret intent. Konoye was not told that the President would not meet with him; he was told that he would not do so until more progress had been made toward defining what the Japanese Government was prepared to propose.

The same basic question had to be faced in the final crisis of negotiation in November, 1941: whether to relax restraints on Japan and leave it in a position to keep on trying to control much of Asia in return for a promise not to press on farther for the time being.

The opinion that the Japanese truce offer made at this last juncture accepted the main purposes and principles for which the American Government had been standing may be summarily dismissed. It was ambiguously worded, it was silent about the alliance with Germany, and it would have required the American Government to end its support of China – for the last of its numbered five points read: "The Government of the United States undertakes to refrain from such measures and actions as will be prejudicial to the endeavors for the restoration of general peace between Japan and China." This scant and unclear proposal was at once deemed "entirely unacceptable." Furthermore, there seemed little use and much possible damage in making a counter truce-offer of the same variety. The intercepted Japanese messages stated flatly that this was Japan's last and best offer. They told of the swift dismissal of a much more nearly acceptable one that Nomura and Kurusu asked their superiors in Tokyo to consider. A deadline had been set. Thus it was all but sure that the reduced counteroffer which had been patched together in Washington would be unheeded. But it might shake the coalition to which by then the opponents of the Axis had pledged their lives and national destinies.

This seems to have been the thought uppermost in Hull's mind in recommending to the President that the counter truce-offer be withheld. As set down in his historic memo of November 26, he had been led to this conclusion by the opposition of the Chinese, the half-hearted support or actual opposition of the British, Dutch, and Australian governments, and the further excited opposition to be expected because of lack of appreciation of the importance and value of a truce. This I believe to have been the true determining reason for a decision reluctantly taken.

Even if by then Japan was genuinely ready for reform, the repentance had come too late. The situation had grown too entangled by then for minor measures, its momentum too great. Germany-Italy-Japan had forced the creation of a defensive coalition more vast than the empire of the Pacific for which Japan plotted. This was not now to be quieted or endangered by a temporary halt along the fringe of the Japanese advance.

Even though these reasons for dropping the idea of a truce may seem sufficient, they leave the question why the American Government could not have given a softer and less declaratory answer. Why had it to give one so "bleakly uncompromising"? It could have said simply that the Japanese offer did not convey the assurances that would warrant us and the alliance for which we spoke to resume the shipment of war materials to Japan and end our aid to China. Why was it deemed advisable or essential at this juncture to state fully and forcibly our maximum terms for a settlement in the Pacific? Was it foreseen that, scanned with mistrust as it would almost surely be, this would be construed as a demand for the swift abandonment of Japan's whole program? Was it done, as the accusation runs, with the deliberate intent of banning any last chance for an accord? Of propelling the Japanese attack?

That this was not the reason I am as sure as anyone can be on a matter of this sort; but I can offer only conjecture as to what the inspiring purposes were. Perhaps to vindicate past actions and decisions. Perhaps a wish to use the dramatic chance to put in the record a statement of the aims for which the risk of war was being accepted, and of the basis on which the Americans would found the peace when the time came. Such an idea was in accord with the usual mode of thought of the men in charge of the Executive Branch of the Government and of most of the American people. It gave vent to the propensity exemplified in Hull to find a base in general principles meant to be at once political standards and moral ideals. After long caution, it appealed as a defiant contradiction of the Axis program. All this, however, is surmise rather than evidenced history.

But I think it is well within the realm of evidenced history that the memo of November 26 was not in any usual sense of the word an ultimatum. It did not threaten the Japanese with war or any other form of forceful punishment if our terms were not accepted. It simply left them in the state of distress in which they were, with the prospect that they might later have to submit to our requirements. The Japanese Government could have, as Konoye and Nomura pleaded with it to do, allowed the situation to drag along, with or without resuming talks with the American Government. Its power to make war would have been depleted, but neither quickly nor crucially. The armed forces and even the position in China could have been maintained.

Notably, the final Japanese answer which ended negotiations on December 7, 1941, does not accuse the American Government of confronting it with an ultimatum, but only of thwarting the larger Japanese aims. Part 14 – the clinching part of this note – reads: "Obviously it is the intention of the American Government to conspire with Great Britain and other countries to obstruct Japan's efforts toward the establishment of peace through the creation of a New Order in East Asia, and especially to preserve Anglo-American rights and interests by keeping Japan and China at war. This intention has been revealed clearly during the course of the present negotiations. Thus, the earnest hope of the Japanese Government to adjust Japanese-American relations and to preserve and promote the peace of the Pacific through coöperation with the American Government has finally been lost."

This is a more nearly accurate description of the purposes of the American Government under Roosevelt than those attributed to it by hostile and suspicious American critics. Our Government did obstruct Japanese efforts, believing them to be unjust, cruel, and a threat to our national security, especially after Japan became a partner with Hitler's Germany and Mussolini's Italy and bent its efforts toward bringing the world under their combined control.

This determination stood on the proposition that it was better to take the risks of having to share in the suffering of the war than of finding ourselves moved or compelled to fight a more desperate battle against the Axis later on. The American Government, I believe, knew how serious a risk of war was being taken. But in its addresses to the American people it chose to put in the forefront the perils we would face if the Axis won, and to leave in the background, even to camouflage, the risks of finding ourselves plunged into wars which during the election campaign it had promised would not occur. Whether any large number of Americans were fooled by this, or whether most of them, in reality, were content to have the prospect presented that way rather than in a more blunt and candid way, I do not know.

This essay in interpretation has compelled me to recall and stress the aggressive Japanese assault — though I should have been glad to let that slip into the past. The passage of time does not alter facts, but it can bring a fuller and calmer understanding of them. It frees the mind for fairer appreciation of the causes and circumstances which impelled Japan along its tragic course and which impelled us to resist it. For both countries there are many common lessons. One of them is that continued friendliness requires mutual effort to relieve the other, to the extent it can, of deep cause for anxiety — the Japanese people of their anxiety over the means of living decently, the American people of anxiety about their security and power to defend the free world. Another is that they must both feel, speak, and act so honestly and steadily that their view of each other will be cleared of mistrust, and brightened by trust.

9

Postwar America

New Liberalism or New Conservatism?

"A NATION which has made a religion of success," Arthur M. Schlesinger, Jr. shrewdly observed in his critique of American liberalism in 1949, "ought to find it hard to acclimate itself to the middle of the twentieth century. For frustration is increasingly the hallmark of the century — the frustration of triumphant science and rampant technology, the frustration of the most generous hopes and of the most splendid dreams. Nineteen hundred looked forward to the irresistible expansion of freedom, democracy and abundance; 1950 will look back to totalitarianism, to concentration camps, to mass starvation, to atomic war. Yet for the United States the world tragedy still has the flickering unreality of a motion picture. It grips us as we see it; but, lingering over the familiar milkshake in the bright drugstore, we forget the nightmare in the resurgence of warmth and comfort. Anxiety is something we hear about. It is not yet part of our lives — not of enough of our lives anyway, to inform our national decisions." [1]

As Schlesinger tacitly pointed out, the American people after

1. Arthur M. Schlesinger, Jr., *The Vital Center: The Politics of Freedom* (Boston, 1949), pp. 1–2.

World War II were faced with a successive series of external and internal challenges and problems for which no precedent existed. At the close of the Second World War, the United States seemed to be the strongest nation in the world – economically, militarily, ideologically. Having triumphed over the forces of totalitarianism, its citizens looked forward with confidence and optimism to the promise of a brighter future. These hopes and expectations, however, proved extraordinarily short-lived. Within a very brief period of time the United States found itself confronted with a seemingly implacable and relentless foe in the form of the Soviet Union. Instead of peace, the American people soon were engaged in a "cold war," a war that required both economic and military mobilization even in the absence of an overt conflict. When the Soviet Union became an atomic power in 1949, Americans were face-to-face for the first time in their history with the realization that their civilization was threatened with total destruction. Moreover, the rise of nationalism in the Far East and Africa ushered in a period of international instability that posed serious dilemmas for the United States.

To the American people the shock of these changes was profound and for the most part they were caught unprepared. The result was an era of anxiety and self-appraisal in the postwar era. Faced with challenges abroad and at home, the solutions that some groups offered reflected the confused and undecided attitudes then prevalent. Some responded with impatience, anger, and a desire to destroy once and for all the evil symbols responsible for their frustrations; they saw not only an external enemy, but foes in their midst who supposedly were bent on destroying cherished American traditions. Others continued to express their faith in the ability of a democratic society to meet the challenges of totalitarianism, irrespective of the time that would be required to accomplish this task. But whatever the answers given after World War II, it was clear that Americans were engaged in the difficult and arduous task of reexamining the fundamental premises that they had for so long taken for granted.

The historical profession was no exception to this development. Because historical thought had been so closely tied in with twentieth century intellectual currents, historians were to be influenced by changes in social and political attitudes of the American people.

Thus the older Progressive school of historiography — which had accepted the reality of progress in human affairs — began to find itself hard-pressed by critics who denigrated its supposedly facile and superficial optimism and attacked its commitment to change. These critics — who taken as a group can be designated as the neo-conservative school — not only attempted to undermine and discredit their Progressive forebears, but also set out to rewrite American history in the light of their own assumptions.

Since the Second World War, therefore, American historians have tended to divide, generally speaking, into two broad schools. The first — the traditional Progressive school — continued to emphasize the ongoing struggle for economic and political democracy in American history. Such writers had always taken a critical though optimistic view of America and stressed largely the flaws and imperfections that required corrective action in American society. Thus they had portrayed American history in the past in terms of a protracted struggle between liberalism and conservatism, between the people and the special interests, and between democracy and aristocracy, so that periods of reform alternated with periods of conservative consolidation or reaction. Implicit in much of their writing was a moral commitment to the idea of progress; each era of reform brought the American people closer and closer to the realization of a better world. While recent historians writing within the Progressive tradition modified somewhat the optimistic outlook of some of their predecessors, they still shared the hope of social betterment that had always been characteristic of this school.

The neo-conservative school of American historiography that appeared after 1945, on the other hand, reflected the reaction to liberal ideas. Responding to the rise of totalitarianism in Europe and elsewhere, many conservatives began to argue that liberalism, because of its optimism, faith in progress, and commitment to social change, had completely underestimated man's capacity for evil. Liberals, they said, always supported change and consistently ignored these traditions which might have checked the revolutionary movements that took place in other parts of the world. Only a conservative philosophy based upon a respect for tradition, religion, natural law, and stability could provide a viable answer to the challenges of the modern world. The result was the appearance in the postwar period of a self-conscious and articulate conservatism.

The growth of conservative ideas was as evident among historians as it was among other groups. The neo-conservative historians not only reacted against the ideas of their Progressive brethren, but also set out to reinterpret American history in the light of their own assumptions. Rather than criticizing the flaws and imperfections in American society, they praised its stability and moral character. Consequently, they played down social and economic conflicts in the American past and stressed the basic consensus that had united the American people throughout most of their history. In an important sense, the neo-conservative school provided their countrymen with a usable past and a sense of unity to draw upon at a time when external forces seemed to be threatening the nation's security. These historians pictured America as a strong and united nation standing guard over the free world against the menace of Communism as exemplified by the rise of the Soviet Union and China. The struggles of earlier epochs in America's history, they said, had never involved fundamental differences over basic ideology and goals; they had revolved over means, not ends. American parties, these neo-conservative scholars were quick to point out, had fought primarily over political offices and power; their goals and ideology were remarkably similar.

The different approaches by these two schools of historians led to obviously dissimilar evaluations of American society and events in the postwar period. It is true that both Progressive and neo-conservative historians had considerable difficulty in judging the postwar era objectively, if only because they lived through these years and lacked the perspective necessary to evaluate them in a meaningful manner. It is also true that many of the sources needed to write the history of the 1940's, 1950's, and 1960's had not yet been made available to scholars. In spite of these handicaps, both schools attempted to chronicle and interpret the events of the last quarter of a century. Understandably, both arrived at startlingly different conclusions.

In general, Progressive historians continued to write in terms of a conflict between the people and those vested interests which impeded progress by their narrow and self-seeking objectives. The realization of the promise of American life, as far as these scholars were concerned, lay in the future, not in the present. Thus the picture that Progressive writers drew of contemporary America tended to be hostile in tone. In portraying their own era, they reiterated several related themes. One theme was the widespread complacency about domestic conditions and the refusal of many Americans to grapple with serious problems that confronted their society. While admitting that many individuals and groups had achieved a level of prosperity in the postwar period hitherto unheard of, these historians argued that prosperity was by no means as widespread as had been popularly assumed. Indeed, they pointed out, there were elements in American society — the Negroes and urban poor — who remained largely unaffected by the spread of affluence.

Progressive historians were joined by scholars in other disciplines who also viewed their own times in a hostile light. By the early 1960's, there existed an extensive body of critical literature that dealt with a variety of problems. Taken as a whole, these works reflected a growing concern that there were fundamental maladjustments in American society. Thus C. Wright Mills, a radical sociologist, in a series of widely read books depicted the United States under the domination of a small power élite bent on defending its own narrow interests; David Riesman, another sociologist and critic, argued in his influential book *The Lonely Crowd* (1950), that the nineteenth-century American individualist had been replaced by what he termed the "other-directed" person — an individual who was a conformist molded largely by the views of his contemporaries; and William Whyte drew a savage indictment of the "organizational" man who had subordinated his individuality to the requirements of a business-world bureaucracy. Among the historians, Richard Hofstadter subjected the reform or liberal tradition to a merciless critical analysis, placing greater emphasis on its failures and shortcomings than its achievements.

Much of the literature of protest was also inspired more by humanitarian and idealistic motives than it was by a supposedly scientific objectivity. In a moving book published in 1962, for example, Michael Harrington, a contemporary social critic, spoke for a younger generation that had rediscovered the abject poverty and degradation of millions of Americans. In his eyes poverty was much more than simply a lack of money; it was "a culture, a way of life and feeling. . . . In short, being poor is not one aspect of a person's life in this country, it is his life. . . . The other Americans are those who live at a level of life beneath moral choice, who are so submerged in their poverty that one cannot begin to talk about free choice."[2] In underdeveloped societies everyone was poor; hence the entire society was bent on uplifting itself. In the United States, on the other hand, the poor had become invisible because they were isolated from the comfortable middle class groups in their society and lacked any effective means to make their voices heard. America, Harrington emphasized, really constituted two nations. Unless its citizens were prepared to act, he warned, the moral cancer within the body politic would continue to grow.

The widespread disillusionment among Progressive writers with the achievements of postwar America resulted in the publication of a number of hostile critiques of the 1950's. In the first selection, William V. Shannon analyzes the presidency of Dwight D. Eisenhower, the first Republican president to break the New Deal coalition of Franklin D. Roosevelt. Although recognizing Eisenhower's remarkable popularity among the American people, Shannon concludes that as president he was a failure. Eisenhower had taken office at a time when the world was changing rapidly and when new domestic problems were being created by technological innovation. Presented with challenges that offered unparalleled opportunities to strike out in new directions, all that Eisenhower did was to postpone any meaningful discussion of these issues. The Eisenhower Administration, Shannon suggests, was the "time of the great postponement." Eisenhower merely reaffirmed the old consensus that had been forged earlier by Franklin D. Roosevelt and Harry S. Truman; he was unable to offer any new alternatives for the issues of his own day. At best his presidency was a pleasant interlude in an otherwise tragic age; at worst it was a waste of precious time in an era when time was running out.

Complacency, according to Progressive interpreters, was not the only characteristic of the postwar era. Even more dangerous in their eyes were the real threats to liberty that appeared to be

2. Michael Harrington, *The Other America: Poverty in the United States* (first published 1962; Penguin edition, Baltimore, 1963), pp. 156, 158–159.

taking shape as the nation seemed to be girding for a struggle with the Soviet Union — an adversary supposedly bent on revolutionizing the world in accordance with Marxian ideals. The relative isolation of America from the rest of the world — an isolation that grew out of a fortuitous combination of geography and technology — had, at least in the past, prevented certain domestic elements from becoming overly virulent or dangerous. The shift in America's world position after 1945, however, proved a potent influence in releasing reactionary forces and setting the stage for what soon became known as "McCarthyism." To Progressive scholars, therefore, the outstanding characteristic of the 1950's was a drive toward an enforced conformity, the likes of which the American people had never experienced before.

To liberals and Progressives, the early 1950's was a particularly difficult time. The fears and frustrations of those years, particularly those arising out of the Korean conflict and the supposed internal threats of Communist subversion, had given rise to a general demand for enforced loyalty and conformity. Unfortunately, according to many liberals, these reactionary forces found a brilliant and unscrupulous leader in the person of Senator Joseph McCarthy of Wisconsin, who quickly gathered to his side many of the right-wing elements in American society. The intellectual community was in an especially vulnerable position, for the arguments used to discredit scholars were purely emotional in tone and content, thus making rational discussion all but impossible. The result was a near fatal blow to the liberal tradition — according to adherents of that tradition — and one that was destined to leave a profound and lasting imprint upon American institutions. Indeed, the legacy of these years was the creation of an organized and cohesive right wing movement that managed during the presidential campaign of 1964 to seize control of the Republican party under Senator Barry Goldwater.

Because of their vulnerable position, liberals were fascinated with the problem of explaining the roots of a movement alien to their own experiences. The fact that a strong and self-conscious right wing movement should follow the New Deal era made this problem even more intriguing. The assumption of those who identified themselves in the liberal tradition was that each period of reform resulted in the progressive elimination of major sources of discontent. But the years of domestic reform had seemed instead to alienate certain individuals and groups that logically had stood to benefit from these social and economic innovations. Why, then, had the postwar reaction been so extreme and taken the form that it had?

In the second selection Richard Hofstadter attempts to offer an explanation to this question by discussing what he terms the "pseudo-conservative revolt." As has been pointed out several times in earlier chapters, Hofstadter, although within the liberal tradition, has also been one of that tradition's most consistent critics. Indeed, in a series of brilliant and provocative books since 1948, he seemed to be saying that many of the more undesirable features of our national life were directly attributable to the deficiencies and shortcomings of American liberalism itself. Thus Populism was associated with anti-Semitism and Progressivism with a narrow Protestant moralizing. His analysis of the radical right in the 1950's in some respects grew out of his concern with and commitment to liberalism; by treating the latter he could begin to understand the deficiencies of the former, thereby contributing to the task of rebuilding and restating the liberal ideology.

By 1952, Hofstadter argued, American liberals – particularly those who had been associated with the New Deal – had been in power for nearly twenty years. Although they had done much to transform the economic and administrative life of the nation, the liberals lost some of the fervor for reform they had had when they first assumed power during the depression. Their own position in society was now secure; they had shared the wartime and postwar prosperity and their outlook was one of satisfaction rather than revolt. While these liberals were attempting to preserve or simply extend the programs of the 1930's, however, a new type of radicalism had emerged. Terming this new radicalism "pseudo-conservative," Hofstadter maintains that it represents the profound, albeit unconscious, hatred of groups who felt alienated from their own society. Denying that the appearance of the radical right in the 1950's was simply a continuation of an older conservative and isolationist tradition, Hofstadter suggests that this pseudo-conservative movement was derived from the rootlessness and heterogeneity of American life, which had intensified a concern for status and personal identity.

In attributing the pseudo-conservative movement to a quest for status, Hofstadter also identifies two distinct political processes. In periods of economic depression, politics usually involved the clash of interest groups hoping to improve their economic position. In periods of prosperity, on the other hand, status considerations became paramount. Two groups in particular were troubled by status considerations: the older Yankee Protestant middle-class, which found its traditional positions of leadership being eroded by technological changes and the rise of other groups in American society; and the groups of newer immigrants who were determined to prove their basic Americanism. Both groups had seized the opportunity after World War II to proclaim their own brand of super patriotism; in so doing, they had identified as their enemies — as well as the enemies of American society — liberals, intellectuals, and nonconformists. The result was the appearance of the radical right — a movement dominated by an overwhelming desire to enforce its own version of conformity upon the American people. While Hofstadter did not believe that this type of ultra movement would plunge the nation into a totalitarian nightmare, he remained troubled by the pervasiveness of the trend and its potential threat of American liberty.

Hofstadter's explanation of the roots of the radical right, of course, raised many more questions than it answered. He implied that insecurity and an indeterminant social status—both of which were associated with freedom — were responsible for the drive toward conformity by rootless groups seeking means of self-identification. In this respect he was echoing Erich Fromm's famous thesis to explain the rise of Nazism. Fromm had argued in *Escape From Freedom* that the rise of totalitarianism represented Western man's effort to escape from the frightening uncertainties of freedom.

Yet Hofstadter never made clear the implications of his analysis. Was he arguing in favor of a social system having clear and distinct class lines so that each individual and group knew clearly where they stood within the system? Furthermore, were political disagreements, particularly in times of prosperity, mere façades for deeper underlying psychological and sociological maladjustments? As a matter of fact, Hofstadter's writings, taken as a whole, revealed the crisis that some liberal historians faced in the postwar era. In The *Age of Reform* Hofstadter had characterized Populism, Progressivism, and the New Deal in more or less negative terms; but he was equally critical of the rise of right wing extremism in the 1950's and 1960's. Although hostile to both left- and right-wing movements, Hofstadter never spelled out precisely the standards by which he measured the failures or successes of either liberalism or conservatism. By omitting from his discussion any suggestion of meaningful alternatives or constructive criticism, Hofstadter weakened his own critique. The result was a negativism that left him ideologically rootless in terms of American political and intellectual traditions.

Not all Progressive historians followed the path trod by Hofstadter. One of the outstanding exceptions was Arthur M. Schlesinger, Jr., who continued to uphold a modified version of the Progressive tradition of American historiography. While committed to reform through social and class conflict, Schlesinger never assumed that the failure to reach utopia was a criticism of the entire American liberal tradition. Having been influenced by Reinhold Niebuhr, the outstanding Protestant theologian who had built an imposing ideology that rested upon the assumption that human nature was essentially sinful, Schlesinger saw human history as an unfinished, even tragic, drama. The failure to establish the millennium on earth, therefore, was no reason to despair; the yardstick by which to judge human affairs had to be a more modest one.

In his analysis of American history, Schlesinger continued to emphasize the constant tensions between economic groups that led to the alternate cycles of periods of reform with periods of conservative consolidation and reaction. Whether discussing the 1830's, the 1930's, or the 1960's, his theme was much the same; American history had been marked by a never-ending struggle between classes and interest groups. "American democracy," wrote Schlesinger in *The Age of Jackson,* "has come to accept the struggle among competing groups for the control of the state as a positive virtue — indeed, as the only foundation for liberty. The business community has been ordinarily the most powerful of these groups, and liberalism in America has been ordinarily the movement on the part of the other sections of society to restrain the powers of the business community. This was the tradition of Jefferson and Jackson, and it has been the basic meaning of American liberalism." [3]

Both as an assistant to President John F. Kennedy as well as in his capacity as the late president's biographer, Schlesinger continued to apply his cyclical approach to American history. The Eisenhower years had been "a period of passivity and acquiescence in our national life"; the Kennedy era, on the other hand, would be "a time of affirmation, progressivism and forward movement." Prior to Kennedy's election Schlesinger had co-authored a memorandum embodying this analysis: the new liberal epoch of the 1960's, he argued, "would resemble the Progressive period of the turn of the century more than it would the New Deal. The New Deal had taken its special character from the fight against depression; but the Progressive revolt grew out of spiritual rather than economic discontent." A revival of a new sense of the public interest, he suggested, would be the central theme of the 1960's. Such was the thesis that Schlesinger stressed in his masterful and brilliant biography of John F. Kennedy.[4]

In the third selection Richard H. Rovere echoes Schlesinger's interpretation of the 1950's, though adding a novel touch of his own. To Rovere many of the charges of liberal commentators to the effect that the Eisenhower years were ones of self-satisfaction and complacency were indeed true. Yet to understand the period requires a larger view. By the time of Eisenhower's election, Rovere suggests, there were many things about American life that were less than desirable. Under Truman — a "good and gallant President" — there was considerable corruption in half a dozen federal agencies. Moreover, the Korean War and the charges of Senator McCarthy had aroused profound unrest. Most Americans tended to resent their nation's international commitments and were responsive to a demagogic explanation that fixed the sources of all difficulties on a small band of evil conspirators (New Dealers, Communists, radicals). The Eisenhower interregnum, according to Rovere, was a time when a new consensus was reached, when the

3. Arthur M. Schlesinger, Jr., *The Age of Jackson* (Boston, 1945), p. 505.
4. Arthur M. Schlesinger, Jr., *A Thousand Days: John F. Kennedy in the White House* (Boston, 1965), pp. 17–18.

Korean War was ended, and when McCarthyism was destroyed by the excesses of the Wisconsin Senator as well as by the opposition of his own party. Moreover, until Eisenhower's victory in 1952, the Republican party had still been fighting the Democratic party over the major issues of the 1930's. To many Republicans welfare state legislation and the internationalist nature of American diplomacy – both of which had been associated with Franklin Delano Roosevelt and Harry S. Truman – remained a menace to American ideals. When in power, on the other hand, Republicans found it both undesirable and impossible to return to a pre-New Deal state of affairs. Thus Eisenhower, particularly during his first administration, consolidated the domestic gains of the previous two decades and confirmed the direction taken by American foreign policy since 1938. His second administration, Rovere sadly admits, was an abysmal failure because of his refusal to confront the newer realities of his day. The stage, therefore, was set for a new leader to deal with problems that could no longer be evaded.

The general approach of the Progressive school of historiography to the postwar era has, therefore – at least in its broad outlines – already taken shape. Eisenhower, in many respects, represents in the 1950's what Hoover had been in the 1920's. Similarly, John F. Kennedy occupies the same relationship to his times that the two Roosevelts did to their own. Reacting to the sterility of American life during the 1950's, Progressive scholars have said, John F. Kennedy was the individual who reawakened the American people from their long slumber and made them aware of the problems and issues of their day. Unlike Eisenhower, he actively committed the nation to a set of ideals as well as to the realization that their national power was less than omnipotent.

In the final selection Richard E. Neustadt attempts a preliminary appraisal of the career of John F. Kennedy. At the outset Neustadt lays down the standards by which he judges a president: his purposes, sensitivity, feel for his office and its powers; his ability to perform under pressure; and finally, his legacy to posterity. To judge Kennedy, of course, is a difficult task because an assassin's bullet removed him prematurely from office. On the whole, Neustadt concludes, Kennedy will go down in history as one of the better presidents. In foreign affairs, his sense of realism was such that he taught his nation that "total victory" in a nuclear age was an unrealistic illusion. On the domestic side, Kennedy undertook an irreversible commitment to civil rights and a pledge to make the economy function effectively for meaningful growth, thus providing a better life for all Americans. According to Neustadt, Kennedy created also an atmosphere in which intelligent discussion of controversial issues was possible. Above all, he showed how a president ought to deal with the problem of nuclear confrontation.

Oddly enough, neo-conservative historians, as compared with their Progressive counterparts, have written relatively little about the postwar era. On the contrary, much of their writings were concerned with the broader problem of interpreting the nature of the American experience as a whole and delineating the unique characteristics of Americans. Unlike Progressive historians, therefore, they did not periodize American history nor did they see the past in terms of a conflict between the democratic masses struggling to free themselves from the dominance of the aristocratic class — however the latter might be identified in different periods of American history. Americans, these neo-conservative writers emphasized, were not divided by hostile and competing ideologies; the differences between individuals and groups were differences that arose out of efforts to elaborate a common theme in various ways. To put it another way, the genius of America lay in the fact that its people subordinated rigid ideological formulas to a sensible pragmatism in meeting the problems that they faced.

Since they interpreted the American national character in such pragmatic and nonideological terms, these historians found it difficult, if not impossible, to write about the 1950's and 1960's in terms of conservative and liberal categories. Precisely because of their emphasis on the idea of consensus, they could not find any differences on fundamentals separating Americans. Instead, they stressed the underlying assumptions that all Americans had in common. The result was an inability to write about the post-World War II era in terms of conflict or to separate succinctly the differences between Democratic and Republican policies. Since the American people as well as their political representatives were in accord on fundamentals, there was no need to write about recent history by polarizing or conceptualizing differences where such differences were nonexistent.

The direction taken by the neo-conservative school of historiography was especially evident in the writings of Daniel J. Boorstin, one of the outstanding contemporary American historians. In 1953 Boorstin attempted to define the essential traits of American civilization. To make his point, he used a biblical analogy. When the Temple of Solomon in Jerusalem fell in 63 B.C. and Pompey entered it, he found much to his amazement that it was empty. "This was, of course," wrote Boorstin, "a symbol of the absence of idolatry, which was the essential truth of Judaism. Perhaps the same surprise awaits the student of American culture, if he finally manages to penetrate the arcanum of our belief. And for a similar reason. Far from being disappointed, we should be inspired that in an era of idolatry, when so many nations have filled their sanctuaries with ideological idols, we have had the courage to refuse to do so." [5] To Boorstin Americans did not need ideologies or plans to remake their society; the absence of fundamental antagonisms rendered this superfluous. Celebrating the uniqueness and morality of American institutions, Boorstin saw no reason to write about differences.

The split between the Progressive and neo-conservative schools of American historiography should not, of course, be overly exaggerated; many contemporary historians fall midway between the two extremes. Nevertheless, the different assumptions that are characteristic of both schools raise important issues for students seeking to understand the significance of the American experience. Obviously, the neo-conservative argument has some element of truth in its contention that all societies, if they are to survive, must hold some values and assumptions in common. Yet to deny, as many neo-conservative scholars have done, the absence of real (as compared with psychological or imaginary) conflicts gives rise to a portrait of the American past that would probably be unintelligible to earlier generations. As John Higham, an outstanding contemporary historian whose sympathies clearly lie with the Progressive school, has perceptively written:

> The advantages of this [neo-conservative] point of view for American historians have not been slight. It has enabled them to cut through the too easy dualisms of progressive historiog-

5. Daniel J. Boorstin, *The Genius of American Politics* (Chicago, 1953), p. 170.

raphy. It is inspiring them to do important and original work in understanding American institutions. They should continue to do so. The conservative frame of reference, however, creates a paralyzing incapacity to deal with the elements of spontaneity, effervescence, and violence in American history. . . .

Moreover, contemporary conservatism has a deadening effect on the historian's ability to take a conflict of ideas seriously. Either he disbelieves in the conflict itself (Americans have been pretty much of one mind), or he trivializes it into a set of psychological adjustments to institutional change. In either case, the current fog of complacency, flecked with anxiety, spreads backward over the American past.

It is not likely in the near future that many critical scholars will emphasize the polarities that fascinated the great progressive historians, nor is it desirable that they should. Certainly no one contends today that the debate between Jefferson and Hamilton, or between human rights and property rights, frames our intellectual history. But to stand Parrington and Beard on their heads does not solve the problem. American thought has had other dialectical patterns, which the present cult of consensus hides. Above all, perhaps, that cult neutralizes some moral issues that have played a not entirely petty or ignoble part in the history of the United States. To rediscover their grandeur and urgency, historians do not need the categories of Beard and Parrington. . . . But we pay a cruel price in dispensing with their deeper values: an appreciation of the crusading spirit, a responsiveness to indignation, a sense of injustice.[6]

6. John Higham, "The Cult of the 'American Consensus': Homogenizing Our History," *Commentary,* XXVII (February, 1959), 100.

William V. Shannon

ACROSS a divided and militarily defenseless Europe, the shadow of Stalin's armies fell; in Korea, Communist Chinese forces pushed American armies back toward the sea; in the United States, Joseph McCarthy scored his first major political triumph, and the Fulbright Committee investigation began to uncover a vein of corruption in the national administration. It was a grim time for Americans. It was November 1950.

When President Truman summoned General Dwight D. Eisenhower to his private study in the White House one afternoon that month to ask him to return to active duty and become chief of the NATO forces in Western Europe, he called upon one of the few Americans who commanded universal respect and admiration. The image of Eisenhower, the liberator of Nazi-occupied Europe, stood bright and untarnished. He was a symbol of the nation's triumphant and united national purpose in a time when the national consensus was fracturing and the national mood becoming querulous and ugly. Eisenhower's acceptance of his new military assignment ended his brief civilian career as president of Columbia University. It restored him to the center of the public scene where in the decade to follow he was to be the dominant figure. His dominance of the age did not derive from any personal mastery of its diverse forces. A central personality may epitomize the spirit of an era and symbolize its prevailing balance of political forces without necessarily transforming the one or controlling the other. As the decade of the 20's is inextricably linked with Calvin Coolidge and the 30's with Franklin Roosevelt, the 1950's in our political history is likely to be known as the age of Eisenhower.

Although Eisenhower has two years still to serve, his place in

"Eisenhower as President: A Critical Appraisal of the Record," reprinted from *Commentary,* XXVI (November, 1958), by permission; copyright © 1958 by the American Jewish Committee.

WILLIAM V. SHANNON (1927–) is a member of the editorial board of *The New York Times.* He has contributed regularly to the *New Republic, Commonweal,* and other periodicals, and has also written *The American Irish* (1963).

history and the significance of his presidency are already becoming clear. Eisenhower is a transitional figure. He has not shaped the future nor tried to repeal the past. He has not politically organized nor intellectually defined a new consensus. When he leaves office in January 1961, the foreign policies and the domestic policies of the past generation will be about where he found them in 1953. No national problem, whether it be education, housing, urban revitalization, agriculture, or inflation, will have been advanced importantly toward solution nor its dimensions significantly altered. The Eisenhower era is the time of the great postponement. Dwight Eisenhower, the executor and trustee of the programs of his two Democratic predecessors whose contemporary he was (Eisenhower is only eight years younger than Franklin Roosevelt and six years younger than Harry Truman), already looms in history not as the first great figure of a new Republican age but the last of an old Democratic generation.

In assessing Eisenhower's status, it is worth recalling the somber, impassioned national mood which the sudden, savage turn in the Korean war created eight years ago this autumn. The emotions aroused by that war endangered the great double consensus on foreign affairs and domestic affairs which had been in the making since 1933. Eisenhower's historic function when he entered political life two years later was to end the war and preserve that consensus against the attacks of its enemies.

The domestic consensus had emerged out of the violent political struggles and intellectual gyrations of the New Deal period from 1933 to 1938. It rested on an irreversible common agreement that the Federal government has a responsibility to maintain the rudiments of a welfare state. Social security, unemployment compensation, and minimum wages were the basic features of this program, and its chief guarantors were the trade unions to whom the Wagner Act of 1935 had given firm legal status. The unionists and their unorganized but sympathetic fellow workers were the guarantors of the consensus because they were the most numerous and, compared to the farmers, the old-age pensioners, and other groups, the most politically dependable of all the New Deal beneficiaries. The Full Employment Act of 1946, the first year of the Truman administration, set a seal of official approval on this consensus but did not extend its range.

The other half of the national consensus, the half on foreign policy, had also begun under Roosevelt but had reached its more significant development during the Truman years. Roosevelt, by his aggressive championing of an internationalist position during the bitter isolationist-interventionist debate of 1940–41, established the basis for a national policy. His actions and his education of the public were essential first steps. He carried it further in his negotiations during the war with various Republican party personalities, looking toward our entry into a world organization. Truman completed this undertaking by leading the country into the United Nations. A genuine bipartisan collaboration during the next five years carried through the Marshall Plan, the Greek-Turkish program, the Berlin airlift, the Point Four program, and other achievements abroad. By 1950, the consensus on foreign policy was well established. It rested on the concept of containment. If Russian aggression in all its forms was firmly resisted, if the military and economic strength of the West were maintained and increased, and if the neutral, underdeveloped countries were not lost to Communism, it would be possible to avoid a third war and to leave the resolution of the cold war to the slow working of history.

Communist China's entry into the Korean war put the foreign policy consensus in jeopardy. The shocking defeats, the capture of thousands of our troops by the Communists, and the eventual bloody stalemate aroused many doubts and profound dissatisfaction. The scope of the war and its inherent nature intensified popular resentment and bafflement. It was clearly not a major war evoking the instinctive zeal and emotional commitment of the whole population; yet its duration and the thousands of dead and wounded made it more burdensome than the brief "brushfire wars" that the containment policy had seemed to postulate. If it was only "a police action," as President Truman called it, how could the government ask for wartime sacrifices? If it was a glorious struggle on behalf of the United Nations, why did the other UN members leave almost all of the fighting to us?

The anxieties were deep and shaking. The public, half-unconsciously and inarticulately, began the search for an alternative to the existing consensus. First, there was a brief, wild resurgence of the old isolationist impulse in early December 1950 when the drive to the Yalu turned into disastrous defeat. The momentary impulse to get our forces out of Korea and abandon the Asian mainland to the Chinese Communists receded once General Ridgway rallied our forces and stabilized the military situation. Second, there was the alternative of smashing our way out of the dilemmas of a containment policy by adopting a more venturesome course. This alternative drew upon feelings and posed choices ranging from the proposals for bombing across the Yalu in Manchuria to launching a preventive war "to get the whole thing over with." The popularity of this alternative policy of aggressive venturesomeness reached its height in the spring of 1951 when General MacArthur made his triumphant tour through the United States after his dismissal. This alternative began to fade during the prolonged, anti-climactic MacArthur hearings. There was yet a third alternative. Senator Joseph McCarthy and a few other senators propounded the view that the real source of danger was treason within. The tendency of those who propagated this alternative was to deprecate the importance of the Soviet Union's power and enormously inflate the real but limited and secondary dangers of Soviet espionage and political infiltration within this country. The minimizing of the Soviet Union's menace flattered many naively chauvinistic ideas about our own relative place in the sun; the exaggeration of the espionage-infiltration problem catered to a congeries of notions about foreigners, radicals, and Communists. And McCarthy's unexpectedly rich talents for political invention and propaganda gave this alternative a raging vitality which was only beginning in 1950 and did not lose force for more than four years.

As against the alarms and confusions of the isolationist, MacArthurian, and McCarthyite alternatives, Harry Truman and Dean Acheson, the two chief official exponents of the containment policy, made an ineffective defense. Truman was without the resources of rhetoric and the mastery of a grand style which would have enabled a Roosevelt or a Wilson to make an early and overpowering counterattack. Acheson was impaled by his own verbal indiscretions and his starchy public manner. They could only mechanically repeat the familiar platitudes about collective security, the United Nations, and the importance of having allies.

The times called for a man who could restate national purposes, reassert in more winning terms the basic truths underlying the foreign policy consensus, and thereby make possible once again the full concentration of national energies. The situation seemed to require a political figure who would personify the causes that united us rather than those which divided us. It was a situation, in a word, that was historically right for a conservative. The conservative aspiration in politics is always toward the ideal of unity, toward the assertion of proved values and established rationales, and directed toward the deliberate blurring of economic and political conflicts. Even more, the times were right for a certain kind of conservative whose appeal had proved valid in the American past. This was the military hero who had a conservative social background but was basically apolitical and who, although a military man, had the plain, even drab, style suitable in the chief of state of a profoundly civilian country. No "fancy Dans" like the elegant General George Brinton McClellan in 1864 or the imperial, proconsular General Douglas MacArthur in 1952 need apply. What was wanted was another Washington, another Grant. What was wanted, and what was so splendidly and self-evidently available for the asking, if the asking were insistent enough, was Dwight D. Eisenhower.

The connection between the conservative aspiration (one can scarcely call it, at least in this country, an ideology or a philosophy) and the military hero candidate is more than an expedient alliance. The ideal of national unity dominates the military ethos. Soldiers are trained to defend the existing social order rather than to examine it critically. Military officers see social and economic groups as components in the great design of national strength, not as dynamic participants battling one another in the social arena. If Eisenhower found the conservative Republicans with their dedication to the status quo and their resistance to rapid change more intellectually congenial than the liberal Democrats with their reformist tradition, he was no different from the great majority of his fellow officers. The military services are not a training school for liberals.

The natural affinity between political conservatives and a military hero has deep roots in the American past. George Washington, our first conservative president and also our first soldier president, set the mold. The conservative Whigs managed to elect only two presidents, General William "Tippecanoe"

Harrison in 1840 and General Zachary Taylor in 1848. The Republican politicians seeking to consolidate their hold on the country after the Civil War chose General Grant. Each of these men was relatively innocent of political ideas. Their appeal was based on the exploitation of their personality as a symbol of integrity and unity. Their campaigns were usually keyed to a simple idea. Grant, for example, said in 1868: "Let us have peace." Eisenhower, with the air of a man expressing a crystal clear idea, said repeatedly in 1952: "I believe our test should be — what is good for 155,000,000 Americans."

In the fall of 1949, Senator Arthur Vandenberg wrote in a private letter to a friend that he might support General Eisenhower in the next presidential contest. "I think the specifications call for a personality of great independent magnitude who can give our splintering American people an 'evangel' instead of an ordinary campaign," he wrote.

Three years in advance, Vandenberg had forecast Eisenhower's "Great Crusade." It was as the candidate of the more responsible Republicans interested in protecting the foreign policy consensus that the General entered politics. (In 1948 he had privately favored Vandenberg's own nomination with Harold Stassen as a running mate.) Lacking any alternative to Senator Taft, the Eastern Republicans successfully and plausibly argued with Eisenhower that he would only be carrying out his NATO mission in a different way. By blocking the coming to power of Taft and his neo-isolationist backers, Eisenhower would make certain that a foreign policy oriented toward the defense of Europe and aligned with the principles of the UN would continue to prevail.

Once nominated, Eisenhower necessarily took into account the three principal strains of Republican party criticism of existing foreign policy. Speaking about the Korean war in Peoria, Illinois, he projected the goal of the ultimate withdrawal of American troops from mainland Asia. If there had to be wars there, "let Asians fight Asians." This remark delighted the devout readers of the Chicago *Tribune*. It evoked glowing words of praise from troglodyte politicians like ex-Senator C. Wayland "Curly" Brooks. But it was meaningless. As army chief of staff in 1946–48, Eisenhower had repeatedly and successfully recommended the withdrawal of American troops from Korea. Moreover, it was settled national military policy to avoid stationing troops on the Asian mainland. But this was quite different from disengaging ourselves completely from our interests and responsibilities on that continent. The Peoria speech was only a fugitive gesture to the isolationists.

Eisenhower made more ambiguous gestures in the direction of the aggressive alternative symbolized by General MacArthur. He allowed himself the liberty of condemning the "negativism" of the containment policy and of referring vaguely to the "liberation" and the "rolling back" of the Communist empire. He promised to go to Korea but he left open the question whether he would end the war by extending it to gain a decisive military victory, or try to end it by continuing the armistice negotiations. The campaign rhetoric unfortunately persisted after election day. In his first State of the Union message, Eisenhower "unleashed" Chiang Kai-shek. Secretary of State Dulles wordily threatened the Communists with "massive retaliation" at times and places of our own choosing. The administration strengthened the government's propaganda forces to wage psychological warfare, seize the strategic initiative, liberate the satellite states by radio broadcasts, and attain various other doubtlessly worthy if uncertain ends. Two crises in the Formosa Straits have demonstrated Chiang Kai-shek is not a free agent; the Hungarian revolution proved the United States had no intention of risking anything to liberate the satellite peoples.

Eisenhower, during the 1952 campaign and for a period thereafter, accommodated himself in small, symbolic ways to the emotional thrust of McCarthyism. He deleted a brief word of praise for General Marshall, his patron, from his Milwaukee speech; he affirmed vigorously his determination to clear the Communists out of government, to encourage the work of the Federal Bureau of Investigation, and to cooperate with the investigating committees of Congress, clearly implying the Truman administration had been remiss, if not treasonable, in these matters. He did not avow belief in the McCarthyite conspiracy theory of the origin of the country's troubles but, to the dismay of some of his admirers in both parties and former colleagues in the Roosevelt and Truman administrations, neither did he disavow it.

Eisenhower's strategy in waging the "Great Crusade" was the only one possible for him given the plasticity of his temperament, his unintellectual cast of mind, and his confident, optimistic nature. He did not separate the sheep from the goats; he welcomed all dissidents to his cause, committed himself in an irretrievable way only to invulnerable platitudes, and hinted genially that in his new synthesis a reconciliation of all divergent elements would be possible. This may not have been the internationalist "evangel" that Vandenberg and his other original supporters had in mind, but it is typical of successful party leaders in our country. Franklin Roosevelt, for example, was able in 1932 to hold the loyalty and quicken the hopes of Huey Long and Bernard Baruch, of Harry Byrd and George Norris. Roosevelt organized his coalition with care and calculation while Eisenhower, gifted with some of the instincts if not the insight and expertise of a successful politician, apparently only did what came naturally to him. If his tactics did not rally a newly broadened and better informed support for the foreign policy consensus, they served at least to deaden and to dissipate the pressures for any serious change from that policy. Eisenhower's fabian tactics carried through successfully the defensive holding action which Truman and Acheson after 1950 could no longer sustain.

As against this negative but vitally important accomplishment, Eisenhower's own positive initiatives in foreign affairs dwindled into insignificance. The Baghdad pact in the Middle East and the SEATO pact in the Far East are pale imitations of the NATO pact in Europe. They have proved irrelevant, if not noxious, diplomatic devices. The administration's ambivalent attitude toward Nasser brought the Atlantic Alliance almost to the breaking point in the Suez affair, but our common interests with Britain are so strong they can survive almost any shock; under Prime Minister Macmillan's soothing ministrations, the alliance re-formed itself. Eisenhower has given hospitality in his administration to MacArthurite tendencies in the persons of Assistant Secretary of State Walter Robertson and Admiral Arthur Radford, but he has heeded their counsel scarcely more than his predecessor did the words of MacArthur himself. Eisenhower has tried the "great man theory" of diplomacy at the summit in Geneva and Dulles has subjected himself to innumerable conferences and journeyings, but no new approaches to the Soviet monolith have developed and none of the old has availed much. Eisenhower settled for truces in Korea and

Indo-China, leaving those countries divided and their future unsettled. This is the kind of minimum accommodation between the Communist and non-Communist worlds which the original containment concept had envisaged.

Holding the line and protecting the gains of the past worked well enough in Europe where in the Eisenhower years the situation has remained virtually stable. Secretary Dulles threatened the French with an agonizing reappraisal, but the French were supremely indifferent. So in the end was the Secretary of State. The European Defense Community died, the British and French patched up a reasonable substitute, and the only agonizing was done by the Secretary's Democratic critics. Career diplomats worked out a compromise solution of the Trieste affair, the Russians relinquished their grip on Austria, and the United States kept the line open to Tito in Belgrade. Germany remained divided. Europe remained divided.

In the Middle East and the Far East, however, creative policy making was called for. The situations were less stable and the inherited guide lines of policy were less well developed. Eisenhower had no contribution to make to the hard problems of Arab and Israeli, of African nationalism, of Communist China's menace to Southeast Asia, of Indonesia's interior decay, and of India's economic viability. He held the line and beyond that he could not go. When he got in trouble on a foreign policy issue in these areas of the world, it was usually because he applied the lessons of the post-war past rigidly and almost mechanically. He reacted to the Anglo-French-Israeli war with Egypt as if it were the Communist invasion of South Korea all over again. When the Chinese Communists shelled Quemoy and Matsu in 1958, he again reacted: hold the line. When Democratic critics attacked him for a lack of discrimination in applying the principle of resisting Communist pressure, Eisenhower responded only with a stubborn reiteration of the principle. At his press conference on October 15, 1958, a reporter asked him if he believed the expression of opposition views on Quemoy "actually weakens the administration's position or ability to negotiate." Eisenhower replied:

> No, not always, but I will tell you: there is a very clear distinction to be made with respect to foreign policy as I see it. One is the policy and one is its operation.

Every single day there are new and tough decisions that have to be made within a foreign policy, but if you go back to 1947 [the date of the Truman Doctrine and the beginning of the Marshall Plan] and see the statements that are made about opposing the territorial expansion of Communism by force, when you go back and see what our policy went into in the effort to develop collective security, mutual aid, technical assistance, that kind of thing that . . . at least will help to make the free world stronger collectively and each individual nation as opposed to Communism, that when you come down to it are the basic parts of the policy.

At times, humans, being human, are going to make errors. And therefore I do not, by any means, decry intelligent questioning and criticism of any particular point. But when it comes to the policy that is being established, *I think it has been standing pretty well on its own feet for a long time* (italics added).

Eisenhower's clear distinction between a policy and the carrying out of that policy may be simpleminded, but future historians are not likely to find a better or more revealing extemporaneous tribute to the foreign policy consensus. Eisenhower's caretaker attitude is clear. His and Dulles's day-to-day decisions do not matter; only the policy matters, and it has an autonomous life of its own not really greatly dependent on their daily actions and judgments.

When Harry Truman ordered American troops into Korea in June 1950, he did not know that he was killing his Fair Deal domestic program. War and liberalism always go ill together, but when the Korean conflict began few foresaw how it would transform the domestic economic scene and jeopardize the national consensus on domestic policy. When the war broke the country was just pulling itself out of the mild recession of 1949–50. With more than 4,000,000 unemployed and farm prices drifting downward, the overriding problem seemed to be how to avoid a possible depression. The Truman administration was ready to adopt the familiar Keynesian solutions of deficit financing and easier credit. Meanwhile, Truman in the 81st Congress of 1949–50 pushed hard for an extension of the welfare state program. He recommended the Brannan farm plan, Federal health insurance, fair employment practices legislation, increased slum clearance, and Federal aid to education. The country seemed lethargic and a bit hesitant about these proposals. The Democratic congressional majorities elected in 1948 were not quite large enough to pass them. Except for the Wagner-Ellender-Taft Housing Act of 1949 which passed with Republican cooperation, all of these measures failed by a few votes. Yet it would require only small Democratic gains in the November 1950 elections to insure their passage.

The Korean war, however, not only benefited the Republicans at the polls and made the 82nd Congress in 1951–52 considerably more conservative than its predecessor, but also touched off a severe inflation. Unemployment vanished, farm prices soared, and the high cost of living replaced the threat of joblessness as a key domestic issue.

The emergence of the inflation issue played an important part in Eisenhower's first victory and has been significant in influencing the tone of his administration. The fear of inflation greatly helped him to organize a new majority coalition in the country and end the Republican party's chronic minority status. Before 1952, the Republican party drew its strength principally from three groups. One was the more sophisticated Eastern industrial and financial community and its allies in the press, clergy, and universities, this was an elite group, small in numbers but important in terms of wealth, prestige, and influence in the mass communication industries. By a British analogy, these voters, overwhelmingly but not exclusively Republican, make up what might be called the American Establishment. These were the people who had organized the successful Willkie boom in 1940 and had subsequently more or less accepted Governor Dewey and his associate Herbert Brownell as their political agents. A second group was the less sophisticated, much more numerous but relatively less effective, hard-shelled conservative business and commercial people of the smaller cities and towns of the Midwest. Their idol was Robert A. Taft. These voters gave, at most, grudging acceptance to the great consensus; some hoped for a withdrawal into isolation, others resented labor unions. The strongest conviction they shared was that government cost too much, that the budget should always be balanced, and taxes reduced promptly. The third group were the farmers who had voted predominantly Republican since the midterm election of 1938. These three groups were not enough to make a majority. The

Democrats were able to maintain themselves in power with the support of the captive South and the second and third-generation immigrant community voters in the nation's dozen largest metropolitan areas.

Eisenhower cracked the Democratic big cities and the high cost of living was probably his most potent weapon. He made sharp gains among housewives. Moreover, he broke into the ranks of the young voters. During the 1930's and 40's, voters under thirty had been heavily Democratic. By 1952, however, many young war veterans bore a burden of fixed charges in their mortgaged suburban homes, with appliances bought on the installment plan, driving cars purchased through a finance company. In abstract economic theory, debtors benefit from inflation, but as a practical matter many of these voters felt they were losing in the dollar race. They feared their wages and salaries would not keep pace with rising prices. They voted for Eisenhower.

However, there were other causes bidding for the allegiances of these voters being detached from the old Democratic urban coalition. One of them was McCarthyism. McCarthy had an entree to these voters because, like many of them, he was Catholic and of immigrant ancestry. He was also relatively young and a war veteran. He was a demagogue with a simple issue to exploit who made a biting, raucous, emotional appeal. For these voters, his appeal was quite a new and different experience contrasted to the stodgy, Chamber of Commerce rhetoric they had been accustomed to hear from Republican orators.

The only real threat to the domestic economic consensus established in the New Deal and perpetuated in Truman's Fair Deal would come from a genuine linkage between working-class- and lower-middle-class urban voters, attracted by a non-economic issue like McCarthyism, and the regular Republican voters of the more hard-shelled, conservative, Midwestern school. If the Republican ticket in 1952 had been Taft and Knowland instead of Eisenhower and Nixon, this linkage might have had serious consequences. A right-wing Republican administration much indebted to the emotional dynamism of the McCarthyites for its victory might have attempted a genuine counter-revolution to reverse many of the verdicts of the 30's and 40's embodied in the economic consensus. Eisenhower's nomination forestalled this eventuality. He absorbed the McCarthyite frenzy into his own "Great Crusade" where in subsequent years it died of inanition.

In terms of the internal dynamics of the Republican party, therefore, Eisenhower's victory in November 1952 had several meanings. It meant much of the potential McCarthy following had been detached from his orbit and their fears, dissatisfactions, and status tensions given a different kind of political expression. "I Like Ike" was a harmless substitute for hating the targets McCarthy singled out. The Eisenhower victory meant that millions of lifelong Republican voters were doomed to a new frustration. The "hard-shells" hoping for a permanent cut in foreign aid, a crackdown on labor, or a big reduction in taxes and the budget had contributed to a victory that in terms of these objectives had no meaning. The Eisenhower victory also meant that there were now millions of voters momentarily enlisted in the Republican cause who had never been in the party before; they had been attracted by "Ike" 's personality, by his promise to bring down the cost of living, and by a desire to escape the Korean stalemate. And finally the victory meant that the predominant Republican wing of the American Establishment was, for the first time in a generation, in power in an administration of its own choosing.

The Eisenhower performance was bound to disappoint at least some of these divergent groups. In practice, it has disappointed them all, and for an odd reason. Upon taking Office, Eisenhower, the choice of the more sophisticated Republicans, turned out to have many of the convictions of the most Tory adherents of Taft: he did not share their animus against union labor, but otherwise he was a true disciple of the Old Guard orthodoxy. He believed in the absolute primacy of thrift, he wanted to return government functions to the states, he believed deficit financing was sin, he believed high taxes and government regulations were "stifling free enterprise." Eisenhower in the White House was closer to an Iowa Rotarian than to a Wall Street banker. He was the man from Abilene, Kansas, not the man from Morningside Heights.

The Eisenhower administration vaguely disappointed many in the Eastern elite who had hoped for more positive leadership. Nelson Rockefeller symbolized this discreet discontent when he left the administration and financed a series of reports on public issues urging ambitious programs far more costly than Eisenhower would countenance. The blue-ribbon members of the committee which presented the Gaither Report on national defense filed, in effect, a dissent to Eisenhower's concept of the national interest.

Eisenhower and Agriculture Secretary Benson, committed to the view that subsidies were intrinsically wrong and that what farmers desired above all was the liberation from government marketing and production restraints, did not abolish subsidies, restraints, or surpluses, but they did manage to alienate the farmers, a dwindling but still sizable Republican voting bloc.

The newer Republicans, converted in 1952 in the cities and the suburbs, should have been reassured by the administration's preoccupation with the inflation problem and "the stable dollar." To some extent they were, but they had other tangible concerns such as the schools their children attended and the cost of medical care for their aged parents. The Eisenhower administration, penny-pinched and budget-obsessed, sabotaged the annual legislative drives for Federal aid to schools, cut back the slum clearance program almost to a nullity, and on the whole failed to demonstrate that it was vitally concerned with the needs of the urban and lower-income voters. The latter retained their "liking for Ike," but as early as 1954 and in increasing numbers they, like many farmers, began to re-identify their own economic welfare with the Democratic party. The gap between Eisenhower's popularity and that of the Republican party widened rather than narrowed as his years in the White House progressed.

The hard-shell Republicans who should have been most pleased at the President's unanticipated sharing of their convictions have been disillusioned by his lack of fighting zeal. If the budget were to be balanced at a modest level, income taxes substantially reduced, the balance of functions between the Federal and state governments shifted, and the trend to big government reversed, it would require as many violent political struggles as it took to pass the New Deal in the first place. It would probably be necessary, for example, to pass a national right-to-work law, forbid industry-wide collective bargaining, and break the political activities of the labor unions. On no front has Eisenhower undertaken a struggle of this magnitude. If his limited physical strength and his limited intellectual interest in this sort of problem were not sufficient to debar such a conflict, his desire for national unity and harmony would in any case prevent it. The domestic consensus rests secure in his hands.

Arthur Larson, the quondam philosopher of "Modern Republicanism," propounded the thesis in his book *A Republican Looks At His Party* (1956) that the Republican party under Eisenhower's leadership had "for the first time in our history discovered and established the Authentic American Center in politics." The Eisenhower administration expressed an "American Consensus." The steady decay of the Republican party at the state and congressional district level throughout the Eisenhower years is enough to discredit this thesis. Parties which have formulated a widely accepted consensus on the big contemporary issues and are united behind a great leader do not show these alarming signs of disaffection and disrepair.

There is an American Consensus on the issues, but it was developed by Franklin Roosevelt and developed further in some respects by Truman. Eisenhower has been content to leave it undisturbed. His few attempts to return to the "little government" of a bygone day have been abortive. Two statistics alone are enough to account for his defeat: there are 40,000,000 more Americans than there were twenty years ago and more than one-third of all Americans now live in states other than those in which they grew up. The growing population makes the pressure for increased government services irresistible and the mobility of that population makes it equally inevitable that the people look to the Federal government to supply those services as state loyalties disappear and state boundaries become unreal.

Eisenhower did disturb the old political balance of power as distinguished from the consensus on issues, but he had not the energies, the talents, nor the experience to exploit his personal triumphs for his party's advantage.

Eisenhower has been the great leader *manqué*. His dignified bearing, his warm flashing smile, his easy manners made him seem a man with whom most voters could feel at ease, and his hero's reputation made him seem a man in whom they could safely trust their destiny. Has their trust been misplaced? The answer lies in America's margin for error. Eisenhower and his administration have lived off the accumulated wisdom, the accumulated prestige, and the accumulated military strength of his predecessors who conducted more daring and more creative regimes. If our margin for error is as great as it has traditionally been, these quiet Eisenhower years will have been only a pleasant idyll, an inexpensive interlude in a grim century. If our margin for error is much thinner than formerly, Eisenhower may join the ranks of history's fatal good men, the Stanley Baldwins and the James Buchanans. Their intentions were good and their example is pious, but they bequeathed to their successors a black heritage of time lost and opportunities wasted.

Richard Hofstadter

TWENTY YEARS AGO the dynamic force in American political life came from the side of liberal dissent, from the impulse to reform the inequities of our economic and social system and to change our ways of doing things, to the end that the sufferings of the Great Depression would never be repeated. Today the dynamic force in our political life no longer comes from the liberals who made the New Deal possible. By 1952 the liberals had had at least the trappings of power for twenty years. They could look back to a brief, exciting period in the mid-thirties when they had held power itself and had been able to transform the economic and administrative life of the nation. After twenty years the New Deal liberals have quite unconsciously taken on the psychology of those who have entered into possession. Moreover, a large part of the New Deal public, the jobless, distracted and bewildered men of 1933, have in the course of the years found substantial places in society for themselves, have become home-owners, suburbanites and solid citizens. Many of them still keep the emotional commitments to the liberal dissent with which they grew up politically, but their social position is one of solid comfort. Among them the dominant tone has become one of satisfaction, even of a kind of conservatism. Insofar as Adlai Stevenson won their enthusiasm in 1952, it was not in spite of, but in part because of the air of poised and reliable conservatism that he brought to the Democratic convention. By comparison, Harry Truman's impassioned rhetoric, with its occasional thrusts at "Wall Street," seemed passé and rather embarrassing. The change did not escape Stevenson himself. "The strange alchemy of time," he said in a speech at Columbus, "has

"The Pseudo-Conservative Revolt," *The American Scholar,* XXIV (Winter, 1954–1955), 9–27. Reprinted with omissions by permission of Alfred A. Knopf, Inc., from *The Paranoid Style in American Politics* by Richard Hofstadter. The essay is reprinted in its original version.

RICHARD HOFSTADTER (1916–   ) is Professor of American History at Columbia University. He is the author of more than half a dozen books in American history, including *The American Political Tradition and the Men Who Made It* (1948) and *Anti-Intellectualism in American Life* (1963).

somehow converted the Democrats into the truly conservative party of this country — the party dedicated to conserving all that is best, and building solidly and safely on these foundations." The most that the old liberals can now envisage is not to carry on with some ambitious new program, but simply to defend as much as possible of the old achievements and to try to keep traditional liberties of expression that are threatened.

There is, however, a dynamic of dissent in America today. Representing no more than a modest fraction of the electorate, it is not so powerful as the liberal dissent of the New Deal era, but it is powerful enough to set the tone of our political life and to establish throughout the country a kind of punitive reaction. The new dissent is certainly not radical — there are hardly any radicals of any sort left — nor is it precisely conservative. Unlike most of the liberal dissent of the past, the new dissent not only has no respect for nonconformism, but is based upon a relentless demand for conformity. It can most accurately be called pseudo-conservative — I borrow the term from the study of *The Authoritarian Personality* published five years ago by Theodore W. Adorno and his associates — because its exponents, although they believe themselves to be conservatives and usually employ the rhetoric of conservatism, show signs of a serious and restless dissatisfaction with American life, traditions and institutions. They have little in common with the temperate and compromising spirit of true conservatism in the classical sense of the word, and they are far from pleased with the dominant practical conservatism of the moment as it is represented by the Eisenhower Administration. Their political reaction express rather a profound if largely unconscious hatred of our society and its ways — a hatred which one would hesitate to impute to them if one did not have suggestive clinical evidence.

From clinical interviews and thematic apperception tests, Adorno and his co-workers found that their pseudo-conservative subjects, although given to a form of political expression that combines a curious mixture of largely conservative with occasional radical notions, succeed in concealing from themselves impulsive tendencies that, if released in action, would be very far from conservative. The pseudo-conservative, Adorno writes, shows "conventionality and authoritarian submissiveness" in his conscious thinking and "violence, anarchic impulses, and chaotic destructiveness in the unconscious sphere. . . . The pseudo conservative is a man who, in the name of upholding traditional American values and institutions and defending them against more or less fictitious dangers, consciously or unconsciously aims at their abolition."

Who is the pseudo-conservative, and what does he want? It is impossible to identify him by class, for the pseudo-conservative impulse can be found in practically all classes in society, although its power probably rests largely upon its appeal to the less educated members of the middle classes. The ideology of pseudo-conservatism can be characterized but not defined, because the pseudo-conservative tends to be more than ordinarily incoherent about politics. The lady who, when General Eisenhower's victory over Senator Taft had finally become official, stalked out of the Hilton Hotel declaiming, "This means eight more years of socialism" was probably a fairly good representative of the pseudo-conservative mentality. So also were the gentlemen who, at the Freedom Congress held at Omaha over a year ago by some "patriotic" organizations, objected to Earl Warren's appointment to the Supreme Court with the assertion: "Middle-of-the-road thinking can and will destroy us"; the general who spoke to the same group, demanding "an Air Force capable of wiping out the Russian Air Force and industry in one sweep," but also "a material reduction in military expenditures"; the people who a few years ago believed simultaneously that we had no business to be fighting communism in Korea, but that the war should immediately be extended to an Asia-wide crusade against communism; and the most ardent supporters of the Bricker Amendment. Many of the most zealous followers of Senator McCarthy are also pseudo-conservatives; although there are presumably a great many others who are not.

The restlessness, suspicion and fear manifested in various phases of the pseudo-conservative revolt give evidence of the real suffering which the pseudo-conservative experiences in his capacity as a citizen. He believes himself to be living in a world in which he is spied upon, plotted against, betrayed, and very likely destined for total ruin. He feels that his liberties have been arbitrarily and outrageously invaded. He is opposed to almost everything that has happened in American politics for the past twenty years. He hates the very thought of Franklin D. Roosevelt. He is disturbed deeply by American participation in the United Nations, which he can see only as a sinister organization. He sees his own country as being so weak that it is constantly about to fall victim to subversion; and yet he feels that it is so all-powerful that any failure it may experience in getting its way in the world — for instance, in the Orient — cannot possibly be due to its limitations but must be attributed to its having been betrayed. He is the most bitter of all our citizens about our involvement in the wars of the past, but seems the least concerned about avoiding the next one. While he naturally does not like Soviet communism, what distinguishes him from the rest of us who also dislike it is that he shows little interest in, is often indeed bitterly hostile to such realistic measures as might actually strengthen the United States vis-à-vis Russia. He would much rather concern himself with the domestic scene, where communism is weak, than with those areas of the world where it is really strong and threatening. He wants to have nothing to do with the democratic nations of Western Europe, which seem to draw more of his ire than the Soviet Communists, and he is opposed to all "give-away programs" designed to aid and strengthen these nations. Indeed, he is likely to be antagonistic to most of the operations of our federal government except Congressional investigations, and to almost all of its expenditures. Not always, however, does he go so far as the speaker at the Freedom Congress who attributed the greater part of our national difficulties to "this nasty, stinking 16th [income tax] Amendment."

A great deal of pseudo-conservative thinking takes the form of trying to devise means of absolute protection against that betrayal by our own officialdom which the pseudo-conservative feels is always imminent. The Bricker Amendment, indeed, might be taken as one of the primary symptoms of pseudo-conservatism. Every dissenting movement brings its demand for Constitutional changes; and the pseudo-conservative revolt, far from being an exception to this principle, seems to specialize in Constitutional revision, at least as a speculative enterprise. The widespread latent hostility toward American institutions takes the form, among other things, of a flood of proposals to write drastic changes into the body of our fundamental law. Last summer, in a characteristically astute piece, Richard Rovere pointed out that Constitution-amending had become almost a major diversion in the Eighty-third Congress. About a hundred amendments were introduced and referred to committee. Several of these called for the repeal of the income tax. Several embodied formulas of various kinds to limit non-military expenditures to some fixed portion of the national income. One proposed to bar all federal expenditures on "the general welfare"; another, to prohibit American troops from serving in any foreign country except on the soil of the potential enemy; another, to redefine treason to embrace not only persons trying to overthrow the government but also those trying to "weaken" it, even by peaceful means. The last proposal might bring the pseudo-conservative rebels themselves under the ban of treason: for the sum total of these amendments might easily serve to bring the whole structure of American society crashing to the ground.

As Mr. Rovere points out, it is not unusual for a large number of Constitutional amendments to be lying about somewhere in the Congressional hoppers. What is unusual is the readiness the Senate has shown to give them respectful consideration, and the peculiar populistic arguments some of its leading members have used to justify referring them to the state legislatures. While the ordinary Congress hardly ever has occasion to consider more than one amendment, the Eighty-third Congress saw six Constitutional amendments brought to the floor of the Senate, all summoning simple majorities, and four winning the two-thirds majority necessary before they can be sent to the House and ultimately to the state legislatures. It must be added that, with the possible exception of the Bricker Amendment itself, none of the six amendments so honored can be classed with the most extreme proposals. But the pliability of the senators, the eagerness of some of them to pass the buck and defer to "the people of the country," suggests how strong they feel the pressure to be for some kind of change that will give expression to that vague desire to repudiate the past that underlies the pseudo-conservative revolt.

One of the most urgent questions we can ask about the United States in our time is the question of where all this sentiment arose. The readiest answer is that the new pseudo-conservatism is simply the old ultra-conservatism and the old isolationism heightened by the extraordinary pressures of the contemporary world. This answer, true though it may be, gives a deceptive sense of familiarity without much deepening our understanding, for the particular patterns of American isolationism and extreme right-wing thinking have themselves not been very satisfactorily explored. It will not do, to take but one example, to say that some people want the income tax amendment repealed because taxes have become very heavy in the past twenty years: for this will not explain why, of three people in the same tax bracket, one will grin and bear it and continue to support social welfare legislation as well as an adequate defense, while another responds by supporting in a matter-of-fact way the practical conservative leadership of the moment, and the third finds his feelings satisfied only by the angry conspiratorial accusations and extreme demands of the pseudo-conservative.

No doubt the circumstances determining the political style of any individual are complex. Although I am concerned here to discuss some of the neglected social-psychological elements in pseudo-conservatism, I do not wish to appear to deny the presence of important economic and political causes. I am aware, for instance, that wealthy reactionaries try to use pseudo-conservative organizers, spokesmen and groups to propagate their notions of public policy, and that some organizers of pseudo-conservative and "patriotic" groups often find in this work a means of making a living — thus turning a tendency toward paranoia into a vocational asset, probably one of the most perverse forms of occupational therapy known to man. A number of other circumstances — the drastic inflation and heavy taxes of our time, the dissolution of American urban life, considerations of partisan political expediency — also play a part. But none of these things seem to explain the broad appeal of pseudo-conservatism, its emotional intensity, its dense and massive irrationality, or some of the peculiar ideas it generates. Nor will they explain why those who profit by the organized movements find such a ready following among a large number of people, and why the rank-and-file janizaries of pseudo-conservatism are so eager to hurl accusations, write letters to congressmen and editors, and expend so much emotional energy and crusading idealism upon causes that plainly bring them no material reward.

Elmer Davis, seeking to account for such sentiment in his recent book, *But We Were Born Free,* ventures a psychological hypothesis. He concludes, if I understand him correctly, that the genuine difficulties of our situation in the face of the power of international communism have inspired a widespread feeling of fear and frustration, and that those who cannot face these problems in a more rational way "take it out on their less influential neighbors, in the mood of a man who, being afraid to stand up to his wife in a domestic argument, relieves his feelings by kicking the cat." This suggestion has the merit of both simplicity and plausibility, and it may begin to account for a portion of the pseudo-conservative public. But while we may dismiss our curiosity about the man who kicks the cat by remarking that some idiosyncrasy in his personal development has brought him to this pass, we can hardly help but wonder whether there are not, in the backgrounds of the hundreds of thousands of persons who are moved by the pseudo-conservative impulse, some commonly shared circumstances that will help to account for their all kicking the cat in unison.

All of us have reason to fear the power of international communism, and all our lives are profoundly affected by it. Why do some Americans try to face this threat for what it is, a problem that exists in a world-wide theater of action, while others try to reduce it largely to a matter of domestic conformity? Why do some of us prefer to look for allies in the democratic world, while others seem to prefer authoritarian allies or none at all? Why do the pseudo-conservatives express such a persistent fear and suspicion of *their own government,* whether its leadership rests in the hands of Roosevelt, Truman or Eisenhower? Why is the pseudo-conservative impelled to go beyond the more or less routine partisan argument that we have been the victims of considerable misgovernment during the past twenty years to the disquieting accusation that we have actually been the victims of persistent conspiracy and betrayal — "twenty years of treason"? Is it not true, moreover, that political types very similar to the pseudo-conservative have had a long history in the United States, and that this history goes back to a time when the Soviet power did not loom nearly so large on our mental horizons? Was the Ku Klux Klan, for instance, which was responsibly estimated to have had a membership of from 4,000,000 to 4,500,000 persons at its peak in the 1920's, a phenomenon totally dissimilar to the pseudo-conservative revolt?

What I wish to suggest — and I do so in the spirit of one setting forth nothing more than a speculative hypothesis — is that pseudo-conservatism is in good part a product of the rootlessness and heterogeneity of American life, and above all, of its peculiar scramble for status and its peculiar search for secure identity. Normally there is a world of difference between one's sense of national identity or cultural belonging and one's social status. However, in American historical development, these two things, so easily distinguishable in analysis, have been jumbled together in reality, and it is precisely this that has given such a special poignancy and urgency to our status-strivings. In this country a person's status — that is, his relative place in the prestige hierarchy of his community — and his rudimentary sense of belonging to the community — that is, what we call his "Americanism" — have been intimately joined. Because, as a people extremely democratic in our social institutions, we have had no clear, consistent and recognizable system of status, our personal status problems have an unusual intensity. Because we no longer have the relative ethnic homogeneity we had up to about eighty years ago, our sense of belonging has long had about it a high degree of uncertainty. We boast of "the melting pot," but we are not quite sure what it is that will remain when we have been melted down.

We have always been proud of the high degree of occupational mobility in our country — of the greater readiness, as compared with other countries, with which a person starting in a very humble place in our social structure could rise to a position of moderate wealth and status, and with which a person starting with a middling position could rise to great eminence. We have looked upon this as laudable in principle, for it is democratic, and as pragmatically desirable, for it has served many a man as a stimulus to effort and has, no doubt, a great deal to do with the energetic and effectual tone of our economic life. The American pattern of occupational mobility, while often much exaggerated, as in the Horatio Alger stories and a great deal of the rest of our mythology, may properly be credited with many of the virtues and beneficial effects that are usually attributed to it. But this occupational and social mobility, compounded by our extraordinary mobility from place to place, has also had its less frequently recognized drawbacks. Not the least of them is that this has become a country in which so many people do not know who they are or what they are or what they belong to or what belongs to them. It is a country of people whose status expectations are random and uncertain, and yet whose status aspirations have been whipped up to a high pitch by our democratic ethos and our rags-to-riches mythology.

In a country where physical needs have been, by the scale of the world's living standards, on the whole well met, the luxury of questing after status has assumed an unusually prominent place in our civic consciousness. Political life is not simply an arena in which the conflicting interests of various social groups in concrete material gains are fought out; it is also an arena into which status aspirations and frustrations are, as the psychologists would say, projected. It is at this point that the issues of politics, or the pretended issues of politics, become interwoven with and dependent upon the personal problems of individuals. We have, at all times, two kinds of processes going on in inextricable connection with each other: *interest politics,* the clash of material aims and needs among various groups and blocs; and *status politics,* the clash of various projective rationalizations arising from status aspirations and other personal motives. In times of depression and economic discontent — and by and large in times of acute national emergency — politics is more clearly a matter of interests, although of course status considerations are still present. In times of prosperity and general well-being on the material plane, status considerations among the masses can become much more influential in our politics. The two periods in our recent history in which status politics has been particularly prominent, the present era and the 1920's, have both been periods of prosperity.

During depressions, the dominant motif in dissent takes expression in proposals for reform or in panaceas. Dissent then tends to be highly programmatic — that is, it gets itself embodied in many kinds of concrete legislative proposals. It is also future-oriented and forward-looking, in the sense that it looks to a time when the adoption of this or that program will materially alleviate or eliminate certain discontents. In prosperity, however, when status politics becomes relatively more important, there is a tendency to embody discontent not so much in legislative proposals as in grousing. For the basic aspirations that underlie status discontent are only partially conscious; and, even so far as they are conscious, it is difficult to give them a programmatic expression. It is more difficult for the old lady who belongs to the D.A.R. and who sees her ancestral home swamped by new working-class dwellings to express her animus in concrete proposals of any degree of reality than it is, say, for the jobless worker during a slump to rally to a relief program.

Therefore, it is the tendency of status politics to be expressed more in vindictiveness, in sour memories, in the search for scapegoats, than in realistic proposals for positive action.

Paradoxically the intense status concerns of present-day politics are shared by two types of persons who arrive at them, in a sense, from opposite directions. The first are found among some types of old-family, Anglo-Saxon Protestants, and the second are found among many types of immigrant families, most notably among the Germans and Irish, who are very frequently Catholic. The Anglo-Saxons are most disposed toward pseudo-conservatism when they are losing caste, the immigrants when they are gaining.

Consider first the old-family Americans. These people, whose stocks were once far more unequivocally dominant in America than they are today, feel that their ancestors made and settled and fought for this country. They have a certain inherited sense of proprietorship in it. Since America has always accorded a certain special deference to old families — so many of our families are *new* — these people have considerable claims to status by descent, which they celebrate by membership in such organizations as the D.A.R. and the S.A.R. But large numbers of them are actually losing their other claims to status. For there are among them a considerable number of the shabby genteel, of those who for one reason or another have lost their old objective positions in the life of business and politics and the professions, and who therefore cling with exceptional desperation to such remnants of their prestige as they can muster from their ancestors. These people, although very often quite well-to-do, feel that they have been pushed out of their rightful place in American life, even out of their neighborhoods. Most of them have been traditional Republicans by family inheritance, and they have felt themselves edged aside by the immigrants, the trade unions, and the urban machines in the past thirty years. When the immigrants were weak, these native elements used to indulge themselves in ethnic and religious snobberies at their expense. Now the immigrant groups have developed ample means, political and economic, or self-defense, and the second and third generations have become considerably more capable of looking out for themselves. Some of the old-family Americans have turned to find new objects for their resentment among liberals, left-wingers, intellectuals and the like — for in true pseudo-conservative fashion they relish weak victims and shrink from asserting themselves against the strong.

New-family Americans have had their own peculiar status problem. From 1881 to 1900 over 8,800,000 immigrants came here, during the next twenty years another 14,500,000. These immigrants, together with their descendants, constitute such a large portion of the population that Margaret Mead, in a stimulating analysis of our national character, has persuasively urged that the characteristic American outlook is now a third-generation point of view. In their search for new lives and new nationality, these immigrants have suffered much, and they have been rebuffed and made to feel inferior by the "native stock," commonly being excluded from the better occupations and even from what has bitterly been called "first-class citizenship." Insecurity over social status has thus been mixed with insecurity over one's very identity and sense of belonging. Achieving a better type of job or a better social status and becoming "more American" have become practically synonymous, and the passions that ordinarily attach to social position have been vastly heightened by being associated with the need to belong.

The problems raised by the tasks of keeping the family together, disciplining children for the American race for success, trying to conform to unfamiliar standards, protecting economic and social status won at the cost of much sacrifice, holding the respect of children who grow American more rapidly than their parents, have thrown heavy burdens on the internal relationships of many new American families. Both new and old American families have been troubled by the changes of the past thirty years — the new because of their striving for middle-class respectability and American identity, the old because of their efforts to maintain an inherited social position and to realize under increasingly unfavorable social conditions imperatives of character and personal conduct deriving from nineteenth-century, Yankee-Protestant-rural backgrounds. The relations between generations, being cast in no stable mold, have been disordered, and the status anxieties of parents have been inflicted upon children. Often parents entertain status aspirations that they are unable to gratify, or that they can gratify only at exceptional psychic cost. Their children are expected to relieve their frustrations and redeem their lives. They become objects to be manipulated to that end. An extraordinarily high level of achievement is expected of them, and along with it a tremendous effort to conform and be respectable. From the standpoint of the children these expectations often appear in the form of an exorbitantly demanding authority that one dare not question or defy. Resistance and hostility, finding no moderate outlet in give-and-take, have to be suppressed, and reappear in the form of an internal destructive rage. An enormous hostility to authority, which cannot be admitted to consciousness, calls forth a massive overcompensation which is manifest in the form of extravagant submissiveness to strong power. Among those found by Adorno and his colleagues to have strong ethnic prejudices and pseudo-conservative tendencies, there is a high proportion of persons who have been unable to develop the capacity to criticize justly and in moderation the failings of parents and who are profoundly intolerant of the ambiguities of thought and feeling that one is so likely to find in real-life situations. For pseudo-conservatism is among other things a disorder in relation to authority, characterized by an inability to find other modes for human relationship than those of more or less complete domination or submission. The pseudo-conservative always imagines himself to be dominated and imposed upon because he feels that he is not dominant, and knows of no other way of interpreting his position. He imagines that his own government and his own leadership are engaged in a more or less continuous conspiracy against him because he has come to think of authority only as something that aims to manipulate and deprive him. It is for this reason, among others, that he enjoys seeing outstanding generals, distinguished secretaries of state, and prominent scholars browbeaten and humiliated.

Status problems take on a special importance in American life because a very large part of the population suffers from one of the most troublesome of all status questions: unable to enjoy the simple luxury of assuming their own nationality as a natural event, they are tormented by a nagging doubt as to whether they are really and truly and fully American. Since their forebears voluntarily left one country and embraced another, they cannot, as people do elsewhere, think of nationality as something that comes with birth; for them it is a matter of *choice,* and an object of striving. This is one reason why problems of "loyalty" arouse such an emotional response in many Americans and why it is so hard in the American climate of opinion to make any clear distinction between the problem of national security and the question of personal loyalty. Of course there is no real reason to doubt the loyalty to America of the immigrants and their descendants, or their willingness to serve the country as fully as if their ancestors had lived here for three centuries. None the less, they have been thrown on the defensive by those who have in the past cast doubts upon the fullness of their Americanism. Possibly they are also, consciously or unconsciously, troubled by the thought that since their forebears have already abandoned one country, one allegiance, their own national allegiance might be considered fickle. For this I believe there is some evidence in our national practices. What other country finds it so necessary to create institutional rituals for the sole purpose of guaranteeing to its people the genuineness of their nationality? Does the Frenchman or the Englishman or the Italian find it necessary to speak of himself as "one hundred per cent" English, French or Italian? Do they find it necessary to have their equivalents of "I Am an American Day"? When they disagree with one another over national policies, do they find it necessary to call one another un-English, un-French or un-Italian? No doubt they too are troubled by subversive activities and espionage, but are their countermeasures taken under the name of committees on un-English, un-French or un-Italian activities?

The primary value of patriotic societies and anti-subversive ideologies to their exponents can be found here. They provide additional and continued reassurance both to those who are of old American ancestry and have other status grievances and to those who are of recent American ancestry and therefore feel in need of reassurance about their nationality. Veterans' organizations offer the same satisfaction — what better evidence can there be of the genuineness of nationality and of *earned* citizenship than military service under the flag of one's country? Of course such organizations, once they exist, are liable to exploitation by vested interests that can use them as pressure groups on behalf of particular measures and interests. (Veterans' groups, since they lobby for the concrete interests of veterans, have a double role in this respect.) But the cement that holds them together is the status motivation and the desire for an identity.

Sociological studies have shown that there is a close relation between social mobility and ethnic prejudice. Persons moving downward, and even upward under many circumstances, in the social scale tend to show greater prejudice against such ethnic minorities as the Jews and Negroes than commonly prevails in the social strata they have left or are entering. While the existing studies in this field have been focused upon prejudice rather than the kind of hyper-patriotism and hyper-conformism that I am most concerned with, I believe that the typical prejudiced person and the typical pseudo-conservative dissenter are usually the same person, that the mechanisms at work in both complexes are quite the same, and that it is merely the expediencies and the strategy of the situation today that cause groups that once stressed racial discrimination to find other scapegoats. Both the displaced old-American type and the new ethnic elements that are so desperately eager for reassurance of their fundamental Americanism can conveniently converge upon liberals, critics, and nonconformists of various sorts, as well as Communists and suspected Communists. To proclaim themselves vigilant in the pursuit of those who are even so much as accused of "disloyalty" to the United States is a way not only of reasserting but of advertising their own loyalty — and one of the chief characteristics of American super-patriotism is its constant inner urge toward self-advertisement. One notable quality in this new wave of conformism is that its advocates are much happier to have as their objects of hatred the Anglo-Saxon, Eastern, Ivy League intellectual gentlemen than they are with such bedraggled souls as, say, the Rosenbergs. The reason, I believe, is that in the minds of the status-driven it is no special virtue to be more American than the Rosenbergs, but it is really something to be more American than Dean Acheson or John Foster Dulles — or Franklin Delano Roosevelt. The status aspirations of some of the ethnic groups are actually higher than they were twenty years ago — which suggests one reason (there are others) why, in the ideology of the authoritarian right-wing, anti-Semitism and such blatant forms of prejudice have recently been soft-pedaled. Anti-Semitism, it has been said, is the poor man's snobbery. We Americans are always trying to raise the standard of living, and the same principle now seems to apply to standards of hating. So during the past fifteen years or so, the authoritarians have moved on from anti-Negroism and anti-Semitism to anti-Achesonianism, anti-intellectualism, antinonconformism, and other variants of the same idea, much in the same way as the average American, if he can manage it, will move on from a Ford to a Buick.

Such status-strivings may help us to understand some of the otherwise unintelligible figments of the pseudo-conservative ideology — the incredibly bitter feeling against the United Nations, for instance. It is not understandable that such a feeling might be, paradoxically, shared at one and the same time by an old Yankee-Protestant American, who feels that his social position is not what it ought to be and that these foreigners are crowding in on his country and diluting its sovereignty just as "foreigners" have crowded into his neighborhood, and by a second- or third-generation immigrant who has been trying so hard to de-Europeanize himself, to get Europe out of his personal heritage, and who finds his own government mocking him by its complicity in these Old-World schemes?

Similarly, is it not status aspiration that in good parts spurs the pseudo-conservative on toward his demand for conformity in a wide variety of spheres of life? Conformity is a way of guaranteeing and manifesting respectability among those who are not sure that they are respectable enough. The nonconformity of others appears to such persons as a frivolous challenge to the whole order of things they are trying so hard to become part of. Naturally it is resented, and the demand for conformity in public becomes at once an expression of such resentment and a means of displaying one's own soundness. This habit has a tendency to spread from politics into intellectual and social spheres, where it can be made to challenge almost anyone whose pattern of life is different and who is imagined to enjoy a superior social position — notably, as one agitator put it, to the "parlors of the sophisticated, the intellectuals, the so-called academic minds."

Why has this tide of pseudo-conservative dissent risen to such heights in our time? To a considerable degree, we must remember, it is a response, however unrealistic, to realities. We do live in a disordered world, threatened by a great power and a powerful ideology. It is a world of enormous potential violence, that has already shown us the ugliest capacities of the human spirit. In our own country there has indeed been espionage, and laxity over security has in fact allowed some spies to reach high places. There is just enough reality at most points along the line to give a touch of credibility to the melodramatics of the pseudo-conservative imagination.

However, a number of developments in our recent history make this pseudo-conservative uprising more intelligible. For two hundred years and more, various conditions of American development — the process of continental settlement, the continuous establishment in new areas of new status patterns, the arrival of continuous waves of new immigrants, each pushing the preceding waves upward in the ethnic hierarchy — made it possible to satisfy a remarkably large part of the extravagant status aspirations that were aroused. There was a sort of automatic built-in status-elevator in the American social edifice. Today that elevator no longer operates automatically, or at least no longer operates in the same way.

Secondly, the growth of the mass media of communication and their use in politics have brought politics closer to the people than ever before and have made politics a form of entertainment in which the spectators feel themselves involved. Thus it has become, more than ever before, an arena into which private emotions and personal problems can be readily projected. Mass communications have aroused the mass man.

Thirdly, the long tenure in power of the liberal elements to which the pseudo-conservatives are most opposed and the wide variety of changes that have been introduced into our social, economic and administrative life have intensified the sense of powerlessness and victimization among the opponents of these changes and have widened the area of social issues over which they feel discontent. There has been, among other things, the emergence of a wholly new struggle: the conflict between businessmen of certain types and the New Deal bureaucracy, which has spilled over into a resentment of intellectuals and experts.

Finally, unlike our previous postwar periods, ours has been a period of continued crisis, from which the future promises no relief. In no foreign war of our history did we fight so long or make such sacrifices as in World War II. When it was over, instead of being able to resume our peacetime preoccupations, we were very promptly confronted with another war. It is hard for a certain type of American, who does not think much about the world outside and does not want to have to do so, to understand why we must become involved in such an unremitting struggle. It will be the fate of those in power for a long time to come to have to conduct the delicate diplomacy of the cold peace without the sympathy or understanding of a large part of their own people. From bitter experience, Eisenhower and Dulles are learning today what Truman and Acheson learned yesterday.

These considerations suggest that the pseudo-conservative political style, while it may already have passed the peak of its influence, is one of the long waves of twentieth-century American history and not a momentary mood. I do not share the widespread foreboding among liberals that this form of dissent will grow until it overwhelms our liberties altogether and plunges us into a totalitarian nightmare. Indeed, the idea that it is purely and simply fascist or totalitarian, as we have known these things in recent European history, is to my mind a false conception, based upon the failure to read American developments in terms of our peculiar American constellation of political realities. (It reminds me of the people who, because they found several close parallels between the NRA and Mussolini's corporate state, were once deeply troubled at the thought that the NRA was the beginning of American fascism.) However, in a populistic culture like ours, which seems to lack a responsible elite with political and moral autonomy, and in which it is possible to exploit the wildest currents of public sentiment for private purposes, it is at least conceivable that a highly organized, vocal, active and well-financed minority could create a political climate in which the rational pursuit of our well-being and safety would become impossible.

Richard H. Rovere

"THE EISENHOWER YEARS," William Shannon wrote, when the period had only a few weeks to run, "have been years of flabbiness and self-satisfaction and gross materialism. . . . [The] loudest sound in the land has been the oink-and-grunt of private hoggishness. . . . It has been the age of the slob." Yes, yes — and then again no. The country did put on a lot of weight that wasn't muscle. But as for "self-satisfaction," was there ever a reasonably stable society that wasn't more pleased with itself than it had a right to be? And isn't "materialism" always "gross"? Still, Shannon has hold of what I think I would call about a two-thirds truth. There is really no denying that the Fifties in the United States were years in which private hoggishness reached some spectacular heights. But "the age of the slob" — no, I don't think that will do.

There is much to be said about the Eisenhower years, a good deal in dispraise, quite a bit in praise, but one must begin, I think, by acknowledging that the period itself had a history, that it took some of its character from what had gone before, that there were important differences between the early period and the late period, and that in any case American life is never all of a piece. As one who in 1956 published a book called *The Eisenhower Years,* I am in a rather poor position to point out that historians and journalists who try to write history have a way of misleading themselves and their readers by associating epochs and pivotal events with the names of ruling or presiding figures. There is, to be sure, a sense in which an American President stamps his character on a period and a sense in which his countrymen tend to become like him. At the same time, there are powerful currents that are scarcely touched by him and, always, currents that run powerfully against him. I hap-

"Eisenhower Over the Shoulder," *The American Scholar,* XXXI (Spring, 1962), 176–79.

RICHARD ROVERE (1915–   ) writes for *The New Yorker.* He has also written a number of books on contemporary issues, including *The General and the President* (1951) with Arthur M. Schlesinger, Jr.

pen to believe that during the Eisenhower years — and in part because they *were* the Eisenhower years — many currents of great promise were running. We were a self-satisfied people, as Shannon said, yet we were terribly uneasy in our complacency and elected as Eisenhower's successor a man whose entire campaign was an assault on complacency. During the Eisenhower years, we developed — great numbers of us — an enormous dissatisfaction with our educational systems and with American intellectual life in general. Of course, it was largely the prodding of the Russians that did it. But that hardly seems to me to matter; we made, I think, some vigorous responses. It was during the Eisenhower years, too, that we became more alert than ever before to civil rights and civil liberties. It was in Eisenhower's day and Joe McCarthy's that the United States Supreme Court did more than in any preceding time to protect and secure the rights of minorities and of individuals.

And it has to be said, neither in praise nor in dispraise, that the election of Dwight Eisenhower in 1952 did not mark an abrupt transition from an elevated concern for the private interest to a base absorption with the private interest. Eisenhower's predecessor was, on balance, a good and gallant President, but not everything about his Administration, or about American life in his time, was admirable. The oink-and-grunt of private hoggishness was more than audible in the Truman years; indeed, as the end drew near, it was almost deafening. There was corruption in half a dozen government agencies, and some of it was laid at the door of persons very close to the President. Much of the corruption was picayune; there was little grandeur in the larcenies. Still, hoggishness in the middle-income brackets is not much lovelier than hoggishness among the very rich. In his last year in office Truman sought to tidy things up by investigation and reorganization, but his efforts were frustrated by his subordinates, particularly in the Department of Justice where things were in the sorriest mess, and nothing of moment was done.

Corruption played a part in the retirement of the Democrats in 1952. So did the Korean war, which was as unpopular as it was just. So did Senator McCarthy's blather about Communists in the State Department, which was as popular as it was unjust. The fact is that the American people in 1952 were a confused, bitter, divided lot. We were prosperous but far from content in our prosperity. We were performing large and necessary services to freedom but not fully persuaded of the need for what we were being called upon to do, and although we had put isolationism behind us, as a simply impossible way of looking at the world, we nevertheless resented a world that asked so much of us. In the preceding decade we had fought and won two overseas wars that not too many of us, at the outset, had acknowledged to be our proper concern. We had been led by Franklin Roosevelt to believe that our sacrifices (small alongside those of our major allies, but less clearly related in the minds of citizens to national security) would rid the world of its principal troublemakers. No sooner had those troublemakers — the German and Japanese militarists and the political structures that supported them — been destroyed than we were asked to arm against a new global menace, said to be even worse than the enemies so recently vanquished. In Korea we were asked to fight a particularly nasty kind of war and were told that it would be in very bad taste to seek victory of the traditional sort; having only a few years earlier absorbed the doctrine of "total war" and "unconditional surrender," we were called upon to make a quick shift to limited war and highly conditional victory.

The disagreeable turn that events had taken in the early Fifties invited demagogic explanation. And a really first-rate demagogue arose to explain them with that most effective of devices for interpreting history to the masses — the conspiracy theory. McCarthy said that things were as they were because the governors had encouraged betrayal. There was a time, in late 1953 and early 1954, when, according to the polls, half the people thought he was performing a useful service.

It seems to me now that Eisenhower's election in 1952 was a good thing for the country and that the first four Eisenhower years are not to be regretted. It was a time in which a new consensus was reached and a time in which tensions were considerably eased. It would have been agreeable, no doubt, to have had a more imaginative and more eloquent President — a Willkie, a Republican Adlai Stevenson, a Charles Evans Hughes. But the Republicans are our only alternative to the Democrats, and in 1952 *their* only alternative to Eisenhower was Robert A. Taft, an honorable and intelligent man but hardly a reducer of tensions. As Walter Lippmann once pointed out, it *had* to be Eisenhower in 1952 in the same sense that it *had* to be George Washington in 1789. In his first term, he did many of the things that needed doing and that could not have been done by a Democratic administration.

He had, for one thing, to end the Korean war. By 1953, when he took office, the time had come to liquidate this enterprise. By their intervention in Korea in 1950, the United States and the United Nations had made the point that they would not flinch from resisting direct aggression by international communism and that they could find the resources for resistance. This was a great turning point in the cold war; the Communist bloc recognized it, and there were no more Koreas, and "containment" remained a feasible American policy. But by the time of Eisenhower's election, when the North Koreans and the Chinese Communists were being effectively contained north of the thirty-eighth parallel, further bloodshed was insupportable. The Truman Administration had entered into negotiations with the Communists and had reached the point where the basic terms of the settlement were clear. But the Truman Administration, intent on giving its domestic critics no grounds for charging it with appeasement, could not possibly have concluded the negotiations. Nor could a Stevenson administration. McCarthy and his animals would have set upon it and quite possibly have destroyed it as the effective agency of American power. There were times, indeed, when it looked as if the Republicans in Congress, ably led by Senator Knowland of California, would not let the Republican Administration negotiate a settlement. The President had to use all the prestige he had, and he did just that.

Eisenhower threw only a small amount of his prestige into the destruction of McCarthy, and for this he was constantly being faulted, as doubtless he deserved to be. It is very easy for anyone to say that McCarthy should have been stopped far sooner than he was. In my judgment, those who think this might have been done at little cost by the use of Presidential powers greatly underrate McCarthy's talents and the force of those currents of opinion he exploited. What seems to me remarkable is that by late 1954, less than two years after Eisenhower took office, McCarthy was done for. Eisenhower's contribution may have been slight. McCarthy did a great deal to destroy himself. But it seems to be doubtful in the extreme that the desirable end would have been reached in 1954 if the Democrats had been enjoying their sixth consecutive term in office and if the casualty lists from Korea had still been appearing every day in the papers. McCarthy had to be destroyed by his own party, and his own party out of power would not have attempted to destroy him — first, because it would have wished to use him; second, because he would not have been compelled to turn against it.

There is more to be said for the first four Eisenhower years. As James Reston once said, the President brought to NATO a valuable new member — the Republican Party. For all their rhetoric about Quemoy and Matsu and Formosa and Chiang Kai-shek, he and Secretary Dulles fashioned a China policy that probably saved us from some bloody and pointless engagements in the Far East. In foreign affairs, I can see little to regret in the Eisenhower Administration's stewardship during its first term.

It has never been easy for an American President to work his way out of the White House in four years. Bad luck and weak management must be combined, as they were in Herbert Hoover's day, to persuade the voters to deny a President a second term. The voters who put Eisenhower in office in 1952 made almost certain his reelection in 1956, and one can hardly say that they did the wise thing the first time and served themselves badly the second time. Nevertheless, the second four years go a long way toward justifying William Shannon's harsh impeachments. If there is anything much to be said for them, it has escaped my notice and understanding. By 1956, the tasks that had seemed to call for the bland Eisenhower treatment had all received it, and the rest, in Washington anyway, was drift and near-slumber. The cold war had taken on many new aspects. It had become in part a technological struggle, the kind that Americans should have relished more than any other, and Washington's response was feeble and grudging. The President, who by then had no political future to worry about, had a magnificent opportunity to take the Negro American's part in the struggle for elementary decency; he refused even to say with any vigor that he himself favored the one ideal that, historically, has been associated with this Republic as with no other. He increasingly surrounded himself with mediocrities and increasingly proclaimed as his own highest ideal the simple-minded, indeed semiliterate political economy of George Humphrey. Although he had never in his life been known as a military thinker, as distinct from a military executive, he became more and more impatient of criticism and more and more confident of his unique qualifications for deciding what we needed and what we did not need for the defense of the national interest in the mid-twentieth century.

It can be argued that he was an older soldier by several years, that he had done his work, that he had lost the men who had been closest to him in the first term, that he should not be made responsible for everything in a time that seemed somehow destined to be squalid. On the whole, this is so. He had the same faults and virtues after 1956 that he had had before — only the faults seemed to count for more, the virtues for less. He had always been a rather irritable Dr. Pangloss, but a time came when the irritability seemed merely self-indulgent. The last half of the Fifties was not made for a President who was unhurried and untroubled, disapproving only of the disapprovers. In a way, the tragedy, if that is not too large a word for it, of that period was that we did not have a President who wanted to keep abreast of the more salutary developments within American society — the intellectual ferment, the technological ferment, the struggles for equality. His growing cantankerousness and stubbornness were responses to the demands that he be more troubled, more in a hurry, more alive.

Many of the things that make us think of it as a squalid period cannot be laid at his door. He bears some responsibility for Sherman Adams and Dixon-Yates, but little for Jimmy Hoffa or Orval Faubus. The loudest of the oink-and-grunt set — the newly rich of Texas and the Southwest — were protected by Lyndon Johnson, Sam Rayburn and Robert S. Kerr. The tide of superciliousness had begun to run before Eisenhower and is running pretty strong today. (The only youth movements that attracted much attention — the conservatives who flocked to William F. Buckley, Jr.'s banner and the beatniks — were alike in their superciliousness and in their flagrant selfishness.) But it would have helped greatly, it would have gone a long way toward redeeming the bad time, if the President of the United States had had some convictions of his own and had said what they were.

Richard E. Neustadt

THERE are many ways to look at the performance of a president of the United States. One way — not the only one — is to assess his operational effectiveness as man in office, a single individual amidst a vast machine. This has been my own approach in previous writings on past presidents. Regarding our most recent President, John F. Kennedy, it is foolhardy to attempt appraisal in these terms. He died too soon and it is too soon after his death. Still, the POLITICAL SCIENCE QUARTERLY has asked me to attempt it. And assuming that my readers will indulge the folly, I shall try.

[I]

In appraising the personal performance of a president it is useful to ask four questions. First, what were his purposes and did these run with or against the grain of history; how relevant were they to what would happen in his time? Second, what was his "feel," his human understanding, for the nature of his power in the circumstances of his time, and how close did he come in this respect to the realities around him (a matter again of relevance)? Third, what was his stance under pressure in office, what sustained him as a person against the frustrations native to the place, and how did his peace-making with himself affect the style and content of his own decision-making? This becomes especially important now that nuclear technology has equipped both Americans and Russians with an intercontinental capability; stresses on the presidency grow apace. Fourth, what was his legacy? What imprint did he leave upon the office, its character and public standing; where did he leave his party and the other party

"Kennedy in the Presidency: A Premature Appraisal," reprinted with permission from the *Political Science Quarterly,* LXXIX (September, 1964), 321–334. Professor Neustadt has made several minor changes in the present text.

RICHARD E. NEUSTADT (1919–) is a former Professor of Government at Columbia University. He served as an advisor to President Kennedy, wrote *Presidential Power* (1960), and is presently at Harvard University.

nationally; what remained by way of public policies adopted or in controversy; what remained as issues in American society, insofar as his own stance may have affected them; and what was the American position in the world insofar as his diplomacy may have affected it?

With respect to each of these four questions, the outside observer looks for certain clues in seeking answers.

First, regarding purpose, clues are found in irreversible commitments to defined courses of action. By "commitment" I mean nothing so particular as an endorsement for, say, "medicare," or anything so general as a pledge to "peace." (All presidents desire peace.) By "course of action" I mean something broader than the one but more definable than the other: Harry S. Truman's commitment to "containment," so called, or Dwight D. Eisenhower's to what he called "fiscal responsibility." By "commitment" I mean personal involvement, in terms of what the man himself is seen to say and do, so plain and so direct that politics — and history — will not let him turn back: Truman on civil rights, or Eisenhower on the Army budget.

Second, regarding feel for office, sensitivity to power, clues are drawn from signs of pattern in the man's own operating style as he encounters concrete cases, cases of decision and of following through in every sphere of action, legislative and executive, public and partisan, foreign and domestic — Truman seeking above all to be decisive; Eisenhower reaching for a place above the struggle.

Third, regarding pressure and its consequences, clues are to be drawn again from cases; here one examines crisis situations, seeking signs of pattern in the man's response — Truman at the time of the Korean outbreak, or of Chinese intervention; Eisenhower at the time of Hungary and Suez, or of Little Rock — times like these compared with others just as tough in terms of stress.

And fourth, regarding the man's legacy, one seeks clues in the conduct of the *next* administration. Roosevelt's first New Deal in 1933 tells us a lot about the Hoover presidency. Truman's troubled turnabout in postwar foreign policy casts shadows on the later Roosevelt presidency. And Kennedy's complaint at Yale two years ago about the "myths" retarding economic management is testimony to one part of Eisenhower's legacy, that part identified with the redoubtable George Humphrey.

To list these sources of the wherewithal for answers is to indicate the folly of pursuing my four questions when the object of the exercise is Kennedy-in-office. He was President for two years and ten months. Were one to assess Franklin Roosevelt on the basis of performance before January 1936, or Harry Truman on his accomplishments before enactment of the Marshall Plan, or Eisenhower had he not survived his heart attack — or Lincoln, for that matter, had he been assassinated six months after Gettysburg — one would be most unlikely to reach judgments about any of these men resembling current judgments drawn from the full record of their terms. We cannot know what Kennedy's full record would have been had he escaped assassination. Still more important, we can never know precisely how to weigh events in his truncated term.

Truman's seven years and Eisenhower's eight suggest a certain rhythm in the modern presidency. The first twelve to eighteen months become a learning time for the new president who has to learn — or unlearn — many things about his job. No matter what his prior training, nothing he has done will have prepared him for all facets of that job. Some aspects of the learning process will persist beyond the first year-and-a-half. Most presidents will go on making new discoveries as long as they hold office (until at last they learn the bitterness of leaving office). But the intensive learning time comes at the start and dominates the first two years. A president's behavior in those years is an uncertain source of clues to what will follow after, unreliable in indicating what will be the patterns of performance "on the job" once learning has been done. Yet the fourth year is also unreliable; traditionally it brings a period of pause, dominated by a special test requiring special effort — the test of re-election. The way that test is taken tells us much about a president, but less about his conduct on the job in others years. The seventh year is the beginning of the end — now guaranteed by constitutional amendment — as all eyes turn toward the coming nominations and the *next* administration.

So in the search for signs of pattern, clues to conduct, the key years are the third, the fifth, the sixth. Kennedy had only one of these.

Moreover, in this presidential cycle, retrospect is an essential aid for sorting evidence. What a man does in his later years sheds light on the significance of what he did in early years, distinguishing the actions which conform to lasting patterns from the aspects of behavior which were transient. The man's early performance will include a host of clues to what is typical throughout his terms of office. But it also will include assorted actions which turn out to be unrepresentative. Looking back from later years these become easy to distinguish. But in the second or the third year it is hard indeed to say, "This action, this behavior will be dominant throughout." That is the sort of statement best reserved for retrospect. Kennedy's case leaves no room for retrospect; he was cut off too early in the cycle. (And when it comes to sorting out the legacy he left, Lyndon Johnson has not yet been long enough in office.)

No scholar, therefore, should have the temerity to undertake what follows.

[II]

Turning to appraise this President in office, I come to my first question, the question of purpose. This is not a matter of initial "ideology," fixed intent; far from it. Franklin Roosevelt did not enter office bent upon becoming "traitor to his class." Truman did not swear the oath with any notion that he was to take this country into the cold war. Lincoln certainly did not assume the presidency to gain the title of "Great Emancipator." The purposes of presidents are not to be confused with their intentions at the start; they are a matter, rather, of responses to events. Nor should they be confused with signs of temperament, with "passion." Whether Kennedy was "passionate" or not is scarcely relevant. Truman certainly deserves to have the cause of civil rights cited among his purposes, but were he to be judged in temperamental terms according to the standards of, say, Eastern liberals, he scarcely could be called a man of passion on the point. And FDR goes down historically as "Labor's friend," although his coolness toward the greatest show of that friendship in his time, the Wagner Act, remained until he sensed that it was sure to be enacted. What counts here is not "passion," but the words and acts that lead to irreversible *commitment*.

In his three years of office, what were Kennedy's commitments? Never mind his private thoughts at twenty, or at forty; never mind his preferences for one thing or another; never mind his distaste for a passionate display — taking the real world as he found it, what attracted his commitment in the sense that he identified himself beyond recall?

The record will, I think, disclose at least three purposes so understood: First, above all others, most compelling, most intense, was a commitment to reduce the risk of holocaust by *mutual* miscalculation, to "get the nuclear genie back in the bottle," to render statecraft manageable by statesmen, tolerable for the rest of us. He did not aim at anything so trite (or unachievable) as "victory" in the cold war. His aim, apparently, was to outlast it with American society intact and nuclear risks in check. Nothing, I think, mattered more to Kennedy than bottling that genie. This, I know, was deeply in his mind. It also was made manifest in words, among them his address at American University on June 10, 1963. That speech is seal and symbol of this purpose. But other signs are found in acts, as well, and in more private words accompanying action: from his Vienna interview with Khrushchev, through the Berlin crisis during 1961, to the Cuban missile crisis and thereafter — this commitment evidently deepened with experience as Kennedy responded to events.

Another speech in June of 1963 stands for a second purpose: the speech on civil rights, June 11, and the message to Congress eight days later launched Kennedy's campaign for what became the Civil Rights Act of 1964. Thereby he undertook an irreversible commitment to Negro integration in American society, aiming once again to get us through the effort with society intact. He evidently came to see the risks of social alienation as plainly as he saw the risks of nuclear escalation, and he sought to steer a course toward integration which could hold inside our social order both impatient Negroes and reactive whites — as tough a task of politics as any we have known, and one he faced no sooner than he had to. But he faced it. What Vienna, Berlin, Cuba were to his first purpose, Oxford and then Birmingham were to his second purpose: events which shaped his personal commitment.

A third speech is indicative of still another purpose, a speech less known and a commitment less apparent, though as definite, I think, as both of the others: Kennedy's commencement speech at Yale on June 11, 1962, soon after his short war with Roger

Blough. He spoke of making our complex economy, our somewhat *sui generis* economy, function effectively for meaningful growth, and as the means he urged an end-of-ideology in problem-solving. His speech affirmed the notion that the key problems of economic growth are technical, not ideological, to be met not by passion but by intellect, and that the greatest barriers to growth are the ideas in people's heads — "myths" as he called them — standing in the way of reasoned diagnosis and response. Kennedy, I think, was well aware (indeed he was made painfully aware) that only on our one-time Left is ideology defunct. Elsewhere it flourishes, clamping a lid upon applied intelligence, withholding brainpower from rational engagement in the novel problems of our economic management. He evidently wanted most of all to lift that lid.

Failing a response to his Yale lecture, Kennedy retreated to the easier task of teaching one simple economic lesson, the lesson of the recent tax reduction: well-timed budget deficits can lead to balanced budgets. This, evidently, was the most that he thought he could manage in contesting "myths," at least before election. But his ambition, I believe, was to assault a lot more myths than this, when and as he could. That ambition measures his commitment to effective growth in the economy.

Stemming from this third commitment (and the second) one discerns a corollary which perhaps would have become a fourth: what Kennedy's successor now has named "the war against poverty." During the course of 1963, Kennedy became active in promoting plans for an attack on chronic poverty. His prospective timing no doubt had political utility, but it also had social utility which evidently mattered quite as much. Historically, the "war" is Lyndon Johnson's. All we know of Kennedy is that he meant to make one. Still, for either of these men the effort, if sustained, would lead to irreversible commitment.

Each purpose I have outlined meant commitment to a course of action which engaged the man — his reputation, *amour propre,* and sense of self in history — beyond recall. The question then becomes: how relevant were these, historically? How relevant to Kennedy's own years of actual (and of prospective) office? Here I can only make a judgment, tentative of course, devoid of long perspective. These purposes seem to me entirely relevant. In short perspective, they seem precisely right as the pre-eminent concerns for the first half of this decade.

[III]

So much for Kennedy as man-of-purpose. What about the man-of-power?

He strikes me as a senator who learned very fast from his confrontation with the executive establishment, particularly after the abortive Cuban invasion which taught him a great deal. On action-issues of particular concern to him he rapidly evolved an operating style which he maintained consistently (and sharpened at the edges) through his years of office. If one looks at Berlin, or Oxford, Mississippi, or the Cuban missile crisis, or at half a dozen other issues of the sort, one finds a pattern: the personal command post, deliberate reaching down for the details, hard questioning of the alternatives, a drive to protect options from foreclosure by sheer urgency or by *ex parte* advocacy, finally a close watch on follow-through. Even on the issues which were secondary to the President and left, perforce, primarily to others, Kennedy was constantly in search of means and men to duplicate at one remove this personalized pattern with its stress on open options and on close control. Numbers of outsiders – Hans Morgenthau and Joseph Alsop for two – sometimes viewed the pattern with alarm and saw this man as "indecisive." But that was to consult *their* preferences, not his performance. Kennedy seemed always keen to single out the necessary from the merely possible. He then decided with alacrity.

Not everything was always done effectively, of course, and even the successes produced side effects of bureaucratic bafflement, frustration, irritation which were not without their costs. Even so, the pattern testifies to an extraordinary feel for the distinction between president and presidency, an extraordinary urge to master the machine. This took him quite a way toward mastery in two years and ten months. We shall not know how far he might have got.

Kennedy's feel for his own executive position carried over into that of fellow rulers everywhere. He evidently had great curiosity and real concern about the politics of rulership wherever he encountered it. His feel for fine distinctions among fellow "kings" was rare, comparable to the feel of Senate-Leader Johnson for the fine distinctions among fellow senators. And with this Kennedy apparently absorbed in his short time a lesson Franklin Roosevelt never learned about the Russians (or de Gaulle): that in another country an *effective* politician can have motives very *different* from his own. What an advantageous lesson to have learned in two years' time! It would have served him well. Indeed, while he still lived I think it did.

The cardinal test of Kennedy as an executive in his own right and also as a student of executives abroad was certainly the confrontation of October 1962, the Cuban missile crisis with Khrushchev. For almost the first time in our foreign relations, the President displayed on that occasion both concern for the psychology of his opponent and insistence on a limited objective. Contrast the Korean War, where we positively courted Chinese intervention by relying on Douglas MacArthur as psychologist and by enlarging our objective after each success. "There is no substitute for victory," MacArthur wrote, but at that time we virtually had a nuclear monopoly and even then our government hastened to find a substitute. Now, with mutual capability, the whole traditional meaning has been taken out of "victory." In nuclear confrontations there is room for no such thing. Kennedy quite evidently knew it. He also knew, as his performance demonstrates, that risks of escalation lurk in high-level misjudgments *and* in low-level momentum. Washington assuredly was capable of both; so, probably, was Moscow. Accordingly, the President outstripped all previous efforts to guard options and assure control. His operating style was tested then as not before or after. It got him what he wanted.

In confrontations with Congress, quite another world than the executive, the key to Kennedy's congressional relations lay outside his feel for power, beyond reach of technique; he won the presidency by a hair, while in the House of Representatives his party lost some twenty of the seats gained two years earlier. The Democrats *retained* a sizeable majority as they had done in earlier years, no thanks to him. With this beginning, Kennedy's own record of accomplishment in Congress looks enormous, indeterminate, or small, depending on one's willingness to give him credit for enactment of the most divisive, innovative bills he espoused:

the tax and civil rights bills passed in Johnson's presidency. Certainly it can be said that Kennedy prepared the way, negotiating a bipartisan approach, and also that he took the heat, stalling his whole program, in the process. Equally, it can be said that with his death – or by it – the White House gained advantages which he could not have mustered. Johnson made the most of these. How well would Kennedy have done without them? My own guess is that in the end, with rancor and delay, both bills would have been passed. But it is a moot point. Accordingly, so is the Kennedy record.

Whatever his accomplishment, does it appear the most he could have managed in his years? Granting the limits set by his election, granting the divisiveness injected after Birmingham with his decisive move on civil rights, did he use to the fullest his advantages of office? The answer may well be "not quite." Perhaps a better answer is, "This man could do no more." For Kennedy, it seems, was not a man enamored of the legislative way of life and legislators knew it. He was wry about it. He had spent fourteen years in Congress and he understood its business, but he never was a "member of the family" on the Hill. "Downtown" had always seemed his native habitat; he was a natural executive. They knew that, too. Besides, he was a young man, very young by Senate standards, and his presence in the White House with still younger men around him was a constant irritant to seniors. Moreover, he was not a "mixer" socially, not, anyway, with most members of Congress and their wives. His manners were impeccable, his charm impelling, but he kept his social life distinct from his official life and congressmen were rarely in his social circle. To know how Congress works but to disdain its joys is an acquired taste for most ex-congressmen downtown, produced by hard experience. Kennedy, however, brought it with him. Many of the difficulties he was to encounter in his day-by-day congressional relations stemmed from that.

But even had he been a man who dearly loved the Congress, even had that feeling been reciprocated, nothing could have rendered their relationship sweetness-and-light in his last year, so long as he persisted with his legislative program. As an innovative President confronting a reluctant Congress, he was heir to Truman, and to Roosevelt after 1936. Kennedy's own manner may have hurt him on the Hill, but these were scratches. Deeper scars had more substantial sources and he knew it.

In confrontations with the larger public outside Washington (again a different world), Kennedy made a brilliant beginning, matched only by the start in different circumstances of his own successor. The "public relations" of transition into office were superb. In three months after his election, Kennedy transformed himself from "pushy," "young," "Catholic," into President-of-all-the-people, widening and deepening acceptance of his presidency out of all proportion to the election returns. The Bay of Pigs was a severe check, but his handling of the aftermath displayed again superb feel for the imagery befitting an incumbent of the White House, heir to FDR *and* Eisenhower. That feel he always had. I think it never failed him.

What he also had was a distaste for preaching, really for the preachiness of politics, backed by genuine mistrust of mass emotion as a tool in politics. These attitudes are rare among American politicians; with Kennedy their roots ran deep into recesses of experience and character where I, as an outsider, cannot follow. But they assuredly were rooted in this man and they had visible effects upon his public style. He delighted in the play of minds, not of emotions. He doted on press conferences, not set performances. He feared "over-exposure"; he dreaded over-reaction. Obviously he enjoyed responsive crowds, and was himself responsive to a sea of cheering faces, but I think he rarely looked at their reaction – or his own – without a twinge of apprehension. He never seems to have displayed much fondness for the "fireside chat," a form of crowd appeal without the crowd; television talks in evening hours evidently struck him more as duty than as opportunity, and dangerous at that; some words on air-raid shelters in a talk about Berlin could set off mass hysteria – and did. At the moment when he had his largest, most attentive audience, on the climactic Sunday of the Cuban missile crisis, he turned it away (and turned attention off) with a two-minute announcement, spare and dry.

Yet we know now, after his death, what none of us knew before: that with a minimum of preaching, of emotional appeal, or of self-justification, even explanation, he had managed to touch millions in their private lives, not only at home but emphatically abroad. Perhaps his very coolness helped him do it. Perhaps his very vigor, family, fortune, sense of fun, his manners, taste, and sportsmanship, his evident enjoyment of his life and of the job made him the heart's desire of all sorts of people everywhere, not least among the young. At any rate, we know now that he managed in his years to make enormous impact on a world-wide audience, building an extraordinary base of public interest and affection (interspersed, of course, with doubters and detractors). What he might have made of this or done with it in later years, nobody knows.

[IV]

So much for power; what of pressure? What sustained this man in his decisions, his frustrations, and with what effect on his approach to being president? For an answer one turns to the evidence of crises, those already mentioned among others, and the *surface* signs are clear. In all such situations it appears that Kennedy was cool, collected, courteous, and terse. This does not mean that he was unemotional. By temperament I think he was a man of mood and passion. But he had schooled his temperament. He kept his own emotions under tight control. He did not lose his temper inadvertently, and never lost it long. He was observer and participant combined; he saw himself as coolly as all others — and with humor. He always was a witty man, dry with a bit of bite and a touch of self-deprecation. He could laugh at himself, and did. Often he used humor to break tension. And in tight places he displayed a keen awareness of the human situation, human limits, his included, but it did not slow his work.

Readers over forty may recognize this portrait as "the stance of junior officers in the Second World War"; Elspeth Rostow coined that phrase and, superficially at least, she is quite right. This was the Kennedy stance and his self-confidence, his shield against frustration, must have owed a lot to his young manhood in that war.

This tells us a good deal but not nearly enough. At his very first encounter with a crisis in the presidency, Kennedy's self-confidence seems to have been severely strained. The Bay of Pigs fiasco shook him deeply, shook his confidence in methods and associates. Yet he went on governing without a break, no change in manner, or in temper, or in humor. What sustained him? Surely much that went beyond experience of war.

What else? I cannot answer. I can only conjecture. His family life and rearing have some part to play, no doubt. His political successes also: in 1952 he bucked the Eisenhower tide to reach the Senate; in 1960 he broke barriers of youth and of religion which had always held before; on each occasion the Conventional Wisdom was against him: "can't be done." Beyond these things, this man had been exceptionally close to death, not only in the war but ten years after. And in his presidential years his back was almost constantly a source of pain; he never talked about it but he lived with it. All this is of a piece with his behavior in a crisis. His control, his objectivity, his humor, and his sense of human limits, these were but expressions of his confidence; its sources must lie somewhere in this ground.

Whatever the sources, the results were rewarding for this President's performance on the job. In the most critical, nerve-straining aspects of the office, coping with its terrible responsibility for use of force, Kennedy's own image of himself impelled him neither to lash out nor run for cover. Rather, it released him for engagement and decision as a reasonable man. In some of the less awesome aspects of the presidency, his own values restrained him, kept him off the pulpit, trimmed his guest list, made him shy away from the hyperbole of politics. But as a chief *executive,* confronting action-issues for decision and control, his duty and his confidence in doing it were nicely matched. So the world discovered in October 1962.

[V]

Now for my last question. What did John Kennedy leave behind him? What was the legacy of his short years? At the very least he left a myth: the vibrant, youthful leader cut down senselessly before his time. What this may come to signify as the years pass, I cannot tell. He left a glamorous moment, an engaging, youthful time, but how we shall remember it depends on what becomes of Lyndon Johnson. He left a broken promise, that "the torch has been passed to a new generation," and the youngsters who identified with him felt cheated as the promise, like the glamor, disappeared. What do their feelings matter? We shall have to wait and see.

May this be all that history is likely to record? Perhaps, but I doubt it. My guess is that when the observers can appraise the work of Kennedy's successors, they will find some things of substance in his legacy. Rashly, let me record what I think these are.

To begin with, our first Catholic president chose and paved the way for our first Southern president since the Civil War. (Woodrow Wilson was no Southerner *politically;* he came to the White House from the State House of New Jersey.) While Texas may be suspect now in Southern eyes, it certainly is of the South in Northern eyes, as Johnson found so painfully in 1960. Kennedy made him President. How free the choice of Johnson as vice-presidential candidate is subject to some argument. But what appears beyond dispute is that once chosen, Johnson was so treated by his rival for the White House as to ease his way enormously when he took over there. Johnson may have suffered great frustration as Vice-President, but his public standing and his knowledge of affairs were nurtured in those years. From this he gained a running start. The credit goes in no small part to Kennedy.

Moreover, Kennedy bequeathed to Johnson widened options in the sphere of foreign relations: a military posture far more flexible and useable than he himself inherited; a diplomatic posture more sophisticated in its whole approach to neutralists and Leftists, markedly more mindful of distinctions in the world, even among allies.

On the domestic side, Kennedy left a large inheritance of controversies, opened by a youthful, Catholic urbanite from the Northeast, which his Southwestern, Protestant successor might have had more trouble stirring at the start, but now can ride and maybe even "heal." This may turn out to have been a productive division of labor. However it turns out, Kennedy lived long enough to keep at least one promise. He got the country "moving again." For in our politics, the *sine qua non* of innovative policy is controversy. By 1963 we were engaged in controversy with an openness which would have been unthinkable, or at least "un-American," during the later Eisenhower years.

Events, of course, have more to do with stirring controversy than a president. No man can make an issue on his own. But presidents will help to shape the meaning of events, the terms of discourse, the attention paid, the noise-level. Eisenhower's years were marked by a pervasive fog of self-congratulation, muffling noise. The fog-machine was centered in the White House. Perhaps there had been need for this after the divisive Truman years. By the late nineteen-fifties, though, it fuzzed our chance to innovate in time. Kennedy broke out of it.

Finally, this President set a new standard of performance on the job, suitable to a new state of presidential being, a state he was the first to face throughout his term of office: the state of substantial, deliverable, nuclear capability in other hands than ours. Whatever else historians may make of Kennedy, I think them likely to begin with this. There can be little doubt that his successors have a lighter task because *he* pioneered in handling nuclear confrontations. During the Cuban missile crisis and thereafter, he did something which had not been done before, did it well, and got it publicly accepted. His innovation happened to be timely, since the need for innovation was upon us; technology had put it there. But also, in his reach for information and control, his balancing of firmness with caution, his sense of limits, he displayed and dramatized what presidents must do to minimize the risk of war through mutual miscalculation. This may well be the cardinal risk confronting his successors. If so, he made a major contribution to the presidency.

Index

Index